Oracle Press™

Oracle9*i*:
A Beginner's Guide

Oracle Press™

Oracle9*i*:
A Beginner's Guide

Michael Abbey
Michael Corey
Ian Abramson

McGraw-Hill/Osborne

New York Chicago San Francisco Lisbon
London Madrid Mexico City Milan New Delhi
San Juan Seoul Singapore Sydney Toronto

McGraw-Hill/Osborne
2600 Tenth Street
Berkeley, California 94710
U.S.A.

To arrange bulk purchase discounts for sales promotions, premiums, or fund-raisers, please contact **McGraw-Hill**/Osborne at the above address. For information on translations or book distributors outside the U.S.A., please see the International Contact Information page immediately following the index of this book.

Oracle9*i*: A Beginner's Guide

1234567890 FGR FGR 01987654321

ISBN 0-07-219279-8

Publisher	**Copy Editor**
Brandon A. Nordin	Judith Brown
Vice President & Associate Publisher	**Proofreader**
Scott Rogers	Linda Medoff
Acquisitions Editor	**Indexer**
Lisa McClain	Karin Arrigoni
Project Editor	**Computer Designers**
Leslie Tilley, Wordjones	Carie Abrew, Tabitha M. Cagan, & Lucie Ericksen
Acquisitions Coordinator	**Illustrators**
Athena Honore	Michael Mueller & Lyssa Wald
Contributing Author	**Series Design**
Peter Smith	Jani Beckwith
Technical Editors	
Jim Lopatosky, Shakir Sadikali, & David Teplow	

This book was composed with Corel VENTURA™ Publisher.

We dedicate this book to those who suffered,
directly and indirectly, as a result of the events in
the United States on September 11, 2001.

About the Authors

MICHAEL ABBEY   Michael S. Abbey is a seasoned writer in the Oracle Press series, this being his tenth work. Michael is past director of conferences for the IOUG-Americas, orchestrating the delivery of its successful user-driven event IOUG-A Live! from 1997 until 2000. He has presented at conferences in Europe and North America, and is a member of the faculty for the IOUG-A's University Master Class series. Michael has been working exclusively with Oracle's technology since the 1980s, having experienced the product all the way from desktop to large mainframes. He is currently the lead DBA for the Pythian Group's dbaSource initiative, delivering  off-site services to clients in North America and Europe. Michael can be reached at **masii@ottawa.com**. He enjoys feedback on these works and is happy to respond to quick questions.

IAN ABRAMSON   Ian Abramson is based in Toronto, Ontario, in the position of CTO of Data Warehousing for Cognicase Inc., Toronto. He has over 15 years of IT and Oracle experience, focusing in all areas of the IT life cycle. His Oracle skills include design, development, and administration, having served in almost every capacity on numerous Oracle projects. Ian is also director of education for the International Oracle Users Group (IOUG),  where he is a regular instructor of Oracle and data warehousing topics. In his spare time, Ian likes to play goalie at cold hockey rinks, still hoping to one day fulfill his dream of hockey stardom. Ian can be reached at **ian@abramson.to**.

MICHAEL COREY   Michael Corey is the founder and chief executive officer of Ntirety (**www.ntirety.com**). Prior to founding Ntirety, Mike was CEO of Database Technologies (DBT), the first consulting company on the East Coast to specialize in Oracle. In 1997 and 1998 Deloitte & Touche, and Hale and Dorr recognized Database Technologies as the fastest growing technology company in New England and the 51st fastest growing high-tech company in the United States.

Mike is a recognized expert on relational databases and data warehousing. He has written a number of articles and books and is a frequent guest speaker at technology conferences around the world. Mike is also a past president of the International Oracle User Group and a past member of the Microsoft Corporation Data Warehousing Advisory Group. He has a B.S. in Management Information Systems from Bentley College, in Waltham, Massachusetts. Feel free to contact Mike at **michael.corey@ntirety.com**.

Contributing Author

PETER SMITH   Peter C. Smith has been playing with relational databases since 1987, when he started programming in Quel-Fortran on an Ingres database. Peter saw the light and started working exclusively with Oracle databases in 1992.

Peter has been president of the Ottawa Oracle Users Group since 1993, where he has given many technical presentations. He has also been a supporter and presenter at IOUG-A Live! events.

Contents at a Glance

1 Oracle: The Company and the Software 3

2 Road Map to Services 15

3 The Oracle Server 59

4 Database Objects 89

5 SQL*Plus 101 113

6 PL/SQL 101 141

7 DBA 101 177

8 More SQL*Plus 203

9 More PL/SQL 241

10 More DBA 259

11 Oracle Enterprise Manager 285

12 Distributed Computing 315

13 The *i* in Oracle9*i* 333

14 All Things WWW 349

15 Forms and Reports Overview 375

16 Partitioning Data 401

17 Data Warehousing and Summarization 431

A Answers to End-of-Chapter Questions 483

Contents

ACKNOWLEDGMENTS xxi
INTRODUCTION xxiii

PART I
Getting Up to Speed

I Oracle: The Company and the Software   3
Terminology   4
Oracle Corporation: A Timeline   4
    1977: In the Beginning   4
    1978: Relational Software Inc. Is Born   5
    1979: First Commercial Database Product Ships   6
    1980: Oracle Systems Is Born   6
    1981–1983: First RDBMS to Run on Mainframes and
        Minicomputers   6
    1984: Version 4 (Read Consistency)   6
    1985: Oracle Enters the Application Business   7
    1986: The First DBMS with Distributed Capabilities   8
    1987: The Beat Goes On   8
    1988: Oracle Financials/Oracle CASE   8
    1989: Oracle 6.2 Is Born   8
    1990–1991: The $1 Billion Mark   9

1992: Ray Lane Is Hired 9
1993: The Applications Business 10
1994–1995: $2 Billion in Sales and the Network PC 10
1996: Oracle Enters the Consumer Marketplace 11
1997: Oracle8 Released 11
1998: Oracle Supports Linux 11
1999: Oracle8i Released 12
2000: Number One 12
Current Offerings 12
Chapter 1 Questions 13

2 Road Map to Services **15**
Terminology 16
Oracle Support Services 18
Logging TARs with OSS
(the Old-Fashioned Way) 20
Providing Documentation to Support Your TAR 21
MetaLink 23
The Technical Libraries 24
The Forums 28
iTars 30
Client Tombstone Information 32
Brief TAR Description 32
Oracle Technology Network 35
Oracle AppsNet 37
Newsgroups and List Servers 40
Newsgroups 41
List Servers 43
Online Documentation 48
Out of Site! 51
Internet Search Engines 51
Some of Our Favorite Sites 54
Chapter 2 Questions 56

3 The Oracle Server **59**
Terminology 60
Architecture of the Server 63
Background Support Processes 65
Database Writer (dbw0) 66
Process Monitor (pmon) 66
System Monitor (smon) 66
Log Writer (lgwr) 67
Checkpoint (ckpt) 67

Recoverer (reco) 67
Archiver (arc0) 67
INIT.ora 68
Location Entries 68
Limiting Entries 70
Feature Entries 70
Making Changes to Parameters 71
The Control File 73
Redo Logs 74
The Database Data Files 77
Rollback Segments/Undo Tablespace 78
Significant Memory Structures 80
The Data Cache 80
The Library Cache 81
Locks and Latches 82
Locks 82
Latches 83
So, You're the New Oracle9*i* Database 84
Chapter 3 Questions 86

PART II
So You've Just Started?

4 Database Objects 89
Terminology 90
Tables—Where Your Data Is Stored 91
create table, an Example 92
create table as, an Example 93
Views—Customized Selections of One or More Tables 94
create view, an Example 94
Materialized Views—The View That Stores Data 95
create materialized view (Formerly snapshot), an Example 95
Query Rewrite 96
Indexes—A Fast Way to Get at Your Data 96
Advantages of Presorted Order 97
Unique and Non-unique Indexes 97
The 95/5 Rule 98
The Bitmap Index—An Index for Low Variations of
Distinct Rows 98
Triggers—Event-Driven Programs 99
create trigger, an Example 99
Synonyms—Object Nicknames 101
create synonym, an Example 102

Sequences—A Fast Way to Obtain a Unique Number   102
    create sequence, an Example   103
create role—A Way to Manage Privileges   103
    create role, an Example   103
Functions, Procedures, and Packages   104
    create function   104
    create procedure   105
    create package   106
Other Database Objects   107
    create operator   107
    create directory   108
    create library   108
    Database Links   108
    create cluster   110
Chapter 4 Questions   111

5 SQL*Plus 101 . . . .   **113**
How to Access SQL*Plus   114
    Access from the Command Line   115
    Icon-Based Access   116
    Ending Your SQL*Plus Session   116
Data Definition Language (DDL)   116
    create/drop Statement   117
    Data Types   118
The describe Command   118
    Not Null   120
Data Manipulation Language (DML)   120
    The insert Statement   121
    The select Statement   122
    The SQL*Plus Environment   128
Joining Tables   133
    Primary Keys and Foreign Keys   133
The break on Clause   135
    Using break on with the skip Option   136
    Computing Column Values at Break   137
    break on report   138
Chapter 5 Questions   140

6 PL/SQL 101 . . . .   **141**
Terminology   143
PL/SQL: The Oracle Programming Language   144
PL/SQL Character Set   146
    Supported Characters   146
    Arithmetic Operators and Relational Operators   147

PL/SQL Structure 147
    PL/SQL Variables 149
Control Structures 152
    if Logic Structures 154
    case Expressions 156
    Loops 158
SQL in Your PL/SQL Programs 160
    Cursors 161
    The Cursor for Loop 163
Exception Handling 165
Stored Procedures and Functions 167
    Stored Procedures 167
    Functions 171
Basic Debugging 173
Moving On 174
Chapter 6 Questions 175

7 DBA 101 . . . . **177**
Terminology 178
What Is a Database? 179
What Is an Oracle Instance? 180
    The System Global Area (SGA) 180
    Oracle Background Processes 181
    startup open 182
    shutdown 184
The Oracle Tablespace 186
    Create Tablespace—extent management dictionary 186
    Create Tablespace—extent management local autoallocate 187
    create undo tablespace 188
    alter tablespace add data file 188
    alter tablespace offline 189
    Drop a Tablespace 189
Rollback Segments 190
    create rollback segment 190
    alter rollback segment online 192
    Shrinking a Rollback Segment Manually 192
    drop rollback segment 193
Redo Logs 193
    Mulitplexed Redo Logs 193
    Dropping a Redo Log 194
    Adding a Redo Log 195
Control Files—The Database Safety Checklist 196
    How Control Files Are Created 196

Creating a User Account 197
    grant connect, resource 197
Chapter 7 Questions 198

PART III

Beyond the Basics

8 More SQL*Plus 203
Terminology 204
Deploying SQL*Plus in Production 205
    Commenting Your Code with rem, --, and /*...*/ 205
    SQL*Plus Include Files 206
union, intersect, and minus Set Operators 209
    union Operator 210
    union all Operator 210
    minus Operator 211
    intersect Operator 211
    Don't Mix Apples with Oranges 211
SQL*Plus Command-Line Editing 212
    Using the Command-Line Editor 212
    If Only I Could Use VI or Emacs 213
Dual Table 213
Oracle Functions 214
    Math Functions and Operators 214
    String Functions 216
    The Date Data Type 219
    Date Functions in SQL*Plus 220
    group by Functions 225
    Using group by to Find Duplicate Data 228
    Using group by to Delete Duplicate Data 229
SQL Generating SQL 231
    SQL Creating a Data File 232
Query Within a Query 233
The Decode Statement 236
    update with decode Statement 237
Chapter 8 Questions 238

9 More PL/SQL 241
Terminology 242
Packages and Program Overloading 243
Advanced Error Handling in PL/SQL 244
    User-Defined Exceptions 245
    Oracle-Supplied Variables for Error Handling 246

Autonomous Transactions 248
PL/SQL Security with Invoker Rights 249
Oracle-Supplied Packages 250
    utl_file Package 250
    Dynamic SQL 254
Chapter 9 Questions 257

10 More DBA **259**
Terminology 260
Backup and Recovery 261
Export 261
    Export's Role in Backups 261
    Parameters Used with Export 262
    Export Modes of Operation 263
    Types of Exports 269
Import 269
    Import's Role in Recovery 270
    Parameters Used with Import 270
    Import Modes of Operation 271
    Types of Imports 273
Media Recovery Features 274
    Hot and Cold Backups 275
    Running in Archivelog Mode 276
    Writing a Hot Backup 279
    Media Recovery—An Example 279
Chapter 10 Questions 283

11 Oracle Enterprise Manager **285**
Terminology 286
What Can Be Done with OEM: A Quick Tour 287
Startup 290
Shutdown 293
Tablespace Maintenance 295
    Resizing a Data File 298
    Adding a Data File 298
    Shrinking a Data File 299
User Maintenance 300
    Creating a New Use 301
    Rights to Occupy Space in the Database 303
    Granting Object Privileges 304
Object Maintenance 307
    Object Maintenance Using SQL*Plus Worksheet 309
Chapter 11 Questions 312

12 Distributed Computing 315
   Terminology 316
   Partitioning Applications via Distributed Processing 317
   Oracle Net 318
      listener.ora 318
      tnsnames.ora 320
      The Network Configuration Assistant 322
      Placement of tnsnames.ora 326
      Establishing a Connection via Oracle Net 327
   Chapter 12 Questions 329

PART IV
I Is for Internet

13 The *i* in Oracle9*i* 333
   Terminology 334
   The Oracle Internet Database 336
      Communicating with the Database 338
   Java in the Database 340
   High Availability 342
      Protection from System Crashes 342
      Protection from Disk Failures 343
      Protection from Human Errors 343
      Management of Planned Outages 344
   Real Application Clusters 345
   The Internet File System (*i*FS) 346
   Chapter 13 Questions 347

14 All Things WWW 349
   Terminology 350
   The Oracle9*i* Application Server 352
      Communication Services 355
      Business Logic Services 357
      Presentation Services 358
      Caching Services 362
      Content Management Services 364
      Portal Services 364
      Business Intelligence Services 366
   Java for the Database 367
   Questions for Chapter 14 370

PART V
Who Said You Were a Beginner?

15 Forms and Reports Overview 375
  Terminology 376
  Sample Data 376
  Introduction to Forms and Reports 378
    Forms and Reports Components 378
    Initiating a Database Connection 378
  Building a Form 380
    The Data Block Wizard 382
    The Layout Wizard 384
    Editing an Existing Form 386
  Report Builder 394
    The Report Wizard 394
    Modifying the Report 398
  Chapter 15 Questions 399

16 Partitioning Data 401
  Terminology 402
  Why Partition Your Data? 403
    Volume of Data 403
    Ease of Management Offered by Partitioning 405
    Performance Benefits 405
  Range-Based Partitioning 406
    Choosing a Partition Key 406
    Range-Based Partitioning—The SQL 409
  Indexing Partitioned Tables 411
    Local Partitioned Indexes 412
    Global Partitioned Indexes 415
    To Local or Not to Local, That Is the Question 417
    Prefixed and Non-prefixed Partitioned Indexes 420
  List Partitioning 421
  Hash Partitioning 423
  Which Approach to Use When 424
    Row Count 424
    Access Method 425
    Composite Partitioning—A Hybrid 427
  Chapter 16 Questions 429

17 Data Warehousing and Summarization **431**
   Terminology 433
   What Is a Data Warehouse? 434
   Designing the Data Warehouse 435
      Dimensional Database Design 437
   Data Warehouse Partitioning 438
   Backing Up the Warehouse 441
   Loading Your Data Warehouse 443
      Using SQL*Loader to Load the Warehouse 444
      Using External Tables to Load the Warehouse 447
      Using PL/SQL to Load the Warehouse 449
   Oracle9i Data Warehousing Functions 452
      Materialized Views 452
   Extended Aggregate Operations 467
      The rollup Function 469
      The cube Function 470
      Ranking Functions 472
      Windowing Functions 477
      Statistical Functions 479
   Chapter 17 Questions 481

A Answers to End-of-Chapter Questions **483**
   Chapter 1: Oracle: The Company and the Software 484
   Chapter 2: Road Map to Services 484
   Chapter 3: The Oracle Server 485
   Chapter 4: Database Objects 485
   Chapter 5: SQL*Plus 101 486
   Chapter 6: PL/SQL 101 486
   Chapter 7: DBA 101 487
   Chapter 8: More SQL*Plus 487
   Chapter 9: More PL/SQL 487
   Chapter 10: More DBA 488
   Chapter 11: Oracle Enterprise Manager 488
   Chapter 12: Distributed Computing 489
   Chapter 13: The i in Oracle9i 489
   Chapter 14: All Things WWW 490
   Chapter 15: Forms and Reports Overview 490
   Chapter 16: Partitioning Data 491
   Chapter 17: Data Warehousing and Summarization 492

Index **493**

Acknowledgments

Michael S. Abbey

I would first of all like to recognize the four most significant people in my private life—my teenagers Naomi, Jordan, Nathan, and Ben. They are all great young adults, and I love them dearly. Second, I want to thank my soon-to-be wife, Sandy Kronick, for turning me into a hermit and making me hide in my dungeon until I finished the seven chapters I contributed to this book. Her apricot chicken is great, her brisket divine, and her kindness to me and my family exquisite! Thanks as well to my professional colleagues Ian Abramson, Mike Corey, Jim Lopatosky, Shakir Sadikali, Peter Smith, the gang at McGraw-Hill/Osborne, Paul Vallée, Steve Pickard, ManyTrees, Grégoire Leger, BTU, Bob Hamel, Ken Jacobs, and David Teplow, to name a few of many. Booluh and Jooluh—you're great!

Ian Abramson

There are points in people's lives when they evaluate where they are and where they are going. This is one of those times, in this world that seems to have redefined the spirit of individuals and brought us closer together. It is humanity that will survive all those that try to destroy. I dedicate my efforts on this book to all those impacted by terrorism around the world. We are all part of the solution, and our reward will be peace.

I would also like to acknowledge those who have made my life richer. As always, I would like to thank my wife and children. Thank you Susan Abramson,

Baila Abramson, and Jillian Abramson. You are my biggest supporters, and I know I often forget to tell you each how much I appreciate and love you. To my friends Mark Kerzner (and the Kerzner clan), Jack Chadirjian and Toula, Ted and Vanessa Falcon, and all the guys I play hockey with, thanks for helping keep pucks away. To my extended family, the Orleans, Abramsons, Astroffs, Weiskopfs, and Rzepas; thanks to all. To everyone at Cognicase, thanks for your continuing support. To my coauthors, Michael and Mike, you guys are great! Thank you for allowing me to be part of this book journey, number 6 and counting; YATFG! Finally, I want to thank my father, Joe Abramson, and my stepmother, Saundra Adeski, for everything. You really know how to keep a family together. Finally, I wish us all peace!

Michael Corey

It is very clear to me why most acknowledgments start off with "Thanks to my family…" It is true the family suffers the most. I am very, very grateful that they have tolerated me through it all, especially after I lost three computers and a much-needed Internet connection, among the many other things that happened.

To bring this book to press required a lot of time and effort from a lot of great people. Thank you to the people at McGraw-Hill/Osborne. They are great to work with. Special thank you for Lisa McClain and Jessica Wilson at Osborne for working with us as we developed the book. Thank you to the team at Ntirety for all their help. My hat goes off to Lisa Smith, Aldo Castaneda, Mike Calisi, and Ed Barry. To the rest of the great people at Ntirety, thanks: Claire Higgins, John Kirby, John McManus, Ed Casey, Eric Weiss, Cindylou Chapman, Ruthann Spengler, and Pat Mcdonald.

Special thanks to Jim Lopatosky and Shakir Shadikali for all their help in developing the finished product. Their comments and guidance have been great.

Thank you to the many special people who have helped me in my career. This list is by no means complete: Rama Velpuri, Ed Marram, Julie Silverstien, Merrilee Nohr, Bert Spencer, Scott Martin, Ray Lane, Mark Porter, Ken Jacobs, Terry Carlin, Dana Spratt, Gerry Tischler, Dave Smith, Jim Hussey, and so many more people.

Last of all, thanks to my coauthors.

Introduction

racle9*i*—the subject material of this book. As the Abbey, Corey, Abramson team places more and more works under its corporate belt, more and more people wonder, "What is Oracle anyway?" While watching CTV Newsnet in Canada, the red letters O-R-A-C-L-E sit on the right margin of your TV screen, reminding you who is responsible for bringing you this fabulous information. In the beginning, some thought Oracle manufactured casual clothing, what with the gamut of T-shirts, golf shirts, and the like populating many work spaces. Oracle software powers the Internet—a saying as well as a fact.

Many of us have our whole IT career invested in one piece of software—Oracle—and yes, thank you very much, business is very good. Unbeknownst to many Internet users, they have had peripheral contact with the Oracle8*i* software and bit by bit Oracle9*i* as the software of choice by most web sites serving up the data that we all enjoy as we surf the net. In the beginning, Oracle was simply a data server, delivering state-of-the-art solutions to corporate business communities. Version 3 is the first many of us saw in the mid-1980s. It ran in RAM—the first 640KB of memory attached to the PCs strewn all over many companies' offices. Version 3, alongside some early tool offerings by Oracle Systems Corporation, had some heavy competition with the likes of Ashton Tate's dBASEII to mention one of many. Peter, Paul, and Mary sang "Where Have All the Flowers Gone"; we might reword this familiar teenage classic as "Where Has All the Competition Gone."

Oracle is the undisputed leader in software solutions that drive the Internet. Is that why you are reading this book? Are you reading it because someone insisted? We believe you fall into that large group of hungry consumers who strive to be on top of the leading-edge technology, whatever the cost. Familiarity and fluency with the technology leader in the 21st century is fundamental to your career, whether you use, manage, help procure, or program with the Oracle9i offering.

We've been around Oracle the company and Oracle the software for many years. We have rubbed shoulders with senior management, hung out with kernel developers, and built up some significant relationships with some of its players over the past 17 years.

Oracle9i: A Beginner's Guide takes you on a journey through the backbone of Oracle's technology. We start by looking at the company, where it has been, and how it has gotten there. There are so many places to go to whet your voracious appetite for Oracle technology. We guide you through where to go to feed that appetite as you ingest Chapter 2. We explain the fundamentals of Oracle's development offerings—SQL*Plus and PL/SQL—then delve into the role of the almighty Oracle techie, the database administrator, affectionately called the DBA. We pay special attention to Oracle Enterprise Manager, a GUI database management offering that has been around since early releases of Oracle7, circa 1992. We finish off the journey looking at the Internet-specific pieces in Oracle9i's offering, paying attention to its data warehousing features.

The intended audience for this book is very wide. Many take it on after having been an end user for many years. They want to look behind the scenes and see what makes their systems tick. Others are transitioning from other pieces of software, looking for a fast route to understanding Oracle9i and how it is put together. Oracle started putting the *i* in their software version name in the late 1990s. We have been putting the *u* in understanding what Oracle is doing, where they have come from, and where their technology is going since our first *Beginner's Guide* offering in 1994. Who knows, perhaps it's superstition that has allowed so much to be accomplished in such a little amount of time. As you enter beginner's land, keep one coincidental piece of information in mind—the structured query language, abbreviated SQL, is the undisputed front end to the world's most powerful Internet software. Oracle headquarters in Redwood Shores, California, is closest to the San Carlos airport—guess what that landing strip's call letters are—*SQL*. A coincidence? We think not!

PART
I

Getting Up to Speed

CHAPTER
1

Oracle: The Company
and the Software

ith Oracle quickly approaching its 25th anniversary, we thought it would be appropriate to spend some time reviewing its history. Understanding the company's roots will give you better insight into how and why the company operates the way it does today. We will then wrap up the chapter with an overview of Oracle's current product and services offerings.

This chapter covers the following topics:

- History of Oracle Corporation
- Five areas of Oracle software

Terminology

The following terminology will arm you with the technical jargon to get through this chapter.

- *DBMS* stands for database management system. Think of it as a file manager for files in a database, rather than files in a file system. The most common type of database today is an RDBMS.

- *Java* is a programming language expressly designed for the distributed environment of the Internet.

- *RDBMS* stands for relational database management system, a database implemented according to Dr. E. F. Codd's relational model.

Oracle Corporation: A Timeline

What does SDL (Software Development Laboratories) have to do with Oracle Corporation? Very little, but now that I have your attention, it is one of the many names of the company before it became known as Oracle Corporation. We have found this to be a great trivia question among our high-tech friends. Here is another trivia question: what is the origin of Scott/Tiger, the username and password used in many of the examples shipped with the database? Bruce Scott is the name of the developer, and Tiger is his cat. But enough fun—on to the history of Oracle.

1977: In the Beginning

The year is 1977, and Larry Ellison, Bob Miner, and Ed Oates have founded SDL. Yes, Ed Oates. Many times you hear only of Larry Ellison and Bob Miner—but to be fair, it was all three. We have been fortunate enough to meet all three individuals.

Larry Ellison and Ed Oates are still with us today. Only Larry Ellison is still with Oracle Corporation.

The new corporation was formed so that they would be able to bid on government contracts. Ellison and his co-founders were already familiar with an IBM research paper by Dr. E. F. Codd about a new type of database that would better organize the way information was stored within a database and a new language called SQL, which would allow you to sort through large amounts of information quickly.

The CIA had an inherent need to store large volumes of information and retrieve it quickly, so it was sufficiently intrigued by this research paper to put some funding behind the idea. SDL was awarded a bid and began work on this top-secret project. The code name for this CIA project was Oracle.

If you think about it, Oracle was a great name for this project. The word *oracle* means a prophecy or someone who delivers such predictions. It was believed that, if one asked a question of an oracle, the answer came straight from the gods. In his paper, Codd theorized that, using the new SQL language, one would be able to navigate vast amounts of information—and derive an answer to one's query—very quickly.

Like many projects the government funds, after a while its funding was canceled. But early on, Larry and his co-founders had recognized the commercial possibilities of a database that could store vast amounts of information and allow you to retrieve it quickly. This, coupled with the belief that IBM was planning on incorporating this new relational database and SQL language into future computers, led Larry, Bob, and Ed to decide to continue work on the project.

They decided to implement this database on a minicomputer built by Digital Equipment, an IBM competitor. At that time, mainframes were still king (IBM dominated computer sales), so a minicomputer was not the obvious choice. Nonetheless, through a combination of their savings and the consulting work they could pick up along the way, they struggled on, developing this new concept in databases.

1978: Relational Software Inc. Is Born

Oracle version 1.0 is written in assembly code on Digital Equipment computer PDP-11 under the RSX operating system. It uses only 128KB of maximum memory. Imagine trying to write any program that uses 128KB of memory, never mind a database. Ellison, Miner, and Oates had hopes that the database would be ready by now, but this version was never released. But the success they had inspired the team to continue.

They change the name of the company from Software Development Laboratories to Relational Software Inc. (RSI). They are completely focused on developing the first production release of a relational database.

1979: First Commercial Database Product Ships

Two years late, Relational Software Inc. ships the first commercial relational database product implementing the SQL language. Not only are Ellison, Miner, and Oates right that IBM is developing a relational database product, but they also beat IBM to the market. Quite a feat, when you consider that IBM dominates the computer industry at this time, with well over 80 percent market share. The first customer to purchase the RSI database is Wright Patterson Air Force Base, Advance Technology Division.

Another great trivia question: what was Oracle Corporation's first implementation of the SQL language called? It was called UFI, which stood for *user friendly interface*. This was done to avoid any issues with IBM, which invented the concept of a structured query language (SQL).

1980: Oracle Systems Is Born

Oracle version 2 is released on a Digital Equipment Corporation (DEC) PDP-11 machine. The underlying database is still written in assembly language. Another release of the database is developed to run under the DEC VAX/VMS operating system, which is also implemented using assembly language.

In 1980, Relational Software Inc. officially changes its name to Oracle Systems Corporation (later to Oracle Corporation). It is decided that the next version of the database will be rewritten using the C programming language. Rewriting the database in C is a key strategic decision, making Oracle Corporation an early adopter of this new programming language.

1981–1983: First RDBMS to Run on Mainframes and Minicomputers

Oracle Corporation hits $2.5 million in sales and releases Oracle version 3 . This is the first relational database to run on mainframes and minicomputers. Since the database is written in C, the same core source code can be used across all platforms. This ability to migrate source code across machines gives Oracle a serious advantage over the competition.

This year, Oracle opens its first international office—Oracle Denmark. Even at this very early stage, the founders have great aspirations. In many ways, Oracle is a reflection of its founders. Bob Miner and Ed Oates lend it its inner personality of soft-spoken technical excellence. From Larry Ellison, it receives its outer personality—proud, bold, and always aspiring to be number one.

1984: Version 4 (Read Consistency)

Oracle Corporation reaches $13 million in sales and releases Oracle version 4. With this release, the Oracle database attains true interoperability between servers (mainframes and minicomputers) and PCs. At Honeywell Systems, where one of us (Mike Corey) worked at the time, we developed Oracle code on PCs and then recompiled that same source code on our servers. It worked as expected. The same code that was written on the PC would actually run on a server. This was unheard of at the time.

All other vendors at this time could not attain true interoperability. Part of the problem was that they were still developing the database in assembly language. This meant that the code set was different on each machine. Code written on one machine would not necessarily behave the same on another machine.

The PC version of Oracle used under 256KB of memory. Imagine a database running in less than 256KB of memory!

At this time, there was no GUI (graphical user interface) to develop forms-based front ends to an Oracle database. Oracle had a product known as Fast Form, which was the predecessor of SQL*Forms (known later as Oracle Forms). The program asked a series of questions, and then, based on the answers, it produced a form-based front end to the database.

In 1984 Oracle also introduced the read consistency model. An SQL query that started running, say, at 12:01 would give users a view of the database exactly as it looked at the time the query started, regardless of what had changed inside the database since the query began executing. Competitors were still doing dirty reads. Dirty reads meant that on a long-running query, if someone changed the data, when the SQL query reached that portion of the database, it would pick up the changed data. The resulting query would not retrieve a consistent view of the database.

Imagine working in a financial institution and trying to determine whether you had made money at 12:01 or not. With non-Oracle products, you would have to stop all updates to the database, and then execute the SQL query to receive an accurate position. With Oracle's read consistency, you could execute the query with confidence that the database would return an accurate portrayal of your position at 12:01 when the query first started executing.

One final note for 1984: Oracle moves its corporate offices to 20 Davis Drive, Redwood City, California. This is touted as the last corporate office they will ever need.

1985: Oracle Enters the Application Business

Oracle attains $23 million in sales, and Jeff Walker joins the company as CFO. Jeff Walker is the founder of Walker Interactive Products, a producer of financial software. Based on the fact that it will sell more databases, Jeff Walker convinces Larry Ellison to enter the financial application business. This proves to be a second key decision point for Oracle Corporation. Oracle's main competitors remain pure database companies, and ultimately, Oracle's financial products alone will bring in more revenue than the competitors' databases sales.

By this time, Oracle is becoming very popular, and all major hardware vendors are asking Oracle to port its database onto their platform. To meet this need, Oracle allows hardware vendors to port the Oracle database directly.

1986: The First DBMS with Distributed Capabilities

Oracle Corporation reaches $55 million in sales and goes public one day before Microsoft Corporation. With an opening price of $15 a share, Oracle reaches a market value of $270 million. Larry Ellison is worth over $90 million by the end of the day. Microsoft goes public the following day at $21 a share and reaches a market value of $700 million.

Oracle version 5 is released with distributed capabilities known as SQL*Star. Now users can have databases all over the world that can share information using the capabilities of SQL*Star. It is possible to join the contents of a database in Boston with the contents of a database in San Francisco.

1987: The Beat Goes On

The company reaches $131 million in sales and has another record year of growth. The performance of distributed capabilities is further refined, and Oracle is running on virtually every machine in existence. Larry Ellison is still personally interviewing every candidate before a job offer can be made. In fact, the company becomes even larger before Larry stops interviewing candidates.

1988: Oracle Financials/Oracle CASE

The company reaches $188 million in sales and releases Oracle version 6. Version 6 represents a major rewrite of significant portions of the database code and is designed to handle larger and larger transactional processing systems. Functionality such as sequence number caches is added; the financial suites of products as well as a CASE (computer-assisted software engineering) development suite are released. For the first time, an Oracle product does not originate in the United States, but from the leadership of Richard Barker and Geoff Squire in Britain, where Oracle CASE is developed.

Also in 1988, Oracle Corporation moves its headquarters from 20 Davis Drive to 500 Oracle Parkway, in Redwood City, where it is located today.

1989: Oracle 6.2 Is Born

Oracle reaches $571 million in sales and releases Oracle version 6.2 on a Digital Equipment VAX/VMS cluster. This marks the first time that two computers that do not share physical memory can share the same disk farm at the same time. In other words, machine A and machine B can both use the same database at the same time. What makes this so special is the fact that there is very little degradation of performance as machines are added. Oracle is a *scalable* architecture as users add machines.

Imagine a hospital where you need uptime 24 hours a day. You could now have two machines working on the same database. If machine A failed, you still had access to the database from machine B. This ability made Oracle a nearly fault-tolerant solution. The only other alternative at the time was to use Tandem computers, which were 100 percent fault tolerant, but also cost ten times more than other machines. A Tandem computer at this time also used a proprietary operating system.

Many people had tried to make a database scalable as machines were added, but all had failed. Andy Laursen, Mark Porter, and Scott Martin convinced Larry Ellison to let them give it a try. To accomplish this task, they ended up writing a generic Distributed Lock Manager. From Oracle 6.2 came the Oracle Parallel Server. Today, any Oracle shop can add computers and expect database performance to scale up, with nearly fault-tolerant capabilities at a fraction of the traditional cost.

1990–1991: The $1 Billion Mark

Oracle finishes the fiscal year 1990 with $916 million in sales, and it appears that nothing can stop the company. Ironically, in 1991, the year that it reaches $1,028 million in sales, Oracle loses money for the first time.

Jeff Walker leaves Oracle as CFO and is quickly replaced by Jeff Henley. Oracle takes scalability to a new level, and Larry Ellison embraces a new type of computer known as a *massively parallel* computer. Until now even mainframes might have four or five CPUs. A massively parallel system (MPS) could have 1,000 CPUs. Using this technology, Oracle is the first database to process 1,000 transactions per second. The Oracle database can take a query that would ordinarily take 12 hours to run and run it in minutes, harvesting the power of an MPS.

1992: Ray Lane Is Hired

Oracle reaches $1,179 million in sales, and Ray Lane joins the staff. This marks a major turning point for the company in many ways. Before Jeff Henley joined the company, most of Oracle management was homegrown. As Oracle comes of age, Ellison and others realize that they need to bring in seasoned management, and Ray Lane is added to the team.

Next to the founders, the most important hire the company ever made would prove to be Ray Lane. He quickly assumes day-to-day operations of the company. Larry Ellison's attentions are drawn elsewhere, and Lane masterfully moves the company forward. He understands how to get a billion-dollar company focused and moving in one direction. Lane has a clear vision of where Oracle needs to go and the skills to make it happen. In many ways, he is the perfect complement to Ellison.

Also in 1992, Oracle Corporation acquires N-Cube Corporation, a pioneer of massively parallel processing. Like IBM, Oracle can now couple software with hardware. The company now sets its sights on intensive multimedia applications.

1993: The Applications Business

Oracle reaches $1,503 million in sales, and Oracle 7 is released under the UNIX operating system. This marks a major shift away from Digital Equipment Corporation; Larry Ellison sees that UNIX is going to dominate the marketplace. Oracle 7 is designed for very large databases (VLDBs)—any database over 5 terabytes in size. Oracle now has the capability to meet the growing need of organizations to build massive databases known as *data warehouses.*

While Jeff Walker was aggressively growing the applications business, he let quality slip to a low priority. Many customers bought the promise of a financial suite based on Oracle, but are struggling to make it work. To solve this problem, Ellison assigns one of his most trusted lieutenants, Ron Wohl, to day-to-day control of Oracle financials. Wohl's job is to stabilize the business and improve the overall quality of the product suite.

Under this dark cloud, Oracle Industries is launched. Ellison sees a clear race ahead to dominate the applications business and pushes the company full steam ahead. His object is to develop a full suite of interrelated applications, not just financials, for business, just as Microsoft owns the desktop, with a suite of interrelated applications (Word, Excel, PowerPoint). Oracle starts to develop a customized suite of applications in key industries, in direct competition with many of its strategic partners. Also in 1993, Oracle releases the first annual report ever to be delivered on a CD-ROM.

1994–1995: $2 Billion in Sales and the Network PC

Oracle reaches $2,001 million in sales and releases Oracle 7 for the PC. One very sad note in 1994: Bob Miner passes away from cancer. If Larry Ellison is Oracle's vision and drive, Bob Miner is its heart and soul. In 1995, the company reaches $2,967 million in sales; and capitalizing on its ability to harness the power of massively parallel systems, Oracle pursues Interactive TV with British Telecom.

While at the Annual European Information Technology Forum in Paris, Ellison introduces the concept of the network computer. He envisions an appliance, much like the telephone for dialing the Internet. It will be a low-cost computer, very simple to use, without the Windows operating system. Users will simply plug it in, like the telephone. The complexity of installing and maintaining all the software will be done at the back end.

1996: Oracle Enters the Consumer Marketplace

The company reaches $4,223 billion in sales, and Oracle Corporation spins off Network Computer, Inc., to build the network computer envisioned by Ellison. Oracle's first foray into the consumer marketplace puts the company at odds with Sun, IBM, and other computer manufacturers. Since the network computer is not based on the Windows operating system, it also puts Oracle in direct competition with Microsoft. Larry Ellison is awarded the Business Times Award for Executive of the Year for the network computer.

Oracle's applications business reaches over $500 million in sales. Because the database is associated with each of those sales, this represents a large portion of Oracle business. Oracle's application suite now includes

- Oracle Financials
- Oracle Supply Change Management
- Oracle Manufacturing
- Oracle Project Systems
- Oracle Human Resources
- Oracle Market Management

Also in 1996, Oracle acquires IRI Software, providing a full suite of OLAP (Online Analytical Processing) tools. This technology will bolster Oracle's data warehousing offering.

1997: Oracle8 Released

Oracle reaches $5,684 million in sales and releases version 8, supporting more users, more data, and higher availability than ever before. Once again making a key strategic technical decision early in the game, Oracle embraces the Java programming language and abandons the client-server architecture to concentrate on Internet-based applications.

The company starts to build a suite of browser-based applications utilizing Microsoft Internet Explorer or Netscape Navigator. The goal is to have a suite of applications that will require no customization or costly installation to use. Larry Ellison donates $100 million worth of network computers to schools.

1998: Oracle Supports Linux

The company reaches $7,144 million in sales and embraces the Linux operating system. Oracle is on a collision course with Microsoft and is doing everything in its power to support non-Microsoft-based solutions.

Building on its groundwork of browser-based applications, Oracle Business Online is founded on the principle that Oracle can run mission-critical software more economically and efficiently as a service for other businesses than they can for themselves.

1999: Oracle8*i* Released

The corporation tops $8 billion in sales, and Oracle 8*i* is released with major Java integration. Oracle is now built with the Internet in mind. Larry Ellison feels that the best advertising Oracle can use is itself and puts the corporation on a mission to shave $1 billion off the bottom line by using its own E-Business Suite of integrated business software.

2000: Number One

Oracle reaches $10,139 million in sales, and is the number one database of choice for the Internet and the number one ERP vendor. Larry Ellison becomes the richest man in the world as Microsoft stock plummets and Oracle stock rises on the Internet wave. The company cuts $1 billion in a year through centralizing software and IT worldwide, using its newly launched E-Business Suite of integrated business software. Oracle 9*i* is released.

Current Offerings

Oracle is a force to be reckoned with. Its take-no-prisoners attitude is a reflection of one of its founders, Larry Ellison. Ellison plays to win; Oracle plays to win.

When a business opportunity arises, the people at Oracle seize the moment. For example, Ellison helped fund Salesforce.com, which was founded by Oracle employee Marc Benioff. Today, Oracle is a competitor. An early Ellison protégé, Tom Siebel, left Oracle after Ellison turned down his idea for sales automation. Today, Oracle is a competitor. Oracle has taken on many of its partners and today competes with some of the biggest names in the industry, such as

- Computer Associates with the Ingres database
- IBM with DB/2 database
- Informix with the Informix database
- Microsoft with Access and SQL Server database
- Software AG with ADABAS
- PostgressSQL (free open source database)

With all these different competitors, it is sometimes difficult for people to understand what business Oracle is in. Oracle Corporation is a supplier of software for the management of information. This includes database management, application development, business intelligence, and the development of Internet-based business applications. Oracle also offers a full range of integrated industry packages that can be brought in-house and customized or purchased as a service, whereby Oracle maintains the application for the customer.

They offer a wide range of supporting services, including one of the largest educational/training businesses in the world, consulting, and full system integration, no matter how small or large the project.

As a product set, Oracle can be broken into five areas:

- Oracle 9*i* database

- Oracle 9*i* Application Server

- Internet Development Suite

- Data Warehousing and Business Development

- Oracle E-Business Suite

Chapter 2 will describe how to make the Oracle services work for you. We will provide a summary of services within and without Oracle that are available for support and guidance.

Chapter 1 Questions

Answers to questions can be found in Appendix A.

1. Larry Ellison, Bob Miner, and _____ founded Oracle.

   A. Ken Jacobs

   B. Ray Lane

   C. Ron Wohl

   D. Ed Oates

2. Oracle shipped the first commercial release of a relational database in what year?

   A. 1979

   B. 1961

    C. 1984

    D. 1982

3. Oracle competes with

    A. IBM

    B. Computer Associates

    C. Software AG

    D. Microsoft

    E. All of the above

4. Oracle's database was the first to introduce the _____ consistency model.

    A. read

    B. write

    C. update

    D. dirty read

5. Oracle's first international office was located in what country?

    A. United Kingdom

    B. Japan

    C. India

    D. Denmark

CHAPTER 2

Road Map to Services

o, you say, Oracle is a large software company with lots of products and lots of clients. We looked at the company and its offerings in Chapter 1. This chapter is dedicated, in part, to one of the other sides of this multitalented organization—their services organization. The balance of the chapter looks at resources all over the place, where you can go for assistance with this very complex and very strong product set. In this chapter, we will look at the following topics:

- Oracle Support Services (an organization we affectionately call *OSS*), what they are and the best way to work with them.

- TARs and how to log them with OSS (the old-fashioned way)

- MetaLink, Oracle's online support forum

- *i*TARs

- Oracle Technology Network

- Oracle AppsNet

- Newsgroups and list servers

- Online documentation

- Popular and useful Internet sites—out of site!

Terminology

The following terminology will arm you with the technical jargon to get through this chapter.

- *OSS* stands for Oracle Support Services, the wing of the organization that provides postsales support.

- A *TAR* is a technical assistance request, used by Oracle Support Services to initiate and follow up on calls for assistance.

- *Severity* is a ranking system used by OSS to assess and then rate the nature of support calls. Severity 1 is reserved for a down production database with complete loss of services. The most common rankings for TARs are as follows:

  - Severity 2—You are experiencing a severe loss of service, but work can carry on with some restrictions.

- Severity 3—The loss of service is minor, and more of an inconvenience, and a workaround is usually available.

- Just about any printable character from the computer keyboard is referred to as *alphanumeric*. This class of characters includes digits (0–9), upper- and lowercase letters of the alphabet, and the assortment of special characters such as ~`!@#$%^&*()_−+={}|[]\:";'<>?,./.

- When creating electronic requests for information or simply filling in an application form, data—such as name, address, city, and country—are referred to as *tombstone information*.

- Oracle uses the industry standard query language to look at and manipulate data, called Structured Query Language, or *SQL* for short.

- A *workaround* is a method used to circumvent a problem and allow the use of a feature, even though it may not be functioning as planned. In the nontechnical arena, suppose the bridge over Redmond Creek is under repair, only handling northbound traffic between 8:00 a.m. and 4:30 p.m. The workaround would be simply to use another route!

- An *error stack*, sometimes just called a *stack*, is a set of error messages that are commonly returned together. The next listing illustrates such a stack:

```
ORA-00604: error occurred at recursive SQL level 1
ORA-06553: PLS-707: unsupported construct or internal error [2603]
```

- *URL* stands for Uniform Resource Locator and is a technical name for an Internet address commonly starting with "http://" or simply the familiar "www" when entered in a browser's Address area.

- The characters entered as search criteria when looking up subject matter in an Internet search engine are called a *search string*. If you wanted to get a list of sites pertaining to *Oracle9i Application Server*, that text could be entered as a search string.

- A windows-based activity driven by data entry from the keyboard and mouse clicks is referred to as a graphical user interface, or *GUI*.

- One of the most popular protocols used to transfer files back and forth between two computers is called *ftp* for file transfer protocol.

A virtual plethora of information exists out there in the written, spoken, and electronic world; let's get started by tackling the heart of Oracle Corporation's world—their support organization—followed by some of their electronic offerings, such as MetaLink, Oracle Technology Network, and AppsNet.

Oracle Support Services

OSS is the heart of Oracle Corporation's services offerings. Talk about the force—this is it. We have a great deal of admiration for the workers in the trenches of this organization. Picture the following scenario illustrating how difficult their jobs must be.

You recently started work in a restaurant as a dishwasher, amidst plans to work toward becoming a server. It's the third week, and even though you reminded your immediate superior of the promise that was made upon hiring, you are still in the dish pit. Week four arrives, and you yet again pass a friendly but firm reminder to that very same person who claims, "That's going to be very difficult to put together for you until things slow down and we find more good dishwashers." The support analysts at OSS are you, and the dishes they are washing are the simple, easy to deal with, beginner-oriented TARs that occupy their time. They are longing for the opportunity to work with more in-depth and technical issues, but the dishes clutter their workspace and they can't move up to something more exciting.

Figure 2-1 shows the current (but ever-changing) support services home page.

NOTE
Due to the ever-changing nature of the Internet, and home pages used by many state-of-the-art software vendors such as Oracle, the home page you look at after reading this chapter may differ.

Our first stop in this journey into the bowels of OSS is at the logging of a technical assistance request, affectionately referred to as a TAR. You must have an appropriate support agreement in place to be able to log TARs by phone. There are currently three levels of support, but only the second of the following three levels, in conjunction with the first, allows you to call in to create TARs:

- Oracle Updates Subscription Services provides for program and documentation updates, access to MetaLink, and limited access to software patches via MetaLink; general maintenance and selected functionality releases are part of this offering.

- Oracle Product Support provides for TAR assistance "24 x 7," access to MetaLink for TAR creation, and nontechnical customer service during the normal business day in your geographical areas.

- Incident Support is Internet based, vended in packages of ten TARs at a time, and is only available to clients running one of the following:

  - **Oracle Database Standard Edition**   A streamlined version of the Enterprise Edition, stripped of some of the most popular and useful functionality such as data partitioning and cluster support.

- **Oracle Database Personal Edition** A full-featured version of the Oracle database, targeted at individuals.

- **Oracle Database Lite** A version that allows you to build and deploy mobile enterprise applications, and easily interface and share data with more industrial-strength Standard and Enterprise Edition versions of Oracle.

Wasn't that the phone ringing? Must be Oracle calling about your latest TAR.

FIGURE 2-1. *Oracle Support Services home page*

Logging TARs with OSS (the Old-Fashioned Way)

OSS encourages you to use the electronic TAR intake interface using MetaLink, as discussed later in this chapter. We are going to discuss opening a TAR by phone, an activity you will no doubt experience when your Internet connection is down (that never happens!) or access to a connection is impossible.

There is a fairly intuitive phone tree to follow when calling support, but let's look at what you should assemble before making the call:

- Your customer support identifier, commonly referred to in North America as a *CSI,* or in parts of Europe as a *SAC.* It doesn't matter what acronym you use, it's the same thing.

- The operating system version of the machine upon which you are logging the TAR. Common O/S versions include the assortment of Linux variants (including SuSE, Red Hat, Mandrake, and OpenLinux eServer); Windows 98, Me, or 2000 (with the appropriate Service Pack level); and a few common UNIX ports such as Compaq Alpha, Sun Solaris, and HP-UX.

- The version of Oracle you are running, including all the numbers to the right of all decimal places in the numbering system of the release. For example, telling OSS you are using release 9.1.0.3.1 means a lot more than simply 9.1.

- Any Oracle errors pertinent to the exercise. These errors commonly take the format of three alphanumeric characters, the most common being *ORA,* followed by a five-digit number with leading zeros where required. Common error messages are ORA-00942: table or view does not exist, or ORA-01034: ORACLE not available. If there is an error stack, it should be reported in its entirety, not just the first or last.

When calling the toll-free number for OSS, the electronic greeting will remind you of the electronic MetaLink web site for non-business-critical issues. If you do have access to the Internet, you will probably be happier with the response using the *i*TAR approach discussed later in this chapter. Seasoned users with telephone-based support tend to jump fairly quickly through the phone tree; beware, as options change, new ones appear, and old ones disappear from time to time. Once you arrive at a human being, you are asked to confirm your support identifier and provide contact information, including a phone number and email address.

NOTE
If you reside in one country but support clients in another, be aware that in many locations throughout the globe (yes, North America, from our experience), TARs are routed based on the area code of the contact number provided at their creation.

Once a TAR has been created, you will be given a reference number. Be sure to specify with the analyst your preferred way of contact. Next, we will look at what types of documentation you may be asked to provide in support of your TAR.

Providing Documentation to Support Your TAR

After receiving your TAR number from the Oracle support analyst, you may be asked to provide relevant documentation in the form of trace files written as your database operates. In the "*iTARs*" section, later in this chapter, we look at uploading this documentation from within your web browser. Here, we are going to look at the more old-fashioned way, using your favorite ftp software. Without necessarily getting into the nitty-gritty details of what to send to Oracle support, let's look at getting files to the appropriate site as backup to your request.

NOTE
*Since we all (the three authors of this book that is) reside in North America, we use an ftp server with the text **us.oracle.com** in the address. Readers elsewhere may use different text, such as **uk.oracle.com** in Europe or **au.oracle.com** in the Asia Pacific region.*

Figure 2-2 illustrates part of the sign-in process to facilitate uploading documentation for your TAR. (The TAR number we use for this example is 1926678.999.)

Once the DOS window shown in Figure 2-2 opens, follow these steps:

1. Enter the command **ftp oracle-ftp.us.oracle.com** to access the support services site.

2. Enter the text **anonymous** in response to the User prompt.

3. Enter your email address as suggested in response to the Password prompt.

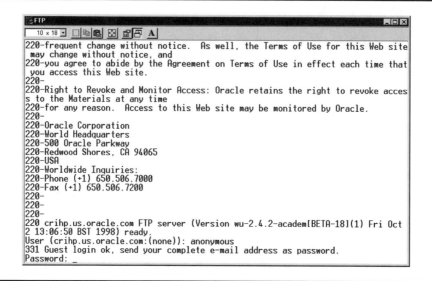

FIGURE 2-2. *Initiating connection and logging into Oracle ftp server*

4. Once logged into the server, some people find it interesting to look at where they are and what sits on the Oracle server. The next listing shows the output of the **ls -l** command:

```
230-Worldwide Inquiries:
230-Phone (+1) 650.506.7000
230-Fax (+1) 650.506.7200
230-
230-
230-
230 Guest login ok, access restrictions apply.
ftp> ls -l
200 PORT command successful.
150 Opening ASCII mode data connection for /bin/ls.
total 10
drwxr-xr-x   6 0          0           1024 Jan  2 09:56 apps
dr-xr-xr-x   2 0          3             96 Aug 21 2004  bin
drwxr-xr-x   7 0          3           1024 Jun 29 2004  dev_tools
dr-xr-xr-x   3 0          3           1024 Aug 21 2003  etc
drwxr-xr-x   3 0          3             96 Dec  9 2000  lms
drwxr-xr-x   2 0          0             96 Dec 18 2002  lost+found
```

```
drwxr-xr-x   7 0          0           1024 Nov 10 18:38 server
drwxr-xr-x   4 0          1             96 Apr  6  2002 tmp
drwxr-xr-x   7 0          3             96 Dec 15 13:03 vendors
drwxr-xr-x   2 10007     22           1024 Dec 11 12:31 wwed
226 Transfer complete.
ftp: 662 bytes received in 0.00Seconds 662000.00Kbytes/sec.
ftp>
```

5. It's the server directory we go to next by issuing the command **cd server**.

6. Underneath that directory, we then proceed to the incoming directory by issuing the command **cd incoming**.

7. Using the sample TAR number, make a directory for the stuff you are about to upload using the command **mkdir 1926678.999**.

8. Change to that directory just made with the command **cd 1926678.999**.

You are now ready to upload files that, for most requests for intervention, include

■ **The instance alert log**   A file that is continually written to as the Oracle9*i* database operates, containing descriptive information and verbiage that may mean something to the support analyst with whom you end up working.

■ **Trace files**   These are session-dependent files that are written as your applications interact with the 9*i* database.

Congratulations! You are now a full-fledged expert at logging a TAR with Oracle Support. Not only that, you can do it by phone; fancy that. In the next section, we are going to look at logging the famous *i*TAR—standing for Internet technical assistance request. Oracle is pushing clients toward the *i*TAR route. It makes most sense to concentrate their efforts in one area; they have chosen the Internet, and we think this makes sense. Before looking at *i*TARs, we will delve into the MetaLink support site and establish a flavor of what Oracle has out there on the Internet.

MetaLink

At the time we went to press with this book, the MetaLink home page was situated at **http://metalink.oracle.com**, shown in Figure 2-3. After entering your login credentials, you are presented with your own MetaLink home page, with a layout similar to that shown in Figure 2-4. The Preferences button shown in this figure is where you go to customize your MetaLink welcome screen.

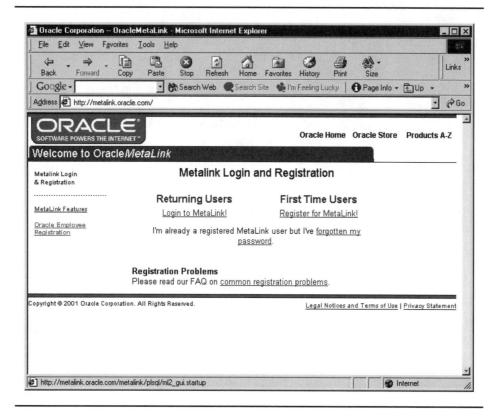

FIGURE 2-3. *MetaLink registration and login*

The answers to most of the questions you could ever think of asking on Oracle can be found using this web interface. There is a plethora of information accessible through the technical libraries; most of the information we get here is the result of browsing these libraries, or simply entering some text in the field beside the Search area on the screen. Let's take a quick peek at the technical libraries, and then test-drive a simple search.

The Technical Libraries

The knowledge base that populates the technical libraries is gleaned from decades of experience in the Oracle support organization. Information on the technology is split into interest areas and product-specific articles, scripts, tips, and techniques.

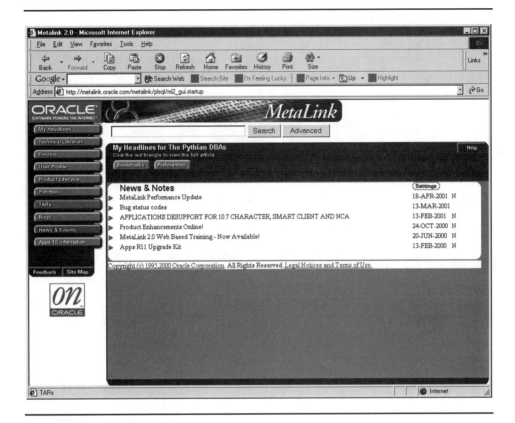

FIGURE 2-4.   *MetaLink welcome screen*

NOTE
Due to the ever-changing face of many Internet sites, the look and feel of MetaLink's technical libraries may be different at the time you visit them after reading this chapter. This material is designed primarily to give you a flavor of the type of information MetaLink provides.

Let's follow one of the areas of expertise in these libraries, called Servers, whose three most popular sections are

■   Database Administration, where you go for assistance with basic administration, architecture, corruption, migration, partitions, security, and storage.

- Performance, the place to go for help with database tuning, SQL tuning, and locking.

- Recovery, which is the spot for articles on general database recovery issues, as well as Oracle Recovery Manager (nicknamed *RMAN*).

Suppose we are looking for help with database and SQL tuning. After selecting an interest area, each is divided into the following five sections:

- Documentation is where product-specific information resides, with material for the user and the administrator.

- Scripts is where you can find snippets of code that will assist in managing the Oracle9i database and its assorted tools.

- White Papers is where you go to peruse technical information, such as data sheets, statements of direction, and feature release information.

- Release Notes/ReadMe discusses issues related to what's new and what's not, as well as product installation specifics.

- Platform Information highlights technical issues, some of which are hardware specific. Herein you will find tools that assist diagnostic activities and the overall database tuning process.

We have now clicked Scripts, presenting a screen similar to that shown in Figure 2-5.

Stand back—cover your eyes. The amount of code that presents itself in the technical libraries is overwhelming. For the beginner all the way up to the advanced reader, there's more than enough code in this section of the libraries to whet your appetite. You are encouraged to download as much as you desire, with the same caveat mentioned in most places where any form of code is dispensed (you assume any and all risk).

NOTE
Some of the code you download from this or other Internet sites requires preliminary setup before it can run error free. This setup may take the form of account setup, database privileges, the database environment, or a handful of other situations.

To illustrate this point before we move on, picture the following two listings that run the same code in different Oracle9i databases.

```
SQL> select count(*)
  2    from dba_tables
  3  where last_analyzed < sysdate-10;
                              *
ERROR at line 1:
ORA-00942: table or view does not exist
. . .
. . . connect to another database
. . .
SQL> select count(*)
  2    from dba_tables
  3  where last_analyzed < sysdate-10;
  COUNT(*)
-----------
       341
```

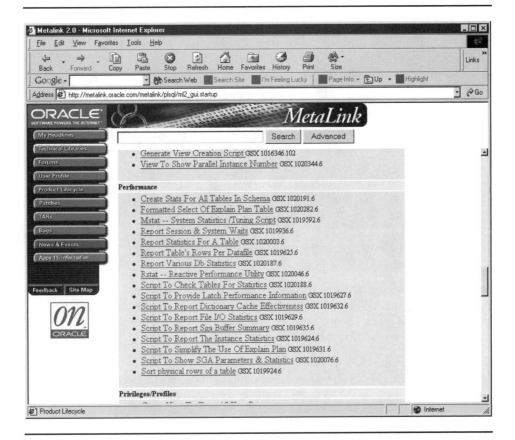

FIGURE 2-5.   *Performance Scripts table of contents*

If and when code from other sources does not work in your Oracle database, look inward (the configuration in place) rather than outward (blaming the creators of code for not testing their SQL statements) for answers. Now let's take a look at another area of interest on MetaLink—the forums.

The Forums

After clicking Forums on the MetaLink main page, as shown in Figure 2-4, you are presented with the initial forum search screen where you can specify

- The product that you are interested in. You can read about it or participate in an online dialogue with other users and Oracle technical experts.

- Threads, where you specify what type of conversation you wish to inspect. Think of *thread* as a fancy word for electronic dialogue.

- Time, which lets you choose items from anywhere in the previous 24 hours to the last 360 days. We have found the Last Visit option the most useful. This one helps you ignore information you have already studied.

- Participation, which strips out items to which you have made a contribution.

Suppose the criteria chosen are Oracle Server Enterprise Edition, New, and Since 2 Days, leaving Participation unselected. Let's get started by clicking Open Forum. The next screen shows a list of qualifying articles, and you select one entitled Getting ORA-02067 Error When Long Column Remote Update Fails, presenting the screen shown in Figure 2-6.

The interesting thing about these articles is that many of them track the dialogue between different Oracle users, with and without the participation of Oracle support personnel. You must pay attention to the following details when studying articles:

- **RDBMS version**   Oracle software version, with numbers like 9i Release 1, or perhaps 8.1.7.2, or even 8.0.6.1.

- **Operating system and version**   The information here will be familiar to most readers, taking the form of text similar to Sun Solaris 5.8, Compaq TRU64 UNIX 5.1F, or Linux 2.2.16-3smp #1. This is the applicable hardware platform and O/S version.

- **Error number (if applicable)**   Generally taking the form of a three-character prefix like ORA followed by a five-digit number. As you get more and more experience with the Oracle9i software, you will start to recognize the error message numbers.

- **Product** The Oracle product in use when the event occurred that led to someone's posting the article in the first place. You will often see entries here like SQL*Plus or PL/SQL.

- **Product version** Most products have a version number matching the server edition version, but some use a different numbering system.

This type of tombstone information is invaluable when you are looking for assistance and you need solutions. You can often quickly find information about the gamut of Oracle server and product versions by browsing these forums, hunting for answers to your questions. Figure 2-7 shows such an answer, more than likely pumped into MetaLink by one of your colleagues.

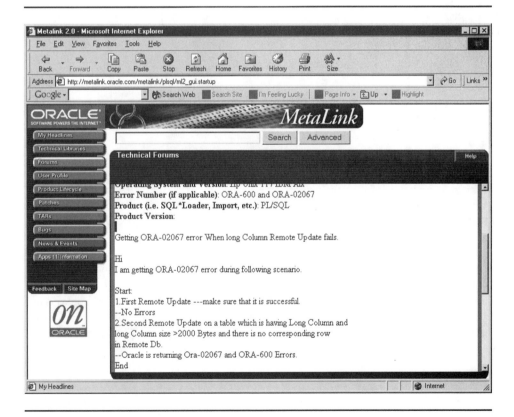

FIGURE 2-6. *Technical forums selection results*

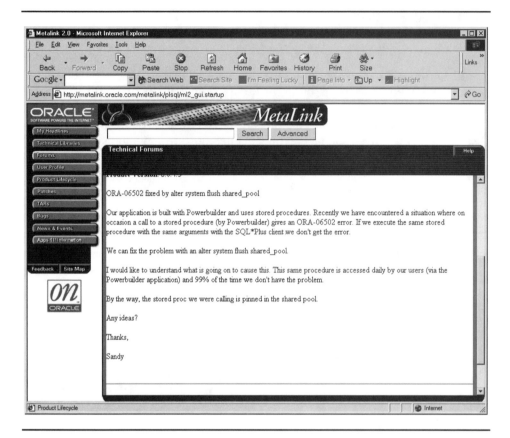

FIGURE 2-7. *User posting to MetaLink forum*

Another thing we like about these forums is that it's mostly your everyday Jill and Jack techie just like ourselves that hangs out on these forums. The exchange of information and advice can be extremely helpful, especially when working with a product so deep as the Oracle9*i* server and its associated product lines. Before closing the door on this brief introduction to MetaLink, let's discuss the *i*TAR process.

*i*Tars

Even though we are showing you how to perform this activity, there are prerequisites that have to be in place before you can go about the *i*TAR creation process covered here.

NOTE
You must register for MetaLink with an appropriate customer support identifier, given to you by Oracle when you signed a support contract. Not all readers are necessarily going to be able to log iTARs; this is something to take up with your Oracle contacts if you fall into this category.

So, let's get started already! After selecting the Tar button on the left side of the screen, you are given the opportunity to view or create TARs. Let's click Create a TAR, as shown in Figure 2-8, and then quickly look at the creation process, starting with entering tombstone information.

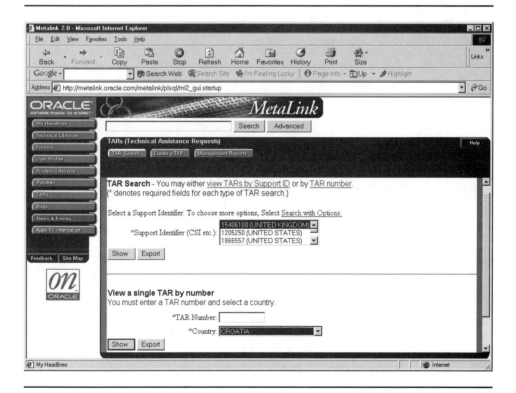

FIGURE 2-8. *Proceeding to TAR creation process*

NOTE
More than likely, you will create TAR profiles to use with subsequent visits to MetaLink; for this exercise, we will simply enter profile-related information without using an existing one.

Client Tombstone Information

Oracle support wants to get to know you better, and asks for the following information before the TAR creation process begins.

- **Contact me via** Enter your preferred communication method for support analysts, be it electronic (the *i*TAR interface), phone, fax, or telephone.

- **Product** Enter the Oracle product that you are calling about.

- **Product version** Enter the version of the product you're working with, for example, SQL*Plus 9.0.1.0.0.

- **Platform** Enter the manufacturer of your computer.

- **Operating system version** Enter the appropriate release number of your O/S.

- **Database version** Enter just that; go as far as you can in this number—9.1.3.0 is more meaningful than 9.1.

- **Support identifier** Select a number from the drop-down list of the CSI numbers you are allowed to log an *i*TAR against.

- **Phone** Enter (you guessed it) your phone number—fancy that!

When you're finished, click Continue to carry on.

Brief TAR Description

This is where you start to enter information related to the nature of your request for technical assistance. Thoroughness is the secret of using the *i*TAR interface successfully. To illustrate, suppose you had a car accident on International Drive South near the Marriott World. Calling for assistance and saying you're on the boulevard beside the red hotel doesn't mean as much as the name of the street, the direction you are pointing, and the brand name of the red hotel. In the theme of being thorough, you enter the following:

- **Type of problem** There is a drop-down list for this field, helping support services classify the nature of your request. Networking and Connectivity

Issues, Oracle Applications General Issues, and Database Issues are some of the choices in that list.

■ **Error message**   This is where you enter the Oracle error numbers, starting with the three-character facility (usually, but not always, ORA) and the five-digit message number. Entries such as ORA-00600 or ORA-07445 are frequent.

■ **Brief subject statement**   This is where you enter some short descriptive text about the problem that led to the *i*TAR creation, for example, "I was trying to install 9*i* and was told that a script had to be run by root."

You're just about there. When you click Continue, MetaLink ingests the information you have entered and places you on a screen similar to that shown in Figure 2-9. You can often find the answer to the problem you are having on this page; bonus—if this happens, *fait accomplis*! No need to go any further.

If you do not find what you are looking for in this list of technical bulletins, as the page suggests, click Continue with TAR Creation. If you go this route, you will be presented with a series of Q&A screens requesting more detailed information about your request for intervention. We are not going to take the time to walk through this electronic dialogue any further; it is not a very time-consuming process. Before we move on to a quick look at Oracle Technology Network and Oracle AppsNet, let's spend a minute on suggestions for making your professional relationship with Oracle Support Services the best for both of you. Follow these guidelines, and you will get the most out of your hard-earned support contract dollars (pounds, francs, guilders, yen, deutsche mark, or lira, in some other popular locations around the world).

■ Assemble pertinent version information and error message numbers before looking at MetaLink and beginning the TAR creation process.

■ Prepare a list of supporting documentation that you will eventually upload to OSS to support the TAR you may end up logging.

■ Ensure that support services has the correct contact information for the person (normally yourself) who will be driving the intervention request from your end. If for some reason you are going to be at alternative email or phone locations and do not inform Oracle, don't complain when you are not contacted.

■ Be realistic with your expectations. Suppose you are having difficulty mapping a key sequence to a certain activity. The documentation you are reading suggests a list of steps to follow that is just not working. You call Oracle, open a TAR, and then expect them to drop everything and attend to your needs. Suppose, at the same time, a handful of large Internet clients' production databases are down, costing one $120,000 per hour in lost revenue, the other a potential missed opportunity to enroll 1,500 new clients per hour. Put yourself in their position; be thankful Oracle is attending to your request, and have realistic expectations.

■ Ensure that you have all your bases covered. Suppose you are having problems with some newfangled functionality of the Oracle9i server, and you are tearing your hair out. You do some research beforehand and find that an entry in an initialization parameter file on your server is not set properly. It must be set to 9.1.1.0, and you know very well it is. At the last minute, before opening an iTAR, you look in this file on your server and, to your horror, see an entry **compatible = 8.1.7.1.1**. Voilà! Problem solved.

I think we've spent enough time on iTAR. Oracle AppsNet and Oracle Technology Network are two places many of you will frequent from the second you enter the Internet world of Oracle9i.

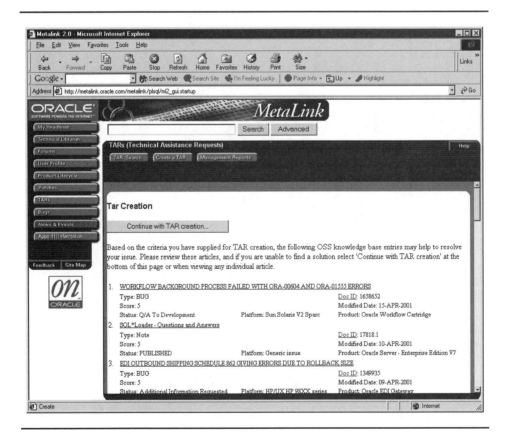

FIGURE 2-9. *Precreation technical bulletins*

Oracle Technology Network

According to Oracle Corporation and a large part of the user community, Oracle Technology Network is *the* place to hang out on the Internet. Point your browser to **http://otn.oracle.com/index.html** for a whirlwind look at the site nicknamed *OTN*. Talk about one-stop shopping; this is a veritable supermarket. Figure 2-10 shows the OTN startup screen. Notice the bubble help that reads FREE Membership; funny how that four-letter word starting with *F* is such an attraction.

NOTE
There is a lot you can do on OTN without becoming a member; certain areas and functionality are not available until you join.

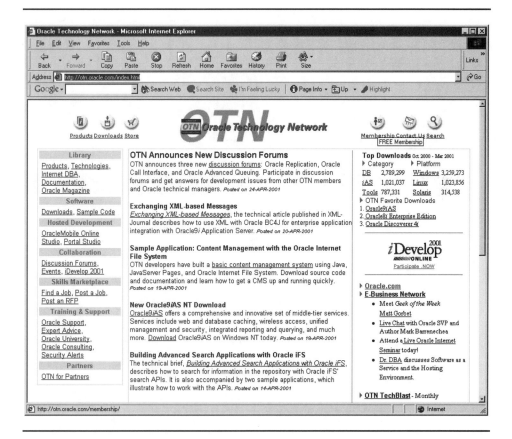

FIGURE 2-10. *Oracle Technology Network*

Let's take a quick peek at a few offerings from OTN. Start by clicking Downloads in the Software menu on the left of Figure 2-10, taking you to a screen entitled Download Oracle Products, Drivers, and Utilities. Suppose you are looking for the 9*i* Application Server (9*i* AS). Select that item from the pick list on the left, which positions you at a page similar to that shown in Figure 2-11.

Suppose you're looking for Oracle9*i* AS v1.0.2 for Linux (Intel). You click that link, which takes you to a screen where you must answer some legal questions about your eligibility to download this fabulous software; then you click I Accept to move to the actual download area. When the download screen appears, select the ias9i_linux.tar link to finish this exercise. Oracle packages their software for download in a number of ways:

■ When the software is destined for a UNIX environment, it is usually in a *tar* compressed format that you transport to your server and uncompress.

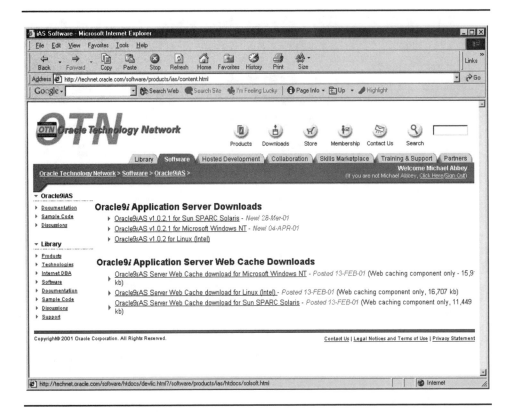

FIGURE 2-11. *Ready to download*

- When packaged for Windows 98, Me, or 2000, the software is usually available in one large WinZip (**www.winzip.com**) format, sized anywhere from around 150MB to sometimes over 500MB. Once downloaded, you have to uncompress the software before installation.

- Sometimes for these desktop environments, you can download the software in smaller pieces along with an accompanying batch file to reassemble the pieces on the desktop in preparation for installation.

Regardless of what you are looking for and the nature of the hardware on which it will reside, we have been happy with the throughput of the download from this web site. We think back to the dark ages of Internet access via a 9,600-baud modem when we consider downloads in the hundreds of megabytes—that was next to impossible! There are other places to obtain software on the OTN site. There are places where you can purchase *technology tracks*—hardware- or solution-based packages of software vended together for the purchaser's convenience. These packages are fully functional products designed for application developers, with free upgrades for 12 months from initial purchase date.

Oracle AppsNet

AppsNet membership, unlike MetaLink where we just visited, is free. If you have already registered, click Sign In. If this is your first visit to **http://www.oracle.com/ appsnet/index.html**, fill out registration information. After completing the registration process, you are presented with a screen similar to that shown in Figure 2-12.

NOTE
Oracle uses the term "Applications" to refer to their commercial off-the-shelf suite of business solutions, such as Financials, HR, and Accounts Payable, to name a few. Your systems written using Oracle's technology can also be referred to as Oracle applications; the terminology is confusing.

To give you a flavor of what is on this high-traffic web site, click the Member tab of this screen to bring up the Members-Only information areas. Many customers spend most if not all of their time in this area, split into the following sections:

- User and Implementation documentation is where you find late-breaking information made available since the latest product release dates.

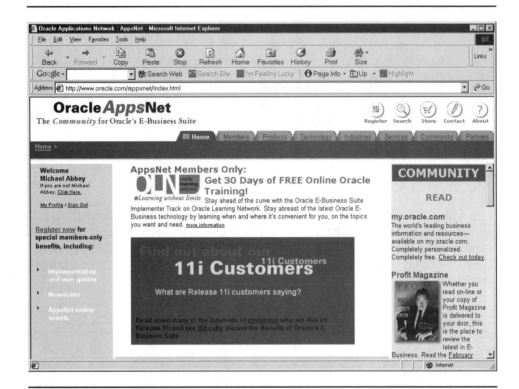

FIGURE 2-12. *AppsNet customized member welcome screen*

■ The Newsletters section contains new product and partner information, bundled under the title Oracle AppsNet eNews. Oracle's E-Business Suite is the heart of the technical information contained herein.

■ E-Business Suite information contains details on issues related to language and platform availability.

■ Presentations is where you go to look at technical conference–related information stemming from inside Oracle Corporation and the most popular user-group–driven forum called Oracle Applications User Group (OAUG).

■ White papers presents information on topics such as applications manageability and multilingual issues.

Regardless of where you go from here, you could end up spending a lot of time on the pages accessible from this members-only section. The peer-to-peer discussion forums under the Community tab shown in Figure 2-12 are where many people go to interact with fellow professionals. Figure 2-13 shows the startup screen for those discussion groups.

Interaction with fellow users of the Oracle technology is the best way to keep adding to your knowledge. Oracle's E-Business Suite, along with many other components of their product lines, is very complex. Many times, you find yourself struggling with some obscure piece of functionality embedded in the E-Business Suite and find a handful of other users in the same predicament. Suppose you are in charge of mapping out the delivery of the upgraded applications—a list of tasks and some time-to-market estimates for each one. For starters, you toddle off to the AppsNet discussion forum and retrieve some information posted by fellow users, as shown in Figure 2-14. The person who responded to this question says at the end of his answer, "I hope this helped!! Good luck"; you say to yourself, "I'll say it helped!"

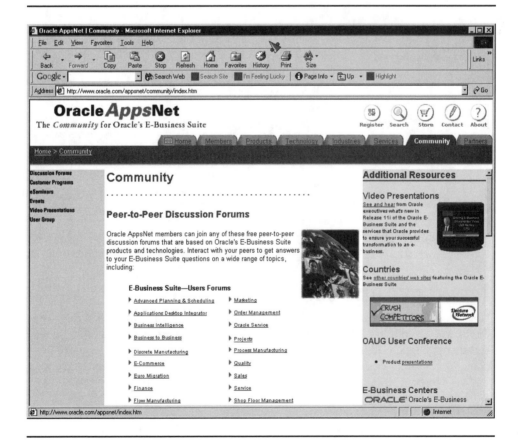

FIGURE 2-13. *Peer-to-peer discussion forums*

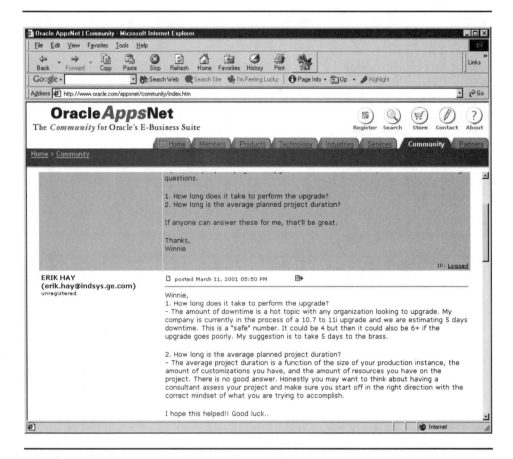

FIGURE 2-14. *Technical assistance gleaned from AppsNet Forum*

Newsgroups and List Servers

Newsgroups and list servers—the best thing on the Internet and the worst thing on the Internet. Wouldn't it be nice if you could go somewhere and hang out with your Oracle cybertech buddies and get just about any question answered? It's a dream come true, and for perhaps 10–15 percent of the messages posted via newsgroups and list servers, they suit your needs just fine. There are essentially two problems with information exchange via these two mechanisms:

■ Many people who post messages here have difficulty staying on topic; we're not talking about a mild dose of "straying off topic syndrome"—we mean an advanced case. Nobody who frequents the **comp.databases.oracle.**

server newsgroup cares whether Betty Houlihan in Beijing has two Springsteen tickets for the 27th in Los Angeles since her trip to the United States was canceled. The fact that Sydney Fricker in Alabama is looking for the left chrome headlight rim for a '56 DeSoto four-door means nothing to the business at hand.

■   The sheer volume of emails that you receive when subscribed to some of these list servers is overwhelming. When you subscribe, you will no doubt anticipate the pending arrival of a handful of useful emails that will immediately solve all your problems. Try again—sometimes you may receive 200–300 or more emails per day! The volume is so staggering, many subscribers cancel their membership in a matter of days. The last thing any of us needs is more emails—we already receive more than we can handle anyway.

With that said, let's look at a handful of list servers and newsgroups that, after you weed through the nuisance postings, can sometimes prove helpful.

Newsgroups

A number of you have probably already hung out in other newsgroups, but the heart of the Oracle newsgroups, from our experience, have been **comp.databases.oracle.server**, **comp.databases.oracle.misc**, and **comp.databases.oracle.tool**. There are different programs out there to access your Internet provider's newsgroups; we are using Forté Free Agent.

NOTE
It is your responsibility to install and configure your own news reader. The screen shots and material we cover in this section assume this has already been done and you can successfully download and post messages.

Browsing Messages

Anyone can post just about anything on any topic related to the Oracle server and have input from around the world. You will judge after you have started using these newsgroups how valuable they are to you. Figure 2-15 shows the screen presented after successfully subscribing to the three groups mentioned in the previous paragraph.

This being our first tour of Free Agent, let's look at some important areas of the screen and buttons you will use the most:

■   As the bubble help in Figure 2-15 shows (Get New Headers in Subscribed Groups), the leftmost menu button retrieves new headers for subscribed groups. The length of time for this activity depends on how many groups you have subscribed to plus the time since you last refreshed.

■ The next button to the right (Get New Headers in Selected Groups) is used to retrieve headers in a subset of subscribed groups.

■ The screen is divided into three areas, as shown in Figure 2-15:

   ■ Area 1 is where the newsgroups are displayed. You can toggle between showing all groups or subscribed groups by selecting Group I Show, and then All Groups or Subscribed Groups from Group on the menu bar.

   ■ Area 2 shows a list of messages sorted in ascending order of date posted. Forté's commercial version, called Agent, allows you to sort any way you want by clicking the appropriate column header. This is the behavior we are used to from Windows Explorer.

   ■ Area 3 is where retrieved messages are displayed. When browsing headers in Area 2, a message is fetched from the news server by a double-click.

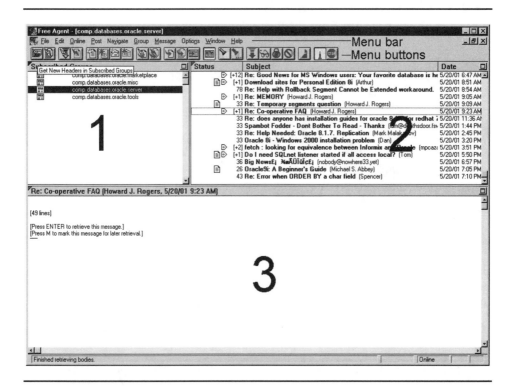

FIGURE 2-15. *Forté Free Agent subscribed groups*

Many users of the newsgroups are in read-only mode—meaning they simply browse and do not post. In the next section, let's follow part of a dialogue to illustrate how useful these groups can be.

A Newsgroup Dialogue

While hanging out at the Oracle server newsgroup, we posted a question in three parts. Figure 2-16 shows a portion of our original question and the response from Randall Roberts, an instructor at Learning Tree University in Costa Mesa, California. Interestingly, Randall, being the educational expert that he is, got full marks on his responses. Some of them were so thorough, we are going to present him with an honorary Ph.D. in Oracle!

List Servers

List servers are like electronic chain letters, except there is nothing to send in and nothing to distribute to thousands of your closest email buddies. One of the most

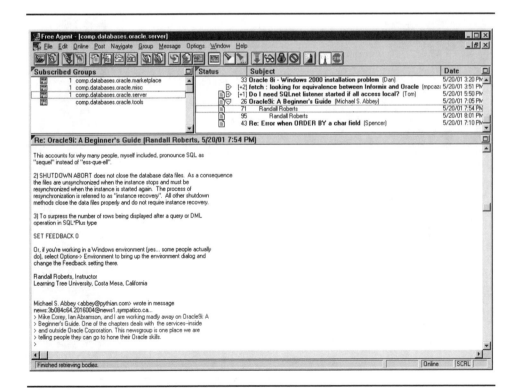

FIGURE 2-16. *Dialogue on comp.databases.oracle.server*

popular list servers is called LazyDBA. Let's look at signing up for this list to get a flavor of the chitchat that goes on inside it.

Subscribing to LazyDBA

The simplest way to subscribe to the list is by going to the Internet site shown in Figure 2-17. After clicking the Subscribe link, you will be positioned in your favorite email program, hopefully with your correct email address showing. Click Send or whatever you are used to, and enter LazyDBA land. You will receive an acknowledgment email similar to that shown in the next listing; as suggested, simply respond to activate your account.

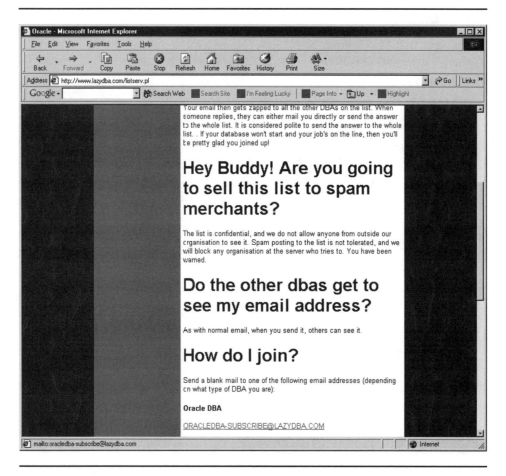

FIGURE 2-17. *Signing up for LazyDBA via its web site*

```
Mailing-List: contact oracledba-help@lazydba.com; run by ezmlm
List-Help: <mailto:oracledba-help@lazydba.com>
List-Post: <mailto:oracledba@lazydba.com>
List-Subscribe: <mailto:oracledba-subscribe@lazydba.com>
Date: 31 May 2004 23:39:56 -0000
From: oracledba-help@lazydba.com
To: abbey@pythian.com
Delivered-To: responder for oracledba@lazydba.com
Reply-To: oracledba-sc.990401996.eihddbofbgoinjgdmpie-
          abbey=pythian.com@lazydba.com
Subject: confirm subscribe to oracledba@lazydba.com
Hi! This is the ezmlm program. I'm managing the
oracledba@lazydba.com mailing list.
I'm working for my owner, who can be reached
at oracledba-owner@lazydba.com.
To confirm that you would like
   abbey@pythian.com
added to the oracledba mailing list, please send
an empty reply to this address:
```

Picking up Email from the List Server

One of the things we like so much about this type of facility is that there is nothing else to do. Simply sit back and enjoy. When you respond to an email from the list server, your email address appears in the response and is then viewable to the world. Is that a problem? You decide. Some people prefer to use the web-based facility to view the most recent 300 messages on the list. An example of this is shown in Figure 2-18.

Unsubscribing from LazyDBA

The assortment of administrative information for LazyDBA is shown in the next listing, with instructions italicized for unsubscribing.

```
--- Administrative commands for the oracledba list ---
I can handle administrative requests automatically. Please
do not send them to the list address! Instead, send
your message to the correct command address:
For help and a description of available commands, send a message to:
   <oracledba-help@lazydba.com>
To subscribe to the list, send a message to:
   <oracledba-subscribe@lazydba.com>
To remove your address from the list, just send a message to
the address in the "List-Unsubscribe" header of any list
message. If you haven't changed addresses since subscribing,
you can also send a message to:
   <oracledba-unsubscribe@lazydba.com>
```

```
or for the digest to:
   <oracledba-digest-unsubscribe@lazydba.com>
For addition or removal of addresses, I'll send a confirmation
message to that address. When you receive it, simply reply to it
to complete the transaction.
If you need to get in touch with the human owner of this list,
please send a message to:
   <oracledba-owner@lazydba.com>
```

Before we move on and have a look at some of our favorite Internet sites, we must spend a few minutes on list server etiquette and a caveat or two about its technical information.

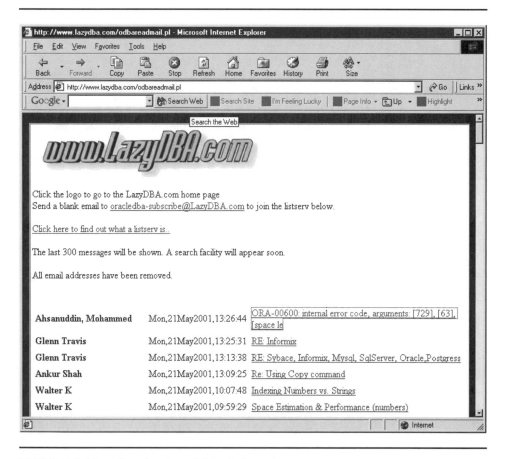

FIGURE 2-18. *Reading LazyDBA via browser*

Etiquette and Caveats

Two words describe the one and only way to behave on this and all other list servers—be nice! Unfortunately, the language and behavior of some people who post information on these lists is less than exemplary. Try to stay on topic and be brief. The most useful information comes from clear, concise, and to-the-point postings. The downside of the lists can be the volume of information you will end up receiving once subscribed. It's easy to tire quickly based on the number of emails you will receive. Keep the following in mind when posting and responding to emails on a list server:

- A lot of people who post to this and other list servers end up straying into territory with which they are not too familiar. It is tempting to respond to questions you are not qualified to answer. Take on only the material you are comfortable with handling and confident you really know well enough to instruct others.

- Before responding, keep in mind that the material you post will be taken as the "law," so to speak, by many readers. If you post code snippets, please run them before you send them into the list server abyss to be run, untested, by the throngs.

To give you an example of how easy it is to inadvertently mislead someone, here is some advice we read on LazyDBA:

```
Original question: Does anyone know how to turn on auto tracing for SQL
statements using release 8.1.7 on Sun? As well, does auto tracing trace
DELETE statements of just SELECT? Thanks in advance! -MG
Original response: We use autotrace, abbreviated to set auto on, which
will display SQL statement access paths rather than run the statements.
Yes, it will  trace DELETE statements. - MC
```

You would not believe how disappointed MG must have been when she tried to autotrace some statements, as shown in the next listing. The comments in the listing explain the problem with the response received from MC. The problem with the advice given by MC is that **set auto on** is a short form for **set autocommit on**, which commits transactions as soon as they are processed by Oracle9*i*.

```
SQL> -- Turn on auto tracing, according to MC abbreviated as set auto on,
SQL> -- when the true abbreviation is set autot on!
SQL> set auto on
SQL> select count(*),event
  2     from v$waitstat
  3     group by event;
   COUNT(*) EVENT
```

```
---------- ------------------------
         1 PX Deq Credit: send blkd
         1 PX Deq: Execute Reply
         3 PX Deq: Execution Msg
         4 PX Deq: Table Q Normal
        47 SQL*Net message from client
         2 SQL*Net message to client
         9 buffer busy waits
         2 db file parallel read
         6 db file scattered read
        11 db file sequential read
         1 enqueue
         4 latch free
         1 lock manager wait for remote message
         1 pmon timer
        25 rdbms ipc message
         1 smon timer
16 rows selected.
SQL> -- Delete rows in ST_WIDE table for the state of Missouri,
SQL> -- mistakenly abbreviated MI in this snippet rather than MO.
SQL> -- MI is the abbreviation for Michigan! Imagine the horror when
SQL> -- finding out that not only were the Michigan rows deleted, but
SQL> -- the transaction was immediately committed!
SQL> delete st_wide
  2    where st_code = 'MI';
346 rows deleted.
Commit complete.
```

Next, let's take a peek at accessing online Oracle9i documentation. In the olden days (circa 1992, for example), we used to order docs from Oracle and spend hundreds of dollars on boxes of paper we never even opened. The medium upon which Oracle software is distributed contains technical and user documentation in HTML and Adobe PDF format; the same material is online, as we discover in the next section.

Online Documentation

Around the time Oracle was releasing version 7, they were in the midst of transitioning to documentation on CD-ROM. At the time, many of us could not imagine how we could ever get along without the paper docs we had become so used to. Figure 2-19 shows one of our favorite online documentation sites. This URL has worked for a few years, but as many of us find out all too often, it could cease to function before this book goes to press.

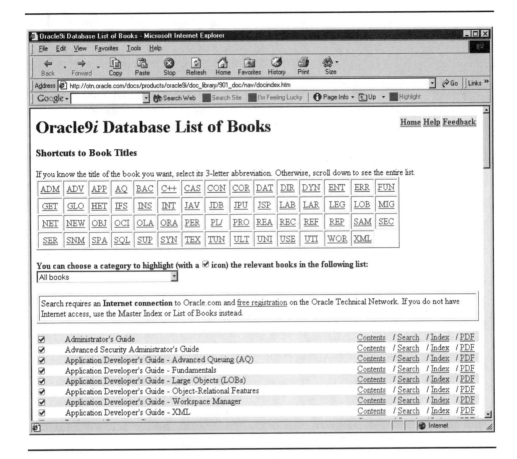

FIGURE 2-19. *Online documentation welcome screen*

Many readers may already have their favorite online documentation site, and the following URLs may prove useful:

■ Buried with the Oracle Technology Network web site is **http://technet.oracle.com/docs/content.html**, where the material is grouped by server release (9*i*, in this case), related features and products (for example, Spatial or Enterprise Manager), Oracle9*i* Application Server, the Internet Development Suite, Data Warehousing and Business Intelligence, and Oracle's E-Business Suite with a hot link pointing to Oracle AppsNet.

- An unofficial third-party site resides at **http://www.oradoc.com/index.html**. They have an interesting search facility here, where you enter one or more keywords and the engine looks through a preselected list of server versions (such as 9.0.1 and 8.1.7).

- Michael Dahlinger, an Oracle server person at GSI, a heavy ion research center funded by the federal government of Germany and the state of Hesse, is responsible for the link at **http://www-wnt.gsi.de/oragsi/oracle_ documentation.html**. The site has quick access links to some of the most popular and useful components of the documentation set—installation and SQL Language Reference in particular.

One issue that comes up regularly with DBAs and other Oracle technical personnel involves resolution of Oracle error message numbers. An online error message utility on UNIX platforms is illustrated in the next listing.

```
/home/oracle/product/9.0.1 -->(o9ibeg)
oracle> oerr ora 20
00020, 00000, "maximum number of processes (%s) exceeded"
// *Cause:  All process state objects are in use.
// *Action: Increase the value of the PROCESSES initialization parameter.
oracle> oerr imp 8
00008, 00000, "unrecognized statement in the export file: \n  %s"
// *Cause:  Import did not recognize a statement in the export file. Either
//          the export file was corrupted, or an Import internal error has
//          occurred.
// *Action: If the export file was corrupted, retry with a new export file.
//          Otherwise, report this as an Import internal error and submit
//          the export file to customer support.
```

The **oerr** command expects two arguments—the facility (shown in italics in the listing, as in *ora* for Oracle server or *imp* for Oracle's import utility) and the error message number shown in bold.

We prefer the documentation in HTML format, as it provides quicker navigation around an online documentation web site. The documentation is also available online in Adobe Acrobat Reader format (**www.adobe.com**), a free utility, available just about anywhere on the Internet. The Adobe format is more easily searchable, but the link mentioned in the previous list of online documentation links (**http:// www.oradoc.com/index.html**) provides a nice search facility of its own.

In the last part of this chapter we are going to highlight a few of our favorite web sites for Oracle technical information. Get familiar with these sites; you may be spending a great deal of time on them now and well into the future.

Out of Site!

Before we get started on the meat of this part of the chapter (or the carrots, for the noncarnivorous readership), let's look at some reasons why we visit these sites.

- Oracle, regardless of the version, is a very complex product. There is always something you can learn from your fellow technical counterparts. Suppose there were 12,000 units of technical knowledge embedded in the Oracle 9*i* software. Your day-to-day job covers less than a quarter of these units. The other 9,000 units involve issues that you have not yet encountered. Instead of waiting for the opportunity to experience these issues firsthand, familiarize yourself with some of them by visiting these sites.

- Oracle Corporation's online technical offerings, for most people, make up the backbone of the Internet sites they visit. Looking into the user community's experiences with the Oracle products and services rounds out any information you may find on Oracle corporate sites.

- There's nothing like learning it from the experts. Be it beginner, intermediate, or advanced, there is such a vast assortment of technical information out there, it's staggering! Why struggle needlessly with a problem, when the answer is not hard to find on the Internet?

In many cases, until you find your own favorite sites, your favorite Internet search engine is a good place to start—and that's where we are going to start.

Internet Search Engines

Discussing search engines is tantamount to looking at the types of lead pencils manufactured. There is such a vast assortment of engines out there, and we all have our favorites! For the sake of this part of the chapter, we will concentrate on where these search engines send you rather than the engine itself. With that said, we will use **www.google.com** as an example. After the web browser is opened, and positioned at this URL, you will see a screen similar to that shown in Figure 2-20.

Your browser, be it Internet Explorer or Netscape Navigator, may look different from what is shown in Figure 2-20. We used one that displays the Google toolbar that we installed by following a link on their site. We entered the text **9i database**, clicked Google Search, and were presented with a results screen similar to the one in Figure 2-21.

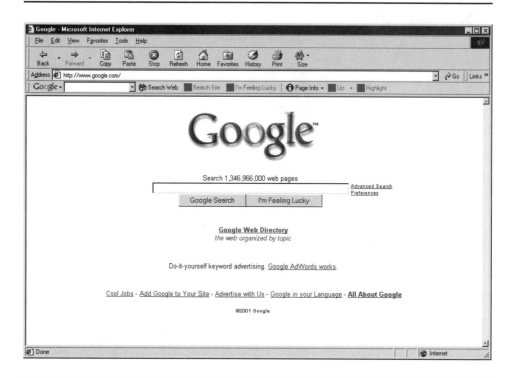

FIGURE 2-20. *Google search engine home page*

One thing we especially like about Google is the I'm Feeling Lucky button—no nonsense please, just take me directly to the site with the heaviest hit on our search string. Oddly enough, we have also found that Internet search engines can be our best friends as well as our worst. Suppose, as a newbie, you wanted to find information on Oracle9*i* Personal Edition software and entered the text **oracle** as a search string. Table 2-1 illustrates our concept of "worst friend"—more web sites than you could even think of visiting.

Let's spend a few minutes on some web searching tips, helpful to both the neophyte and many veterans on the Internet.

Internet Search Engine Tips

Without spending an enormous amount of time on this, search engine math is about the most useful tool at your disposal. Table 2-2 describes the most useful math that may help you narrow down a search from returning millions to hundreds of sites.

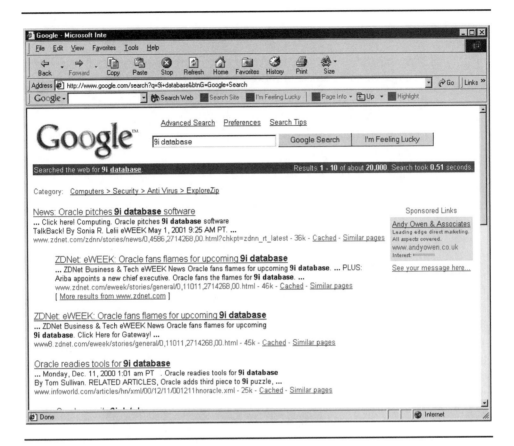

FIGURE 2-21.   *Search results for 9i database*

Search Criteria	Hits
Oracle	~4,100,000
Oracle personal	~571,000
Oracle personal edition	~70,400
Oracle9*i* personal edition	~305

TABLE 2-1.   *Web Hits for Different Search Criteria*

Symbol	Meaning	Example
+	Search for sites containing all of the words entered, not just one or more.	+unix +redhat +oracle +developer +tools
–	Search for sites containing words prefixed by + and deliberately not containing those prefixed by –.	+oracle9i –suse +b2b +oracle –server
" "	Find the enclosed words in the exact order they appear in the lookup string.	"oracle9i locks latches"

TABLE 2-2.   *Basic Search Engine Math*

Some of Our Favorite Sites

Enough said about searching—most if not all of us have a favorite search engine and have been using it for years. There is such a plethora of technical information out there on Oracle technology; here's a handful of our favorite sites:

- Oracle User Forum and Fan Club at **www.orafans.com** is helpful due to the volume of postings. When on the site's home page, we selected rdbms, sql, pl/sql from a pick list of discussion forums, which brought us to the page shown in Figure 2-22. Notice how there are over 65 pages of items, with a good chance you will find what you are looking for.

- Oracle Magazine at **www.oracle.com/oramag/index.html** is a well-rounded information site, with something for just about all readers, especially those getting started. The Online Only section of this site has links to position you at some very useful code, and tips you may find useful from day one.

- Steve Adams, an experienced Oracle server resource in Australia, offers a wealth of information at **www.ixora.com.au/home.htm**. Steve has been living and breathing Oracle's technology for many years, and has gleaned some very useful and technical information for his busy web site. Figure 2-23 shows the menu presented after selecting Scripts from Ixora's home page.

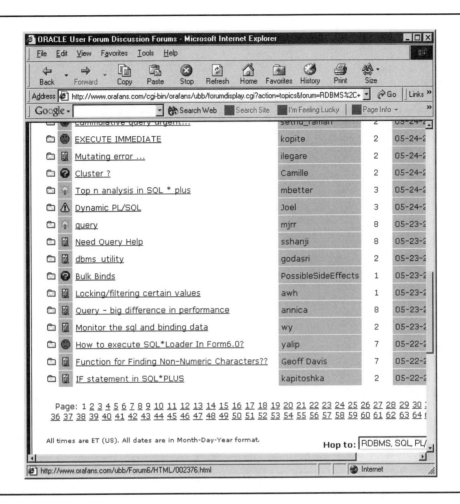

FIGURE 2-22. *orafans.com discussion forum*

Now that was a handful. Whatever your experience level, you will find more than enough help out there on the Internet. Often we think back to the days before this information explosion and wonder how we ever managed. It's time to move on. In the next chapter, we will have a look at the all-encompassing foundation of the current Oracle software offering—the 9*i* server. Enjoy!

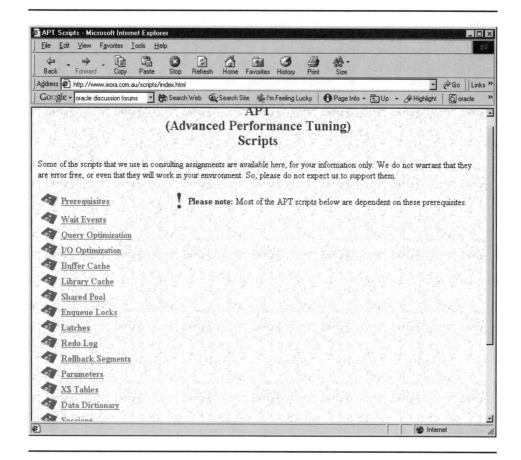

FIGURE 2-23. *Ixora—a distinct Oracle technical resource*

Chapter 2 Questions

Answers to questions can be found in Appendix A.

   I. The TAR, or technical assistance request, is the vehicle used to access the following organization at Oracle:

     A. Sales

     B. Feature Acquisition

C. Tech Support

D. MetaLink

2. If you use command-line ftp to transfer files to support services when logging TARs, what username or login account would you use to access Oracle's servers?

A. Your CSI

B. oracle9i_help

C. anonymous

D. This cannot be done.

3. When logging an *i*TAR, what is the single most helpful thing you can do to speed up the process?

A. Describe in great detail exactly what you were doing when you encountered the problem leading to the TAR creation.

B. Assemble relevant trace and log files and upload them somehow to Oracle Support Services.

C. Do not log a TAR unless your production database is down.

D. Do not call until you can reproduce the error.

4. Oracle's one-stop shop for software downloads and technical information on their products is

A. Oracle Support

B. Technet

C. LazyDBA

D. MetaLink

5. The best corporate site to go for E-Business and Oracle Applications information is

A. Oracle Support

B. Technet

C. MetaLink

D. AppsNet

CHAPTER
3

The Oracle Server

his chapter is about the ever-popular Oracle server. Regardless of its version number, this product is the backbone of Oracle's technology offering. Whether you're an Internet company, charged with providing "25 × 8" (the familiar 24 × 7 to the max) to a hungry worldwide community, or a multinational bank, the server is your best friend. This is what we are going to discuss in this chapter:

- Introduction to the architecture of the server

- Background support processes and the role each plays

- Makeup of the database instance, paying attention to the four main components—the initialization parameter file, data files, redo logs, and control files

- Rollback segments and the functionality they support with Oracle9i

- Highlights of the significant Oracle9i memory structures

- Locks and latches

Terminology

The following definitions will arm you with the technical jargon to make it through this chapter.

- An *executable* is a special kind of computer code that, when invoked, runs a program to accomplish a desired task. For example, the word processing program we used to write this book, Microsoft Word, is invoked by running an executable called *winword.exe*.

- An Oracle9i *instance* is a set of shared memory processes that provide the mechanism for accessing a set of Oracle database files. We discuss the components of the files that support an Oracle9i instance later in this chapter.

NOTE
It is possible to have multiple instances of Oracle9i running on the same server with separate memory space to support each occurrence.

- The act of opening an Oracle9i database is called *startup*; the closing of and suspension of access to the same database is called *shutdown*.

- Computer memory on a personal computer is often called *RAM,* or random access memory.

- The processor on most classes of computer systems is called a *CPU,* or central processing unit.

- The file read by Oracle9*i* when the database is started is called its *initialization parameter file,* nicknamed an INIT.ora file.

- A *distributed network* is a collection of central and remote computers, interconnected by some form of network transport hardware and software. The nodes in a distributed computing environment can communicate with one another.

- An *application server* is a program in a computer in a distributed network that provides the business logic for an application program.

- *Client server* refers to an architecture in which there is a central network of one or more database servers, a middle-tier application server where most software resides, and a desktop with which users interact with the database.

- In a *checkpoint* activity, Oracle9*i* performs tasks such as data synchronization and integrity checking that assist the smooth operations of the database. Certain activities are associated with the checkpoint operations, which run unattended as the Oracle9*i* database runs.

- A *buffer* is a chunk of memory used by Oracle9*i* to store data as it is massaged by users' sessions. These buffers are periodically and systematically written to disk.

- *Recovery* is a process whereby one or more Oracle9*i* processes restore the database to a consistent state to protect the integrity of the instance. Sometimes, due to a hardware or even human error, an Oracle9*i* database aborts; recovery would be performed when it is restarted.

- The operating system upon which the Oracle9*i* server operates is referred to as the *O/S.*

- Many Windows-based programs use a graphical user interface for user interaction, commonly called *GUI.*

- Oracle Enterprise Manager, or *OEM,* is a GUI that the database administrator may use to interact with the Oracle9*i* database.

- A *TAR* is a technical assistance request, requesting help from Oracle Support Services with some component of the Oracle9*i* server or auxiliary tools.

- Oracle uses the word *commit* in the same context as *save*. When a transaction completes and the user wants the data written back to the database, the transaction is committed.

- When transactions interact with data, Oracle9i keeps an image of the data before it is changed or deleted. It's not a sure thing that when an address is changed from 44 Bourne to 60 Cocksfield that the update will be committed. Until it is, *undo information* is kept by Oracle9i so the change can be undone if necessary. In addition, until the update is committed, other sessions still read the affected row with column values as they were before changes were initiated. This undo can be managed automatically by Oracle9i or stored in DBA-configured *rollback segments,* discussed later in this chapter.

- *Cache* is another word for a portion of memory. There are various types of cache used by Oracle9i—data and SQL statements being the two biggest consumers of memory.

- Oracle9i protects the integrity of data using a *lock*; this mechanism ensures that the same data cannot be changed by more than one user at the same time. Oracle9i uses a facility called *latches* to perform similar activity on shared memory structures.

- *Contention* occurs when more than one process fights for a resource in the Oracle9i database. Suppose a process spins while a different session is using a resource in the database; this can be said to be causing a form of contention. A mad scramble for the last chocolate bobka at a bakery is a form of contention.

- The Structured Query Language—or *SQL,* for short—is an industry-standard mechanism for accessing data in the Oracle9i database. The familiar **select** statement is a construct used in SQL to look at data.

NOTE
It drives some of our readers crazy that we use an rather than a in front of the letters SQL. That is because we pronounce the letters by name; so "an SQL" is pronounced "an-es-kew-ell." Some people say "seequel" instead of the letter names and use the a in front of the acronym, for "a-see-quell."

Architecture of the Server

The server product is simply an executable that performs important activities when it is run. Access to the Oracle9*i* database is supported by the Oracle executable and a series of support routines and files that fall into the categories described in the following list.

NOTE
These are the common players; they are available but may not be used in all Oracle9i installations.

- **INIT.ora**   This file contains entries that determine the runtime environment of the Oracle9*i* database as it operates. The values for the entries in this file control items such as the amount of memory allocated to the instance and the breakdown of the structures within that memory.

- **Shared memory**   Often referred to as RAM on the PC, this is an amount of a computer's memory that is acquired when an Oracle9*i* database is started. This chunk of memory is acquired when the Oracle9*i* server is started and is affectionately called the *SGA*, or system global area.

- **Database files**   These fall into three categories—data files, control files, and redo log files—each of which is discussed in its own section later in this chapter. Figure 3-1 shows a listing of these three types of files on the Ntirety.com server we used to write this book. The files that end in .dbf are data files, the ones in .ctl are control files, and .log files are online redo logs.

NOTE
Even though Oracle9i runs on a wide assortment of computers, we will concentrate on Sun Solaris 5.8 throughout this book. The screen print shown in Figure 3-1 and most figures throughout this book are UNIX.

- **Support processes**   These are workers that are spawned when an Oracle9*i* instance is started, and they help facilitate access to a set of Oracle database files. We spend more time on these in the next few sections under the heading "Background Support Processes."

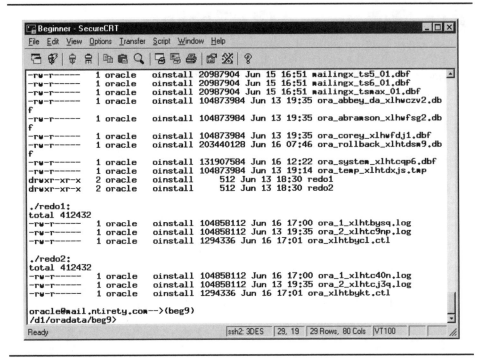

FIGURE 3-1. *Control files, redo logs, and database files*

NOTE
Most of us use the terms database *and* instance
*synonymously. Even though there are subtle
differences between the two, they have the same
meaning throughout this book.*

- **Network access**   This is enabled by Oracle9i's Oracle Net product,
  discussed in more detail in Chapter 12. Its precursors were SQL*Net,
  delivered with versions up to and including Oracle7, and Net8 with
  all releases of Oracle8.

- **Trace files**   These are continually written to as Oracle9i operates
  and are deposited in locations specified in an instance's INIT.ora. They
  contain primarily two kinds of descriptive information—certain types
  of Oracle errors and timestamp information related to some significant
  instance activities.

- **Runtime libraries**   These are the equivalent of PC dynamic link libraries, containing routines and service components that allow the Oracle9*i* server to operate and perform a suite of sophisticated functionality on its user community's behalf.

Let's have a brief look at what goes on as the Oracle9*i* server operates. We will pretend that the software has just been installed, a database created, and the appropriate accounts set up, both on the computer where Oracle9*i* resides and within the Oracle9*i* repository itself.

Background Support Processes

Several background processes support the operation of an Oracle9*i* instance and accept connection requests from users. Figure 3-2 shows the instance support processes; we will discuss the role each plays in supporting this phenomenal piece of software.

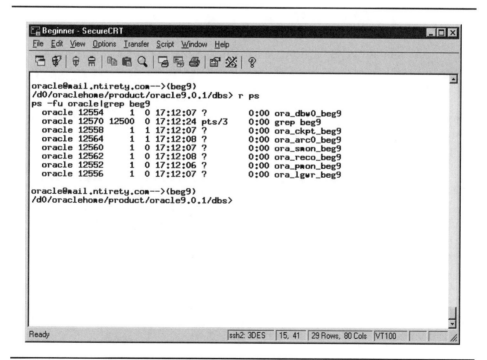

FIGURE 3-2.   *Oracle9i instance support processes*

Database Writer (dbw0)

The database writer is responsible for writing contents of database buffers to disk. Oracle marks buffers in memory as *dirty* when the data they contain is changed. There is one database writer process by default, but you can instruct Oracle9i to spawn up to an additional nine. When a user process needs to access data that is not in the buffer cache, dbwr ensures that these sessions can have access to free buffers to go about their work.

NOTE
Even though we call it dbwr, the Oracle9i processes start with 0, as in dbw0, with increasing sequential integer numbers to 9.

This is the only process that writes data to the database—think of it as the keeper of all the write activities, taking minutes as the database operates. Let's call it the Director of Communications.

Process Monitor (pmon)

The process monitor is responsible for carrying out cleanup if and when any user sessions are ended abnormally and they do not do it themselves. An all-too-common activity is when users abruptly end sessions against the database by pressing CTRL-ALT-DELETE and rebooting their desktop computers. Resources that may have been tied up by aborted sessions are cleaned up and released by pmon. Let's call pmon the Secret Agent, slinking around the database, assuming identities of aborted user sessions, and performing cleanup on their behalf.

System Monitor (smon)

The system monitor has a number of responsibilities, the primary one only happening when the Oracle9i instance is started. At startup, smon's job is to ensure that all the database files are consistent and perform recovery if required. There is also an assortment of other cleanup activities that may need to be done, which are smon's responsibility. Other background processes can wake up smon if work needs doing. The smon process by itself checks every so often to see whether there are any tasks waiting for its attention. The work performed by smon is integral to the smooth operation of any Oracle9i instance. Let's call this process the Comptroller, ensuring that everything is being done according to the book on an ongoing basis.

Log Writer (lgwr)

The log writer is responsible for redo log buffer management. We will discuss redo logs in more detail later in this chapter. Suffice it to say for now that the redo logs are Oracle9*i*'s transaction logs. Almost all activity against the database is tracked in the online redo logs. As transactions are initiated, and eventually committed (saved) or rolled back (abandoned), a record of this activity is written to these log files. The log writer can write records of multiple transactions to the redo log files, thereby maximizing its throughput and performance. Writing this transaction information in batches rather than serially, one at a time, is less time consuming and uses less resources. The log writer is our Bank Teller, recording all the transactions against the virtual Oracle9*i* database bank.

Checkpoint (ckpt)

When a checkpoint activity begins, this process updates all the database data files with the details of the checkpoint. The database writer is the only process that writes data to these database files, whereas the ckpt process ensures the data files are in synch with one another after a checkpoint completes. This process we call the Dispatcher—ensuring all is in synch.

Recoverer (reco)

The recoverer process's primary responsibility is to resolve failed transactions in a distributed Oracle9*i* environment. This process automatically connects to remote nodes involved in a distributed transaction and resolves the failed transactions, removing rows where appropriate from all nodes involved in the failure. This recoverer process may attempt to connect to remote nodes more than once for transaction resolution, with the delay time between consecutive connections increasing each time.

Archiver (arc0)

The archiver process automatically saves copies of redo logs in a DBA-specified storage location when media recovery is enabled. We discuss the circular usage of the online redo logs and the special form of media recovery called *archivelog mode* in the upcoming section "Redo Logs." This is an optional process spawned by **log_ archive_start = true** in the INIT.ora.

So, Grasshopper—it's not magic after all; a network of background processes supports the operation of an Oracle9*i* database. We feel it is relevant to the understanding of the Oracle software, and the management of the 9*i* database in particular, to cover details on how the support processes do just that—support. Let's move on to the INIT.ora, the first piece in the Oracle9*i* server O/S file layer.

INIT.ora

The INIT.ora file is read when an Oracle9*i* instance is started. A snippet of this file is
shown in the next listing. (The lines terminating in "..." were truncated for the listing.)

```
###############################
#
# INIT file for beg9 instance
#
# Created by Michael S. Abbey
#          June 13, 2004
#          abbey@pythian.com
###############################
#
audit_trail = none
background_dump_dest = /d0/oraclehome/product/oracle9.0.1/. . .
compatible = 9.0.0.0
control_files = (/d1/oradata/beg9/redo1/ora_xlhtbycl.ctl,
                 /d1/oradata/beg9/redo2/ora_xlhtbykt.ctl)
core_dump_dest = /d0/oraclehome/product/oracle9.0.1/. . .
cursor_sharing = force
db_block_size = 16384
db_cache_size = 50m
db_create_file_dest = /d1/oradata/beg9
db_create_online_log_dest_1 = /d1/oradata/beg9/redo1
db_create_online_log_dest_2 = /d1/oradata/beg9/redo2
db_name = beg9
distributed_transactions = 10
hash_area_size = 8388608
java_pool_size = 20971520
large_pool_size = 614400
log_archive_start = true
log_checkpoint_interval = 0
log_checkpoint_timeout = 0
log_checkpoints_to_alert = true
max_dump_file_size = 10000
open_cursors = 200
```

Let's look at the type of parameters found in the INIT.ora file and a few examples
of each.

Location Entries

The first category of parameters describes the location of one or more files required
by or written to as the instance operates. In some cases, it contains the fully pathed

location, directory, and file name, as in **control_files**. In other cases, it simply contains a directory name, as in **db_create_file_dest**. When the instance is started, Oracle9*i* verifies that the directories and files mentioned in INIT.ora exist and can be written to and read from. If there are any problems, Oracle9*i* displays one or more error messages along the lines of those shown in the next listing.

```
SQL> startup
ORA-00444: background process "LGWR" failed while starting
ORA-07446: sdnfy: bad value '' for parameter .
SQL>
SQL> startup
ORACLE instance started.
Total System Global Area  537691548 bytes
Fixed Size                   279964 bytes
Variable Size             469762048 bytes
Database Buffers           67108864 bytes
Redo Buffers                 540672 bytes
ORA-00205: error in identifying controlfile, check
           alert log for more info
```

NOTE
*Unfortunately, some error messages can be misleading; the first message really has nothing directly to do with lgwr, simply the fact that the file name specified for **background_dump_dest** does not exist.*

This illustrates something we want you to take with you into the land of Oracle9*i*. Often, the error messages spit out by the database software are cryptic and, if taken at face value, will end up sending you on a wild-horse chase (changed with the respect due to all the geese reading this book). Oracle9*i* land is not the only place this happens. Picture yourself leaving your friendly neighborhood Chevron station, mounting the I-95, and pulling into the next rest area after noticing that the "Engine needs service soon" lamp is illuminated. The problem? Your gas cap is not fully tightened; the engine is fine, but the error message is cryptic. Let's take control—moving on to the like-named file and the role it plays in the Oracle9*i* database.

NOTE
*In Windows 2000, sometimes Oracle seems to ignore the **background_dump_dest** setting and places the trace file in the rdbms/trace directory underneath %ORACLE_HOME%.*

Limiting Entries

Parameters that list a number for controlling implementation of a feature of the Oracle9i server usually fall into one of two categories:

- **Resource limiters** How many resource items should be made available to the instance upon startup. The entries **open_cursors**, **open_links**, and **timed_statistics** fall into this realm.

- **Memory allocations** How much memory should be set aside for the piece of functionality described by these entries. The most commonly changed parameters in this class are **db_cache_size**, **shared_pool_size**, and **sort_area_size**. Some of these entries accept "k" for kilobytes, "m" for megabytes, and "g" for gigabytes; others simply accept an integer number of bytes.

There are some operating system– and Oracle9i-enforced minimums and maximums that can be specified for these entries, and if they exist on your hardware platform, you will be told when the instance is started. An occurrence of this is shown in the next listing.

```
/d0/oraclehome/product/oracle9.0.1/dbs> sqlplus /nolog
SQL*Plus: Release 9.0.1.0.0 - Production on Sun Jun 17 13:44:09 2009
(c) Copyright 2001 Oracle Corporation.  All rights reserved.
SQL> connect / as sysdba
Connected to an idle instance.
SQL> startup
ORA-00093: shared_pool_reserved_size must be between 5000 and 8388608
```

Feature Entries

Feature entries also fall into two categories:

- Those that can only specify keywords like **true**, **false**, **partial**, or **full**. A few parameters that fall into this category are **max_dump_file_size**, **oracle-trace_enabled**, and **row locking**. Any values other than those in the approved list for each parameter will be rejected, as shown next.

  ```
  SQL> ORA-01078: failure in processing system parameters
  LRM-00105: 'always' is not a legal boolean for 'oracle_trace_enable'
  ```

- Those that determine the level to which a feature is enabled. A good example of this type of entry is **compatible**. As the version number of the Oracle9i software increases, more and more newfangled functionality is added. To leverage the new features, this parameter must be set to reflect the new version number. In our beg9 Oracle9i database, it is set to 9.0.1.0.

Before moving on to the control file, let's spend a minute on making changes to the parameter values in INIT.ora.

Making Changes to Parameters

Not all parameters in INIT.ora can be changed. The more you work with the software, and the more TARs you log with support services, the more familiar you will become with the details of this statement. Often, changes to the INIT.ora are put in place to attempt to deal with performance issues. Sometimes tuning books or the Oracle9*i* documentation suggests increasing the likes of **shared_pool_size** or **db_cache_size** to assist the speed and throughput of the database.

NOTE
This is one spot where the Oracle9i documentation must be consulted unless you are fluently familiar with the ramifications of making changes to the entries in this file. The Oracle9*i* Database Reference *(part number A90190-01) should be looked upon as the scripture in this subject area.*

In earlier releases of the Oracle server, the only way to change parameter values was to edit the INIT.ora file, shut down, and start up the database. Since Oracle7, and more so with Oracle8 and Oracle9*i*, more and more changes can be made with the database running. The v$parameter data dictionary view shown in the next listing is where you can deduce what parameters can be changed without *bouncing* (shutdown followed by startup) the database.

```
SQL>   desc v$parameter
   Name                   Null?    Type
   ------------------     --------  -------------
   NUM                              NUMBER
   NAME                             VARCHAR2(64)
   TYPE                             NUMBER
   VALUE                            VARCHAR2(512)
   ISDEFAULT                        VARCHAR2(9)
   ISSES_MODIFIABLE                 VARCHAR2(5)
   ISSYS_MODIFIABLE                 VARCHAR2(9)
   ISMODIFIED                       VARCHAR2(10)
   ISADJUSTED                       VARCHAR2(5)
   DESCRIPTION                      VARCHAR2(64)
   UPDATE_COMMENT                   VARCHAR2(255)
```

The **issys_modifiable** column contains the values **false**, **deferred**, or **immediate**, as shown next.

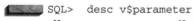
```
SQL> col issys_modifiable form a9 heading CHANGE?
SQL> col name form a30
SQL> set pages 90
```

```
SQL> break on issys_modifiable
SQL>
SQL> -- IMMEDIATE means the change affects every session at once,
SQL> -- even those connected
SQL>
SQL> select issys_modifiable,name
  2    from v$parameter
  3   where issys_modifiable = 'IMMEDIATE'
  4     and rownum < 6
  5     and name like 'db%'
  6   order by 1,2;

CHANGE?    NAME
---------  -----------------------------
IMMEDIATE  db_2k_cache_size
           db_4k_cache_size
           db_block_checksum
           db_keep_cache_size
           db_recycle_cache_size
SQL>
SQL> -- DEFERRED means the change affects only sessions that
SQL> -- connect after the statement complete; current sessions
SQL> -- are not affected.
SQL>
SQL> select issys_modifiable,name
  2    from v$parameter
  3   where issys_modifiable = 'DEFERRED'
  4   order by 1,2;

CHANGE?    NAME
---------  -----------------------------
DEFERRED   backup_tape_io_slaves
           object_cache_max_size_percent
           object_cache_optimal_size
           sort_area_retained_size
           sort_area_size
           transaction_auditing
SQL>
SQL> -- FALSE means there must be a bounce to affect the change.
SQL>
SQL> select issys_modifiable,name
  2    from v$parameter
  3   where issys_modifiable = 'FALSE'
  4     and rownum < 6
  5     and name like 'db%'
  6   order by 1,2;
```

```
CHANGE?    NAME
--------   ----------------------------
FALSE      db_block_buffers
           db_block_size
           db_file_name_convert
           db_writer_processes
           dbwr_io_slaves
```

The INIT.ora right from the start is somewhat of a black hole—you keep pouring time and effort into it, wondering what benefit you gain. You now have a preliminary knowledge of what this file is all about—carry on.

The Control File

Oracle9*i* builds a control file when a database is created; you require only one control file per instance, but best practices dictate at least two of these files at all times. This file is a road map to the Oracle9*i* database and contains instance-specific information such as

- The name of the database.

- Fully pathed names of all database files and redo log files.

- The time and date that the database was created.

- The current log sequence number—Oracle9*i* uses its online redo logs in a circular fashion, allocating this sequence number at the start of a new log file.

- Relevant checkpoint information.

NOTE
Control file information is available in the v$controlfile data dictionary view as Oracle9i operates. This view is shown next.

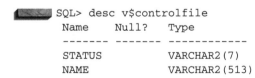

```
SQL> desc v$controlfile
   Name      Null?    Type
   -------   -------  ------------
   STATUS             VARCHAR2(7)
   NAME               VARCHAR2(513)
```

As we will discuss in Chapters 7 and 10, the startup and shutdown of the Oracle9*i* database uses the instance control files for consistency and completeness checking.

When we speak of consistency, we refer to the cross-file dependencies all over the Oracle9i database that are checked and rechecked on startup and shutdown. In this context, completeness means a check for the presence of and accessibility to all the files mentioned in the control files. Let's look now at the redo or transaction logs.

Redo Logs

The redo log files are the heart of the proprietary Oracle9i server. Some other vendors may have a similar facility for tracking the activity against their database, but this one is a beauty! Oracle will write to any number of redo log files that the DBA chooses to specify. Redo logs were introduced in Oracle V6 (circa 1988), and with Oracle7 in February 1993, redo log files were enhanced to become multimembered redo log groups. When DBAs now talk about the online redo logs, they really mean online redo log groups.

NOTE
When we mention redo logs in this section and elsewhere throughout this book, we are really speaking of redo log groups. There are Oracle9i and operating system constraints on the number of members you can have for each online redo log group.

When redo log groups are created, we give them an integer number, which becomes the group number to which they are referred by the DBA. We then speak of redo log group 1 or redo log group 2, and so on. As users interact with the Oracle9i database, a record of their activities is written to the online redo logs at commit or rollback time. Redo logs are a finite size, and when they fill up, Oracle switches to another set of log files. An example of four two-membered redo log groups on the beg9 database is shown in Figure 3-3.

NOTE
Each member of the same redo log group is a mirror image of the other members in the same group.

Oracle9i needs at least two single-membered redo log groups to operate, though we recommend at least three two-membered redo log groups. These must be made manually using a GUI such as OEM or SQL*Plus. When a redo log group fills up, Oracle switches to the next available group. Before a group is marked available, Oracle marches through each redo log group reconciling any outstanding activities, and then marks the group "able to be used" the next time a switch occurs. The

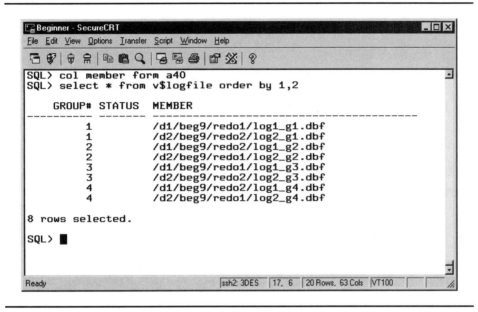

FIGURE 3-3.   *Four two-membered redo log groups*

question you may have already asked yourself is "What if a group has not yet been marked as reusable and its turn comes up?" Oracle9*i* suspends activity against the database until the group is marked reusable, and then operations carry on. Figure 3-4 illustrates this concept.

NOTE
Online redo log file information can be viewed in the v$logfile data dictionary view shown in the next listing.

```
SQL> desc v$logfile
 Name          Null?     Type
 ----------    --------  ------------
 GROUP#                  NUMBER
 STATUS                  VARCHAR2(7)
 TYPE                    VARCHAR2(7)
 MEMBER                  VARCHAR2(513)
```

We have now looked at the major players—background support processes, redo logs, and control files; these files track activities and pertinent information about the

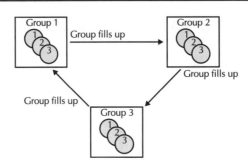

FIGURE 3-4. *The circular reuse of the online redo log groups*

Oracle9*i* instance. Figure 3-5 illustrates who interacts with what (adapted with permission from *Oracle9i Database Concepts*, Oracle Corporation, 2001, part number A88856-01). The only piece we have not yet touched on, the database data files, is the subject of the next section.

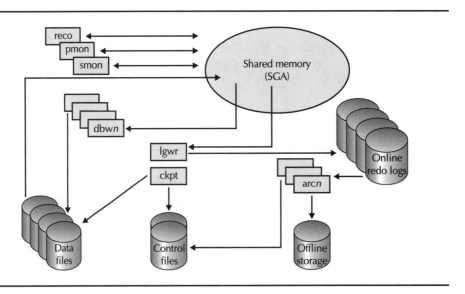

FIGURE 3-5. *SGA, support process, and file interaction*

NOTE
*With some Oracle9i installations, there may be
other processes (for example, queue monitor or lock
monitor), but this discussion highlights the most
standard configuration.*

The Database Data Files

Your data is stored in data files. These O/S files are created using one of the tools
supplied with Oracle9*i*, be it SQL*Plus or OEM. Data files themselves are not
allocated to the database directly; they are hooked into the instance using an
Oracle9*i* tablespace. As tablespaces are created, one or more data files are
included, as shown in the next listing—part of a **create tablespace** command.

```
create tablespace gl
datafile '/d0/oradata/ntirety/beg9/gl01.dbf' size 2000m,
         '/d1/oradata/ntirety/beg9/gl02.dbf' size 2000m,
         '/d2/oradata/ntirety/beg9/gl03.dbf' size 2000m
blocksize 2048
default storage . . .;
```

NOTE
*When the **blocksize** keyword is used to create a
tablespace, there must be a corresponding parameter
(in this case, **db_2k_cache_size**) in INIT.ora for that
sized block. Consult Chapters 6 and 10 for further
details. If you include the **blocksize** keyword without
its corresponding **size** parameter, you will get error
ORA_29339.*

Once this command is written, an entry is written to DBA_DATA_FILES, part of
Oracle9*i*'s data dictionary, and the tablespace is acquired by the instance. Table 3-1
illustrates the hierarchical relationship between the database, a tablespace, and the
database data files.

When a tablespace is added to an Oracle9*i* instance, a record of its size, name,
and location is written to the control files and the data dictionary. The tablespace
map in the data dictionary tracks the Oracle data blocks that have been allocated
to a tablespace. Once the file exists, space is available to users with appropriate
credentials. The Orace9*i* **create database** statement produces the SYSTEM tablespace
where the data dictionary resides. As soon as the database exists, the DBA runs a

Entity	Is a superset of	Belongs to
Database	Tablespace/data file	
Tablespace	Data file	Database
Data file		Tablespace

TABLE 3-1. *Relationship Between Database, Tablespace, and Data File*

handful of administration scripts that set up the remainder of the data dictionary. One use for tablespaces over and above SYSTEM is for Oracle9i's rollback segments. A discussion of architecture would be deficient without paying some attention to these components of each and every Oracle database.

Rollback Segments/Undo Tablespace

Whatever format you choose for the management of your database's undo, that information plays a crucial role in the implementation of Oracle's *read consistent* model. With multiple user sessions working with the data concurrently, this model ensures that a session has access to column values within a database table for the life cycle of the transaction. When necessary, Oracle9i automatically saves a before image of data in case the transaction that initiated the change is not committed. Suppose a banking application is receiving a deposit for $1,200 into a savings account with a current balance of $940. The first try at the update, the operator enters 12,000 instead of 1,200. Table 3-2 illustrates how read consistency is implemented, assuming the session that is performing the updates shown has a session identifier, or *SID,* of 99.

Notice how when SID 99 has no active transaction, there is no undo. When the transaction started (State 2), Oracle9i allocates an undo area to keep a copy of the pretransaction balance. Before the transaction started, the information for account 55524 was on disk, not having yet been read into memory. As the transaction begins, the data is scooped into memory, the update applied, and undo space reserved for the sake of other users. When the **rollback;** is issued, the data that was supposed to have been updated is left in memory, with its old value, and the undo released. It's the same story when the transaction is reinitiated, and upon **commit;**, the undo is released and the new value, in memory, is available to SID 99 and all other sessions. The secret of this read consistent model is illustrated in another way in Table 3-3, showing how the concurrent user community sees the data in account 55524.

State	Activity	Account Balance at End of Activity		
		Undo	Data in Memory	Seen by Others
1	Pretransaction #1	Empty	940	940
2	update savings set balance = balance + 12000 where account = 55524;	940	12,940	940
3	rollback;	Empty	940	940
4	update savings set balance balance + 1200 where account = 55524;	940	2,140	940
5	commit;	Empty	2,140	2,140

TABLE 3-2.   *Read Consistency and the Role Played by Undo*

The *m* word (memory) keeps surfacing in this section. Speaking of memory, let's move on and look at two significant areas in shared memory—the library cache and the data cache. The next section will just about round out the discussion of Oracle9*i* architecture.

State	Balance Value Seen and from Where (D = database, M = memory, U = undo)	
	SID 99	Other Sessions
1	940 (D)	940(D)
2	12,940 (M)	940 (U)
3	940 (M)	940 (M)
4	2,140 (M)	940 (U)
5	2,140 (M)	2,140 (M)

TABLE 3-3.   *Who Views What Value and from Where*

Significant Memory Structures

Many kinds of software take a lot of heat because they are memory hogs—so what else is new. "Hog-schmog," we say; Oracle9*i* is a fabulous user of computer memory. End of story! Here, we are going to have a look at the two most significant memory structures—the library cache and the data cache. What about the infusion of cash?

The Data Cache

Oracle9*i* sets aside a portion of its SGA to hold data read from the database files and/or getting ready to be written back to those same files. The size of the data cache is determined by a handful of INIT.ora parameters, the most common being **db_cache_size**. This entry specifies a default cache size in megabytes (using **m**) or an absolute number of bytes.

NOTE
Readers with Oracle8 experience may remember sizing the data cache as a product of **db_block_size** *and* **db_block_buffers***. Oracle9*i* handles this a little bit differently.*

Figure 3-6 highlights how Oracle9*i* uses its data cache. User sessions read and manipulate data in this cache. They do not directly interact with the database files. All data, regardless of what ends up happening to it, passes through memory on its way to these user sessions.

Oracle9*i* deliberately uses memory to store data as it is massaged by the user community. Remember back to when you went hiking at summer camp. The counselors always told you to let the slowest children set the pace for everyone else. It's handled exactly the same way with computers. Printing, reading from disk drives, and memory access are common activities performed as systems operate, listed from slowest to fastest. One can justifiably claim that the speed with which the printer churns out the printed word sets the standard for the speed of the computer. The point of all this? If you had a choice between reading Oracle9*i* data directly from disk or memory, which would you choose—access at the speed of the printer or from memory? Here's a hint— when read from memory, the access is virtually at the speed of light, or 280,000 kilometers per second.

Oracle9*i* moves data into memory before making it accessible to user sessions. These sessions work with the data in memory, the data gets marked as changed where appropriate, and eventually gets written back to disk. Oracle9*i* performs all its data manipulation in the data cache, a finite amount of computer memory. Cache sizes of 400MB to 500MB are common on some of the higher-end UNIX

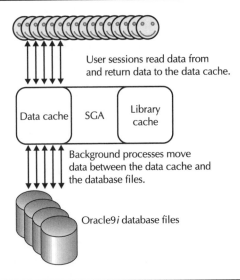

FIGURE 3-6. *How Oracle9i uses the data cache*

servers. Oracle9*i* manages the space in the data cache using a *least recently used,* or LRU, algorithm. Data gets aged out of the cache when the space it occupies is required for other data. The LRU rule ensures that data used the longest time ago is flushed before the more active data. Once an Oracle9*i* instance is started, you need not perform any manual maintenance of the data cache. Enough said—now the other biggest customer in the SGA.

The Library Cache

The library cache is where all the SQL and PL/SQL statements reside in memory. Chapters 5, 6, 8, and 9 look at these two products in some detail. All the Oracle9*i* database engine understands is SQL; regardless of what you use to facilitate user interaction with the database, SQL is what gets sent off to the software for processing. This cache is sized primarily by **shared_pool_size** in INIT.ora, with absolute values in bytes or the megabyte measurement followed by the **m** abbreviation. In a nutshell, the following steps are how Oracle9*i* processes SQL:

1. Statement is passed to Oracle9*i* for processing.

2. Before it is placed in the library cache, a hash value is computed that represents a number of characteristics of the SQL.

3. Oracle compares the computed hash value against those values in a hash table it maintains for SQL statements already in the cache.

4. If a match is found, the new SQL statement is thrown away and the one sitting in the cache is executed on its behalf.

5. If no match is found, further processing is done on the new SQL statement, an entry is made in the library cache hash table for the newly arrived code, and it is placed in the library cache.

NOTE
Naturally, the processing is not this straightforward; this simplification is designed to give you a flavor of how the library cache is managed.

Any SQL statement executed against the Oracle9i database must first be placed in the library cache and marked ready-to-execute. This library cache, also referred to as the shared pool, is discussed in a number of places throughout the book.

Locks and Latches

Locks and latches are fundamental to the protection of your data and shared memory structures. Oracle9i runs in a multiuser environment, and without these protection mechanisms, the smooth and consistent operation of the database would be in question.

Locks

Oracle9i uses locks to ensure that different sessions are not able to interact with the same data in use by other sessions. *Interact* in this context means anything other than **select**. This protects the integrity of the data and is managed automatically by Oracle9i, without need for manual intervention. Locks are acquired as SQL statements begin their interaction with data and last for the duration of a transaction. Transactions commonly end with a **commit** or **rollback**, the latter restoring data to its pretransaction state. Oracle9i uses two locking modes:

- Exclusive mode will not allow the locked resource to be shared whatsoever by any concurrent sessions. This lock is acquired to modify data or define the structures within which data resides.

- Share mode allows concurrent read access to the same chunk of data, with escalation to an exclusive mode lock when change is initiated.

Oracle9*i* obtains a share mode lock on a row of data as it is accessed as part of the result set to a query. If, and only if, that query leads to an **update** or **delete** statement, the lock is escalated to an exclusive row lock, if the row is not already locked in that mode. Oracle9*i* allows simultaneous updates to rows sitting in the same data block. If two sessions request **update** access to the same row in the same data block, they queue up and go about their business in a serial fashion. There are two types of locks Oracle9*i* acquires on its data:

- *DML locks,* or data manipulation locks, ensure data integrity in multiuser environments for the purposes of protecting data.

- *DDL locks,* or data definition locks, protect the structure of objects and are acquired for data definition activities.

Oracle9*i* requests a lock in the least restrictive mode possible and, from time to time, may convert a number of row locks to a table lock to reduce the number of locks being acquired. Oracle9*i* chooses this path when the management of a table lock requires less overhead than the protection provided by multiple row locks. Let's tackle latches next.

Latches

Latches are low-level mechanisms that help manage the internal operations of the Oracle9*i* software. They can be thought of as a type of lock, acquired and released in subsecond time periods. Latches are almost always obtained when requested but, as the activity on an Oracle9*i* database increases, often queue behind one another for getting hold of precious resources. Remember the redo logs and how transaction information is written to these files as the database operates. A special redo copy latch ensures that one and only one process writes to the redo logs at a time. Obtaining a latch is only part of the work; there is a cleanup phase that comes into play as a latch is released. Think of this cleanup process as a swarm of buspeople who descend on a table at Monk's Café when Jerry and Shmoopie leave for the Soup Nazi's.

Latches are required when working with shared memory structures in the SGA. If working with a particular structure requires a latch and that structure is in use, a wait situation is created. There are two types of latches:

- Willing to wait means that if a latch cannot be obtained at once, a persistent request is resubmitted until it can be satisfied. Latches in the library cache are examples of ones that fall into this category.

- Requests for no-wait latches are canceled if the latch cannot be obtained immediately and are resubmitted as a new request. Latches related to redo log copies fall into this class.

.

DBAs need not worry themselves about latches unless they cause problems in their databases, if they ever do. Suffice it to say, latches are part of the puzzle fundamental to the operation of the Oracle9i database and, most of the time, go about their work unnoticed. They are an essential player in the running of the instance and are like busy ants scurrying around in memory. We find it almost ironic that the words *lock* and *latch* both start with the same letter—*l*—and the words *look out* start with the same letter, which is what you will do if your locks and latches lead to significant wait situations. The hourglass displayed by the mouse cursor when a window is busy is a familiar example of a wait situation.

We have given you a framework of how the Oracle9i database is put together and what pieces play what role. Each component in the software equation may not be all that important on its own; bring all of them together and you have a powerful, robust, and fast database management system we affectionately call 9i. Let's finish off by looking at a day in the life of an Oracle9i database and bring this chapter's magic carpet ride to a conclusion.

So, You're the New Oracle9i Database

We are going to do a high-level, step-by-step walkthrough of putting up your first Oracle9i database. Get yourself a cup of coffee and a comfortable chair; for those of you in business class, raise the footrest beforehand … here we go:

1. Choose a location on the disk for Oracle's home directory, commonly called ORACLE_HOME. We chose the location /d1/app/oracle/product/ 9.0.1. Install the software using Oracle9i's Universal Installer.

NOTE
In earlier releases of the Beginner's Guide, *we walked you through the Oracle server installation. With Oracle8i and now Oracle9i, it's just too big a topic to cover in a book this size.*

2. Choose an Oracle system identifier for the new database, affectionately referred to as the ORACLE_SID. We chose the text beg9.

3. Construct the INIT.ora file, using the O/S name that corresponds to the chosen ORACLE_SID, and place it in a directory called dbs ("database" for Win2000) underneath your ORACLE_HOME. With a beg9 database, the INIT.ora will be called initbeg9.ora.

4. Build and run a create database script, sensitive to whether you are using Oracle Managed files, an Oracle9i feature that instructs Oracle

to self-manage activities such as creating a database. If you are not using this feature, you will have to specify the name and location of the control files in INIT.ora, as well as the following in the SQL statement used to create the database:

- The name, location, and size of the first data file that will be the SYSTEM tablespace

- The name, size, and location of your online redo log groups

5. Run an assortment of administration scripts to populate the data dictionary.

6. Run even more scripts to enable special features of the Oracle9*i* server, such as PL/SQL, discussed in Chapters 6 and 9. Even though PL/SQL is embedded in the Oracle9*i* server software, some admin scripts enliven special PL/SQL functionality in the form of packages, procedures, and functions.

7. If not using Oracle Managed files, build

- A tablespace to be used when sessions that access the database require sorting space—commonly, though not always, called **temp**.

- One or more tablespaces to hold undo information.

8. Create tablespaces to hold the data your applications will end up pumping into your information repository.

9. Create the users who own the data created and updated by your applications.

10. Create accounts for the user community who will interact with your data.

11. Ensure the appropriate people in your organization know how to get in touch with you if anything goes wrong.

12. Read the rest of this book.

Closing time for Chapter 3. The next piece in the never-ending Oracle9*i* puzzle addresses the types of objects in the database. The most familiar object we work with is the *table*. As the version numbering of the software increases, Oracle keeps inventing more and more objects to assist the information storage and retrieval process that drives users and administrators of electronic systems. There are far too many and some much-too-complex objects to cover each and every one. We will look at ones that make the most sense to you as you come up to speed with and/or become more familiar with this incredibly rich piece of technology called Oracle9*i*.

Chapter 3 Questions

Answers to questions can be found in Appendix A.

1. Which background process is responsible for cleanup of aborted user sessions?

   A. dbwr

   B. lgwr

   C. smon

   D. pmon

2. The online redo logs contain

   A. a record of all committed transactions

   B. the names of all the files associated with the Oracle9i instance

   C. a list of all the users who have logged into the database

   D. a record of all transactions whether committed or rolled back

3. Which of the following INIT.ora parameters is the primary determining entry that controls what features are enabled when the Oracle9i instance starts?

   A. version

   B. compatible

   C. db_cache_size

   D. sga_size

4. Ready-to-execute SQL statements are placed where in the SGA?

   A. Redo buffer cache

   B. Library cache

   C. Data cache

   D. Data block

5. As Oracle9i runs, what portion of the instance is protected by latches?

   A. Database files

   B. Redo log files

   C. System monitor process

   D. Memory structures in the SGA

PART II

So You've Just Started?

CHAPTER

4

Database Objects

his chapter contains definitions and examples of database objects that you will most likely encounter when working with the Oracle9*i* database. It also contains some database objects that you might not encounter, but you should be aware of their existence.

You could think of a database object as any database item that begins its existence with the SQL **create** statement. In Chapter 5 you will learn more about the **create** statement and other DDL (data definition language) statements available to you. Upon execution of a successful **create** statement, you will have created a new database object. These objects come in many sizes and shapes, and in this chapter you will learn how to create each one. We will also explain in easy-to-understand terms their purpose within the database. This chapter covers the following topics:

■ Tables

■ Views, including materialized views

■ Indexes

■ Triggers

■ Synonyms

■ Sequences

■ Roles

■ Functions, procedures, and packages

Terminology

The following terminology will arm you with the technical jargon to help you through this chapter.

■ The *data dictionary* is maintained by the database and contains all the information on how data is stored in the database, where it is, and how the database can work with it.

■ *DDL* stands for *data definition language*. These are the SQL statements that begin with **create**, **revoke**, **grant**, and **drop**. These are statements that are used to created and remove database objects. They are also statements that are used to create permissions to access the database and database objects.

- *DML (data manipulation language)* are SQL statements that begin with **select**, **insert**, **delete**, or **update**. These are statements used to manipulate the contents of a database.

- *Grants* are privileges given out by owners of objects, allowing other users to work with the owner's data. Grants fall into two categories: object-level grants and system-level grants. Object-level grants give users the ability to select, insert, update, or delete against a database object like a table. Examples of system-level grants are giving a database user the ability to connect to the database or permission to create an object in the database.

- An *index* is a minicopy of an Oracle table stored in a presorted manner. Index entries for a table allow rapid access to the data within your tables. Think of the index in a book, which makes it quicker to find a particular point of interest within the pages of the book.

- *Integrity constraints* are business rules associated with the database. For example, in order for a customer to exist, it must have a unique customer ID.

- A *synonym* is an alternative name for an object within the database.

- A *table* is a database object that holds your data. Information about every table is stored in the Oracle9*i* data dictionary; with this information, Oracle allows you to maintain the data residing in your tables.

- Database *triggers* are programs that are stored in the database and are triggered by certain events. Inserting a row of data into a table is an example of an event that might cause a trigger to execute.

- A *view* allows database users to see a customized selection of one or more tables within the database. A *view* is created based on a SQL statement stored within the database. When you access the view, the stored SQL statement is executed and the results of that query are made available to the user.

- A *role* is a group of privileges that are collected together and granted to users. Once privileges are granted to a role, a user inherits the role's privileges by becoming a member of that role.

Tables—Where Your Data Is Stored

A table is the database object that holds all the data. Every piece of information that gets loaded into an Oracle database must be placed inside an Oracle table. In fact, all the information needed by an Oracle database to manage itself is stored in a series of tables that are commonly known as the data dictionary. Think of the data dictionary as tables about tables. The data dictionary tables tell the database what kind of data is stored in the database, where it is located, and how the database can work with it.

A table is made up of columns. Each column must be given a unique name within that table and assigned a data type (such as **varchar2**, **date**, or **number**) with an associated width (which could be predetermined by the data type, as in **date**). Each table column can also be designated as **null** or **not null**. **Not null** means the column data is mandatory for that column. In other words, for rows of data to be entered into that table, all columns assigned **not null** designation must contain valid data values.

To enforce defined business rules (integrity constraints) on a table's data, Oracle9i allows you to associate integrity constraints and triggers for a table. Later in this chapter, we will go into greater detail on database triggers.

create table, an Example

Let's take a look at an example table called PETS:

```
SQL> CREATE TABLE PETS (
  2    PET_ID           INTEGER        PRIMARY KEY,
  3    PET_KIND         VARCHAR2 (20)  NOT NULL,
  4    PET_NAME         VARCHAR2 (20),
  5*   PET_SEX_FLAG_MF  CHAR(1)        CHECK (PET_SEX_FLAG_MF IN ('M','F')))
SQL> /
Table created.
```

PETS has four columns associated with it. The first column is PET_ID, which is of type integer. It has an integrity constraint of **primary key** associated with it, which means the database will enforce the business rule that each pet ID must be unique within this table. This means that no two entries in the table PETS could share the same pet ID. If you attempted to place a duplicate pet ID in the table PETS, you would receive an error.

The next column is PET_KIND, which is of type **varchar2** with a width of up to 20 characters. The **not null** attribute means that whenever an entry is made in the PETS table, it must contain a valid value for the PET_KIND column.

The next column is PET_NAME, which is also of type **varchar2** with a width of up to 20 characters. Unlike the PET_KIND column, whenever a row of data is entered into PETS, an associated data entry is optional for the PET_NAME column.

The last column in the PETS table is PET_SEX_FLAG_MF. This is of type **char** with a width of one character. Like the PET_ID column, it also uses an Oracle9i integrity constraint. In this case, the **check** option only allows this column to accept a value of **M** or **F**. This tells the database to check the proposed value of the PET_SEX_FLAG_MF and make sure it equals a value of **M** or **F**.

create table as, an Example

A very useful feature within the Oracle9*i* database is the ability to create a table based on an existing table. You can use this feature to create a quick copy of the entire table or just a subsection. This is a great way to create a test environment. Here is a very simple example of it in action:

```
SQL> CREATE TABLE mass_newhire
  2    AS select *
  3          from newhire
  4*        where state_cd = 'MA'
SQL> /
Table created.
```

Let's take a look at the contents of the original table:

```
SQL> select * from newhire;

LNAME                          ST HIREDATE    SALARY
------------------------------ -- --------- ----------
corey                          MA 01-JAN-01     20000
calisi                         NJ 10-JUN-01     30000
smith                          CA 15-AUG-01     40000
abby                           TX 12-DEC-01     50000
tony                           CT 12-NOV-01     60000
larry                          VT 11-MAY-01     90000
tom                            MA 15-AUG-01     55000
dick                           NJ 02-FEB-01     30000
harry                          NJ 05-JUN-01     20000
lisa                           MA 26-JUN-01     75000
cheryl                         MA 08-MAY-01     80000

11 rows selected.
```

Now let's take a look at the contents of the newly created MASS_NEWHIRE table. Remember, this new table only contains entries from the **state_cd = 'MA'**.

```
SQL> select * from mass_newhire;

LNAME                          ST HIREDATE    SALARY
------------------------------ -- --------- ----------
corey                          MA 01-JAN-01     20000
tom                            MA 15-AUG-01     55000
```

```
lisa                        MA 26-JUN-01      75000
cheryl                      MA 08-MAY-01      80000
```

Views—Customized Selections of One or More Tables

A view is a customized slice of data retrieved from one or more base tables. Base tables can, in turn, be tables or can themselves be views. Unlike a table, a view contains no data, just a stored SQL statement. When a user executes a query that accesses the view, the database goes out to the data dictionary, retrieves the stored SQL statement, and executes the statement. The data retrieved from this query is presented like a table.

In fact, if you did not create the view, you would think you were dealing with a table. As with a table, you may insert, update, delete, and select data from the view. All changes made to the view would be pushed down to the underlying base tables.

Views are used for many reasons. In a payroll table, you might give a payroll clerk access to employees' contract information but not their salary information. Other times, a view is used to hide data complexity. You might give your users access to a view, when, in fact, the SQL statement that created the view is a complex multitable join. This way, users don't have to deal with the complexity of a relational database.

create view, an Example

This example demonstrates joining two tables:

```
SQL> CREATE VIEW emp_dept_vw AS
  2    SELECT e.emp_name_first, e.emp_name_last, d.dept_name
  3      FROM employee e,
  4           department d
  5*    WHERE e.dept_id = d.dept_id
SQL> /
View created.
```

Now we will issue a select against the view. To the user, the view EMP_DEPT_VW acts just like a table; but in reality, it is a stored SQL statement in the database, with no data associated with it until it is executed.

```
SQL> SELECT * FROM emp_dept_vw;
EMP_NAME_FIRST          EMP_NAME_LAST               DEPT_NAME
--------------------    --------------------------  --------------------
LISA                    HALEY                       Finance
CHRISTOPHER             SMITH                       Sales
```

```
HANNAH          RINALDI                    Human Resources
MICHAEL         CALISI                     Marketing
```

Materialized Views— The View That Stores Data

Unlike an ordinary view, which only contains an SQL statement, a materialized view contains the rows of data resulting from an SQL query against one or more base tables. Whenever a change is made to one of the underlying base tables, the database stores a log of each change. The materialized view can be set up to automatically keep itself in synch with those base tables, updating itself at user-defined intervals. The materialized view can be stored in the same database as the source base tables or in a completely different remote database.

Let's see how you might use materialized views in a data warehouse. Many times they are used to precompute and store aggregated data such as sums and averages. If the materialized view were of monthly sales, when a new month's sales figures were entered into the base tables, the materialized view would automatically update its summary totals to reflect this change to the base tables. Many times, having information precomputed and summarized is an easy way to increase the speed of queries on large data warehouses.

In distributed environments, you can use materialized views to replicate data at distributed sites and to synchronize updates between those sites. In a mobile computing environment, materialized views can be used to download a subset of data from a central server to mobile clients, with periodic updates between the server and mobile clients.

create materialized view (Formerly snapshot), an Example

First, all of the tables that the materialized view is based on must be logged. Here is an example of how to do that:

```
SQL> CREATE MATERIALIZED VIEW LOG ON department
  2      WITH PRIMARY KEY,
  3      ROWID (dept_name)
  4*     INCLUDING NEW VALUES
SQL> /
Materialized view log created.

SQL> CREATE MATERIALIZED VIEW LOG ON newhire
  2      WITH PRIMARY KEY,
  3      ROWID (dept_id, salary)
```

```
   4*     INCLUDING NEW VALUES
SQL> /
Materialized view log created.
```

Now let's create the materialized view itself:

```
SQL> CREATE MATERIALIZED VIEW dept_salary_mvw
  2       REFRESH FAST ON COMMIT
  3       ENABLE QUERY REWRITE
  4  AS select d.dept_name,
  5             sum(n.salary) as sum_salary
  6        from department d,
  7             newhire     n
  8       where d.dept_id = n.dept_id
  9   group by d.dept_name;

Materialized view created.
```

Query Rewrite

Materialized views stored in the same database as the underlying base tables allow the query optimizer to take advantage of the query rewrite feature. This means that if the optimizer decided it could obtain the data it needed faster by using the materialized view rather than the source tables the query was pointing at, it would rewrite the query (SQL statement) to go against the materialized view instead of the original source tables.

This ability to rewrite the original query will greatly improve performance of your database. You could use this to set up a reporting database (materialized views) versus a production database. In this case, the materialized views would maintain themselves as the production tables changed.

Indexes—A Fast Way to Get at Your Data

Just as the index in a book helps you navigate the book quicker, an index on a table helps you retrieve your data faster. An index can be much faster than the source table, because it is a much smaller copy of a subset of the source table.

Imagine a table called ALPHABET with 26 columns (A through Z). Imagine an index on the first three columns—let's call it ABC. Say this table has a million rows, and you want to find every occurrence of *Soup* located in column A. When you look at the source table ALPHABET, the database still has to retrieve columns A through Z, just so you can look at the contents of column A.

Since the index is a full copy of the contents of columns ABC, in order to look at the contents of A, it only has to bring along two additional columns, BC. Think of how much work the database has to go through to retrieve a million rows A through Z versus a million rows columns A through C.

Advantages of Presorted Order

In a relational database, the contents of a table are not in any presorted order. Perhaps you have heard of the accounting term FIFO; in the database world, we have FIFL—first in is first loaded. An index, on the other hand, is always in a presorted order. In the example just given, trying to find *Soup* in column A of the source table means we have to inspect all million rows. In the index, we know the data is in a presorted order, so the database can take advantage of that fact to speed things up.

When you create an index on columns ABC you really get the following:

```
A
AB
ABC
```

You get an index on column A. You get an index on column A combined with column B. You also get an index on column A combined with column B and also combined with C.

What you don't get is

```
B
BC
C
```

Also keep in mind that the index is a minicopy of the table. In the example of index ABC, every time a change is made to A or B or C, the index must be updated. Every time you create an index, the database has to maintain all the changes that affect it from the source table it is based on.

Unique and Non-unique Indexes

You can create the standard index either as a unique index or non-unique index. A unique index does not allow duplicate entries. A non-unique index allows duplicate entries within the table columns specified.

```
SQL> CREATE UNIQUE INDEX ui_dept_name
  2*    ON department (dept_name)
SQL> /

Index created.
```

The Primary Key

Another way to ensure there are no duplicates is to use the primary key constraint when creating a table. This tells the database to ensure that the identified columns cannot contain duplicates. In the following example, rather than create a new table, we will alter an existing table using the primary key constraint.

```
SQL> ALTER TABLE department
  2*    ADD CONSTRAINT pk_dept_name PRIMARY KEY (dept_name)
SQL> /
Table altered.
```

Once you identify a column as a primary key, the database makes it very difficult to remove this constraint.

```
SQL>  DROP INDEX pk_dept_name
SQL> /
DROP INDEX pk_dept_name
            *
ERROR at line 1:

ORA-02429: cannot drop index used for enforcement of unique/primary key
```

The 95/5 Rule

There are situations in which using the index can actually slow you down. The 95/5 rule gives you a guideline for gauging the efficiency of an index. When the result of a query is going to bring back less than 5 percent of the rows in a table, the index is almost always the fastest way to retrieve the data. When a query is looking at retrieving more than 5 percent of the data, it's usually fastest not to use the index.

The Bitmap Index— An Index for Low Variations of Distinct Rows

The bitmap index was created with data warehousing in mind. Sometimes your data set has very low variations of distinct rows. Take the example of a data set in which one of the key criteria is gender. In this case, the traditional index would not work. Every query would always return greater than 5 percent of the rows. The bitmap index works best here, for example,

```
SQL> L
  1  CREATE BITMAP INDEX bi_pet_sex_flag_mf
  2*     ON pets(pet_sex_flag_mf)
SQL> /

Index created.
```

Triggers—Event-Driven Programs

Triggers are programs that are stored in the database and are executed when certain events occur. These programs can be written in PL/SQL or Java, or as C callouts. Oracle allows you to define these programs, and then executes them when an **insert**, **update**, or **delete** statement is issued against the associated table, view, or database action.

Triggers can be used to enforce database security, prevent invalid transactions, enforce business rules, provide auditing, or even maintain a replicated table.

create trigger, an Example

We're going to use a trigger to provide an audit trail of all activities against the PETS table. These activities will be recorded in the LOG table.

```
SQL> descr log;
 Name                                    Null?    Type
 -------------------------------- -------- ---------------------------
 LOG_ID                                   NOT NULL NUMBER
 LOG_TABLE                                NOT NULL VARCHAR2(20)
 LOG_DML                                           VARCHAR2(20)
 LOG_KEY_ID                                        NUMBER(38)
 LOG_DATE                                          DATE
 LOG_USERNAME                                      VARCHAR2(20)
```

Now let's create a trigger that will record all **insert**, **update**, or **delete** events into the LOG table:

```
CREATE OR REPLACE TRIGGER trg_pets_upper_pet_kind
      BEFORE
      DELETE OR INSERT OR UPDATE
      ON pets
      FOR EACH ROW
BEGIN
      if INSERTING then
       insert into log
                 (log_id, log_table, log_dml,
                    log_key_id, log_username , log_date)
              values
                 (log_id_seq.nextval,'LOG','INSERT',
                    :new.pet_id, user , sysdate);
          elsif DELETING then
            insert into log
                 (log_id, log_table, log_dml,
                    log_key_id, log_username , log_date)
               values
                  (log_id_seq.nextval,'LOG','DELETE',
```

```
                            :old.pet_id, user , sysdate);
        else
           insert into log
                  (log_id, log_table, log_dml,
                     log_key_id, log_username , log_date)
                  values
                   (log_id_seq.nextval,'LOG','UPDATE',
                        :old.pet_id, user , sysdate);
     end if;


EXCEPTION
   WHEN others THEN
        raise_application_error(-20000,'ERROR trg_pets_upper_pet_kind: '
                               ||SQLERRM);

END trg_pets_upper_pet_kind;
/
```

We need to take a quick look at the LOG table to see that it is currently empty. Then we'll look at the PETS table before issuing the **update**, **insert**, and **delete** commands.

```
SQL> select * from log
SQL> /

no rows selected

SQL> select * from pets;

    PET_ID PET_KIND              PET_NAME             PET_SEX_FLAG_MF
---------- --------------------  -------------------- ----------------
         1 DOG                   OZZIE                M
         2 CAT                   MOGLEY               M
```

Now we're ready to execute **insert**, **update**, and **delete** commands against the PETS table. Remember, these are commands that will cause the database trigger to fire.

```
SQL> insert into pets (pet_id, pet_kind, pet_name, pet_sex_flag_mf)
  2*          values (3,'HORSE','WINDY','F')
SQL> /

1 row created.
```

```
SQL> update pets
  2     set pet_name = 'HOLLY',
  3         pet_sex_flag_mf = 'F'
  4* where pet_id = 1
SQL> /

1 row updated.

SQL> delete from pets
  2* where pet_id = 2
SQL> /

1 row deleted.
```

Here is the current state of the PETS table:

```
SQL> select * from pets;

    PET_ID PET_KIND            PET_NAME             PET_SEX_FLAG_MF
---------- ------------------- -------------------- ----------------
         1 DOG                 HOLLY                F
         3 HORSE               WINDY                F
```

Notice how the trigger did fire and create entries in the LOG table:

```
SQL> select * from log;
    LOG_ID LOG_TABLE  LOG_DML    LOG_KEY_ID LOG_DATE  LOG_USERNAME
---------- ---------- ---------- ---------- --------- -------------
         1 LOG        INSERT              3 09-AUG-01 MCALISI
         2 LOG        UPDATE              1 09-AUG-01 MCALISI
         3 LOG        DELETE              2 09-AUG-01 MCALISI
```

Synonyms—Object Nicknames

A synonym is an alternate name for a table, view, sequence, or program unit. You typically use synonyms for a variety of reasons:

- Hide the true name of the owner of the database object.
- Hide the true location of the database object.
- Provide a name for an object that is less complicated or easier to type.

A synonym can either be *private* or *public*. A private synonym is available only to the user who created it. A public synonym is available database wide.

create synonym, an Example

Here is an example of a private synonym being created:

```
SQL> CREATE SYNONYM salgrade
  2*    for scott.salgrade
SQL> /
Synonym created.
```

Let's try to access the PETS table:

```
SQL> SELECT * FROM pets;
SELECT * FROM pets
              *
ERROR at line 1:
ORA-00942: table or view does not exist
```

Now let's create a synonym:

```
SQL> CREATE SYNONYM pets
  2*    for pets
SQL> /
Synonym created.
```

What happens if we try to access the PETS table again?

```
SQL> SELECT * FROM pets;

PET_KIND             PET_NAME
-------------------- --------------------
DOG                  OZZIE
CAT                  MOGLEY
RABBIT               INKY
HORSE                KING
```

Sequences—A Fast Way to Obtain a Unique Number

Sequences are a super-efficient way to generate a number sequence. Many times in a relational database, you need to create a unique number to act as the primary key. For example, say you get a hot stock tip on a ".com" that may not be ".gone." You call up the stockbroker and make a purchase. Associated with that purchase will be a unique order number. Sequences are used to create that unique number. They are independent of any tables, and cached in memory waiting for a request.

In the past, before there were database objects called sequences, you created tables with a column containing the sequence number. These tables became major bottlenecks in high-performance applications. By the time you locked the table, grabbed the current value of the column, incremented it by 1, and then released all the locks, the stock had gone up. The sequence object sits in memory waiting for your request.

create sequence, an Example

In this example, the cache 1000 tells the database that whenever it runs out of sequence values in the cache, it must create 1,000 more. As a side note, whenever the database is shut down, the sequence cache in memory is lost. This means that you will have gaps in the numbers.

```
SQL> CREATE SEQUENCE project_team_seq
  2     START WITH 1000 INCREMENT BY 1
  3     MINVALUE 1
  4*    CACHE 1000 NOCYCLE  NOORDER
SQL> /
Sequence created.
```

create role— # A Way to Manage Privileges

In the past, if you wanted to grant a user access to an application, it had to be done on a table-by-table basis. Each application had a particular set of permissions depending on who you were. Very quickly, this became a convoluted mess. You needed a database just to keep all the permissions straight. Recognizing this need, Oracle created the role database object.

You create a database role, then grant privileges to the role, and then assign it to the user. For example, in a hospital environment, you might create the role of Doctor and a role of Nurse. A Doctor might have the ability to create an order for a lab result, while a Nurse could only read a lab result.

create role, an Example

Let's look at a very simple role object using the hospital example:

```
SQL> CREATE ROLE nurse
  2*    NOT IDENTIFIED
SQL> /
Role created.
```

In the example of the Nurse role, **not identified** means no additional level of security is needed beyond the initial login to the database. There are other flavors of this statement that would require further action on the user's part before the role would become activated.

NOTE
*With the Oracle database, you can grant users **select**, **insert**, **update**, and **delete** privileges on any Oracle table. This is known as an object-level grant and is just one level of database security that you could create. So, imagine a typical hospital environment of 100+ tables, where on one table a Nurse role has select and insert privileges, while the Doctor role has select, insert, update, and delete. This happens for each table. Instead of having to issue each privilege individually, you can set up the role once, assign all the privileges by role, and then assign the role over and over.*

Functions, Procedures, and Packages

We will talk about functions, procedures, and packages as a unit. They are database objects you can create that have encapsulated PL/SQL code within them. You can use this PL/SQL code to customize programs to meet the needs of your applications.

create function

The **create function** command allows you to create a database object that extends the standard functions provided with the database. For example, Oracle gives you a function named **sqrt()**. This is a program that returns the square root of a number.

A function lets you call a PL/SQL program by name. An important distinction of a function is that it must always return an output value.

create function, an Example
Let's take a look at the NEWHIRE table.

```
SQL> select * from newhire;
LNAME                            STATE_CD HIREDATE    SALARY
-------------------------------- -------- --------- ----------
corey                            MA       01-JAN-01     20000
calisi                           NJ       10-JUN-01     30000
```

```
smith                    CA        15-AUG-01        40000
abby                     TX        12-DEC-01        50000
tony                     CT        12-NOV-01        60000
larry                    VT        11-MAY-01        90000
tom                      MA        15-AUG-01        55000
dick                     NJ        02-FEB-01        30000
harry                    NJ        05-JUN-01        20000
lisa                     MA        26-JUN-01        75000
cheryl                   MA        08-MAY-01        80000
11 rows selected.
```

Next, we'll create a program that adds up all the salary information for the given state and returns a salary total.

```
SQL> CREATE FUNCTION add_salary_for_state(in_state_cd IN VARCHAR2)
  2       RETURN NUMBER
  3       IS state_salary NUMBER(11,2);
  4       BEGIN
  5         SELECT sum(salary)
  6           INTO state_salary
  7           FROM newhire
  8          WHERE state_cd = in_state_cd;
  9       RETURN(state_salary);
 10      END;
 11   /
Function created.
```

Now we can use that function to retrieve the total salaries for **state_cd ='MA'**. Notice how we call the function by the name **add_salary_for_state** and pass it the abbreviation "MA."

```
SQL> var x number;
SQL> exec :x := add_salary_for_state('MA');
PL/SQL procedure successfully completed.
SQL> print x;
        X
----------

    230000
```

create procedure

A procedure is a group of PL/SQL programs that you call out by name. Unlike a function, a procedure does not have to return a value. A procedure may or may not contain input and output arguments.

create procedure, an Example

In the following example, our procedure contains an input and output parameter.
This is how I typically see procedures.

```
SQL> CREATE OR REPLACE PROCEDURE GET_COUNT_EMP_BY_STATE (
  2         in_state_cd      IN  varchar2,
  3         out_count_emp    OUT integer
  4  )
  5  AS
  6  check_output varchar2(6);
  7
  8  BEGIN
  9
 10    select count(e.emp_id)
 11      into out_count_emp
 12      from employee e,
 13        state s
 14     where e.state_cd = s.state_cd
 15       and s.state_cd = in_state_cd;
 16
 17
 18  EXCEPTION
 19      when others then
 20      dbms_output.put_line ('ERROR in GET_COUNT_EMP_BY_STATE'||SQLCODE||SQLERRM);
 21* END;
SQL> /

Procedure created.
```

create package

A package is a collection of procedures and functions bundled together. They
are usually bundled together by similar functionality. All internal procedures and
functions are recorded within the data dictionary as a single stored package.

create package, an Example

Notice how the following package contains multiple functions and a single
procedure all rolled into one.

```
SQL> CREATE OR REPLACE PACKAGE pkg_emp_state AS
  2       PROCEDURE get_count_emp_by_state (in_state_cd VARCHAR2, out_count_emp INTEGER);
  3       FUNCTION add_salary_for_state (in_state_cd VARCHAR2)
  4         RETURN NUMBER;
  5       FUNCTION cap_whole_name (in_name1 VARCHAR2, in_name2 VARCHAR2)
  6      RETURN VARCHAR2;
  7* END pkg_emp_state;
SQL> /

Package created.
```

Other Database Objects

The following sections summarize some additional database objects you may encounter. Some of them are here because they highlight functionality of the Oracle9*i* database; others are here because you are likely to encounter them as you work with the database. The examples are meant to give you a sense of how to work with them.

create operator

The create operator object creates a new operator within the database. In Chapter 8, we go over in great detail the **union**, **intersect**, and **minus** operators. You use the **create operator** command to create a new operator and its bindings. This operator can, in turn, reference functions, packages, and so on.

create operator, an Example

Notice how this operator references the procedure **cap_whole_name**.

```
SQL> CREATE OPERATOR make_whole_name
  2     BINDING
  3       (varchar2, varchar2)       RETURN varchar2
  4         USING cap_whole_name;

Operator created.
```

Now notice how the **cap_whole_name** function is referenced in the newly created operator.

```
SQL> CREATE OR REPLACE FUNCTION cap_whole_name
  2           (in_name1 IN VARCHAR2,
  3            in_name2 IN VARCHAR2)
  4       RETURN VARCHAR2
  5       IS out_whole_name VARCHAR2(50);
  6
  7       BEGIN
  8
  9         SELECT initcap(ltrim(rtrim(in_name1)))||' '||
 10                initcap(ltrim(rtrim(in_name2)))
 11           INTO out_whole_name
 12           FROM dual;
 13
 14         RETURN(out_whole_name);
 15*    END;
SQL> /

Function created.
```

create directory

Sometimes it is advantageous to store objects external to the database in a directory. It is most common to see this when dealing with large graphic files known as *binary files*. The **create directory** command allows you to create a directory object that is an alias for a directory on the computer server file system. Then you can reference this object in your code instead of hard coding the location in the application.

create directory, an Example

This is a typical use of the **create directory** statement. This is a directory that will hold all our binary files.

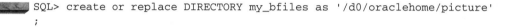

```
SQL> create or replace DIRECTORY my_bfiles as '/d0/oraclehome/picture'
;

Directory created.
```

create library

The **create library** statement creates a database object associated with an operating system shared library. This allows SQL and PL/SQL to call third-generation language functions (such as C functions or COBOL functions) and procedures, which can then call out to the library. Before this object existed, you had to hard code each library reference.

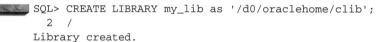

```
SQL> CREATE LIBRARY my_lib as '/d0/oraclehome/clib';
  2  /
Library created.
```

Database Links

A database link allows a user to work with data in a remote database without the need to know where the data actually resides. When a database link is created, login information for the remote database is supplied. Each time the database link is used, a session is initiated over the network to resolve the reference to the remote table or view.

Regardless of who is logged in, the database link will log into the remote database as the user information that is supplied when the link is created. Also, links can be created for both private and public use.

create database link, an Example

In this example, the user **timetrack** will be used on the remote database. In addition, the network service **emile.corp.Ntirety.com** will be used.

```
SQL> CREATE DATABASE LINK dblink_timetrack
  2     CONNECT TO timetrack IDENTIFIED BY timetrack
  3*    USING 'emile.corp.ntirety.com'
SQL> /
Database link created.
```

Now that we have the link, let's use it to retrieve some data.

```
SQL> SELECT *
  2*   FROM color@dblink_timetrack
SQL> /

COLOR_CD COLOR_DESCR
-------- -----------------------------
RD       Red
GN       Green
BL       Blue
BK       Black
```

Think of the database link as a two-way pipe. You can use it in many ways. In the following example, we insert some data into the remote database:

```
SQL> INSERT into color@dblink_timetrack(color_cd, color_descr)
  2*     values ('YL','Yellow')
SQL> /

1 row created.
```

Now let's update some remote data:

```
SQL> UPDATE   color@dblink_timetrack
  2     set  color_cd = 'YW'
  3*  where  color_cd = 'YL'
SQL> /

1 row updated.
```

Let's delete some remote data:

```
SQL> DELETE FROM color@dblink_timetrack
  2*  where color_cd = 'YW'
SQL> /

1 row deleted.
```

You can also use the link to access another user's data on the remote database. The only limiting factor is the privileges of the Oracle9*i* account you are using to log into the remote database.

```
SQL> SELECT *
  2*    FROM scott.salgrade@dblink_timetrack
SQL> /

    GRADE      LOSAL      HISAL
---------- ---------- ----------
        1        700       1200
        2       1201       1400
        3       1401       2000
        4       2001       3000
        5       3001       9999
```

create cluster

Clusters allow for a different way to physically store table data. In the cluster database object, you can take tables and store them in a prejoined manner. This is quite useful when you have two or more tables that are always referenced in a joined manner. A good example of this might be the joining of water meter reads with the domicile information of the house. For all intents and purposes, the water company will never look at meter-read data without also comparing it to the table that contains the domicile information.

Remember that the contents of these two tables are stored together. This means that if you just want to look at the domicile information, you will also force the database to retrieve the meter readings with it.

create cluster, an Example
First, create the cluster key:

```
SQL> CREATE CLUSTER clr_president
  2      (president_number  number(3))
  3      size 512
  4*     storage (initial 100k next 50k)
SQL> /

Cluster created.

SQL> CREATE TABLE presidents
  2      (pres_no       NUMBER(3),
  3       pres_fname    VARCHAR2(20),
  4       pres_lname    VARCHAR2(30),
  5       pres_birth    date,
  6       pres_city     VARCHAR2(20),
  7       state_cd      VARCHAR2(2))
  8*     CLUSTER clr_president (pres_no)
SQL> /

Table created.
```

Notice how the cluster database object is referenced as this table is created.

```
SQL> l
  1  CREATE TABLE president_employees
  2      (pemp_id        integer,
  3    pres_no        NUMBER(3),
  4      pemp_fname    VARCHAR2(20),
  5      pemp_lname    VARCHAR2(30),
  6      pemp_title    VARCHAR2(20))
  7*     CLUSTER clr_president (pres_no)
SQL> /
Table created.
```

At this point, we have gone over the database objects you will most likely encounter. We have also introduced you to more advanced objects like bitmap indexes, database links, and operators. The next chapter will give you a very solid overview of SQL*Plus and how to use it.

Chapter 4 Questions

Answers to questions can be found in Appendix A.

1. A _____ is a database object that contains your data.

   A. view

   B. operator

   C. role

   D. table

2. Until it is executed, a _____ contains no data, just a stored SQL statement.

   A. view

   B. table

   C. index

   D. materialized view

3. A _____ must always return a value.

   A. package

   B. procedure

    C. function

    D. view

4. A _____ allows a user to work with data in a remote database.

    A. view

    B. database link

    C. table

    D. function

5. A _____ is an easy way to manage groups of privileges.

    A. role

    B. view

    C. database link

    D. package

CHAPTER
5

SQL*Plus 101

s you know, SQL is the foundation of an Oracle database; in fact, it is
the foundation of all relational databases. You cannot insert a row of
data into an Oracle database unless you have first issued some basic
SQL statements to create the underlying tables. Yes, even that GUI
interface you are using is issuing SQL statements behind the scenes.
SQL*Plus is the Oracle-specific implementation of SQL with additional features
that let you retrieve, format, and control data to suit your needs. Among all the
choices you have for getting data out of an Oracle database, we think you will
find SQL*Plus to be a great tool when you just need to get the job done.

NOTE
*Not only is SQL the foundation of any relational
database, but it also serves as a top-notch
report writer.*

In this chapter, we will cover the following topics:

- How to log into (access) SQL*Plus

- DDL and DML: what is the difference?

- The basic format of every **select** statement

- How to format retrieved data

- The most common **set** commands

- How to join tables

How to Access SQL*Plus

A very useful person to know in every installation is your site's database administrator,
more commonly known as the DBA. Be nice to your DBAs; they hold the keys to the
kingdom. DBAs are responsible for keeping all Oracle databases up and running. They
are responsible for the installation of all the Oracle software. In many installations,
before you can access Oracle, the DBA may need to install some client-based software
on your PC.

Before you can access SQL*Plus (more commonly known as logging in), you
will need to know some basic information. You need to know whether SQL*Plus
has been installed, you need to know your Oracle username and password, and
you might need to know your site's specific domain information. You will also need
to know whether your site's access to SQL*Plus is command-line based or icon based.
If you do not know the answers to these questions, you know that person I told you

to be nice to? Your site's DBA will know the answers to these questions and many more. Contact the DBA, and get those answers. To help you with this, we have created the SQL*Plus Get Started Checklist, shown in Figure 5-1. Please feel free to use it.

Access from the Command Line

Now that you are armed with all the information from the checklist, at an operating system prompt type **sqlplus** and press ENTER. You will be prompted for an Oracle username and password, for example:

```
$ sqlplus
SQL*Plus: Release 9.0.1.0.0 - Production on Mon Jul 23 12:37:43 2003
<c> Copyright 2001 Oracle Corporation.  All rights reserved.
Enter user-name: mcalsis
Enter password:
```

I hope you were not alarmed when you typed in your password and noticed it came back hidden. This is done for your protection. Be very careful with whom you share your password. If you typed everything correctly, you will see the following:

```
$ sqlplus mcalisi
SQL*Plus: Release 9.0.1.0.0 - Production on Mon Jul 23 12:37:43 2003
<c> Copyright 2001 Oracle Corporation.  All rights reserved.
Enter password:
Connected to:
Oracle9i Enterprise Edition Release 9.0.1.0.0 - Production
With the Partitioning option
JServer Release 9.0.1.0.0 - Production
SQL>
```

Notice how the system prompt you started with has been replaced with "SQL>." This is to let you know that you are now logged into your Oracle 9*i* database.

SQL*Plus Get Started Checklist

☐ Contact your site's database administration and make sure SQL*Plus is installed.
☐ Ask your site database administrator for your Oracle username and password.
☐ Ask for your site's domain information.
☐ Determine SQL*Plus access method:
  ☐ Prompt based (**$sqlplus**)
  ☐ Icon based

FIGURE 5-1. *Getting started with SQL*Plus*

Congratulations! Just as Dorothy took her first step on the yellow brick road, you have just begun your journey.

Icon-Based Access

Examine your desktop to locate an icon like the one you see illustrated here. Once you find it, double-click the icon to activate it.

Ending Your SQL*Plus Session

When you have finished using SQL*Plus, it is important that you properly end the session. This ensures that the database resources you were holding onto are freed up for other users of the database to access. It also saves your site's DBA from spending time looking for database problems caused by users who do not properly end their database sessions.

To end your Oracle session, type **exit** and press ENTER, for example:

```
SQL>EXIT
Disconnect from Oracle9i Enterprise Edition Release 9.0.1.0.0 - Production
With the Partitioning Option
Jserver Release 9.0.1.0.0 - Production
```

You are now ready to learn more about SQL statements and how to use them to create database objects and access information stored in the database.

Data Definition Language (DDL)

All SQL statements fall into one of two categories: DDL, which stands for *data definition language,* and DML, which stands for *data manipulation language.* DDL is the set of SQL statements that define or delete database objects such as tables or views. For the purposes of this chapter, we will concentrate on dealing with tables. Examples of DDL are any SQL statements that begin with **create**, **alter**, and **drop**. Table 5-1 lists all the basic DDL statements. If a statement is not in this list, then consider it DML. For additional information on database objects, refer to Chapter 4.

Command	Description
alter procedure	Recompiles a stored procedure
alter table	Adds a column, redefines a column, or changes storage allocation of the given table
analyze	Gathers performance statistics on database objects to be fed to the Cost-Based Optimizer
alter table add constraint	Adds a constraint to an existing table
create table	Creates a table
create index	Creates an index
drop index	Removes an index
drop table	Removes a table
grant	Grants privileges or roles to a user or another role
revoke	Removes privileges from a user or database role

TABLE 5-1.   *Basic DDL Clauses*

create/drop Statement

The following SQL statement is an example of DDL **create** and **drop** statements in action. In this example, each **create table** command is preceded by a **drop table** command. You will commonly see this in SQL statements. We place the **drop table** command before each table create is done, so that if we find an error in the script, we can modify the source script and reexecute the script immediately. We know that the preceding **drop** statement will remove the table and all its contents. The tables created in this script will be the basis of the examples later in the chapter.

```
SQL> drop table a;
Table dropped.

SQL> create table a
  2  (cola char(1));
```

```
Table created.

SQL> drop table b;
Table dropped.

SQL> create table b
  2   (colb char(1));

SQL> drop table newhire;
Table dropped.

SQL> create table newhire
  2    (lname      varchar2(30),
  3      state_cd  varchar(2),
  4      hiredate  date,
  5      salary    number(8,2));
Table created.

SQL> drop table state;
Table dropped.
SQL>

SQL> create table state
  2    (state_cd    varchar(2) not null,
  3      state_name varchar2(30));
Table created.
```

Data Types

By examining the create table scripts just shown, a few things become obvious. Not only do you have to give each table a name, you must also list all the columns or fields associated with the table. You must also associate a data type with each column. This tells the database what kind of information a particular column can hold. For example, the database would not accept a letter into the SALARY column. The number data type will only accept valid numbers.

Each data type has a set of rules associated with it, and the Oracle9i database engine is designed to support those rules. Table 5-2 gives a partial listing of data types accepted by Oracle9i.

The describe Command

Now that we have created all the tables we will use later in this chapter, let's take a closer look at those tables using the **describe** command.

```
SQL> desc newhire
Name                                               Null?    Type
------------------------------------------------  --------  ------------------
LNAME                                                       VARCHAR2(30)
STATE_CD                                                    VARCHAR2(2)
HIREDATE                                                    DATE
SALARY                                                      NUMBER(8,2)
SQL> desc state;
Name                                               Null?    Type
------------------------------------------------  --------  ------------------
STATE_CD                                          NOT NULL  VARCHAR2(2)
STATE_NAME                                                  VARCHAR2(30)
```

Data Type	Description
char(size)	Stores fixed-length character data.
varchar2(size)	Stores variable-length character data.
number(l,d)	Stores numeric data, where *l* stands for length and *d* for the number of decimal digits.
blob	A binary large object. The BLOB data type stores up to 4GB of binary data (such as text, graphic images, video clips, and sound waveforms) in the database. Oracle recommends that you always use LOB (BLOB, CLOB, NCLOB, and BFILE) data types rather than LONG data types.
raw(size)	Raw binary data. The raw data type is a variable-length data type like varchar2 character data type. It is intended for binary data or byte strings, such as graphics, sound, documents, or arrays of binary data.
date	Stores dates.
long	Stores variable-length character data. Columns defined as LONG can store variable-length character data containing up to 2GB of information. A table can contain multiple LOB columns but only one LONG column.

TABLE 5-2. *Common Oracle Data Types*

Experience suggests that you will find this a very useful command to know as you attempt to access the database using SQL*Plus. Did you notice a slight difference about the STATE_CD column on the STATE table? It will not accept null values. Let's have a quick discussion about what a null is.

Not Null

You are probably wondering what a null value is. Simply put, null is a column that contains no data. In other words, it contains nothing. For you technical types out there, think of it as a character string with a length of 0.

Null values have a way of getting into your database where you least expect them, for example, in numeric columns. This creates a big problem since 1 + null = null. Null is not 0.

It is advisable to create primary key columns with the **not null** clause. This makes it mandatory, before entering a row of data, to specify a valid entry for all the table columns so tagged, or the database will refuse the record. (Primary key columns are discussed later in the chapter.)

Data Manipulation Language (DML)

DML is any SQL statement that begins with **select**, **insert**, **update**, or **delete**:

- **select** is used when you want to retrieve data from an Oracle database. Any report you write always begins with **select**. In fact, this is the most common SQL statement you will see.

- **insert** is used when you want to load data into the database.

- **update** is used when you want to change the contents of a table

- **delete** is used when you want to remove the contents of a table.

Table 5-3 summarizes the DML statements.

Statement	Description
select	Used to retrieve data/information stored within the database; the most common SQL statement
insert	Used to load/add a new row of data into a table
update	Used to update/modify the contents of a table
delete	Used to delete data from a table

TABLE 5-3. *DML Statements*

The insert Statement

Here is an example of using the **insert** statement in its simplest form:

```
SQL> insert into newhire values ('corey','MA','01-Jan-01','20000');
1 row created.
SQL> insert into newhire values ('calisi','NJ','10-Jun-01','30000');
1 row created.
SQL> insert into newhire values ('smith','CA','15-Aug-01','40000');
1 row created.
SQL> insert into newhire values ('abby','TX','12-Dec-01','50000');
1 row created.
SQL> insert into newhire values ('tony','CT','12-Nov-01','60000');
1 row created.
SQL> insert into newhire values ('larry','VT','11-May-01','90000');
1 row created.
SQL> insert into newhire values ('tom','MA','15-Aug-01','55000');
1 row created.
SQL> insert into newhire values ('dick','NJ','2-Feb-01','30000');
1 row created.
SQL> insert into newhire values ('harry','NJ','5-Jun-01','20000');
1 row created.
SQL> insert into newhire values ('lisa','MA','26-Jun-01','75000');
1 row created.
SQL> insert into newhire values ('cheryl','MA','8-May-01','80000');
1 row created.
SQL> insert into newhire values ('nohr','CA','7-May-01','80000');
1 row created.
```

Notice that each time the command is executed you receive the message "1 row created." You get immediate feedback that you are populating the given table with data. When you load data into a table, you may also specify the column to load it into. This ensures that there is no mistaking where you want the data to be placed. In the next example, the columns are specified after the **insert** command:

```
SQL> insert into state (state_cd, state_name) values ('MA','Massachusetts');
1 row created.
SQL> insert into state (state_cd, state_name) values ('NJ','New Jersey');
1 row created.
SQL> insert into state (state_cd, state_name) values ('CA','California');
1 row created.
SQL> insert into state (state_cd, state_name) values ('TX','Dallas');
1 row created.
SQL> insert into state (state_cd, state_name) values ('Fl','Florida');
1 row created.
```

```
SQL> insert into state (state_cd, state_name) values ('MN','Maine');
1 row created.
```

Many times when you first load a very big table, you may not have all the data available for all the columns. For example, let's load a record into the NEWHIRE table omitting salary:

```
SQL> insert into newhire (state_cd, lname) values ('CA','Nohr');
1 row created.
```

The select Statement

As stated before, the **select** statement is used to retrieve information from the database. It has five components, as described in Table 5-4.

Component	Description
select (mandatory)	This tells Oracle which information you want to receive (in other words, the names of the columns you want to retrieve). Note that * means "retrieve all columns" from a table. It is a great time-saver when doing quick selects.
from (mandatory)	This tells the database where to find the information. This is the name of one or more Oracle tables in which the data resides.
where (optional)	This is where you set any special condition(s), or selection criteria, that might restrict the data that is retrieved. It also specifies how the contents of two tables are correlated together. (We will discuss joins in more detail later in this chapter.)
group by (optional)	This tells the database how you want the data summarized.
order by (optional)	This tells the database how you want the data sorted. In a relational database, the data is not stored in a presorted order. Although optional, it's a good rule of thumb to include an **order by** clause in every **select** statement.

TABLE 5-4. *Five Components of the select Statement*

Now that you understand the basic components of a **select** statement, you're ready to put this newfound knowledge to work. Let's start by retrieving the contents of two tables named A and B.

```
SQL> insert into a values ('1');
1 row created.
SQL> insert into a values ('2');
1 row created.
SQL> insert into a values ('3');
1 row created.
SQL> insert into b values ('2');
1 row created.
SQL> insert into b values ('3');
1 row created.
SQL> insert into b values ('4');
1 row created.
SQL>
SQL> select * from a
  2  ;
C
-
1
2
3
SQL> select colb from b;
C
-
2
3
4
```

This very simple example illustrates a couple of important points. Notice the use of the asterisk in the first **select** statement. As noted in Table 5-4, the asterisk means "retrieve all the columns" of a given table. In this example, there is only one column in table A; but in a table with three columns, the asterisk would be the same as typing

```
SQL> select cola, colb, colc from a;
```

Notice the semicolons, which signify that you have completed the given SQL statement. In SQL*Plus there are two ways to signify that you have finished and the SQL statement can be executed:

■ The semicolon at the end of a line

■ The slash on a separate line

Until SQL*Plus encounters the end of a SQL statement, which is signaled by the use of a slash or semicolon, it assumes you need an additional line. The following example highlights this point. Notice the use of the slash and semicolon. Also notice the line continuation.

```
SQL> select *
  2  from a;
SQL> select *
  2  from a
  3  /
```

Formatting Output from the select Statement

With every **select**, you always have the option of preceding its execution with some **column** commands. In that case, any **select** statement that is executed will pick up the settings established by the previous **column** command and present the results accordingly. Once a **column** command has been issued, it stays in effect until another **column** command overrides its setting or you exit SQL*Plus.

The **column** statement has four sections, as described in Table 5-5.

Section	Description
column <column name>	Specifies the column you want to format.
format <mask applied>	Specifies the size of the output and what mask you want applied to it.
heading 'any string'	Specifies the column heading to use. Note that "|" in the column heading means new line.
wrap/trunc	Specifies what to do with the overflow—it can be truncated or wrapped down to the next line.

TABLE 5-5.   *The Four Sections of a Column Statement*

What we are talking about here is presentation logic. In SQL*Plus you have complete control over how you want the output retrieved. This does not affect the data stored in the table, only the way it is presented from the query. This must seem confusing at this point, so let's see it in action. The following example uses the **column** command to provide some very basic formatting of the output.

```
SQL> column cola format a10 heading 'Col A' truncate
SQL> column colb format a12 heading 'Column|B' Wrap
SQL> select * from a;
Col A
----------
1
2
3
SQL> select * from B;
Column
B
------------
2
3
4
```

Now we'll take a closer look at format masks and how you can use them to present the data in various ways.

Format Masks

Format masks are most commonly used to control the width of the display. In the case of characters, the **format** command determines the width of the field and how you want overflows handled—should the output be truncated or wrapped to the next line? In the case of numbers, you can control how many numbers to display, as well as how you want them to be displayed. Table 5-6 summarizes common format masks you will encounter.

It's time to see this knowledge put to work. The following query demonstrates the points we have discussed:

```
SQL> Column state_cd format a25              heading 'State|Code' trunc
SQL> Column lname     format a10              heading 'Last|Name'  trunc
SQL> Column hiredate format a10              heading 'Hire|Date' trunc
SQL> Column salary    format $999,999,999.00  Heading  'Salary' trunc
SQL> select state_cd, lname, hiredate, salary
  2  from newhire
SQL> /
```

```
State                       Last      Hire
Code                        Name      Date          Salary
-------------------------   --------- ---------- ---------------
MA                          corey     01-JAN-01      $20,000.00
NJ                          calisi    10-JUN-01      $30,000.00
CA                          smith     15-AUG-01      $40,000.00
TX                          abby      12-DEC-01      $50,000.00
CT                          tony      12-NOV-01      $60,000.00
VT                          larry     11-MAY-01      $90,000.00
MA                          tom       15-AUG-01      $55,000.00
NJ                          dick      02-FEB-01      $30,000.00
NJ                          harry     05-JUN-01      $20,000.00
MA                          lisa      26-JUN-01      $75,000.00
MA                          cheryl    08-MAY-01      $80,000.00
CA                          nohr      07-MAY-01      $80,000.00

12 rows selected.
```

Format Character	Example	Description
A	format A10 trunc format a22 wrap	Determines the display width based on the number provided to the right of A. In the first example, if more than 10 characters are retrieved from the table, only the first 10 will be displayed. In the second example, if more than 22 characters are retrieved, they will wrap in increments of 22. Note that you can use any number to define the width.
9	format 999999	Determines the display width based on the number of 9s provided. Note that a number overflow is displayed as ########.
0	format 0999	Displays leading zeros.
0	format 9999990	When value is zero, display a zero instead of the default behavior of displaying a blank.
$	format $999	Place a dollar sign in front of the number.
B	format B999	Display a blank when zero.

TABLE 5-6. *Common Format Masks*

Format Character	Example	Description
MI	format 999MI	Display a minus sign when the value is negative.
PR	format 9999PR	Place <> around a negative number.
,	format 999,999,999	Place a comma in the specified position.
.	format 999.99	Place a decimal point where specified, and round.

TABLE 5-6. *Common Format Masks* (continued)

Let's Bring Some Order to the Situation (order by)

Unlike other types of databases, relational databases store data in no predetermined order. With that in mind, when it's important to present the results in a particular order, use the **order by** clause. As Captain Jean-Luc Picard of the starship *Enterprise* might say, "Make it so order by. "

There are two ways to use the **order by** clause:

- **By numbered position** Specify a number of the ordered position you want to sort on.

- **By column name** Name the particular column you want to sort on.

The only other decision you have to make is whether the named column is retrieved in ascending or descending order. By default, you get ascending order. This is done on a column-by-column basis or a number-by-number basis. The following SQL statement illustrates this point:

```
SQL> select state_cd, lname, hiredate, salary
  2  from newhire
  3* order by state_cd desc, lname;
SQL> select state_cd, lname, hiredate, salary
  2  from newhire
  3* order by 1 desc, 2;
```

To restate the point, the **order by** clause determines how the results of the query will be played back. In the SQL statement shown next, the contents of the STATE_CD column will be presented in descending order; then the contents of the LAST_NAME column will be presented in ascending order. Rather than spell out the column names

in the **order by** clause, we prefer to use positional order as a way to identify the column
we want to sort on.

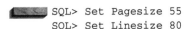

```
SQL> Column state_cd format a25           heading 'State|Code' trunc
SQL> Column lname    format a10           heading 'Last|Name'  trunc
SQL> Column hiredate format a10           heading 'Hire|Date' trunc
SQL> Column salary   format $999,999,999.00  Heading  'Salary' trunc
SQL> select state_cd, lname, hiredate, salary
  2   from newhire
  3*  order by 1 desc, 2
SQL> /


State                      Last    Hire
Code                       Name    Date              Salary
-------------------------- ------- ---------- ----------------
VT                         larry   11-MAY-01      $90,000.00
TX                         abby    12-DEC-01      $50,000.00
NJ                         calisi  10-JUN-01      $30,000.00
NJ                         dick    02-FEB-01      $30,000.00
NJ                         harry   05-JUN-01      $20,000.00
MA                         cheryl  08-MAY-01      $80,000.00
MA                         corey   01-JAN-01      $20,000.00
MA                         lisa    26-JUN-01      $75,000.00
MA                         tom     15-AUG-01      $55,000.00
CT                         tony    12-NOV-01      $60,000.00
CA                         nohr    08-MAY-01      $80,000.00
CA                         smith   15-AUG-01      $40,000.00

12 rows selected.
```

The SQL*Plus Environment

As you have learned by now, SQL*Plus is a powerful tool for retrieving information
from your Oracle database. In fact, it's a whole development environment. Up
until now we have been discussing **column**, the most commonly used SQL*Plus
environmental command. Let's look now at some other commands that you can
use in the SQL*Plus environment to determine how information will be presented.

set pagesize/linesize

Two of the most important environment parameters you can set are **set pagesize** and
set linesize commands. On a report, these determine the number of lines per page
and number of characters available in each line, for example:

```
SQL> Set Pagesize 55
SQL> Set Linesize 80
```

Spooling the Output

After you have created a great report, you can save it to a file with the **spool** command. SQL*Plus saves the contents of everything that happens after the command has been issued into the named output file. The named output file is any valid file name that follows the **spool** command.

The contents will keep being spooled until one of three things happens:

- Another **spool** <output filename> command is issued.

- A **spool off** command is issued.

- The SQL*Plus session is ended. (Remember the proper way to exit SQL*Plus: type **exit**.)

The following is an example of the **spool** command at work:

```
SQL> Spool Staterpt.txt
SQL> select state_cd, lname, hiredate, salary
  2  from newhire
  3* order by 1 desc, 2;
SQL> Spool off
```

set termout on/off

When the SQL statement you have created returns many rows of data, it can be useful to shut off the display of the SQL*Plus session to the terminal you are using. For this, you use the **set termout on/off** command. The most common problem people have with this command is they forget to turn the terminal output back on, and think their screen is broken. Here is an example of this command at work:

```
SQL> Column state_cd format a25              heading 'State|Code' trunc
SQL> Column lname    format a10              heading 'Last|Name'  trunc
SQL> Column hiredate format a10              heading 'Hire|Date' trunc
SQL> Column salary   format $999,999,999.00  Heading  'Salary' trunc
SQL> set termout off
SQL> Spool out.txt
SQL> select state_cd, lname, hiredate, salary
  2  from newhire
  3* order by 1 desc, 2
SQL> /
SQL> Spool off
SQL> Set Termout on
```

show all Command

Once you set an environmental setting, it stays active until the SQL*Plus session has
ended or you change the setting. It's quite useful to be able to see what the current
settings are. For this, you use the **show all** command:

```
SQL> show all
appinfo is OFF and set to "SQL*Plus"
arraysize 15
autocommit OFF
autoprint OFF
autorecovery OFF
autotrace OFF
blockterminator "." (hex 2e)
btitle OFF and is the first few characters of the next SELECT statement
cmdsep OFF
colsep " "
compatibility version NATIVE
concat "." (hex 2e)
copycommit 0
COPYTYPECHECK is ON
define "&" (hex 26)
describe DEPTH 1 LINENUM OFF INDENT ON
markup HTML OFF SPOOL OFF ENTMAP ON PREFORMAT OFF
echo OFF
editfile "afiedt.buf"
embedded OFF
escape OFF
FEEDBACK ON for 6 or more rows
flagger OFF
flush ON
heading ON
headsep "|" (hex 7c)
instance "local"
linesize 80
lno 13
loboffset 1
logsource ""
long 80
longchunksize 80
newpage 1
null ""
numformat ""
numwidth 10
pagesize 55
```

```
PAUSE is OFF
pno 1
recsep WRAP
recsepchar " " (hex 20)
release 900010000
repfooter OFF and is NULL
repheader OFF and is NULL
serveroutput OFF
shiftinout INVISIBLE
showmode OFF
spool ON
sqlblanklines OFF
sqlcase MIXED
sqlcode 0
sqlcontinue "> "
sqlnumber ON
sqlpluscompatibility 8.1.7
sqlprefix "#" (hex 23)
sqlprompt "SQL> "
sqlterminator ";" (hex 3b)
suffix "sql"
tab ON
termout ON
time OFF
timing OFF
trimout ON
trimspool OFF
ttitle OFF and is the first few characters of the next SELECT statement
underline "-" (hex 2d)
USER is "MCALISI"
verify ON
wrap : lines will be wrapped
```

As you can see, this environment is quite configurable. We could write half a book on just these settings. It is out of the scope of this book to discuss them all, but we have given you the tools you need to display the settings. Table 5-7 also describes some common environmental parameters you will set.

repheader and repfooter

What is a report without a header and footer? To create them, you can use the **repheader** and **repfooter** commands. We prefer to use the default behavior of these settings. The default setting of the **repheader** command gives you a nice centered

Command	Description
set heading off	Use this when you want to shut off the headings. It's useful when you are creating a data file.
set pagesize 55	This defines the vertical page size of the output you are using. The most common setting is 55 or 60. When creating a data file for output, you would set this to 0.
set linesize 80/132	This determines the horizontal size of output you are working on. When creating a data file, you would set this to the size of the longest line of data.
set trimspool on	Tells SQL*Plus to trim trailing blanks off spooled output.
set feedback off	Suppresses SQL*Plus from telling you how many rows of data were retrieved.
set echo off	Tells SQL*Plus not to echo the SQL statement as it is run.
spool (output name)	Tells SQL*Plus to send the results of the query to the named file.
spool off	Stops the spooling of output.
set termout on	Suppresses display of the output to the screen.

TABLE 5-7. *Common SQL*Plus Environment Settings*

heading, with page number and today's date. Where the header and footer appear is based on the current setting of **pagesize** and **linesize**.

```
SQL> column state_cd   format a5 trunc heading 'State|Code'
SQL> column state_name format a15 wrap Heading 'State|Name'
SQL> btitle '--Company Confidential--'
SQL> ttitle 'The State Report|WWW.NTIRETY.COM'
SQL> set pagesize 55
SQL> set linesize 80
SQL> Spool 'State.txt'
SQL> select state_name, State_cd
  2  from state
  3  order by STATE_NAME;
SQL> Spool Off
Tue Jul 24
page    1
                          The State Report
                          WWW.NTIRETY.COM
```

```
State           State
Name            Code
--------------- -----
California      CA
Dallas          TX
Florida         Fl
Maine           MN
Massachusetts   MA
New Jersey      NJ
                            --Company Confidential--

6 rows selected.
```

To quote Billy Crystal, "You look marvelous." You now have all the tools you need to build great-looking reports. So don't be afraid to experiment.

Joining Tables

The true power of a relational database (and the source of its name) comes from the ability to relate different tables and their data together. Understanding this concept is critical to harvesting the information held within the database. This is more commonly known as *joining* two or more tables.

Primary Keys and Foreign Keys

You relate (or join) two or more tables together based on common fields. These common fields are known as *keys*. There are two types of keys:

- A *primary key* is what makes a row of data unique within a table. In the STATE table, STATE_CD is the primary key.

- A *foreign key* is the primary key of one table that is stored inside another table. The foreign key connects the two tables together. The NEWHIRE table also contains STATE_CD, which in the case of the NEWHIRE table, is a foreign key.

You relate the two tables together in the **where** clause. In the next example, we join the NEWHIRE table to the STATE table so that we can display STATE_NAME in a NEWHIRE report. Let's take a closer look:

```
SQL> set pagesize 55
SQL> set linesize 80
SQL> repheader 'The New Hire Report|By State'
SQL> repfooter '--- Company Confidential ---'
SQL> column state_name format a15 trunc
```

```
SQL> column state_name heading 'State|Name'   format a15 trunc
SQL> column lname       heading 'Last|Name'    format a12 wrap
SQL> column hiredate    heading 'Hire|Date'    format a12
SQL> column salary      heading 'Salary'       format $999,999.99
  1  select st.state_name, nh.lname,
  2         nh.hiredate, nh.salary
  3  from   newhire nh, state st
  4  where  st.state_cd = nh.state_cd
  5* order by 1,2
SQL> /
```

```
Tue Jul 24                                                      page    1
                          The New Hire Report
                               By State


State            Last         Hire
Name             Name         Date              Salary
---------------  -----------  ------------  ------------
California       nohr         07-MAY-01       $80,000.00
California       smith        15-AUG-01       $40,000.00
Dallas           abby         12-DEC-01       $50,000.00
Massachusetts    cheryl       08-MAY-01       $80,000.00
Massachusetts    corey        01-JAN-01       $20,000.00
Massachusetts    lisa         26-JUN-01       $75,000.00
Massachusetts    tom          15-AUG-01       $55,000.00
New Jersey       calisi       10-JUN-01       $30,000.00
New Jersey       dick         02-FEB-01       $30,000.00
New Jersey       harry        05-JUN-01       $20,000.00
                          --- Company Confidential ---
10 rows selected.
```

Yes, it was that easy. Once you understand what a primary key is, and what a foreign key is, joining them becomes that simple. The foreign key is a direct road map to the source table. Now it's just a matter of telling SQL*Plus in the **select** portion what you want displayed.

SQL*Plus Alternate Names

Once you start joining tables, it can become quite confusing. You might have three or more STATE_CD foreign keys to choose from. Which STATE_CD do you want displayed, and which STATE_CD do you want to join with? This is when it is very helpful to be able to give a table a nickname. Then use that nickname to clarify what you are trying to do. Here is a sample SQL statement to clarify this point. In this example, we use the nicknames **x** and **y**. We also show you the same statement written without the use of nicknames.

```
SQL>REM *** With Alternate Names
SQL>select y.state_name, x.lname,
  2          x.hiredate, x.salary
  3  from    newhire x, state y
  4 where   x.state_cd = y.state_cd;
SQL>REM Without Alternate Names
SQL>select state.state_name, newhire.lname,
  2          newhire.hiredate, newhire.salary
  3  from    newhire, state  4  where   state.state_cd = newhire.state_cd;
```

The break on Clause

One of the most important things we learned to do when we first started coding was to put break logic into our code. Break logic means that you identify key fields in the data set where a change will take place. At the point of change, you trigger an event, such as skipping a line, starting a new page, or computing a total.

In traditional programming languages, the coding to make these sorts of breaks becomes quite convoluted. Fortunately, SQL*Plus makes this a very easy task to accomplish. Let's look at how easy it is to suppress duplicate state names:

```
SQL> set pagesize 55
SQL> set linesize 80
SQL> repheader 'The New Hire Report|By State'
SQL> repfooter '--- Company Confidential ---'
SQL> column state_name format a15 trunc
SQL> column state_name heading 'State|Name'  format a15 trunc
SQL> column lname      heading 'Last|Name'   format a12 wrap
SQL> column hiredate   heading 'Hire|Date'   format a12
SQL> column salary     heading 'Salary'      format $999,999.99
SQL> break on state_name
SQL> Spool state.out
SQL>select st.state_name, nh.lname,
  2          nh.hiredate, nh.salary
  3  from    newhire nh, state st
  4  where   st.state_cd = nh.state_cd
  5* order by 1,2;

Tue Jul 24                                              page    1
                        The New Hire Report
                             By State


State            Last        Hire
Name             Name        Date         Salary
--------------- ------------ ------------ ------------
```

```
California       nohr        07-MAY-01          $80,000.00
                 smith       15-AUG-01          $40,000.00
Dallas           abby        12-DEC-01          $50,000.00
Massachusetts    cheryl      08-MAY-01          $80,000.00
                 corey       01-JAN-01          $20,000.00
                 lisa        26-JUN-01          $75,000.00
                 tom         15-AUG-01          $55,000.00
New Jersey       calisi      10-JUN-01          $30,000.00
                 dick        02-FEB-01          $30,000.00
                 harry       05-JUN-01          $20,000.00
                          --- Company Confidential ---
10 rows selected.
SQL> Spool Off
```

Notice how the STATE NAME column does not repeat the state name over and over. The default behavior of the **break** command is to suppress duplicates. With just the addition of the **break** command, we have a much more effective report. Next, let's see what happens when we add the **skip** option.

Using break on with the skip Option

Many times it is advantageous to insert blank lines at key break points. Let's take a look at the same SQL statement from the previous section with the **break on** command using the **skip** option:

```
SQL> set pagesize 55
SQL> set linesize 80
SQL> repheader 'The New Hire Report|By State'
SQL> repfooter '--- Company Confidential ---'
SQL> column state_name format a15 trunc
SQL> column state_name heading 'State|Name'   format a15 trunc
SQL> column lname      heading 'Last|Name'    format a12 wrap
SQL> column hiredate   heading 'Hire|Date'    format a12
SQL> column salary     heading 'Salary'       format $999,999.99
SQL> break on state_name skip 1
SQL> Spool state.out
SQL>select st.state_name, nh.lname,
  2        nh.hiredate, nh.salary
  3  from   newhire nh, state st
  4  where  st.state_cd = nh.state_cd
  5* order by 1,2;

Tue Jul 24                                              page     1
                        The New Hire Report
                            By State
```

```
State           Last        Hire
Name            Name        Date            Salary
--------------- ----------- ----------- ------------
California      nohr        07-MAY-01       $80,000.00
                smith       15-AUG-01       $40,000.00

Dallas          abby        12-DEC-01       $50,000.00

Massachusetts   cheryl      08-MAY-01       $80,000.00
                corey       01-JAN-01       $20,000.00
                lisa        26-JUN-01       $75,000.00
                tom         15-AUG-01       $55,000.00

New Jersey      calisi      10-JUN-01       $30,000.00
                dick        02-FEB-01       $30,000.00
                harry       05-JUN-01       $20,000.00

                    --- Company Confidential ---
10 rows selected.
SQL> Spool Off
```

Computing Column Values at Break

The most common use of the **break** command is to combine it with a **compute sum** command, which allows you to add up columns based on key break points. In the next example, we add up the salary amounts by state:

```
SQL> set pagesize 55
SQL> set linesize 80
SQL> repheader 'The New Hire Report|By State'
SQL> repfooter '--- Company Confidential ---'
SQL> column state_name format a15 trunc
SQL> column state_name heading 'State|Name'  format a15 trunc
SQL> column lname      heading 'Last|Name'   format a12 wrap
SQL> column hiredate   heading 'Hire|Date'   format a12
SQL> column salary     heading 'Salary'      format $999,999.99
SQL> compute sum of salary on state_name
SQL> break on state_name skip 1
SQL> Spool state.out
SQL> select st.state_name, nh.lname,
  2         nh.hiredate, nh.salary
  3  from   newhire nh, state st
  4  where  st.state_cd = nh.state_cd
  5* order by 1,2;
```

```
Tue Jul 24                                           page    1
                    The New Hire Report
```

```
                                      By State

State            Last          Hire
Name             Name          Date                Salary
---------------  ------------  ------------  ------------
California       nohr          07-MAY-01       $80,000.00
                 smith         15-AUG-01       $40,000.00
***************                              ------------
sum                                          $120,000.00


Dallas           abby          12-DEC-01       $50,000.00
***************                              ------------
sum                                           $50,000.00


Massachusetts    cheryl        08-MAY-01       $80,000.00
                 corey         01-JAN-01       $20,000.00
                 lisa          26-JUN-01       $75,000.00
                 tom           15-AUG-01       $55,000.00
***************                              ------------
sum                                          $230,000.00


New Jersey       calisi        10-JUN-01       $30,000.00
                 dick          02-FEB-01       $30,000.00
                 harry         05-JUN-01       $20,000.00
***************                              ------------
sum                                           $80,000.00

                   --- Company Confidential ---
10 rows selected.
SQL> Spool Off
```

With the simple addition of two lines, our report is even more effective. This same program written in a traditional language would be quite complex. But the next question in your mind should be, "How do I get a final total?" Glad you asked.

break on report

A special break point named "report" is used to signify the end of a report. By using this command, you can now do final totals. Let's look at this statement in action:

```
SQL> set pagesize 55
SQL> set linesize 80
SQL> repheader 'The New Hire Report|By State'
SQL> repfooter '--- Company Confidential ---'
SQL> column state_name format a15 trunc
SQL> column state_name heading 'State|Name'  format a15 trunc
```

```
SQL> column lname       heading 'Last|Name'    format a12 wrap
SQL> column hiredate    heading 'Hire|Date'    format a12
SQL> column salary      heading 'Salary'       format $999,999.99
SQL> compute sum of salary on state_name
SQL> compute sum of salary on report
SQL> break on report skip 1 on state_name skip 1
SQL> Spool state.out
SQL> select st.state_name, nh.lname,
  2          nh.hiredate, nh.salary
  3  from    newhire nh, state st
  4  where   st.state_cd = nh.state_cd
  5* order by 1,2;
```

```
Tue Jul 24                                                    page     1
                        The New Hire Report
                           By State


State            Last        Hire
Name             Name        Date              Salary
--------------   ----------- ------------  -----------
California       nohr        07-MAY-01       $80,000.00
                 smith       15-AUG-01       $40,000.00
**************                             -----------
sum                                         $120,000.00


Dallas           abby        12-DEC-01       $50,000.00
**************                             -----------
sum                                          $50,000.00


Massachusetts    cheryl      08-MAY-01       $80,000.00
                 corey       01-JAN-01       $20,000.00
                 lisa        26-JUN-01       $75,000.00
                 tom         15-AUG-01       $55,000.00
**************                             -----------
sum                                         $230,000.00


New Jersey       calisi      10-JUN-01       $30,000.00
                 dick        02-FEB-01       $30,000.00
                 harry       05-JUN-01       $20,000.00
**************                             -----------
sum                                          $80,000.00


                                          -----------
sum                                         $480,000.00


                    --- Company Confidential ---
SQL> Spool Off
```

There you have it. You have learned all the concepts you need in order to make full use of SQL*Plus. Take these simple examples and try writing some SQL. You will be surprised at how much you can accomplish on your own. SQL*Plus is the workhorse of Oracle; now go put it to work in your environment.

Chapter 5 Questions

Answers to questions can be found in Appendix A.

1. The proper way to terminate a SQL*Plus session is to issue the _____ command.

   A. CTRL-C

   B. end

   C. quit

   D. exit

2. The _____ command displays all the columns and attributes of the named table.

   A. explain

   B. describe

   C. showb

   D. printb

3. Which of the following is an example of DML?

   A. select

   B. create

   C. drop

   D. alter

4. DDL stands for

   A. data description language

   B. data destruction language

   C. data manipulation language

   D. data definition language

CHAPTER
6

PL/SQL 101

ou have already learned that Oracle9*i* is a great place to store your information. We have also shown you how to get data out of your database using SQL*Plus. By now you know that the job of an Oracle DBA is very complex. That stuff is all great, but it is not enough. Our experience in programming has revealed that we need more, and of course, we want more. PL/SQL is Oracle's contribution to the programming world. It stands for Procedural Language Structured Query Language and is a programming environment that resides directly in the database. We will get to architecture in just a bit; first some background.

PL/SQL first appeared in Oracle Version 6 in 1988. It was primarily used within Oracle's user interface product SQL*Forms to allow for the inclusion of complex logic within the forms. It replaced an old step method for logical control and provided a reasonably simple programming language that resembled ADA and C. Looking back at those days, we remember converting old Pro*C programs into PL/SQL so that we could more easily maintain them. Actually, the C programmer took another job, and we had lots of people who wanted to use their new programming language knowledge. So we converted all the code in a relatively short time frame, and here we are 14 years later with some of that original PL/SQL code still in use. We have come a long way since then. Today we use PL/SQL to read data, to populate the database, create stored objects, and even to display web pages. PL/SQL has certainly grown into a mature product. If you are concerned that Oracle is planning to replace PL/SQL with Java, your worries are not based in fact. Oracle has shown a strong dedication to the language, as illustrated by its use of PL/SQL in many of its products, such as Oracle Applications. Oracle is also using the web portion of PL/SQL quite extensively. Have you visited **www.oracle.com** lately? If so, you have seen PL/SQL for the web in action. So let's move on and look more closely at the PL/SQL programming language.

We will cover PL/SQL in three chapters. In this chapter, we discuss the basic concepts and constructs of PL/SQL. Later, in Chapter 9, we will discuss more advanced topics and techniques, including Oracle's built-in packages. Finally, in Chapter 14, we will discuss PL/SQL for the web. There is a lot of stuff to cover, but it is just as important to learn PL/SQL as it is to learn SQL. So, whether you are looking at becoming a DBA or an Oracle developer, knowledge of PL/SQL is a skill that you must have in your database toolkit. In this chapter, we plan to discuss the following:

- Overview of PL/SQL structure

- Components of PL/SQL

- Compilation and execution

- Block structure

- Variables and data types
- Execution control
- Looping
- SQL in PL/SQL
- Cursors
- Exceptions
- Stored procedures and functions
- Basic debugging

Terminology

The following terminology will arm you with the technical jargon to get through this chapter.

- A *program* is a set of commands that perform a specific task.

- *Variables* are programmer-defined names to store information while running a program.

- The *declare section* is where you define the variables in a program.

- The *executable section* is where you define the steps that will run in the program you create.

- An *exception* is a system- or user-defined error-handling mechanism within a program.

- A *data type* defines the class of a piece of information or data. For example, you can think of information as numbers or characters. In programming, the same is true—a character data type would contain any set of characters, and a numeric data type would contain decimals between 0 and 9 and may be either a positive or negative value.

- A *PL/SQL block* is the set of commands that constitute a PL/SQL program.

- An *anonymous PL/SQL block* is a PL/SQL block that may contain a declare section, will always contain an executable section, and may contain an exception section. A *named PL/SQL block* is one that is defined and named for storage in the database.

- An *executable* is the name of a program written using one of an assortment of computer programming languages. When you type the name of an executable, the program runs. For example, when you use SQL*Plus, you enter the command **sqlplus**.

- *Arithmetic operators* are symbols used to define mathematical operations performed on data. The most common operators are **+** (addition), **–** (subtraction), **/** (division), ***** (multiplication).

- *Relational operators* define comparisons or choices made on data. For example, if you wish to see whether two dates are equal, you would use the relational operator. Some common relational operators are = (equal), > (greater than), < (less than), != (not equal).

- A *loop* is a construct in a computer program in which a segment of code is executed repeatedly.

- An *exit condition* is the part of the loop where a test is performed on data. If the test returns a result of "true," then you might exit the loop.

- An *array* is a data set that may be held in a memory structure that can hold many rows of information. You can usually move from row to row in an array. It is a variable, but it is one that may contain more than one value at any one time.

- A *cursor* is an Oracle memory structure that holds an SQL statement and may also hold the result during the running of a program.

- A *stored object* is a PL/SQL program that is saved in the database and may be shared and used by many developers and end users. *Procedures, packages, functions,* and *triggers* are all examples of stored objects. We will discuss these more fully in Chapter 9.

PL/SQL: The Oracle Programming Language

The Oracle9i database is more than just a database. It is also an engine for many languages. It serves as a Java engine with the built-in Java Virtual Machine (JVM), as well as a PL/SQL engine. This means that the code may be stored in the database and then run. So there is no need for another product. The PL/SQL engine is bundled with the database. Imagine a product from Oracle that works really well and is free. How can they make any money? Let's look at how PL/SQL fits into the Oracle database. Figure 6-1 shows you how PL/SQL works from within and from outside the database.

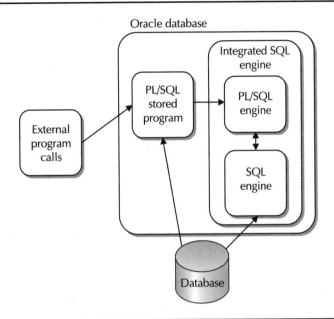

FIGURE 6-1. *PL/SQL architecture*

Int Figure 6-1, you see at the center the Oracle9*i* server, the primary engine for the database. It serves as the coordinator for all calls to the database. When a call is made from a program to the server to run a PL/SQL program, the database (Oracle) loads the compiled program into memory, and then the PL/SQL engine and SQL engine execute the program. The PL/SQL engine will handle the program's memory structures and logical program flow. The SQL engine then issues data requests to the database. It is a closed system and one that allows for very efficient programming.

PL/SQL is used in numerous Oracle products, including

- The Oracle server
- Oracle Forms, discussed in Chapter 15
- Oracle Reports, discusssed in Chapter 15
- Oracle Warehouse Builder
- Oracle Applications
- Oracle Portal

All these programs use PL/SQL to some extent. There may be as many as 5 million lines of PL/SQL code contained in Oracle Applications, for example. PL/SQL programs can be called from these Oracle development environments:

■ SQL*Plus

■ Oracle Enterprise Manager

■ Oracle precompilers (such as Pro*C, Pro*COBOL, etc.)

■ Oracle Call Interface (OCI)

■ Server Manager

■ Oracle9i Application Server

■ Java Virtual Machine (JVM)

As you can see, PL/SQL is well established within most of the Oracle9i line of products. You now have some background in the PL/SQL architecture. Let's rock and roll and discover the basics of the language. Please fasten your seatbelts.

PL/SQL Character Set

As with all programming languages, there are characters that you use to write your programs. Each language has its own rules and restrictions when it comes to the valid characters. In the following sections, we will show you the following:

■ Valid characters when programming in PL/SQL

■ Arithmetic operators

■ Relational operators

Supported Characters

When programming in PL/SQL, you may only use characters as defined here:

■ Upper- or lowercase characters

■ All digits between 0 and 9

■ Symbols: ( ) + - * / < > = ! ~ ; : . - ` @ % , " ' # ^ & _ | { } ? [ ]

Some of these characters are for program commands; others serve as relation or arithmetic operators. Together they form a program. It's like someone asking you what your favorite book is and you say the dictionary, because the dictionary has all the words from all the books in one place.

Arithmetic Operators and Relational Operators

Table 6-1 shows the common arithmetic operators used in PL/SQL. They are listed in the order that they are executed (known as *precedence*, or priority). When the functions appear in the same line, this means they are executed with the same level of precedence, so the position of the expression will decide which goes first. Table 6-2 shows the common relational operators used in PL/SQL.

PL/SQL Structure

It's time to get your feet wet. The structure used in all of PL/SQL is the foundation for all of the language. When you master it, you will be able to move forward; but if you do not take the time to get this first step right, your journey will be difficult. Actually, it's easy. Let's look at the structure that all of your PL/SQL programs will have.

You will have areas for program parameters (used to pass values from outside a program to the program), internal variables, the main program code and logic, and then some ways to handle things when they go wrong. At one time on *Saturday Night Live,* there was a character named Father Guido Sarducci, who lectured on the things you actually know when you graduate from a university. In his economics

Operator	Meaning
**	Exponent
*, /	Multiplication, division
+, −, ‖	Addition, subtraction, concatenation

TABLE 6-1. *Common Mathematical Operators*

Operator	Meaning
=	Equal
<> or !=	Not equal
>	Greater than
<	Less than
>=	Greater than or equal
<=	Less than or equal

TABLE 6-2. *Common Relational Operators*

class, you learned two things: supply and demand; and if you think back to your last economics class, that is probably the main lesson that you remember. In the case of PL/SQL, it is BEGIN and END. Let's look at a sample bit of code:

```
DECLARE
        -- Put Variables Here
BEGIN
        -- Put Program Here
END;
/
```

That's it. This is the basic structure of every PL/SQL program. When we talk about PL/SQL programs, we usually refer to them as PL/SQL blocks. PL/SQL blocks are simply programs that are complete and contain the programming required to run successfully. This structure will form the basis for any program that you will be writing in PL/SQL. As you continue to read, you will learn how to use this simple form to build more complex programs.

NOTE
To add comments to your code, start a comment with /* and end it with */, or you may use the double hyphen, -- (as we have done here). If you use --, make sure to put it either on its own line or after your program code if you place it on the same line.

You will usually need to declare variables in your PL/SQL program. Variables are used in PL/SQL to hold the working storage (constants, variables, **select** statements, data arrays, and so on.) within your program. So, if you need a counter, or a data array, or data variables, or even Boolean variables, you will find them here. Then the program body is the only section that you really need, since you could write a program without variables within it. It is in the program body that you build your program logic and database access. That is why you must always remember BEGIN and END: these are your PL/SQL bookends. It is between these two lines that your program logic is contained. We can now move on and look at the main program areas.

PL/SQL Variables

You will almost always need to use variables in a PL/SQL program. It is here that you will define how your data is to be held while you work it through your program. These variables can be the same types you already learned about in Chapter 5. However, in addition to these standard data types, some special ones have been created specifically for the PL/SQL language. One of the great features of Oracle9*i* is the integration of SQL and PL/SQL into one system. This means that starting with Oracle9*i*, you can run the same commands in PL/SQL that you use in SQL.

So on to the most common data types that you will use when writing PL/SQL programs. There are numerous data types, but mastering these simple ones will allow you to build some complex programs. The following are some of the data types that you will use most often:

- Varchar2
- Number
- Date
- Boolean

Assigning values to variables is a very important task when programming in PL/SQL or any other programming language. You can assign values to variables in any section of your program code. In the declare section, you usually do this to initialize values in advance of their use in the program or to define values that will be used as constants in your program. To assign a value to a variable in the declaration section, you would use the following format:

```
Variable_name      variable_type      := value;
```

The important item that you should notice here is the use of := to assign a value. This is the standard that will be used in PL/SQL.

You may also define variable values in the execution and exception sections of your PL/SQL program. Within the program, you would use the following format to assign a value to a variable:

```
Variable_name      := value;
```

Let's look at a small program that assigns values in each section of a program.

```
-- declaration section of the program
declare
        l_counter  number := 0;       -- initiate value to 0
        l_today    date   := sysdate; -- assign system date to variable
        l_name     varchar2(50);  -- variable is defined but has no value
-- execution section of the program
begin
        l_counter := l_counter + 1;       -- add one to current value of counter
        l_name := 'ESTHER ASTROFF'; -- set a value to name variable
-- Error handling section of the program
exception
-- Generic error handling to handle any type of error
     when others then
-- print out an error message
raise_application_error (-20100, 'error#' || sqlcode || ' desc: ' || sqlerrm);
end;
```

NOTE
*Oracle has some special variables that may be used in a PL/SQL program. In the example, we used the **sqlcode** and **sqlerrm** variables, which represent the Oracle error number and the Oracle error message, respectively. You may use these to capture Oracle errors in your program.*

varchar2

varchar2 is a variable-length alphanumeric data type. In PL/SQL, it may have a length up to 32,767 bytes. When you define the **varchar2** variable in the declare section, remember to terminate the line with a semicolon (;). The following is the form of **varchar2** variable declarations,

```
Variable_name       varchar2(max_length);
```

where the max_length is a positive integer, as in

```
l_name              varchar2(30);
```

You may also set an initial or default value for the variable. This is done on the same line as the variable declaration in the declare section of your program, so you can do this by using the following syntax:

```
l_name       varchar2(30)       := 'ABRAMSON';
```

The preceding statement sets the value of the variable l_name to ABRAMSON.

number

The number variable is used to represent all numeric data. The format of the declaration is

```
Number_field      number(length, decimal_places);
```

where the length can be from 1 to 38 numerical positions, and decimal_places represents the positions for numerical precision of the decimal place for the variable. Keep this in mind when you define your numerical variable, for example:

```
L_average_amount      number(12,2);
```

This describes a variable that may hold up to 10 digits (length (12) – decimal_places (2)) and up to two decimal places, or a number up to a value of 9,999,999,999.99.

date

As you would expect, the date variable is used to store date and time values. (Together these form a data type sometimes called *datetime,* which, in Oracle, is known only as the date data type.) The following is the format of the date declaration:

```
Date_variable      date;
```

By default, Oracle displays values using the format DD-MON-YY; so a value of 14-JAN-03 would be the equivalent of January 14, 2003. When programming in PL/SQL, you should always use this data type to perform date manipulation. It is possible to extend the flexibility of your date manipulations by combining this data type with some built-in Oracle9*i* functions. For example, let's say that you create a variable for a start date and you want to place values into this variable. Let's see how this may be done:

```
Declare
        L_start_date      date;
Begin
-- Sets variable to September 29, 2005.
        L_start_date := '29-SEP-05';
-- Sets variable to September 29, 2083.
        L_start_date := to_date('29-SEP-2083 ', 'DD-MON-YYYY');
-- Sets variable to June 9, 1991, 1:01p.m.
        L_start_date := to_date('09-JUN-91:13:01 ', 'DD-MON-YY:HH24:MI');
End;
```

Here, the date variable is set in three different ways. The first is the simplest; the second uses the **to_date** function and allows for more flexible data declarations, since you can use a four-digit year definition. The final example shows how you may put a datetime into the variable. Again, you use the **to_date** function, but include the time in the value and then define it with the date mask definition.

NOTE

To discover more details on other Oracle9i built-in functions, refer to the gamut of technical resources available.

Boolean

The final basic data type we will discuss is the Boolean data type. Simply put, this variable will hold a value of either **true** or **false**. When you use this data type, you must test its status, and then do one thing if it is true or another if it is false. You can use Boolean expressions to compare arithmetic expressions or character expressions. Here is an example of comparing arithmetic values:

```
L_record_goals := 91;
L_season_goals := 77;
-- Therefore the following expression will be true
L_record_goals > l_season_goals
-- However the next is false
l_record_goals <= l_season_goals
```

You can compare character strings the same way, for example:

```
l_Cognos_developer := 'Falcon';
l_Oracle_dba := 'Ruxpinnah';
-- The following expression will true in a true Boolean value
l_Cognos_developer != l_oracle_dba
```

It is important to understand that comparison provides Boolean results that may then be used during conditional program control; so take the time to know the difference between **true** and **false**. In C++ and other languages, Booleans can be represented as either true or false, or 1 or 0. In PL/SQL, the value is only assigned a true or false.

Control Structures

At the heart of any programming language are its control structures. Since programs are written to handle a number of different situations, the manner in which different conditions are detected and dealt with is the biggest part of program control. Various types of control structures are used for this purpose, including

- **if** logic structures

■ **case** expressions

■ Looping structures

Program control is governed by the status of variables and the data that is read from and written to the database. As an example, picture yourself going into the driver's license office to renew your driver's license. When you enter the office, you are presented with a number of directional signs. One sign reads "Driver Testing"; for this, you go to the second floor. Another sign tells you that "License Renewals" is on the third floor. You are here for a renewal, so you head up to the third floor. Once you arrive in the renewal office, you once again are faced with some new choices. After all, this is a government office; it is not going to be a simple exercise. Now you have to decide whether you are going to pay by cash or credit card. Cash payments are being accepted to the right, and credit cards are to the left. You see that you have enough cash, and you head to the payment wicket on the right. Let's look at Table 6-3 and see how our program control influenced your choices.

Step	Process or Decision to Make	Next Steps	
1	Here for a driver's license transaction	Yes = 2	No = 4
2	Here for a driving test	Yes = 5	No = 3
3	Here for a license renewal	Yes = 6	No = 4
4	Ask for help	Right place = 1	Wrong place = 13
5	Go to second floor	7	
6	Go to third floor	9	
7	Line up for driver's test (we hope)	8	
8	Pass test	6	
9	Payment method	Cash = 10	Credit = 11
10	Cash payment wicket	12	
11	Credit card payment wicket	12	
12	Receive new license	13	
13	Go home, leave building		

TABLE 6-3. *Program Control Decision Matrix*

if Logic Structures

When you are writing computer programs, situations present themselves in which you must test a condition. When you ask a question in your program, you are usually presented with one of two answers: it may be **true** or it may be **false**. Computer programs are black and white; in computer logic, there can only be **true** or **false** answers to your questions, no maybes. PL/SQL provides you with three distinctive **if** logic structures that allow you to test for true and false conditions. In everyday life we are presented with decisions that we need to make; the following sections will show you how to do it using PL/SQL.

if-then

You use the **if-then** construct to test the simplest type of condition. If the condition evaluates to true, then one or more lines of program code will be executed. If the condition evaluates as false, then no action is taken. The following code snippet illustrates how this is performed with a PL/SQL program. Notice the bold text, which shows you the reserved words used in this example.

```
IF l_date > '11-APR-03' then
        l_salary :=  l_salary * 1.15; -- Increase salary by 15%
END IF;
```

NOTE

*Each **if** statement is followed by its own **then**. There is also no semicolon (;) terminator on a line that begins with an **if**.*

In this case, if the value of the variable l_date is greater than the 11th of April 2003, then the salary will be increased by 15 percent. This statement may also be restated using the following statement:

```
IF not(l_date <= '11-APR-03') then
        l_salary :=  l_salary * 1.15; -- Increase salary by 15%
END IF;
```

Also, you may nest **if-then** statements to increase the power of your statements. Let's add a condition to limit who gets the raise:

```
IF l_date > '11-APR-03' then
    IF l_last_name = 'PAKMAN' then
        l_salary :=  l_salary * 1.15; -- Increase salary by 15%
    END IF;
END IF;
```

Now, not only must the date be greater than the 11th of April, 2003, but also your last name must be equal to Pakman in order to get the raise. This is a method that we use to make sure human resource programs give programmers a raise every year.

What you should also notice in this code is that there are now two **end if** statements. This is a required construct, since you must always pair an **if** statement with an **end if;**. So if you are going to have nested **if** statements, you must ensure that each is paired with a matching **end if;**.

NOTE
*Each **if** statement block must have at least one line of program code. If you wish to do nothing within your program code, simply use the **null;** command.*

if-then-else

The **if-then-else** construct is similar to the simple **if-then** construct. The difference is that when the condition executes as false, the program statements that follow the **else** statement are executed. The following code illustrates this logic within PL/SQL.

```
IF l_date >  '11-APR-03' then
        l_salary :=  l_salary * 1.15; -- Increase salary by 15%
ELSE
    l_salary := l_salary * 1.05;  -- Increase salary by 5%
END IF;
```

In the preceding code listing, you see the condition that if the date is greater than the 11th of April, 2003, you will get a 15 percent salary increase. However, when the date is less than or equal to this date, you will only receive a 5 percent increase. As with the simple **if-then** construct, you may nest the **if-then-else** construct. Let's look at how this might appear in our PL/SQL program:

```
IF l_date > '11-APR-03' then
    If l_last_name = 'PAKMAN' then
        l_salary :=  l_salary * 1.15; -- Increase salary by 15%
    ELSE
        l_salary :=  l_salary * 1.10; -- Increase salary by 10%
    END IF;
ELSE
    l_salary := l_salary * 1.05;  -- Increase salary by 5%
END IF;
```

This leads us to another note on using the **if** statement within PL/SQL.

NOTE
*Only one **else** statement is allowed within every **if** statement construct, and there is no semicolon (;) on the line starting with **else**.*

if-then-elsif

The final **if** construct that we will show you is **if-then-elsif**. In this case, you provide yourself with the option to test another condition when the first condition is evaluated as **false**. When you want to test for more than one condition without using nested **if** statements, this is the type of statement that you might use.

```
IF l_last_name = 'PAKMAN' then
    l_salary :=  l_salary * 1.15; -- Increase salary by 15%
ELSIF l_last_name = 'ASTROFF' then
        l_salary :=  l_salary * 1.10; -- Increase salary by 10%
ELSE
        l_salary :=  l_salary * 1.05; -- Increase salary by 5%
END IF;
```

In the preceding statement, if your last name is Pakman, you get a 15 percent raise; if it is Astroff, you get 10 percent; and the rest of us get only a 5 percent raise. There is no limit to the number of **elsif** conditions that you may use within this construct. The following shows you an example of using multiple **elsif** statements within the construct.

```
IF l_city = 'OTTAWA' then
        L_team_name := 'SENATORS';
ELSIF l_city = 'LOS ANGELES' then
        L_team_name := 'KINGS';
ELSIF l_city = 'NEW YORK' then
        L_team_name := 'RANGERS';
ELSIF l_city = 'TORONTO' then
        L_team_name := 'MAPLE LEAFS';
END IF;
```

NOTE
*There is no matching **end if** statement for each **elsif**.*
*Only a single **end if** is required within this construct.*

When writing your PL/SQL program, use indentation to simplify the reading of the program, as in the code segments shown here. As a rule, you should line up each **if-then-else** statement, and indent the program code that lies between each of these words.

case Expressions

The next logical step from the **if** statement is the **case** statement. The **case** statement, which was introduced with Oracle9*i*, is an evolution in logical control. It differs from the **if-then-else** constructs in that you now can use a simple structure to logically select from a list of values. More important, it may be used to set the value of a variable. Let's look at how this may be done. First, let's look at the format:

```
CASE variable
        WHEN expression1 then value1
        WHEN expression2 then value2
        WHEN expression3 then value3
        WHEN expression4 then value4
        ELSE value5
END;
```

There is no limit to the number of expressions that may be defined in a **case** expression. Here is an example of the use of the **case** expression:

```
SQL> run
  1  declare
  2     val      varchar2(100);
  3     city     varchar2(20) := 'TORONTO';
  4  begin
  5     val := CASE city
  6                  WHEN 'TORONTO' then 'RAPTORS'
  7                  WHEN 'LOS ANGELES' then 'LAKERS'
  8                  WHEN 'BOSTON' then 'CELTICS'
  9                  WHEN 'CHICAGO' then 'BULLS'
 10                  ELSE 'NO TEAM'
 11            END;
 12
 13     dbms_output.put_line(val); -- output to the screen
 14* end;
RAPTORS
PL/SQL procedure successfully completed.
```

NOTE
*In order to get Oracle to provide output from a PL/SQL program, you must set the environment variable within SQL*Plus. To do this, type **set serveroutput on size 1000000;** at the SQL prompt.*

Although you can use the **if-then-else** to achieve the same purpose, the **case** statement is easier to read and more efficient. Remember that once Oracle9*i* reaches a value in the **case** statement that meets the condition, the processing of the **case** statement will stop.

Loops

When was the last time you visited an amusement park? If you have been to one in recent years, you will surely have seen a roller coaster. That roller coaster—if it's a really good roller coaster—probably had one or more loops. Well, PL/SQL is that kind of ride. It is a ride that includes loops. Loops are control structures that allow you to repeat a set of commands until you decide that it is time to stop the looping.

Generally, the format that all loops take is the following:

```
LOOP
        Executable statements;
END LOOP;
```

Each time the loop is executed, the statements within the loop are executed, and then the program returns to the top of the **loop** structure to do it all over again. However, if you ever want this processing to stop, you will need to learn about the **exit** statement.

The **exit** statement allows you to stop executing within a loop without a condition. It will then pass control back to the program and will continue on after the **loop** statements.

The following is how to get out of a tight **loop**:

```
LOOP
        IF l_batting_average <= 300 then EXIT;
        ELSE
                L_decision := 'STAY IN MAJORS';
        END IF;
END LOOP;
```

There are many other kinds of loops that provide more control over looping. Each has its uses in PL/SQL programming, and each should be learned so that you have maximum flexibility in your programming needs.

The while Loop

The **while** loop will continue to execute as long as the condition that you have defined continues to be true. If the condition becomes false, then you exit the loop.

Let's look at an example:

```
WHILE l_sales_total < 100000 LOOP
        Select sales_amount into l_sale_amount from daily_sales;
        l_sales_total := l_sales_total + l_sale_amount;
END LOOP;
```

Although you may use the **exit** command to do the same thing, it is better form to
use the **while** expression.

The for Loop

The **for** loop is one of the most common loops that you will encounter in your
PL/SQL travels. This loop allows you to control the number of times that a loop
executes. In the case of the **while** loop, you are never quite sure how many times
a loop is executed, since it will continue to loop until a condition is met. The **for**
loop allows you to define the number of times that you will be looping when you
program the loop itself. You will define the value to start your loop with and the
value that will terminate your loop. Let's look at some syntax:

```
FOR l_counter IN 1 .. 10
LOOP
        Statements;
END LOOP;
```

So, what is important for you to note in the preceding statement? First, you need
to know that the variable **l_counter** will hold the value between 1 and 10. How do
we know it will be between 1 and 10? Well, after the **IN**, we place the counter's
range. In this case, the counter starts at 1, the low bound, and continues to 10. You
should also note the two dots (. .) between the two integer values (1 and 10). This tells
Oracle9*i* that you would like it to count between these two numbers. One more
note: regardless of any previous values that the variable **l_counter** has been set to in
an earlier command in your program, when you use the values in the loop, you will
discover that they are now set to values between 1 and 10.

You can also count backward using the **reverse** clause. The next code listing
shows you how the **reverse** clause may be used.

```
    declare
        l_counter number;
    begin
        FOR l_counter IN REVERSE 1..5
        LOOP
                dbms_output.put_line(l_counter);
        END LOOP;
    end;
/
5
4
3
2
1
PL/SQL procedure successfully completed.
```

Now you can see how easy it is to use simple loops, but loops have much more power. Using loops like the **while** loop or the **for** loop allows you to use variables instead of hard-coded values. This gives you the greatest possible flexibility because you can have the database or external data provide you with the limits within your loop. Let's look at how this might work. In the following example, we select the number of employees in our employee table, and then show how the counter counts from 1 to the number of employees in our small company:

```
SQL> run
  1  declare
  2    l_emp_count number;
  3    i           number;  -- We will use this as our counter
  4  begin
  5    -- Select the number of employees in the l_emp_count variable
  6    select count(*) into l_emp_count from employee;
  7
  8    FOR i IN 1 .. l_emp_count  LOOP
  9         dbms_output.put_line('Employee ' || i);
 10    END LOOP;
 11* end;
Employee 1
Employee 2
Employee 3
Employee 4
Employee 5
Employee 6
PL/SQL procedure successfully completed.
```

As you might have guessed, we have six employees in our company. (It may be small, but it's very good.) The important point is that you may use variables in your loops. The other line that you may have noticed is the **select** statement contained in this PL/SQL block. You might be thinking, what are they talking about and where did this come from? Well, relax, we haven't told you about **select** statements in your PL/SQL programs, but this seems like a perfect time to talk about SQL in your PL/SQL programs.

SQL in Your PL/SQL Programs

We have looked at a lot of structure up until now. You should know that a PL/SQL program will always have a BEGIN and END. It may have variables, loops, or logic control, but your next question must be "Where's the beef?" What gives PL/SQL its beef is SQL. Since you have all these nice control structures, you need to use them in conjunction with information. You may want the information so that you can create a report, update data, create new data, and delete old data, or perform just about any other function that you can think of. It is very important for you to see how you can integrate data into PL/SQL code. Without data, PL/SQL is just PL.

Cursors

How do you get data to your programs? Simple—select it from the database. The previous section actually introduced you to using SQL in your PL/SQL programs. Do you remember the line

```
6     select count(*) into l_emp_count from employee;
```

This is the easiest way to use SQL in your program.

Let's break down the statement and look at what it means to the program. As you look at the **select** statement, you see that it looks pretty much the way a standard **select** statement looks. However, you should also have noticed the **into** word in the statement; so you must be wondering, what is it for? This is how you put a value into a variable using a **select** statement. In addition to selecting one value from the database, you also have the ability to select more than one value. To do this, you use the following cursor format:

```
select emp_name, salary into l_emp_name, l_salary from employee;
```

You can use any SQL statement you want within your program. It can be a **select**, **insert**, **update**, or a **delete** statement. All of these will be supported. When you use a **select** statement like we did in the preceding, this is called an implicit cursor. An *implicit cursor* is a SQL statement that is contained within the executable section of the program and contains an **into** statement in the case of a **select** statement. With an implicit cursor, Oracle will handle everything for you, but there is a cost to doing this. The cost is internal within Oracle and will result in a program running slower. Now you must be wondering, why are they telling me about an inefficient way to use Oracle? Well, you need to understand what you can do; it may not be the best way to perform a **select** statement, but you must use an implicit cursor when you want to run a **delete**, **update**, or **insert** statement. So, let's move on to see the better way to do the same thing. We will revisit our previous example so that you can compare the two.

The better way is by creating an explicit cursor. An *explicit cursor* is a **select** statement that is declared in the declare section of a program. You do this so that Oracle will then prepare your SQL statement in advance of running your program.

This makes for very efficient use of memory by the program. Let's look at what the program would look like with an explicit cursor:

```
1    declare
2         l_emp_count number;
3         i              number;   -- We will use this as our counter
4
5       -- declare our SELECT cursor (explicit)
6       CURSOR get_employee_data IS
7             select count(*)
8             from    employee;
9    begin
10
11      -- open the cursor for use
12      OPEN get_employee_data;
13      -- run your SQL statement and put the value into a variable
14      FETCH  get_employee_data INTO l_emp_count;
15
16          FOR i IN 1 .. l_emp_count  LOOP
17                dbms_output.put_line('Employee ' || i);
18          END LOOP;
19
20      -- Don't forget to tell Oracle that you are done
21      CLOSE get_employee_data;
22*  end;
PL/SQL procedure successfully completed.
```

See how easy that was? OK, so the code looks more complicated, but remember we are building up to more. The important lines are highlighted in the program and explained in Table 6-4.

In this example, Oracle9*i* will retrieve only one row from the database. However, a similar method may be used in conjunction with a loop to retrieve more than one row. We will discuss this in the next section.

NOTE
Always remember to close your cursors when you are done with them. If you don't, you may start getting memory problems, or you could get results that you don't expect.

Line Number	Description
6–8	These lines define your **select** statement in the form of a cursor. This cursor will now be available for use in the program. You must be sure to include the capitalized words in your cursor declaration. Also remember to end the cursor with a semicolon.
12	This line tells Oracle9*i* that you would like to use the cursor, so you use the **open** command. Next you want to get the data.
14	To retrieve the data from the database, you tell Oracle9*i* to fetch the data into the variables.
21	Once you have finished with the **select** statement, you need to tell Oracle to free up the memory that it used for the statement.

TABLE 6-4. *Important Lines in Explicit Cursor Listing*

The Cursor for Loop

You really start getting the power of the cursor by combining it with a loop. The cursor **for** loop is the result of combining the **select** cursor with a **for** loop. This allows you to retrieve multiple rows from the database if your result set should do this. It also is simpler to program, and you don't have to worry about opening or closing your cursor; Oracle will handle all that within the loop. Let's look at an example of the cursor **for** loop. The important lines have been highlighted for you.

```
SQL> set serveroutput on
SQL> run
  1  declare
  2        l_emp_count number;
  3        i           number;  -- We will use this as our counter
  4
  5     -- declare our SELECT cursor (explicit)
  6     cursor get_employee_data IS
  7             select emp_name, salary
  8          from    employee
  9          order by emp_name;
 10     begin
 11
 12       -- The infamous  FOR loop
```

```
13      FOR c1_rec IN get_employee_data
14      LOOP
15          dbms_output.put_line('Employee :' || c1_rec.emp_name ||
16                              ' Salary: $' || c1_rec.salary);
17          END LOOP;
18
19*  end;
Employee :ABRAMSON Salary: $50000
Employee :ASTROFF Salary: $65000
Employee :FALCON Salary: $55000
Employee :HERRON Salary: $67500
Employee :PAKMAN Salary: $75000
Employee :STANFORD Salary: $77500
PL/SQL procedure successfully completed.
```

Now that is what we call a program that starts to put this chapter into perspective. The cursor **for** loop is truly PL/SQL power in action. Let's look a little closer at the preceding example, especially at the lines that are bold, as discussed in Table 6-5.

Notice that you do not include the cursor variable declaration in the declare section. Oracle9*i* will handle this for you—same price. Finally, on line 15, we use a value from the cursor. In order to use this you need to reference it in the following way:

```
Cursor_variable.column_name
```

Line Number	Description
6–9	Here you declare your explicit cursor. We made it a little more complicated than before by including a couple of fields and an **order by** clause. You can use almost any SQL **select** statement here.
13	This line contains the setup for running your cursor loop. The variable **c1_rec** simply tells Oracle to use this variable name to hold the cursor results.

TABLE 6-5. *Discussion of Cursor **for** Loop*

As you can see on line 15, we did just that by using **c1_rec.emp_name** when we wanted to use those values. So, now you know how to get data from the database. Once you master this small skill, you will be able to write just about any PL/SQL that you can think of—except that you are sitting there asking, "Tell me more...I want to know." As you might expect, you get all this, and we are about to throw more into your PL/SQL special at no extra charge. We will now move on to look at how errors are handled.

Exception Handling

When everything is going right, and your best laid programming plans seem to be perfect, you know what happens? You get an error. It might be a small error, or it could be something very big. To you, it's just an error; and when errors happen in computer programs, bad things can happen. Some people might call it a bug. Do you know why they call a problem in a computer a bug? It's because they found a moth inside a computer that caused the computer to crash.

Back to how to handle errors in Oracle PL/SQL programs: to handle errors in PL/SQL, you use a mechanism called an exception handler. An *exception handler* is a facility within a program that makes sure that your program deals with errors in a nice way.

Whenever an error occurs during the running of a PL/SQL program, the program checks to see whether you as a good programmer have dealt with this remote possibility. It checks for this in the exception section to see whether the problem has already been anticipated. Oracle provides certain exception handles within he product. When you need to handle an error that Oracle has not provided a handle for, you can create a user-defined exception.

Table 6-6 describes some of the most common errors that Oracle helps you handle. For a complete list of built-in exceptions, we refer you to the gamut of technical documentation strewn throughout the Internet.

The other important fact that you need to learn here is the raising of errors from within a program. To raise an error from within a PL/SQL program, you use the built-in function named **raise_application_error**. The function requires two arguments. One is for the error number. This number must be between –20000 and –20999. The second argument is the error that you want the user to see.

The following is the line that your program may contain to provide feedback to the user:

```
raise_application_error (-20123, 'This is an error, you have done a bad thing');
```

Exception Name	Explanation	Oracle Error
no_data_found	When a **select** statement returns no rows, this error may be raised. This error usually occurs when you use an implicit cursor and perform a SELECT INTO.	ORA-01403
too_many_rows	When a case that should only return a single row returns multiple rows, this exception is raised.	ORA-01422
dup_val_on_index	This exception is raised when you try to insert a record into a table that has a primary key on it, and the record that you are inserting duplicates one that already exists in the table.	ORA-00001
value_error	This error occurs when you attempt to put a value into a variable, but either the value is incompatible (for example, putting a value of "DATAVISIONS" into a numerical field), or the value is too big (for example, putting a value of "JILLIANABRAMSON" into a variable that is only six characters long).	ORA-06502
Others	This exception is used to catch any errors that are not handled by specific error handles. Note that you must always make this error handle the last one in your program since Oracle will not process any exception handles after this one.	Nonspecific

TABLE 6-6. *Common Exceptions in PL/SQL*

Let's see how these error handlers come together in a single program:

```
SQL> run
  1  declare
  2          l_emp_count number;
  3          i           number;  -- We will use this as our counter
```

```
 4        l_row         employee%rowtype;
 5    begin
 6               select *
 7            into l_row
 8            from    employee
 9            order by emp_name;
10    EXCEPTION
11    WHEN no_data_found then
12     raise_application_error (-20052,'Sorry no data in '||
13                              'this table. TRY AGAIN!');
14    WHEN others then
15      raise_application_error (-20999,'Something has gone ' ||
16                              'really wrong...you better guess');
17*  end;
declare
*
ERROR at line 1:
ORA-20052: Sorry no data in this table. TRY AGAIN!
ORA-06512: at line 12
```

This program will handle the fact that no data is found, as well as anything else that is not a lack of data. With these simple facts, you can now handle problems that may occur in your programs.

Stored Procedures and Functions

Up until now, we have shown you examples in PL/SQL programs that cannot be shared; they are simply run in SQL*Plus one at a time. These are known as *anonymous* PL/SQL programs. However, to optimize the reuse of programs and provide you with the ability to share programs between users and applications, you use stored programs. These programs are stored in the database and can be made available to any of the users of your database. You can create three types of stored programs: procedures, packages, and functions. We will not be discussing packages in this chapter. *Stored procedures* are complete programs that may be run stand-alone or from another program. *Functions* are programs that return specific values.

Stored Procedures

Creating a stored procedure is the same as anything you have done before, but now you frame it with a **create procedure** statement. By adding this at the beginning of a program, you create an object in the database that is known as a *procedure*. Another feature of stored procedures, provided to you at no extra cost, is the ability to pass values in and out of a procedure.

NOTE
*You should put **create or replace procedure** in your*
create procedure commands. If you do not use the
replace portion of the command, you will need to
drop your procedure before trying to re-create it.
*By using **replace**, the procedure will be created*
if it does not exist or replaced if it does.

Let's look at one of the programs that we have already created and convert it to a stored procedure.

```
 1   CREATE OR REPLACE PROCEDURE LIST_EMPLOYEES
 2   BEGIN
 3   declare
 4        l_emp_count number;
 5        i            number;  -- We will use this as our counter
 6     -- declare our SELECT cursor (explicit)
 7     cursor get_employee_data IS
 8              select emp_name, salary
 9          from    employee
10          order by emp_name;
11    begin
12    -- The infamous  FOR loop
13    FOR c1_rec IN get_employee_data
14    LOOP
15       dbms_output.put_line('Employee :' || c1_rec.emp_name ||
16                          ' Salary: $' || c1_rec.salary);
17          END LOOP;
18   end;
19*  END;
20  /
```

```
Warning: Procedure created with compilation errors.
```

Now it looks like we have an error. Even authors get errors when we write PL/SQL. To see what errors you have received from your program, simply enter **show errors**. Oracle9i will then show you the errors that have occurred during the compiling of your program. Let's see what we did wrong:

```
SQL> show errors
Errors for PROCEDURE LIST_EMPLOYEES:
LINE/COL ERROR
-------- ----------------------------------------------------------------
```

```
2/1       PLS-00103: Encountered the symbol "BEGIN" when expecting one of
          the following:
          ( ; is with authid as cluster compress order using compiled
          wrapped external deterministic parallel_enable pipelined
          The symbol "is" was substituted for "BEGIN" to continue.
```

Looks like we simply forgot to include the **is** portion of the create procedure declaration. At times, figuring out what is actually causing your errors is a challenging task. But remember that you learn through experimentation and experience; and, as with other programming languages, the debugging of PL/SQL is an art that you will develop. Let's look at how the code has changed. The change is shown in bold.

```
SQL>   CREATE OR REPLACE PROCEDURE LIST_EMPLOYEES
  2    IS
  3    BEGIN
  4    declare
  5         l_emp_count number;
  6         i           number;   -- We will use this as our counter
  7       -- declare our SELECT cursor (explicit)
  8       cursor get_employee_data IS
  9               select emp_name, salary
 10           from    employee
 11           order by emp_name;
 12     begin
 13       -- The infamous  FOR loop
 14       FOR c1_rec IN get_employee_data
 15       LOOP
 16           dbms_output.put_line('Employee :' || c1_rec.emp_name ||
 17                              ' Salary: $' || c1_rec.salary);
 18            END LOOP;
 19     end;
 20*   END;
 21 /

Procedure created.
```

That's good news. The program has compiled and will now run when we call it. Let's look at how to call a procedure from SQL*Plus. Using the **execute** command, you may run a stored program:

```
SQL> execute list_employees
PL/SQL procedure successfully completed.
```

We have added some parameters to our program to show you how to get information into the program. We use parameters within the program when we supply data to the procedure, and we can then return a value to the program that calls it through another output parameter. It is also possible to define parameters as both input and output. However, to simplify our parameters, we usually define them for only one of the two purposes. In this case, we will use SQL*Plus to call our procedure, since it works. Our example will pass in a province code and we will find out how many employees live in the province.

```
SQL> run
  1   CREATE OR REPLACE PROCEDURE EMPLOYEES_COUNT
  2   (IN_PROVINCE          IN       VARCHAR2,
  3   OUT_EMPLOYEE_COUNT    OUT      NUMBER)
  4   IS
  5   BEGIN
  6   declare
  7          l_emp_count number;
  8          i                number;   -- We will use this as our counter
  9      -- declare our SELECT cursor (explicit)
 10      cursor get_employee_data IS
 11                select count(*)
 12            from    employee
 13            where province = IN_PROVINCE;
 14    begin
 15     open  get_employee_data;
 16     fetch get_employee_data INTO i;
 17
 18     out_employee_count := i;
 19    end;
 20* END;
 21 /

Procedure created.
```

Now, let's see how to describe our procedure, as indicated by the bold text in the next listing. Here, we will learn the name of the program and get a list of any parameters that we may need to pass:

```
SQL> describe employees_count
PROCEDURE employees_count
 Argument Name                  Type                     In/Out Default?
 ----------------------------   ----------------------   ------ --------
 IN_PROVINCE                    VARCHAR2                 IN
 OUT_EMPLOYEE_COUNT             NUMBER                   OUT
```

Next, we need to run the procedure. In our case, we are running it in SQL*Plus. When in this facility, if you want to receive data from a program, you need to declare a variable. This is done in the first line of the next code listing. We will then run the program with the **execute** command. Finally, we will show you how to view the contents of your declared variable, which now contains the number of employees in the province of Ontario.

```
SQL> variable prov_count number; -- create a variable for province count
SQL> describe employees_count
PROCEDURE employees_count
 Argument Name                   Type                       In/Out Default?
 ----------------------------    ----------------------     ------ --------
 IN_PROVINCE                     VARCHAR2                    IN
 OUT_EMPLOYEE_COUNT              NUMBER                      OUT
SQL> execute employees_count('ONTARIO',:prov_count);

PL/SQL procedure successfully completed.
SQL> print   -- shows you the contents of your variables
PROV_COUNT
----------
         4
```

You can see that there are only five employees for this company in the Ontario area. From here, you could share this program with others, use it in a program, or call it from a web application.

If you wanted to call and execute this program from within a PL/SQL program, the following commands would achieve the same result as the previous. Line 6 is bold because this is the command that performs the call to the other program.

```
SQL> run
  1  declare
  2      l_province     varchar2(20);
  3      l_count        number;
  4  begin
  5      l_province     := 'ONTARIO';
  6      employees_count(l_province,l_count);
  7      dbms_output.put_line ('Province of ' || l_province || ': '|| l_count);
  8* end;
Province of ONTARIO: 4
PL/SQL procedure successfully completed.
```

Using stored procedures, you can now share with others. What a nice thought. Let's see what we can do with functions.

Functions

Very much like stored procedures, functions are objects stored in the database, but you have the ability to use functions within SQL commands. This is just like building your very own **substr** function. In the following example, we use the employee count program to make a program that will provide a count of all employees. We will then call the function and see how this all flies.

```
SQL> run
  1  CREATE OR REPLACE FUNCTION COUNT_ALL_EMPLOYEES
  2  RETURN number
  3  IS
  4  BEGIN
  5  declare
  6       i           number;  -- We will use this as our counter
  7    -- declare our SELECT cursor (explicit)
  8    cursor get_employee_data IS
  9             select count(*)
 10          from    employee;
 11    begin
 12    open  get_employee_data;
 13    fetch get_employee_data INTO i;
 14    return i;
 15    end;
 16* END;
 17 /

Function created.
SQL> desc count_all_employees;
FUNCTION count_all_employees RETURNS NUMBER
SQL> select count_all_employees()
  2  from dual;
COUNT_ALL_EMPLOYEES()
--------------------
                   5
```

NOTE
To tell Oracle9i that you have a function but do not have any parameters to send it, you include the () after the name of the function.

The function may be used in **select** statements or **where** clauses or numerous other ways. This is a common example of how to use a function. Functions provide great value to programmers, since we can now provide common utilities to our user base.

Basic Debugging

At this point, you can write programs, you can send in information, and you can get it out. You even now have the ability to deal with things when they go wrong. However, when things go wrong, or even to prove that they are going right, you need to have the ability to look inside a program.

You could purchase a product that lets you step through a program, find out what is going on inside, and then conduct performance tuning tests. But we see this more like learning mathematics. We could give you a calculator in Grade 1 and tell you to learn addition by punching in numbers, but you still have to learn that 2 + 2 = 4. You also need to see how it works. A story goes, that a man walks into a classroom and on the wall is some graffiti. Written on the wall is Albert Einstein's famous formula $E = mc^2$. Right below it someone else has written "B+. Next time show your work." In the case of debugging, we will not show you how to do it with a tool. Instead we will show you some simple methods for debugging a program on your own.

To see data as a program is running or after it has completed, your options include

- Committing data into a database table

- Using the **utl_file** built-in function

- Using **serveroutput** and the **dbms_output** function

We will show you the third option. In the SQL*Plus environment, we will turn the output facility on and then run a program and see its output. We will do this to see our results, but we could have done the same to show the value of variables, or to tell us where we are in the program.

```
SQL> set serveroutput on size 1000000
SQL> run
  1    declare
  2        l_emp_count number;
  3        i            number;   -- We will use this as our counter
  4    -- declare our SELECT cursor (explicit)
  5    cursor get_employee_data IS
  6                select count(*)
  7            from    employee;
  8    begin
```

```
 9      -- open the cursor for use
10      open get_employee_data;
11      -- run your SQL statement and put the value into a variable
12      fetch  get_employee_data INTO l_emp_count;
13         FOR i IN 1 .. l_emp_count  LOOP
14                  dbms_output.put_line('Employee ' || i);
15         END LOOP;
16      -- Don't forget to tell Oracle that you are done
17      close get_employee_data;
18*  end;
19 /
Employee 1
Employee 2
Employee 3
Employee 4
Employee 5
```

As you see in the previous listing, we turned on the output by issuing the
SQL*Plus set command: **set serveroutput on size 1000000**. We may also turn it off,
by switching the **on** to **off** in the command. Next, we run a program. At line 14 of
the program, we use the **dbms_output.put_line** function. For additional functions for
dbms_output, we refer you to the plethora of technical information available via
your favorite search engine.

The **dbms_output.put_line** function will output data to the command line, and
together with serveroutput, the user may see this information. So you can see that
this program appears to be working and reading through the table as we expected.

Debugging can be very complicated. Experience has taught us that finding our
errors is never a task to be taken lightly. Using a simple facility like **dbms_output**,
you already have the ability to perform these tasks.

Moving On

We have shown you just about everything you might need in order to create a
program using Oracle9*i*. The most important thing you should have learned is
BEGIN and END. These two words start and finish everything that you do in PL/
SQL. In addition, there are three sections to your PL/SQL program: the declaration,
the execution, and the exception sections. We have seen loops, cursors, and stored
objects. Once you have mastered PL/SQL, you will see that the uses for PL/SQL in
your everyday Oracle life are endless.

The next chapter introduces you to database administration. That is DBA to you
if you want to come off as a cool Oracle professional. It is the most complicated job
you will ever do, and this book will get your DBA journey started.

Chapter 6 Questions

Answers to questions can be found in Appendix A.

1. Which of the following sections are included in a PL/SQL program?

   A. Execution

   B. Subroutine

   C. Declaration

   D. Exception

   E. Technical

2. Which one of the following may not be included in the declare section of a PL/SQL program?

   A. Variables

   B. Cursors

   C. Loops

   D. Constant variables

3. Which of the following is a valid looping structure?

   A. `for I between 10 and 100 then ...(program) ...; end loop;`

   B. `for l_variable  1 .. 10 loop ...(program)...; else ...(program,)...; end loop;`

   C. `do while l_test is TRUE loop ...(program)...; end loop;`

   D. `Loop; ...(program)...; end loop;`

4. All SQL statements that may be run in SQL*Plus are supported in PL/SQL for Oracle9*i*.

   A. True

   B. False

5. What built-in Oracle function do you use to get output to your
   SQL*Plus session?

   A. dbms_printout

   B. dbms_output

   C. dbms_writetoscreen

   D. dbms_serveroutput

CHAPTER
7

DBA 101

n this chapter, we will focus on the fundamental skills a DBA needs to survive. We will not use any of the GUI tools; instead, we will use SQL*Plus for working with the database. We find it the fastest and easiest way to get things done. In this chapter, we will cover the following topics:

- What a database is

- What an Oracle instance is

- The system global area

- How to start up a database

- How to shut down a database

- The Oracle tablespace

- Rollback segments

- Redo logs

- Control files

- A user account

Considering how important it is for the DBA to understand the structure of an Oracle9i database, we're going to spend a little time reviewing some of the information in Chapter 3.

Terminology

The following terminology will arm you with the technical jargon you need for this chapter:

- The *data dictionary* is maintained by the database. It contains all the information on how data is stored in the database, where it is, and how it can be worked with.

- An *extent* is a contiguous collection of Oracle blocks.

- *Grants* are privileges given out by owners of objects, allowing other users to work with their data.

- A *block* is the smallest unit of space within an Oracle9*i* database. All database reads and writes happen in increments of a block. The smallest increment is 2KB.

- The *system global area* (*SGA*) is an area of memory that is used for database information shared by database users.

- Whenever the database is started, a system global area (SGA) is allocated, and the Oracle background processes are started. The combination of the background processes and SGA is called an *instance*.

- A *user process* executes the code of an application program (such as an Oracle Forms, Cobol, or C++ application) or an Oracle tool (such as Oracle Enterprise Manager).

- Oracle *processes* are server processes that perform work for the user processes and background processes that perform maintenance work for the Oracle9*i* server.

What Is a Database?

A database is a collection of data organized so that its contents can easily be accessed and managed. In a relational database, this data is stored in a very specific manner within database objects called tables. The way these tables are structured is commonly known as *data normalization*. The purpose of data normalization is to structure data so that it can be accessed or reassembled in many ways without having to reorganize the underlying tables. In essence, the database is data driven, based on the relationships of these tables. It is never based on the physical format of the data itself.

To illustrate this point, let's compare what happens in a nonrelational database versus a relational database. In a traditional database, your name is stored in numerous locations. For example, it is in the payroll system, human resources, and so on. When you get married, you may want to change your last name. You notify the payroll system, because you want your paycheck correct, but your name will still be incorrect elsewhere, since in a traditional database, your name is most likely stored separately for each application it is used in.

In a relational database, your name is stored in the EMP table. Everyone else who needs access to information about employees gets that information based on a relationship within the database to the EMP table. The employee name information is stored only once in the database.

When you change your name, the EMP table is updated with the new value. The next time an application requests your name, the database points to the new value in the EMP table.

What Is an Oracle Instance?

Whenever an Oracle database is started up, a system global area (SGA) is allocated, and the Oracle background processes are started. The SGA is an area of memory that is shared by all database users. The combination of the background processes running and the system global area is called an *Oracle instance.*

The System Global Area (SGA)

Whenever an Oracle database is started, the SGA must be allocated. The same is also true whenever an Oracle database instance is shut down; the SGA is deallocated. Note that certain commands, such as the command that follows, can only be issued after you have connected to the database using **connect username/password as sysdba**. While the database is open, the **show sga** command can be issued to see the following information:

```
SQL> show sga
Total System Global Area   235701300 bytes
Fixed Size                    279604 bytes
Variable Size              167772160 bytes
Database Buffers            67108864 bytes
Redo Buffers                  540672 bytes
```

All users who are connected to the Oracle9i database share the SGA. There are several types of memory structures stored within the SGA. These include the following:

- Database buffers
- Redo log buffers
- Shared pool

Database Buffer—Your Data Cache

Think of database buffers as your data cache. Before a user can look at a piece of information in an Oracle9i database, it must first reside in the database buffer cache. Data gets into this cache based upon the most recently used (MRU) algorithm. Because the most recently (and often the most frequently) used data is kept in memory, less disk I/O is necessary, and overall database performance is improved.

Redo Log Buffers—Your Transaction Cache

A redo log file contains all the changes made to the database. Before a redo log entry can be written into the redo logs, it must first reside in the redo log buffer.

The redo log buffer piggybacks transactions and writes them out from the redo log buffer into the physical redo log very efficiently.

Shared Pool—Your Shared Program Cache
Before an SQL program can execute, an entry must be made in the shared pool. Key information about that SQL program is stored with the entry, such as an execution plan. Other users of the database who issue the same SQL statement are able to share this area. This leaves more shared memory for other uses.

Oracle Background Processes
The second key to having an Oracle instance is for the background processes to have started. The background processes all have different jobs and interact with different parts of the database. Here is a partial list of the background processes:

- **smon** System monitor

- **pmon** Process monitor

- **dbwr** Database writer

- **lgwr** Log writer

- **ckpt** Checkpoint

Here is a partial copy of the output of the UNIX **ps–ef** command, which shows you the processes that are currently working on the system. In a working environment, here is how the background processes would typically look:

```
oracle 28840     1  1  Aug 07  ?       163:10 ora_ckpt_dev
oracle 23654 23652  0 08:51:02 pts/3    0:00 -ksh
oracle 16060     1  0  Aug 10  ?        0:12 ora_dbw0_emile
oracle 16078     1  0  Aug 10  ?        0:00 ora_s000_emile
oracle 28852     1  0  Aug 07  ?        0:00 ora_d002_dev
oracle  3465  3032  0  Jul 03  ?        0:00 /usr/dt/bin/dtexec
oracle 28249     1  0  Aug 07  ?        0:00 ./runInstaller
oracle 16070     1  0  Aug 10  ?        0:00 ora_J000_emile
oracle 16066     1  0  Aug 10  ?        0:08 ora_smon_emile
```

Notice the word *emile* in the background process name, which correlates to the particular database name of the instance.

System Monitor

The system monitor process (smon) of an instance performs recovery when a failed instance starts again. Think of instance recovery as what happens when an Oracle9i database starts up after a power failure on the computer system it resides on.

Process Monitor

The process monitor performs process recovery on failed user processes and frees up any resources they may have been using.

Database Writer

The database writer process is responsible for writing changed blocks from the database buffers cache to the data files.

Log Writer

The log writer process is responsible for writing blocks from the log writer buffers cache to the redo logs on disk.

Checkpoint

Based on a number of configurable factors, like the size of the redo log files, an event known as the checkpoint occurs. A *checkpoint* is the point at which all modified database buffers in the SGA must be written back to the data files.

startup open

Before an Oracle9i database can be accessed, it must first be started to get background processes running. As you have learned, these background processes serve many of your requests to the database.

To start an Oracle9i database, first connect to the database using the sysdba privilege. From there, you can then issue the database **startup open** command.

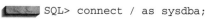

```
SQL> connect / as sysdba;
SQL> startup open test pfile=/d0/oraclehome/admin/test/pfile/init.ora;

ORACLE instance started

Total System Global Area   235701300 bytes
Fixed Size                    279604 bytes
Variable Size              167772160 bytes
Database Buffers            67108864 bytes
Redo Buffers                  540672 bytes
Database mounted.
Database opened.
```

In the preceding example, notice how we issued the command **connect / as sysdba**. This established us with the correct privilege level for starting up or shutting down a database. The name of this particular database is test. Also associated with every database is a parameter file known as the INIT.ora file.

INIT.ora File

Every Oracle9*i* database must have an INIT.ora file associated with it. When a command is given to start up an Oracle9*i* database, the database finds the INIT.ora file, inspects it, and then allocates resources according to what is stated inside the file. If no entry is found inside the INIT.ora file for a particular resource, the database reverts to the default setting.

Once a database has been started, you can use the command **show parameters** to see the current settings of the resources you can allocate in the INIT.ora file. Here is a partial listing:

```
SQL> show parameters;
NAME                                         TYPE         VALUE
-------------------------------------------- ------------ ------------------------------
active_instance_count                        integer
aq_tm_processes                              integer      0
archive_lag_target                           integer      0
audit_file_dest                              string       ?/rdbms/audit
audit_trail                                  string       NONE
background_core_dump                         string       partial
```

startup nomount—An Example

Before you have created the database, there is no database to open. In this situation, you need to access the background processes and SGA, so that you can then issue the **create database** statement. The **create database** statement is unlike the **startup open** command, which really means start up, mount, and open. When you first create a database, you issue the **startup nomount** command.

```
SQL>connect / as sysdba;
SQL>startup nomount pfile=/d0/oraclehome/admin/test/pfile/init.ora

Oracle instance started

Total System Global Area   235701300 bytes
Fixed Size                    279604 bytes
Variable Size              167772160 bytes
Database Buffers            67108864 bytes
Redo Buffers                  540672 bytes

SQL> CREATE DATABASE "test"
```

```
 2          LOGFILE   GROUP 1 ('/d1/oradata/test/redo0101.log',
 3                            '/d0/oraclehome/admin/test/files/redo0102.log')
 4                            SIZE 500k REUSE,
 5                    GROUP 2 ('/d1/oradata/test/redo0201.log',
 6                            '/d0/oraclehome/admin/test/files/redo0202.log')
 7                            SIZE 500k REUSE,
 8                     GROUP 3 ('/d1/oradata/test/redo0301.log',
 9                            '/d0/oraclehome/admin/test/files/redo0302.log')
10                            SIZE 500k REUSE
11                  DATAFILE '/d1/oradata/test/system_001.dbf'
12                            SIZE 250M REUSE
13                            MAXLOGFILES 20
14                            CONTROLFILE REUSE
15                            MAXDATAFILES 500
16;

Database created.
```

shutdown

As Oracle technology has advanced, the need for shutting the database down has decreased. You used to have to shut the database down so that you could make changes to the INIT.ora file and resize the SGA. Today, you frequently need only to shut the database down if it encounters a serious fault or you want to upgrade the software to the newest release.

To shut down an Oracle9i database, first connect to the database using the sysdba privilege. Then you can issue the database **shutdown** command. This is also known as the **shutdown normal** command.

This version of the **shutdown** command waits for all users and processes to disconnect from the database. It also prevents additional users from logging in. The database is closed and dismounted. On the next startup, no instance recovery is needed.

```
SQL> connect / as sysdba

Connected.

SQL> shutdown
Database closed.
Database dismounted.
Oracle instance shut down.
```

As you will quickly learn, even though you ask everyone to exit the database, not everyone will do it. Have no fear; you can issue the next level of shutdown known as a **shutdown immediate** command.

shutdown immediate—An Example

First, connect to the database using the sysdba privilege. From there, you can then issue the database **shutdown immediate** command. This version of the **shutdown** command does not wait for users and processes to disconnect from the database. It also prevents additional users from logging in. The database is closed and dismounted. As with the **shutdown normal** command, no instance recovery is needed on the next database startup.

```
SQL> connect / as sysdba;

Connected.

SQL> shutdown Immediate
Database closed.
Database dismounted.
Oracle instance shut down
```

Sometimes things happen, and the database won't come down even with a **shutdown immediate** command. In those circumstances, you can always use **shutdown abort**.

shutdown abort—An Example

First, connect to the database using the sysdba privilege. From there, you can then issue the database **shutdown abort** command. This version of the **shutdown** command does not wait for users and processes to disconnect from the database. It immediately terminates all user processes against the database. It also prevents additional users from logging in. Unlike **shutdown normal** and **shutdown immediate**, the **shutdown abort** command does require you to do an instance recovery on the next database startup.

The **shutdown abort** command is what you must use when an Oracle background process terminates abnormally.

Using the **shutdown abort** command in an Oracle9*i* database is like rebooting your computer when the Windows operating system freezes. No matter what is happening, the Oracle9*i* database will come down. When it is restarted, the database will have to recover itself. Be patient: sometimes recovery takes a lot of time.

```
SQL> connect / as sysdba;

Connected.

SQL> shutdown abort;

Oracle instance shut down
```

The Oracle Tablespace

Every Oracle9i database has one or more physical data files associated with it. These data files are where all the data in the database is physically held. To help you better manage these data files, they are grouped together into database objects called *tablespaces*. A tablespace is a collection of one or more data files.

Your tables, indexes, and other database objects are placed within these tablespaces. Before you can place a row of data into an Oracle9i database, you must first create a tablespace and associate a physical data file with it. Then you can create the database objects to hold the data.

Create Tablespace— extent management dictionary

When an Oracle9i database is first created, you have only one tablespace, known as the *system tablespace*. This is where all the tables that the database uses to manage itself are kept.

The system tablespace is created using the **extent management dictionary** clause. This means that all the management concerning how space extents are allocated within the tablespace is stored within the data dictionary tables.

What Is an Extent?

An extent is a contiguous collection of Oracle blocks. An Oracle block is the smallest unit of physical space in an Oracle9i database, which the data is ultimately stored in. Until Oracle9i, there was only one choice for an Oracle block within the database, determined by a setting in the INIT.ora file when the database was created. With Oracle9i, different tablespaces can be based upon different block sizes. Here is an example of creating a tablespace named **user02**:

```
SQL>   CREATE TABLESPACE user02
   2     DATAFILE '/d0/oraclehome/admin/test/files/user02_001.dbf'
   3     SIZE  5M REUSE
   4     EXTENT MANAGEMENT DICTIONARY
   5          DEFAULT  STORAGE (INITIAL 25K   NEXT 25K
   6                    MINEXTENTS 5
   7                    MAXEXTENTS 100
   8                    PCTINCREASE 0)
   9   ;

Tablespace created.
```

In the preceding example, we have created the tablespace **user02**, which is associated with the physical operating system file user02_001.dbf. The user02_001.dbf data file was created at a size of 5MB.

Managing how this tablespace allocates extents is done using the data dictionary. This means that whenever a request is made to place an object into this tablespace, it must first access the data dictionary to determine where the available free extents are.

If a user does not specify a size when creating a database object in this tablespace, the object will be created based on the default storage clause. In this example, a table will be created with an initial size of 25KB and will grow in 100KB increments.

Create Tablespace— extent management local autoallocate

Recognizing that it is not always advantageous to have the tablespace manage its space allocations in the data dictionary, Oracle9*i* gives you the option of having the space management of a tablespace done locally.

```
SQL>   CREATE TABLESPACE user03
    2         DATAFILE '/d1/oradata/test/user03_001.dbf'
    3         SIZE 5m REUSE
    4         EXTENT MANAGEMENT LOCAL AUTOALLOCATE
    5   ;

Tablespace created.
```

In the preceding example, we have created the tablespace **user03**, which is associated with the physical operating system file user03_001.dbf. The user03_001.dbf data file was created at a size of 5MB. The management of how this tablespace allocates extents is done within the tablespace itself. If a user does not specify a size when creating a database object in this tablespace, its size is allocated by the database.

Create Tablespace—extent management local uniform size

In the next example, we create the tablespace **user04**, which is associated with the physical operating system file user04_001.dbf. The user04_001.dbf data file is created at a size of 5MB. The management of how this tablespace allocates extents is done within the tablespace itself.

```
SQL>
SQL>   CREATE TABLESPACE user04
    2         DATAFILE '/d1/oradata/test/user04_001.dbf'
    3         SIZE 5m reuse
```

```
4        EXTENT MANAGEMENT LOCAL UNIFORM SIZE 128K
5   ;
```

Tablespace created.

If a user does not specify a size when creating a database object in this tablespace, it is created at an initial size of 128KB and in increments of 128KB chunks.

create undo tablespace

There is a special variation of the **tablespace** command called **create undo tablespace**. This can be issued in the **create database** command, or it can be done after the database has been created. The database understands the primary purpose of undo segments, which is to undo or roll back a transaction that is aborted or canceled.

When you activate a tablespace of type undo, you are telling the database not to use rollback segments but instead to rely on the special type undo tablespace. All undo segments will be managed by the database in the tablespaces of type undo.

```
SQL>    CREATE UNDO TABLESPACE USER05
  2         DATAFILE '/d1/oradata/test/user05_001.dbf'
  3         SIZE 2M
  4         REUSE
  5         AUTOEXTEND ON
  6;
```

Tablespace created.

alter tablespace add data file

We talked about a tablespace being a database object made up of one or more data files. Often, you create multiple data files on a tablespace to spread the I/O across multiple physical devices. Sometimes you initially make the tablespace too small and have to add another data file later. Here is an example of adding a second data file to the tablespace.

```
SQL> ALTER TABLESPACE USER04
  2   ADD DATAFILE '/d1/oradata/test/user04_002.dbf'
  3   SIZE 2M
  4   REUSE
  5   AUTOEXTEND ON
  6   NEXT 1M
  7   MAXSIZE 10M
  8   ;
```

Tablespace altered.

In the preceding example, we added a second data file named user04_002.dbf to the tablespace **user04**. We told the data file that it can automatically grow if it needs additional space. That way we should not have to add an additional data file again. It can grow this data file in 1MB increments to a maximum size of 10MB.

alter database autoextend off—An Example
Sometimes, it is not advantageous to autoextend a data file. Here is the **alter database** command to shut the autoextend feature off for a given data file:

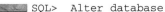
```
SQL>  Alter database
  2       DATAFILE '/d0/oraclehome/admin/test/files/rbs_002.dbf'
AUTOEXTEND OFF;
Database altered.
```

alter tablespace offline
There are many reasons why you may want a tablespace taken on- or offline. Sometimes it is done to ensure no one is using it; other times, it is done for backup purposes. Here is an example of placing the **user04** tablespace offline and then back online:

```
SQL> ALTER TABLESPACE USER04 OFFLINE;

Tablespace altered.

SQL> ALTER TABLESPACE USER04 ONLINE;

Tablespace altered.
```

Drop a Tablespace
Often you create a tablespace to store a group of database objects associated with a particular developer or development effort. When the job is done, you need to remove those database objects. Here is a quick-and-easy way to drop a tablespace and all its objects. (In the past if you tried to drop the tablespace, you would first have to remove its contents.) Remember that it drops every object in the tablespace, no matter who owns it.

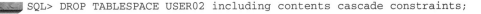
```
SQL> DROP TABLESPACE USER02 including contents cascade constraints;

Tablespace dropped.
```

Here is our favorite variation of the **drop tablespace** command. This one even removes the physical data file associated with the tablespace (finally):

```
SQL> DROP TABLESPACE USER03 including contents and datafiles;

Tablespace dropped.
```

Here is the traditional **drop tablespace** command. It assumes the tablespace is empty, or it will fail when you try to execute the command.

```
SQL> DROP TABLESPACE USER04;

Tablespace dropped
```

In summary, you have learned that a database is made up of tablespaces, which are made up of one or more data files. When you create a database object like a table, it is placed inside a tablespace, which is associated with a physical device via the data file.

Rollback Segments

A rollback segment is a segment in the database that stores a before image, or "undo" copy, of a data block before it was modified. In the event the transaction is canceled or aborted in any way, the rollback segment is used to restore the data block to its original state, before the transaction modified the physical contents of the block.

Every transaction in the database that modifies the contents of the database uses some form of undo in the form of a rollback segment or in a special undo tablespace. Rollback segments are allocated in a round-robin manner.

create rollback segment

Experience has taught us that it is best to place rollback segments in a separate tablespace. We like to call that tablespace **rbs**. Here is an SQL statement that creates a rollback statement named **r77**. As we have just created a private rollback segment, it would need to be named in the INIT.ora file so that the rollback segment could be activated upon instance startup.

```
SQL> create rollback segment R77 tablespace rbs
   2* storage (initial 250k next 250k minextents 2 optimal 1m)
SQL> /

Rollback segment created.
```

In the preceding example, we created the rollback segment **r77** in tablespace **rbs**. It will be created with two initial extents. The first extent will be 250KB, based upon the **initial** parameter. The second extent will also be 250KB, based upon the **next** parameter. There will be two of them because of the **minextents** setting of 2.

The DBA_ROLLBACK_SEGS View

There is a special view named DBA_ROLLBACK_SEGS that gives very useful information about the rollback segments in the database. Here is a **describe** command of that view:

```
SQL> desc dba_rollback_segs
```

Name	Null?	Type
SEGMENT_NAME	NOT NULL	VARCHAR2(30)
OWNER		VARCHAR2(6)
TABLESPACE_NAME	NOT NULL	VARCHAR2(30)
SEGMENT_ID	NOT NULL	NUMBER
FILE_ID	NOT NULL	NUMBER
BLOCK_ID	NOT NULL	NUMBER
INITIAL_EXTENT		NUMBER
NEXT_EXTENT		NUMBER
MIN_EXTENTS	NOT NULL	NUMBER
MAX_EXTENTS	NOT NULL	NUMBER
PCT_INCREASE		NUMBER
STATUS		VARCHAR2(16)
INSTANCE_NUM		VARCHAR2(40)
RELATIVE_FNO	NOT NULL	NUMBER

Let's execute a quick **select** statement off the DBA_ROLLBACK_SEGS view to see the status of our newly created rollback segment:

```
SQL> select tablespace_name, segment_name, status from dba_rollback_segs
SQL> /
```

TABLESPACE_NAME	SEGMENT_NAME	STATUS
SYSTEM	SYSTEM	ONLINE
RBS	RBS0	ONLINE
RBS	RBS1	ONLINE
RBS	RBS2	ONLINE
RBS	RBS3	ONLINE
RBS	RBS4	ONLINE
RBS	RBS5	ONLINE
RBS	RBS6	ONLINE
RBS	**R77**	**OFFLINE**

Notice that it has been created but not activated.

alter rollback segment online

The following **alter rollback segment** command takes an existing rollback segment and changes its status to online. Online status makes the rollback segment available to the database.

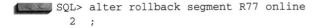

```
SQL> alter rollback segment R77 online
  2  ;

Rollback segment altered.
```

Let's run that same **select** statement against the DBA_ROLLBACK_SEGS view. Notice the status of rollback segment **r77** now.

```
SQL> select tablespace_name, segment_name, status from dba_rollback_segs
SQL> /
```

TABLESPACE_NAME	SEGMENT_NAME	STATUS
SYSTEM	SYSTEM	ONLINE
RBS	RBS0	ONLINE
RBS	RBS1	ONLINE
RBS	RBS2	ONLINE
RBS	RBS3	ONLINE
RBS	RBS4	ONLINE
RBS	RBS5	ONLINE
RBS	RBS6	ONLINE
RBS	**R77**	**ONLINE**

```
9 rows selected.
```

alter rollback segment offline—An Example

Let's now take the **r77** rollback segment offline. This is something you would do if you needed to drop and re-create it.

```
SQL> alter rollback segment r77 offline
  2  ;

Rollback segment altered.
```

Shrinking a Rollback Segment Manually

You can manually decrease the size of a rollback segment using the **alter rollback segment** command. To be shrunk, the rollback segment must be online.

`SQL> ALTER ROLLBACK SEGMENT rbs1 SHRINK TO 100K;`

`Rollback Segment Altered`

drop rollback segment

Here is a sample **drop rollback segment** command. Before this command is issued, you must first take the rollback segment offline.

`SQL> drop rollback segment r77;`

`Rollback segment dropped.`

Redo Logs

Every Oracle9*i* database has at least two redo log groups. No matter how many redo log groups you have, they are collectively known as the database's redo logs. The redo log members contain a copy of every transaction that is executed against the database.

The primary purpose of the redo log is to record all changes made to the data. These transaction logs are used by the database to recover in the event of a failure. The combination of the redo logs working with the data files ensures that every transaction is recorded on physical disk. If a failure were to occur that prevented changes made to the database from being recorded back to the data files, those changes would have been captured by the redo log and stored on a disk, so work is never lost.

Simply put, the redo log contains a copy of every transaction against the database, and the combination of the physical data files and redo log ensure that work is never lost.

Mulitplexed Redo Logs

Redo logs are so critical to ensuring that the database does not lose a transaction that you have the option of creating multiplexed redo logs. A multiplexed redo log is a second redo log created and maintained in tandem with the original. You should always implement redo logs in a multiplexed manner.

To provide that extra layer of protection, it is also very important that the second, shadowed redo log be created on a separate physical device.

NOTE
When working with redo logs, it is always best to create at least three sets. A database must always have at least two valid redo log groups; and in order to perform maintenance work on the redo logs, it is strongly recommended that you create a third one.

In this example of the use of the **create database** command, notice how each redo log is given a twin, or clone.

```
SQL> CREATE DATABASE "test"
  2          LOGFILE   GROUP 1 ('/d1/oradata/test/redo0101.log',
  3                             '/d0/oraclehome/admin/test/files/redo0102.log')
  4                    SIZE 500k REUSE,
  5                    GROUP 2 ('/d1/oradata/test/redo0201.log',
  6                             '/d0/oraclehome/admin/test/files/redo0202.log')
  7                    SIZE 500k REUSE,
  8                    GROUP 3 ('/d1/oradata/test/redo0301.log',
  9                             '/d0/oraclehome/admin/test/files/redo0302.log')
 10                    SIZE 500k REUSE
 11              DATAFILE '/d1/oradata/test/system_001.dbf'
 12                      SIZE 250M REUSE
 13                      MAXLOGFILES 20
 14            CONTROLFILE REUSE
 15            MAXDATAFILES 500
 16        ;

Database created.
```

Notice how the first redo log is created on device /d1, while the clone is created on a separate physical device /d0. Every time a transaction is entered on the redo log redo0101.log, an exact copy of the transaction is entered on redo0102.log.

Dropping a Redo Log

Before you can drop a redo log, you must first make sure it is not active. An easy way to see the status of a redo log is to perform a quick **select** of the V$LOG view.

```
SQL> select group#, thread#, bytes, members, status from v$log;

    GROUP#    THREAD#       BYTES    MEMBERS STATUS
---------- ---------- ---------- ---------- ----------------
         1          1     512000          1 CURRENT
         2          1     512000          1 INACTIVE
         3          1     512000          1 INACTIVE
```

If we wanted to drop the redo logs associated with group 1, we would be forced to do a log switch. The **alter system** command is used for redo log switches:

```
SQL> alter system switch logfile;

System altered.
```

Let's now issue a quick **select** command against the V$LOG view to see that the log has switched:

```
SQL> select group#, thread#, bytes, members, status from v$log;

    GROUP#    THREAD#      BYTES   MEMBERS STATUS
---------- ---------- ---------- ---------- ----------------
         1          1     512000          1 ACTIVE
         2          1     512000          1 CURRENT
         3          1     512000          1 INACTIVE
```

Now we will use the **alter database** command to drop the redo log:

```
SQL> ALTER DATABASE DROP LOGFILE GROUP 1;

Database altered.
```

Let's now issue the **select** statement against the V$LOG table to confirm what happened.

```
SQL> select group#, thread#, bytes, members, status from v$log;

    GROUP#    THREAD#      BYTES   MEMBERS STATUS
---------- ---------- ---------- ---------- ----------------
         2          1     512000          1 CURRENT
         3          1     512000          1 INACTIVE
```

Adding a Redo Log

To add an additional redo log, you use the **alter database** command. Here is an example:

```
SQL> alter database add logfile group 4
  2 ('/d1/oradata/test/redo04.log',
  3 '/d0/oraclehome/admin/test/files/redo04a.log')
  4 size 1m reuse
  5 ;

Database altered.
```

Control Files— The Database Safety Checklist

Every Oracle9i database has at least one control file. Think of the control file as the database safety checklist. It contains a checklist of things that must be correct before the database instance can start up. Think of the database instance as all the programs that must be running in order for Oracle9i to **select**, **insert**, **update**, or **delete** a row of data in the database. This checklist includes

- Database name
- Names and locations of the data files
- Names and location of the redo logs
- Date and timestamp associated with all data files
- Date and timestamp associated with all redo logs

If any one of these items, when inspected, does not match the control file checklist, it considers the database suspect and will not start up. If an extra redo log or data file exists, it will not start up. The database must be in complete agreement with the control file checklist, or else the database will not start up.

How Control Files Are Created

The initial control files are created when you issue the **create database** command. To see what control files you currently have, issue the following **show parameters** command:

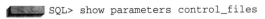

```
SQL> show parameters control_files

NAME                                 TYPE     VALUE
------------------------------------ -------  ----------------------------
control_files                        string   /d1/oradata/emile/control01.ct
                                              l, /d1/oradata/emile/control02
                                              .ctl, /d1/oradata/emile/contro
                                              l03.ctl
```

The easiest way to create an additional control file is to shut down the database. Copy an existing control file where you want the new control file to be located. Edit the INIT.ora file to reference the additional control file. Start up the database.

For example, here is what the INIT.ora file might look like before you create a new control file:

```
CONTROL_FILES = (/u01/oracle/prod/control01.ctl,
                 /u02/oracle/prod/control02.ctl)
```

Here is what it looks like after you make the INIT.ora entry:

```
CONTROL_FILES = (/u01/oracle/prod/control01.ctl,
                 /u02/oracle/prod/control02.ctl,
                 /u03/oracle/newcontrol.ctl)
```

Creating a User Account

To create an Oracle9*i* user, you use the **create user** command. Here is an example of a typical **create user** command being executed:

```
SQL> create user littlemike
  2   identified by bigmike
  3   default tablespace users
  4   quota 10m on users
  5   temporary tablespace temp
  6*  quota unlimited on users
SQL> /

User created.
```

In this example, we have created a new user named littlemike. We have set the password to bigmike. When the user creates database objects and doesn't specify a location, the objects will be placed in the tablespace **users**. They are limited to a total of 10MB of space in the **users** tablespace.

When temporary space is needed (sorts, group by, and views all use temporary space), the database creates those database objects in the temporary tablespace. They are allowed as much space as is available in the temporary tablespace.

grant connect, resource

At this point, littlemike has not been given permission to log into the Oracle9*i* database, nor does he have the right to create database objects. Before he can do that, you must issue the **grant connect, resource** statement. Here is an example:

```
SQL> grant connect, resource to littlemike;

Grant succeeded.
```

A very useful view to know when working with users is DBA_USERS. Here is a quick **select** on that view:

```
SQL> column username format a14 trunc Heading 'Username'
SQL> column default_tablespace format a15 trunc heading 'Default'
SQL> column temporary_tablespace format a15 trunc 'Temp'
SQL> select username, default_tablespace, temporary_tablespace
  2* from dba_users
SQL>/
Username       Default         Temp
-------------- --------------- ---------------
SYS            SYSTEM          TEMP
SYSTEM         TOOLS           TEMP
LITTLEMIKE     USERS           TEMP
DBSNMP         SYSTEM          SYSTEM
NTIRETY        USERS           TEMP
```

Changing the Password

Here is how you change the password of a user's account. In this example, we push the password for the littlemike user to a password of littlemike.

```
SQL> alter user littlemike identified by littlemike;

User altered.
```

In this chapter, you have learned all the basics for getting your database started, adding rollback segments, and creating a user account in the database. This is a very simple pass at what it takes to be a DBA. In the next chapter, you will learn how to harvest the power of SQL*Plus. To be a great Oracle9*i* user, you must have a solid foundation in SQL*Plus and what it can do.

Chapter 7 Questions

Answers to questions can be found in Appendix A.

1. The system global area (SGA) is an area of memory that is

   A. shared by all users

   B. not shared by all users

   C. used by a single user

   D. never used

2. To start and stop the database, you must first connect to the database using

A. connect username/password

B. connect/as dba

C. connect/as sysadmin

D. connect/as sysdba

3. These are all valid shutdown commands except

A. shutdown

B. shutdown now

C. shutdown abort

D. shutdown immediate

4. A segment in the database that stores a before image or "undo" copy of a data block, before it was modified, is called a

A. redo log

B. rollback segment

C. table

D. control file

PART
III

Beyond the Basics

CHAPTER
8

More SQL*Plus

ongratulations! If you are reading this chapter, it means you have recently graduated from SQL*Plus 101. If that is not the case, please turn back and read Chapter 5. To begin this next lesson, you must have completed the prerequisites. This means you have a core understanding of SQL*Plus, because, in this chapter, we concentrate on some of its finer points. At the end of the chapter, we may pull a surprise quiz, so be prepared. This chapter covers the following:

- Some tricks to deploying SQL*Plus in a production environment
- **union**, **intersect**, and **minus** set operators
- The dual table
- Math functions
- String functions
- Date functions
- The **group by** command
- How to find duplicate rows in a table
- How to delete duplicate rows in a table
- SQL generating SQL
- SQL generating a data file
- How to use a real editor from SQL*Plus

Terminology

The following terminology will arm you with the technical jargon you need for this chapter:

- *Set operators* combine the results of two queries into one result.
- An *operator* combines the results of the items being operated upon into a single result. For example, in 3 + 4 = 7, the addition symbol (+) is an *operator*.
- An *include file* is an SQL*Plus command file read in by another SQL*Plus program.

- A *command file* contains a series of commands that are read by a program such as SQL*Plus. The work accomplished by a command file is the same as if you had typed commands interactively one after the other.

- A *flat file* is a subset of data stripped out of one or more tables into a single output file. Think of it as a text document in which all the special characters have been removed. Many users would call a Microsoft Word document that has been saved in text-only format a flat file.

Deploying SQL*Plus in Production

If you want to deploy anything in production, make sure whatever you do is well documented. Experience has taught us that when a piece of software breaks in the middle of the night, documentation comes in very handy, especially if you just happen to be the person on call that weekend rather than the author of the software.

We always find it ironic that the same programmer who is quick to have an opinion on any subject in any conversation is also the last person to use the **remark** command in SQL*Plus. The bottom line is that great code is code that is well documented. It is also a key step in building a production-quality environment.

Commenting Your Code with rem, --, and /*...*/

SQL*Plus gives you the ability to place comments inside your code. This can be done using the **rem** command, **--**, or the **/* */** command. The **rem** command must start at the beginning of the line. If you want to continue the comment on a second line, you must issue another **rem** command.

The **/* */** and the **--** commands are much more flexible. They can span several lines. They can also be placed within a line. The choice is up to you.

Here is an example of some code with comments placed in the command file using the **rem**, **--**, and **/* */** commands.

```
rem ****
rem **** The Newhire.sql
rem *****
Column state_cd format a25              heading 'State|Code' trunc
Column lname    format a10              heading 'Last|Name'  trunc
Column hiredate format a10              heading 'Hire|Date'  trunc
Column salary   format $999,999,999.00  Heading  'Salary' trunc
/* Sorted by State
 in a Descending manner */
-- This is a comment Line
select state_cd, lname, hiredate, salary
from   newhire       --One of my Favorite Tables
order by 1 desc, 2 /* Note state_cd is descending */
```

Remember the old saying: happy code is well-documented code. If you must be on call, hope the code is well documented.

SQL*Plus Include Files

Imagine a year has gone by, and you take the time to review all the SQL*Plus programs that were written. What would you learn? Immediately, you would realize that much of what you have written was repeated over and over again. It would be very obvious to you that you should have created an include file for your reports. An *include file* is an SQL*Plus command file read in by another SQL*Plus program. In this file, you can place all the setup information that rarely changes from program to program. You can also create standard naming conventions that can be used consistently for report after report. By doing this, the quality of the SQL*Plus program is improved greatly, as is the readability of the SQL code.

Experience has taught us that it is actually best to create two report setup files. The first SQL*Plus setup file is for 80-character-wide reports. Here is an example of an 80-character-wide report setup file.

```
Rem *********************************************
Rem ***      RPTSTD.sql
Rem *********************************************
Rem *  Put all Column Commands Here ...
Column state_name format a15 trunc
Column state_name heading 'State|Name'  format a15 trunc
Column lname      heading 'Last|Name'   format a12 wrap
Column hiredate   heading 'Hire|Date'   format a12
Column salary     heading 'Salary'      format $999,999.99
Repfooter '|--- Company Confidential ---'
Set pagesize 55
Set linesize 80
set newpage 0
set feedback off
set timing off
set trimspool on
Rem ***************************************************
```

This example is for a 132-character-wide report setup file:

```
Rem *********************************************
Rem ***      RPTWIDE.sql
Rem *********************************************
Rem *  Put all Column Commands Here ...
Column state_name format a15 trunc
Column state_name heading 'State|Name'  format a30 wrap
Column lname      heading 'Last|Name'   format a25 wrap
Column hiredate   heading 'Hire|Date'   format a12
```

```
Column salary      heading 'Salary'      format $999,999.99
Repfooter '|--- Company Confidential ---'
Set pagesize 40
Set linesize 132
set newpage 0
set feedback off
set timing off
set trimspool on
Rem ****************************************************
```

How to Use the SQL*Plus Include File

Once you have built these two include files, it becomes far quicker and easier to develop SQL*Plus programs. All the standard **set** commands are done. All the standard **column** commands are done. Your time can be spent writing the actual **select** statement and thinking about good documentation.

```
Rem *******************************************
Rem *          newhire.sql
Rem *******************************************
Rem *  This program joins newhire table with state table.
Rem *    A.C.  8/24/01
Rem *
Rem * Bring in include file
Rem *
@rptstd.sql
rem * now lets do report specific commands
rem *
repheader 'The New Hire Report|By State'
spool newhire.lis
rem *
select st.state_name, nh.lname,
       nh.hiredate, nh.salary
from   newhire nh, state st

where  st.state_cd = nh.state_cd
order by 1,2
/
spool off
exit
```

The **@rptstd.sql** tells SQL*Plus to look in its current directory for a program named **rptstd.sql** and execute it. It's not uncommon to place these include files into a central directory. If that is the case, then just include the path before the program name. The command may look something like this:

```
@c:\mycompany\sql\rptstd.sql
```

When you issue the @ sign, it's as if you typed those commands at the SQL prompt one by one.

SQL*Plus Include File with Overrides

Sometimes the standard column size of a heading is not what you want for a particular query. In that case, you override the setting provided by your site's standard SQL*Plus include file. For example,

```
Rem ********************************************
Rem *              newhiretot.sql
Rem ********************************************
Rem *  This program joins newhire table with state table.
Rem *    A.C.  8/24/01
Rem *
Rem * Bring in include file
Rem *
@c:/sql/rptstd.sql
rem * Let's override the setting of the salary column from include file
rem *
column salary      heading 'Salary'      format $999,999.99
rem * Let's add some more complicated report logic
rem *
repheader 'The New Hire Report|By State'
compute sum of salary on state_name
compute sum of salary on report
break on report skip 1 on state_name skip 1
spool newhiretot.lis
rem *
select st.state_name, nh.lname,
       nh.hiredate, nh.salary
from    newhire nh, state st
where   st.state_cd = nh.state_cd
order by 1,2
/
spool off
exit
```

Using SQL*Plus from the Operating System Prompt

Let's execute a SQL*Plus command file program from the operating system prompt. In this example, we will tell SQL*Plus to log into the user's account scott, whose password is tiger. We will also tell SQL*Plus to find a program named newhiretot.sql and execute it. Since the last line of newhiretot.sql is **exit**, the program will return to the operating system prompt when it is done, for example,

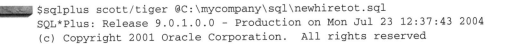

```
$sqlplus scott/tiger @C:\mycompany\sql\newhiretot.sql
SQL*Plus: Release 9.0.1.0.0 - Production on Mon Jul 23 12:37:43 2004
(c) Copyright 2001 Oracle Corporation.  All rights reserved
```

union, intersect, and minus
Set Operators

Unlike a traditional database, a relational database is based upon set theory. In a
traditional database, you read a record, inspect it, and determine a course of action.
The program is designed to work on the data one record at a time. In a relational
database, you work with sets of data versus a single row. You will never issue a read
record command in SQL*Plus. Since you always work with sets of data, the program
may be quite small, but it is also quite powerful. This very strong relationship to set
theory separates a relational database from a traditional nonrelational database.

This next set of examples will use the **union**, **intersect**, and **minus** set operators
to compare the contents of two tables. Let's create Tables A and B, and then populate
them with some data:

```
SQL> create table a
  2  (cola  number);

Table created.

SQL> create table b
  2  (colb  number);

Table created.

SQL> insert into a values (1);
1 row created.
SQL> insert into a values (2);
1 row created.
SQL> insert into a values (3);
1 row created.
SQL> insert into b values (3);
1 row created.
SQL> insert into b values (4);
1 row created.
SQL> insert into b values (5);
1 row created.
```

Let's examine the content of those tables:

```
SQL> select * from a;
     COLA
----------
        1
        2
        3

SQL> select * from b;
     COLB
----------
        3
        4
        5
```

union Operator

We will now use the **union** operator in SQL*Plus to join the contents of Table A with the contents of Table B.

```
SQL> select * from a union select * from b;
     COLA
----------
        1
        2
        3
        4
        5
5 rows selected.
```

Notice how the **union** set operator combines the results of two queries into a single result. Did you notice that it returned no duplicates? Even though both tables contain the value 3, only a single row is returned containing the value 3. It's important to remember that the default behavior of the **union** operator returns no duplicates.

union all Operator

Let's now try the **union** command with the **all** option.

```
SQL> select * from a union all select * from b;
     COLA
----------
        1
        2
        3
```

```
        3
        4
        5

6 rows selected.
```

Did you notice how the **union all** operator returned all the rows in both tables with all duplicates?

minus Operator

Let's now try Table A **minus** Table B.

```
SQL> select * from a minus select * from b;
      COLA
----------
        1
        2
SQL>
```

As you can see, the **minus** operator returns all the rows in Table A minus (subtracted) the rows contained in Table B. Did you notice how the 3, 4, and 5 are missing?

intersect Operator

Let's try the **intersect** operator on Table A and Table B.

```
SQL> select * from a intersect select * from b;
      COLA
----------
        3
```

Did you notice how the **intersect** operator returned all the rows contained in Table A that also reside in Table B?

Don't Mix Apples with Oranges

It is important to note that when using set operators, the contents of both tables are returned into a single result. This means that the data being selected must be of the same type on a column-by-column basis as it is returned.

The first column selected from each table must be of the same type, the second column selected from each table must be of the same type, and so on. You can only compare apples with apples and oranges with oranges. In Oraclespeak, compare number type with number type and characters with characters.

Let's see what happens when you try to violate this rule:

```
SQL> select * from a union select * from c;
                *
ERROR at line 1:
ORA-01790: expression must have same data type as corresponding expression
```

SQL*Plus Command-Line Editing

When you work with SQL*Plus, it becomes apparent very quickly that Oracle9i holds the last command executed in the SQL buffer. To execute this buffer, you merely enter a slash (/) and press the ENTER key. This action causes the last SQL statement entered to be executed immediately.

If you are like us, every time you type a statement into SQL*Plus, you fat-finger a column name. Rather than retype the whole statement back into SQL*Plus, you can use the command-line editor that comes with SQL*Plus. Table 8-1 is a quick reference guide to its functionality.

Using the Command-Line Editor

Let's try a few of the commands listed in Table 8-1. First, let's look at what's currently contained in the SQL buffer. To see the buffer, type the **list** command:

```
SQL> l
    1  Select last_name, salary
    2  from newhire
    3* order by lname
```

Notice the asterisk. It tells us what line we are currently pointing at. Did you also notice that you see only the SQL statement and that none of the column commands are displayed? Let's change the active line the editor is pointing at to Line 1:

```
SQL> l 1
    1* Select last_name, salary
    2  from newhire
    3 order by lname
```

Now that the command-line editor is pointing to Line 1, let's correct the column name we fat-fingered. Let's change LAST_NAME to LNAME:

```
SQL> c/last_name/lname/
    1* Select lname, salary
    2  from newhire
    3 order by lname
```

Editor Command	Name	Purpose
A	Append	Add text to the end of the current line
C/value1/value2/	Change	Replace *value1* with *value2*
DEL	Delete	Delete the current line
I	Insert	Add a line after the current line
L	List current line	Show all the lines in the buffer
L N	List line N	Show line number N in the buffer

TABLE 8-1. *SQL*Plus Line-Editing Commands*

This is a great improvement from retyping the SQL statement each time you make a mistake.

If Only I Could Use VI or Emacs

As you can see, with the command-line editor, it's possible to make simple changes. But what happens when you just can't take it anymore and you want the use of a full-functioning editor? You are in luck.

There is a command in SQL*Plus that allows you to define your favorite editor. The command format is **define_editor = "editor_name"**, where **editor_name** is your favorite editor accessible on that machine.

To access that editor, just type the SQL*Plus command **edit**. SQL*Plus looks at what has been defined in **define_editor** and brings it up.

Dual Table

Simply put, the *dual* table is an Oracle table that is accessible to every SQL*Plus user. What's really important is that the dual table only contains one row of data. This is a fact you can count on. It's a very useful table to know about, especially when you start to work with new SQL*Plus functionality.

You can use the dual table as a way to test many of the Oracle functions you are about to learn. For example, if you want to add two numbers together, you can issue the following **select** statement:

```
Select 102456.56 + 2043 from dual;
```

Oracle Functions

The Oracle 9i database comes with a powerful set of functions. Functions are commands you can issue in SQL*Plus that execute a predetermined algorithm. Sometimes this changes the display of the data; other times, it changes the data type itself or just executes a mathematical formula.

In the case of numbers, it might be the **sqrt** function, which provides the square root of a number. In the case of dates, it might be the function **last_day**. This algorithm is designed to return the last day of the given month. In the case of a string function, it might be the **initcap** function. This function makes the first character in the string uppercase.

Your ability to harness the power of these functions is critical. Often you can use these functions in the **where** clause to help you retrieve the particular data you are looking for, or you can use them in the **select** clause to help you present the data in a certain way.

Math Functions and Operators

With the Oracle 9i database, you have the full complement of mathematical operators and functions available. Table 8-2 shows the basic arithmetic operators.

Many times, the ability to add, subtract, multiply, and divide numeric data is not enough. Have no fear; Oracle9i can still help. Oracle9i supports an extensive list of mathematical functions. Table 8-3 is only a partial listing. Don't be afraid of using the dual table to test a few of these on your own, for example,

```
Select CEIL(34.09) from dual;
```

Operator	Description	Example
+	Addition	select salary + bonus from finance;
−	Subtraction	select year − age from employee;
*	Multiplication	select base * rate from finance;
/	Division	select cost / amount from finance;

TABLE 8-2. *Arithmetic Operators*

Mathematical Function	Example	Result	Description
abs (*value1*)	abs(5604.5) abs(−70) abs('−123')	5604.5 70 123	Returns the absolute value of *value1*. The result is always positive.
ceil (*value*)	ceil(34.09) ceil(34) ceil(−909.98)	35 34 −909	Returns the nearest whole integer greater than or equal to the *value*.
cos (*value*)	cos(180)	0.5984601	Returns the cosine of the *value*.
floor (*value*)	floor(34.09) floor(34) floor(−909.98)	34 34 −910	Returns the largest integer equal to or less than *value*.
mod (*value, divisor*)	mod(100,6) mod(250,5)	4 0	Returns the remainder of *value* divided by the *divisor*. If the divisor equals zero, then the value is returned.
power (*value, exponent*)	power(5,2) power(2,10)	25 1024	*Value* is raised to the power of *exponent*.
round (*value, precision*)	round(456.789) round(4.789, 2) round(456.789, 0)	457 4.79 457	Result is rounded to *precision* places to the right of the decimal place.
sign (*value*)	sign(22) sign(−309.1) sign(0)	1 −1 0	Returns a number indicating whether the *value* is positive or negative: If *value* > 0, returns 1 If *value* < 0, returns −1 If *value* = 0, returns 0
sqrt (*value*)	sqrt(25) sqrt(2209)	5 47	Returns the square root of *value*.

TABLE 8-3.   *Common Math Functions*

Mathematical Function	Example	Result	Description
trunc (*value, precision*)	trunc(456.789)	456	Returns the *value* truncated to the *precision* specified. If a positive number is specified for *precision*, it will truncate the digits to the right of the decimal point to that number of places. If a negative number is specified for *precision*, it will truncate the digits to the left of the decimal point to that number of places. If no *precision* is specified, 0 (zero) is assumed, which means it will truncate to the decimal point.
	trunc(4.789, 2)	4.78	
	trunc(456.7, 0)	456	
	trunc(456.789, −1)	450	
	trunc(456.789, −2)	400	
	trunc('456.789', 2)	456.78	

TABLE 8-3. *Common Math Functions* (continued)

String Functions

SQL*Plus provides you with an army of functions designed to manipulate the character data stored within your database. Character data is any information you are able to store in the char, varchar, and varchar2 column types. Typically, if the data you have is not stored in a table column type (number or date column), it's most likely character data.

Given that you have recently graduated from SQL*Plus 101, we thought it best to provide you with Table 8-4, on character data.

Concatenation Operator

The concatenation operator, ||, deserves special attention before we move on to the next discussion. Technically, it is a string operator, where the results of this operator are returned as a single result. We included it with string functions, since it is too important to be left out. Later in this chapter, you will see it put to some interesting uses.

String Function	Example	Display	Returns
length(*value*)	length ('massachusetts')	13	The **length** function returns the length of *value* whether string, number, date, or expression.
lower(*string*)	lower('boston')	boston	The **lower** function converts the given character *string* to lowercase.
upper(*string*)	upper('boston')	BOSTON	The **upper** function converts the given character *string* to uppercase.
lpad(*string, length [,padding]*)	lpad('Total:',15,'*')	*********Total:	The **lpad** function left-pads a *string* with the padding until the string is the *length* given. If *padding* is not specified, spaces are the default.
rpad(*string, length [,padding]*)	rpad('Chapter 1',15,'.')	Chapter 1...	Same as the **lpad** function except that it pads to the right.
ltrim(*string [,trimming_value]*)	ltrim ('mississippi','mis')	ppi	The **ltrim** function left-trims the *string*, removing any of the characters in the *trimming_value* on the left of the string until a character not in the *trimming_value* is found. If a *trimming_value* is not given, spaces are the default.

TABLE 8-4.   *String Functions*

String Function	Example	Display	Returns
rtrim(*string* [,*trimming_value*])	rtrim ('mississippi','ip') rtrim ('Lisa ')	mississ Lisa	Same as the **ltrim** function, except that it trims to the right. This is very helpful when cleaning data entry by removing unwanted spaces.
string || *string*	select clt_salutation||'. '|| clt_last_name from client;	Mr. Alberto	The concatenation function, (||), joins two strings together. Note: Some machines show this as broken rather than solid lines.
initcap(*string*)	initcap('mr Corey')	Mr Corey	The **initcap** function changes the first character of each *string* to uppercase.
instr(*string*, *value* [,*start* [,*occurrence*]])	instr ('mississippi', 'is', 1,2) instr ('mississippi', 'IS', 1,2)	5 0	The **instr** function returns the location of a *value* in a *string*. If a *start* position is given, **instr** begins searching there. If an *occurrence* is given, **instr** waits to return the location of *occurrence* of the value. Note: A date or number can replace the *string*.

TABLE 8-4.   *String Functions* (continued)

String Function	Example	Display	Returns
replace(*string, if, then*)	replace ('617-555-1212','-') replace ('DOGCATDOG CAT','CAT','GONE')	6175551212 DOGGONEDO GGONE	The **replace** function searches a string for the *if* and replaces it with the *then*.
soundex(*string*)	soundex(mem_first_name) soundex('mike')	Mike M200	The **soundex** function syntax is different from other string functions. It is used to find words that sound like *string*. The results always begin with the same letter as the string.
substr(*string, start [,count]*)	substr ('candlestick', 7) substr ('Just One Wish', 6,3)	stick One	The **substr** function removes a portion of the string beginning in the *start* position and goes for *count* characters. If *count* is not specified, all characters beginning at *start* and going to the end of the string are removed.

TABLE 8-4.   *String Functions* (continued)

The Date Data Type

One of the most important types of information you store in an Oracle database is dates. In our example table NEWHIRE, the HIREDATE column is of the type date.

When dealing with the date column, it is important to remember in an Oracle9i database that a date column is really for a date and particular time. The date data type really contains two values. The first portion of a date column is the year, month, and day. The second portion is time.

In other words, you might have three entries in the NEWHIRE table with May 23:

1. May 23, 2001 10:00 am

2. May 23, 2001 11:00 am

3. May 23, 2001 12:32 am

Even though on a simple select, it just brings back the May 23, 2001, each one of those dates has a particular time associated with it.

Many times people get themselves into trouble because they are comparing two dates that they think are equal, but because of the time element associated with every date, the fields don't match. Don't worry; there are date functions that help you avoid that sort of problem.

Date Functions in SQL*Plus

Oracle software provides you with a very extensive list of date functions. To help understand all the date functions available, please review Table 8-5. Notice how the dual table is used to demonstrate these date functions.

Date Function	Example and Result	Description
| add_months (*date,number*) | ```
select sysdate as today,
       ADD_MONTHS(sysdate,1)  as
next_month,
       ADD_MONTHS(sysdate,-1) as
last_month
  from dual;


TODAY      NEXT_MONTH  LAST_MONTH
---------  ----------  ---------
24-JUL-01  24-AUG-01   24-JUN-01
``` | The **add_months** function adds a *number* of months to a *date*, and returns the resulting date. |

TABLE 8-5. *Date Functions Within Oracle*
```

Date Function	Example and Result	Description

last_day (*date*)	Return the last day of the month for 6/6/2002.
	`select LAST_DAY('06-JUN-2002') as`
	`last_day`
	`  from dual;`
	`LAST_DAY`
	`---------`
	`30-JUN-02`
		The **last_day** function returns the last day of the month for the given *date*.

months_ between (*date1, date2*)	Return the number of months between 9/31/2001 and 12/25/2001.
	`select MONTHS_BETWEEN('25-DEC-2001',`
	`'31-AUG-2001')`
	`  from dual;`
	
	`MONTHS_BETWEEN('25-DEC-2001',`
	`'31-AUG-2001')`
	`-----------------------------`
	
	`3.80645161`
		The **months_ between** function returns *date1* subtracted by *date2* in months. *date1* is usually the future date. The result is usually a fraction.

new_time (*current_date, current_zone, future_zone*)	Return the date in Yukon standard time, if it is 01/01/2002 in Eastern Standard time.
	`select NEW_TIME('01-JAN-2002',`
	`'EST','YST') from dual;`
	
	`NEW_TIME`
	`---------`
	`31-DEC-01`
		The **new_time** function returns the date that it would be in the *future_zone*, according to the *current_date* and *current_zone* supplied. (See the list that follows this table.)

TABLE 8-5. *Date Functions Within Oracle* (continued)

Date Function	Example and Result	Description

next_day (*date*, '*day*')	Return the date of the first Monday for the year 2002.
	
	```select NEXT_DAY('31-DEC-2001', 'MONDAY') from dual;```
	
	```NEXT_DAY```
	```---------```
	```07-JAN-02```
		The **next_day** function gives the next date that lands on the '*day*' after *date*; '*day*' is the day of the week fully spelled out.

round (*date*, '*format*')	Return today's date rounded to the closest month.
	
	```select ROUND(SYSDATE,'month') from dual;```
	
	```ROUND```
	```---------```
	```01-AUG-01```
		The **round** function rounds a *date* to what is specified by '*format*'.

to_char (*date*, '*format*')	Return today's date as a character data type in the format mm/dd/yyyy.
	
	```select TO_CHAR(SYSDATE,'MM/DD/YYYY') from dual;```
	
	```TO_CHAR```
	```----------```
	```07/24/2001```
		The **to_char** function takes in a *date* and returns a character date in the *format* given. Many times this is used to concatenate a date with a character field.

to_date (*string*, '*format*')	Return 10/13/1960 in a date data type.
	
	```select TO_DATE('10/13/1960','MM/DD/YYYY') from dual;```
	
	```TO_CHAR```
	```--------```
	```13-OCT-60```
	The output is based upon the default date format chosen. In this case, the default date format is set to DD_MON_YY
		The **to_date** function takes in a *string* that looks like a date in the *format* supplied. This is helpful when migrating character dates into date fields.

TABLE 8-5.   *Date Functions Within Oracle* (continued)

Date Function	Example and Result	Description

trunc (*date*, '*format*')	Return today's date
	
	`select to_char(sysdate,'MM/DD/YYYY`
	`HH24:MI:SS') before`
	`From dual;`
	`Before`
	`------------------`
	`09/14/2001 15:05:50`
	
	`select to_char(TRUNC(sysdate),'MM/DD/YYYY`
	`HH24:MI:SS')) after`
	`From dual;`
	`Before`
	`------------------`
	`09/14/2001 00:00:00`
		trunc (truncate) used in this manner sets the associated time with every date to 00:00:00.

TABLE 8-5. *Date Functions Within Oracle* (continued)

The *current_zone* and *future_zone* functions described in Table 8-5 are three-letter abbreviations of time zones. Some of the most common ones are listed here:

- **AST/ADT** Atlantic standard/daylight time
- **BST/BDT** Bering standard/daylight time
- **CST/CDT** Central standard/daylight time
- **EST/EDT** Eastern standard/daylight time
- **GMT** Greenwich mean time
- **MST/MDT** Mountain standard/daylight time
- **NST** Newfoundland standard time
- **PST/PDT** Pacific standard/daylight time
- **YST/YDT** Yukon standard/daylight time
- **HST/HDT** Alaska-Hawaii standard/daylight time

When working with dates, you need to understand all the format masks you can work with. Table 8-6 is a complete listing of all the date formats you can use. As you can see, Oracle gives you a quite extensive way of accepting and playing back dates.

Format	Description	Example
fm	Prefix to day of month; suppresses leading zeros	fmDD = 6 (not 06)
TH	Suffix to a number; appends the ordinal suffix (*th* or *nd*)	DDTH = 06TH
SP	Suffix to a number; forces it to be spelled out	DdSP = Six
SPTH	Suffix to a number; both appends the ordinal suffix (*th* or *nd*) and forces the number to be spelled out	DdSPTH = Sixth
MM	Shows number of month	01–12
RM	Shows month as Roman numeral	XII
MON	Shows three-letter abbreviation of month in uppercase	JAN–DEC
Mon	Shows three-letter abbreviation of month with first letter in uppercase	Jan–Dec
MONTH	Shows month spelled out in uppercase	JANUARY
Month	Shows month spelled out with first letter in uppercase	January
month	Shows month spelled out in lowercase	january
DDD	Shows number of the day in the year since January 1	365
DD	Shows number of the day in the month	13
D	Shows number of the day in the week	7
DY	Shows day as three-letter abbreviation in uppercase	WED
Dy	Shows day as three-letter abbreviation with first letter in uppercase	Wed
DAY	Shows day of the week spelled out in uppercase	WEDNESDAY
Day	Shows day of the week spelled out with first letter in uppercase	Wednesday

TABLE 8-6. *Date Format Masks*

Format	Description	Example
day	Shows day of the week spelled out in lowercase	wednesday
YYYY	Shows year in four digits	1965
YY	Shows last two digits of year	65
YEAR	Shows year spelled out in uppercase	NINETEEN SIXTY FIVE
Year	Shows year spelled out with first letter of each word in uppercase	Nineteen Sixty Five
Q	Shows the quarter of year as a number	3
WW	Shows the number of the week in year	45
W	Shows number of week in month	3
HH	Shows hour of day	1–12
HH24	Shows hour of day using a 24-hour clock	1–24
MI	Shows minute of hour	0–60
SS	Shows second of minute	0–60
SSSSS	Shows seconds since midnight	0–86399
A.M. or P.M.	Shows a.m. or p.m. in uppercase with periods	A.M. or P.M.
a.m. or p.m.	Shows a.m. or p.m. in lowercase with periods	a.m. or p.m.
AM or PM	Shows a.m. or p.m. in uppercase without periods	AM or PM
am or pm	Shows a.m. or p.m. in lowercase without periods	am or pm
CC	Shows number of century	21

TABLE 8-6. *Date Format Masks* (continued)

Date Arithmetic

An Oracle9*i* database gives you the ability to perform date arithmetic. For example, if the HIREDATE column contained the value 03-MAR-02, and you issued the SQL statement **select hiredate+14 from dual;**, the resulting value would be 13-MAR-02. Why not try a few experiments of your own and see what happens?

Group Function	Example	Description

avg ([*distinct*] *column_name*)	Average all employees' salaries.
	`select AVG(emp_salary)`
	`    from employee;`
		The average value of all the values in the *column_name*. If the **distinct** option is used, only distinct non-null numbers are used.

count ([*distinct*] *value*)	Count the number of employees.
	`select COUNT(emp_name)`
	`    from employee;`
		Counts the number of rows selected, ignoring nulls for that *value*. If **distinct** is used, only distinct non-null numbers are used. *value* can be either a column name or an expression.

max (*value*)	Return the greatest salary.
	`select MAX(emp_salary)`
	`    from employee;`
		Returns the maximum number/character for the *value* selected, ignoring nulls. *value* can be either a column name or an expression.

min (*value*)	Return the smallest salary.
	`select MIN(emp_salary)`
	`    from employee;`
		Returns the minimum number/character for the *value* selected, ignoring nulls. *value* can be either a column name or an expression.

stddev (*value*)	Return the standard deviation for the employees' salaries.
	`select STDDEV(emp_salary)`
	`    from employee;`
		Returns the standard deviation from the norm of *values* selected.

TABLE 8-7. *group by Functions*

Group Function	Example	Description

sum(*value*)	Return the total amount of salaries paid.
	`select SUM(emp_salary)`
	`   from employee;`
		Adds the *value*, returning the total for the rows selected. *value* can be either a column name or an expression.

variance ([distinct] *value*)	Return the variance of employees' salaries.
	`select VARIANCE(emp_salary)`
	`   from employee;`
		Returns the variance of all values of rows selected, ignoring nulls for that *value*. If **distinct** is used, only distinct non-null numbers are used. *value* can be either a column name or an expression.

TABLE 8-7. *group by Functions* (continued)

group by Functions

You can use the **group by** functions to group sets of data together for the purpose of getting summary information. Think of this as the ability to lump similar types of information together as it is retrieved from the database. Table 8-7 gives a complete list.

group by Functions Without the group by

Did you notice we don't have the **group by** command in any of the examples in Table 8-7? When you don't mention the **group by** clause in a query, you are telling the database you want to treat all the rows in the table as a single group. Many times, this is not the behavior you want. Most people understand the concepts of groups but quickly get into trouble trying to use it.

A good rule of thumb to use is this: if a column is not mentioned in the **group by** clause, then you must aggregate upon it. In other words, you must use one of the functions in Table 8-7 on every column name that is not part of the **group by** clause.

For example, the following SQL statement will not work:

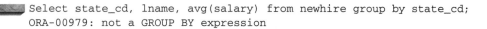
```
Select state_cd, lname, avg(salary) from newhire group by state_cd;
ORA-00979: not a GROUP BY expression
```

Since the column LNAME is not in the **group by** clause, you must do one of two things to it: add it to the **group by** clause or use a **group by** function on it, such as **min**, **max**, or **avg**.

If you can't find a **group by** function you want to use, then add the column name to the **group by** clause.

The having Clause

Just as you use **where** clauses to examine individual rows retrieved by a query, you use the **having** clause to specify a search condition for a group of rows. For example, if you want to see the average salary for states with more than two new hires, using the **having** clause, the query would be as follows:

```
Select state_cd, avg(salary)from newhire
group by state_cd
having count(state_cd) > 2;
```

Using group by to Find Duplicate Data

Using the **group by** functionality, we find duplicate data within an Oracle table. Let's create a table of colors and accidentally put a duplicate entry in it.

```
SQL> create table color (
  2     color_cd varchar2(8) not null,
  3     color_descr varchar2(30));
Table created.
SQL> insert into color (color_cd, color_descr) values('RD', 'Red');
1 row created.
SQL> insert into color (color_cd, color_descr) values('GN', 'Green');
1 row created.
SQL> insert into color (color_cd, color_descr) values('BL', 'Blue');
1 row created.
SQL> insert into color (color_cd, color_descr) values('GN', 'Green');
1 row created.
SQL> insert into color (color_cd, color_descr) values('BK', 'Black');
1 row created.
```

Notice that the COLOR table contains a duplicate entry for the color green:

```
SQL> select * from color;
COLOR_CD COLOR_DESCR
-------- ------------------------------
RD       Red
GN       Green
BL       Blue
GN       Green
BK       Black
```

Using the **group by** function, let's look for color codes having a count greater than 1.

```
SQL> select count(color_cd), max(color_descr)
  2     from color
  3  group by color_cd
  4  having count(color_cd) > 1;
COUNT(COLOR_CD) MAX(COLOR_DESCR)
--------------- ----------------------------
              2 Green
```

Using group by to Delete Duplicate Data

Let's build a more complex example. In this example, the key that determines duplicates will be the combination of the emp_id and proj_id. Using the **group by** command, we will find duplicate entries and then delete them. Let's create the table:

```
SQL> create table project_team (
  2     projteam_id integer  not null,
  3     emp_id     integer  not null,
  4     proj_id    integer  not null,
  5     projteam_name varchar2(20));
Table created.
SQL> insert into project_team
  2     (projteam_id, emp_id, proj_id, projteam_name)
  3     values (1, 10, 221, 'Timetracking');
1 row created.
SQL> insert into project_team
  2     (projteam_id, emp_id, proj_id, projteam_name)
  3     values (2, 30, 221, 'Timetracking');
1 row created.
SQL> insert into project_team
  2     (projteam_id, emp_id, proj_id, projteam_name)
  3     values (3, 10, 221, 'Time Tracking');
1 row created.
SQL> insert into project_team
  2     (projteam_id, emp_id, proj_id, projteam_name)
  3     values (4, 10, 505, 'Account System');
1 row created.
SQL> insert into project_team
  2     (projteam_id, emp_id, proj_id, projteam_name)
  3     values (5, 40, 505, 'Account System');
1 row created.
SQL> insert into project_team
  2     (projteam_id, emp_id, proj_id, projteam_name)
  3     values (6, 102, 21, 'HR Reporting');
1 row created.
```

```
SQL> select * from project_team;
PROJTEAM_ID    EMP_ID     PROJ_ID PROJTEAM_NAME
----------- ---------- ---------- --------------------
          1         10         221 Timetracking
          2         30         221 Timetracking
          3         10         221 Time Tracking
          4         10         505 Account System
          5         40         505 Account System
          6        102          21 HR Reporting
```

Pay close attention to this example; the duplicate entry in this case is

```
          3         10         221 Time Tracking
```

What makes this the duplicate entry is the fact that more than one row in the
PROJECT_TEAM table has the same emp_id when combined with the proj_id.
Let's run our program to find the duplicates:

```
SQL> select count(emp_id||proj_id), max(projteam_id)
  2    from project_team
  3    group by emp_id, proj_id
  4    having count(emp_id||proj_id) > 1;
COUNT(EMP_ID||PROJ_ID) MAX(PROJTEAM_ID)
---------------------- ----------------
                     2                3
SQL>
```

Now let's delete the duplicate entry:

```
SQL> delete from project_team
  2    where projteam_id = (select max(projteam_id)
  3                         from project_team
  4                         group by emp_id, proj_id
  5                         having count(emp_id||proj_id) > 1);
1 row deleted.
```

See how easy that was? Let's see if it worked:

```
SQL> select * from project_team;
PROJTEAM_ID    EMP_ID     PROJ_ID PROJTEAM_NAME
----------- ---------- ---------- --------------------
          1         10         221 Timetracking
          2         30         221 Timetracking
          4         10         505 Account System
          5         40         505 Account System
          6        102          21 HR Reporting
SQL>
```

Had there been more than one duplicate entry, we would have had to run this **delete** statement over and over until no rows were deleted.

With the preceding concepts mastered, you should be well on your way to finding duplicate data in your tables.

SQL Generating SQL

There is no reason why you cannot get SQL to create another SQL program. Many times there is information in the database that you might want to use within another SQL program. For example, let's say you want to drop all the tables in your Oracle account. Let's take a look at how you might do this using the power of SQL.

First, let's issue an SQL statement of all your current tables within the database:

```
SQL> select table_name from user_tables;
TABLE_NAME
------------------------------
A
B
COMPANY
CUST
EMP

X

Y

7 rows selected
```

Now let's build an SQL program that creates another SQL program. Notice how we disable the headings and set **pagesize** to zero. This ensures that we will have no page breaks in the resulting SQL program.

```
Rem ***
Rem *** countmytables.sql
Rem ***
Set heading off
Set pagesize 0
Set feedback off
Set echo off
Set linesize 80
Spool countall.sql
select 'select count(*) from ' || table_name || ';' from user_tables;
spool off
@countall.sql
```

We spool the results of the first SQL statements into a file named dropall.sql. We then terminate the **spool** command. This closes the file. Now that the file has been closed, we can use the @ to execute the recently created dropall.sql file.

The dropall.sql file that was created looks like this:

```
drop table A;
drop table B;
drop table COMPANY;
drop table CUST;
drop table EMP;
drop table X;
drop table Y;
```

SQL Creating a Data File

Often, you need to write a program to dump the contents of an Oracle table into a flat file that can be read by another program.

In our example, we are going to create a comma-delimited file out of the contents of the NEWHIRE table. It is also a requirement that all non-numeric data be encapsulated in single quotes. To refresh your memory about the NEWHIRE table, let's issue the **describe** command and a **select** of the contents.

```
SQL> descr newhire
 Name                                      Null?    Type
 ----------------------------------------- -------- ------------
 LNAME                                              VARCHAR2(30)
 STATE_CD                                           VARCHAR2(2)
 HIREDATE                                           DATE
 SALARY                                             NUMBER(8,2)
SQL> select * from newhire;
LNAME                            ST HIREDATE    SALARY
-------------------------------- -- --------- ----------
COREY                            MA 01-JAN-01    20000
CALISI                           NJ 10-JUN-01    30000
SMITH                            CA 15-AUG-01    40000
ABBY                             TX 12-DEC-01    50000
```

Putting Single Quotes in the Output Query

Since the output is going to be a flat-file strip that will be read into another program, it's important that we issue a few **set** commands first. The **set heading off** command disables the headings. The **set feedback off** command makes sure there is no record count at the end of the query. The **set trimspool off** command makes sure there are no trailing spaces. The **set echo off** command makes sure we don't see the SQL statement replayed. The **set pagesize 0** command makes sure there are no page breaks in the output. The **spool** command captures the results. Here is the program to capture the NEWHIRE table in a comma-delimited format:

```
SQL> set heading off
SQL> set feedback off
SQL> set trimspool on
SQL> set echo off
SQL> set pagesize 0
SQL> Spool out.dat
SQL> select     ''''||LNAME    ||''''||','
  2             ||''''||STATE_CD||''''||','
  3             ||''''||HIREDATE||''''||','
  4                  ||SALARY
  5*   from newhire
SQL> /
SQL> spool off
```

Notice all the quotes. The single quote means something special to Oracle9*i*: it signifies the start and end of a literal string. You must select four of them together if you want a single quote in your query results. Look at the results:

```
'COREY','MA','01-JAN-01',20000
'CALISI','NJ','10-JUN-01',30000
'SMITH','CA','15-AUG-01',40000
'ABBY','TX','12-DEC-01',50000
```

If you wanted to use double quotes in the output, your SQL statement would look like this:

```
SQL> select     '"'||LNAME    ||'"'||','
  2             ||'"'||STATE_CD||'"'||','
  3             ||'"'||HIREDATE||'"'||','
  4                  ||SALARY
  5*   from newhire
SQL> /
```

Notice how we placed a double quote between two single quotes. You now have all the tools you need to build comma-delimited output files.

Query Within a Query

A very powerful feature in SQL*Plus is to have a query within a query, which is also known as a subquery, or subselect. The format for using a subquery is as follows:

```
(Main query text) where (condition)
          ((sub query text));
```

The best way to understand a subquery is to see it in action. Let's set up a real-world example:

```
SQL> create table employee(
  2    emp_id           integer        not null,
  3      emp_first_name varchar2(20),
  4      emp_last_name  varchar2(30),
  5    dept_id          integer,
  6    constraint pk_employee primary key (emp_id));
Table created.
SQL> create table department (
  2    dept_id        integer  not null,
  3    dept_name    varchar2(20) not null,
  4    constraint pk_department primary key (dept_id));
Table created.
```

Let's now populate the department and employee tables with some data:

```
SQL> --  department table data
SQL> INSERT INTO department (dept_id,dept_name)
  2  VALUES(222,'Human Resources');
1 row created.
SQL> INSERT INTO department (dept_id,dept_name)
  2  VALUES(333,'Marketing');
1 row created.
SQL> INSERT INTO department (dept_id,dept_name)
  2  VALUES(444,'Finance');
1 row created.
SQL> INSERT INTO department (dept_id,dept_name)
  2  VALUES(555,'Sales');
1 row created.
SQL> --  employee table data
SQL> INSERT INTO employee (emp_id,emp_first_name,emp_last_name,dept_id)
  2  VALUES(10,'Lisa','Haley',444)
1 row created.
SQL> INSERT INTO employee (emp_id,emp_first_name,emp_last_name,dept_id)
  2  VALUES(20,'Christopher','Smith',555);
1 row created.
SQL> INSERT INTO employee (emp_id,emp_first_name,emp_last_name,dept_id)
  2  VALUES(30,'Hannah','Lynn',222);
1 row created.
SQL> INSERT INTO employee (emp_id,emp_first_name,emp_last_name,dept_id)
  2  VALUES(40,'Aldo','Castaneda',333);
```

```
1 row created.
SQL> INSERT INTO employee (emp_id,emp_first_name,emp_last_name,dept_id)
  2   VALUES(50,'Joan','Edgecomb',444);
1 row created.
SQL> INSERT INTO employee (emp_id,emp_first_name,emp_last_name,dept_id)
  2   VALUES(60,'Nancy','Golden',444);
1 row created.
SQL> -- Save Data
SQL> COMMIT;
Commit complete.
```

Now let's look at the contents of the tables:

```
SQL> select * from employee;
    EMP_ID EMP_FIRST_NAME        EMP_LAST_NAME                      DEPT_ID
---------- --------------------  --------------------------------  --------
        10 Lisa                  Haley                                  444
        20 Christopher           Smith                                  555
        30 Hannah                Lynn                                   222
        40 Aldo                  Castaneda                              333
        50 Joan                  Edgecomb                               444
        60 Nancy                 Golden                                 444
6 rows selected.
SQL> select * from department;
   DEPT_ID DEPT_NAME
---------- --------------------
       222 Human Resources
       333 Marketing
       444 Finance
       555 Sales
```

Finally, let's find out how to put a subquery to work:

```
SQL> select emp_first_name||' '||emp_last_name as  Finance_Employees
  2    from employee
  3   where dept_id = (select dept_id
  4                      from department
  5                     where dept_name = 'Finance');
FINANCE_EMPLOYEES
------------------------------------------------------
Lisa Haley
Joan Edgecomb
Nancy Golden
```

The Decode Statement

Simply put, the **decode** statement is how you implement **if-then-else** logic in SQL*Plus. The **decode** statement is one of the most useful and most powerful abilities you have in SQL*Plus. Most people shy away from it because, like the concatenation operator, the SQL statements get pretty ugly pretty quickly. But like a small dog, its bark is far worse than its bite. With this in mind, let's examine the **decode** statement:

```
Decode (column_name, comparison, action, comparison, action,. . .
else action)
```

The **decode** statement compares the content of the column_name to each of the comparisons. If they are equal, then **decode** does the action. If none of the comparisons match, then the **else action** is performed.

The best way to understand how this works is to see it in action. Let's build a table called SOURCE_TABLE.

```
SQL> CREATE TABLE SOURCE_TABLE (SOURCE_LETTER  CHAR (1)      NOT NULL);
Table created.
SQL> INSERT INTO source_table VALUES ('1');
1 row created.
SQL> INSERT INTO source_table VALUES ('A');
1 row created.
SQL> INSERT INTO source_table VALUES ('B');
1 row created.
SQL> INSERT INTO source_table VALUES ('C');
1 row created.
SQL> select source_letter from source_table;
S
-
1
A
B
C
```

In this table, we have four entries. Notice the number 1. Let's now build a table called LOOK_UP_CASE.

```
SQL> CREATE TABLE LOOK_UP_CASE (UPPER_LETTER  CHAR (1)NOT NULL,
    2 LOWER_LETTER  CHAR (1) NOT NULL);
Table created.
SQL> INSERT INTO look_up_case ( upper_letter, lower_letter)
```

```
   2    VALUES ('A','a');
1 row created.
SQL> INSERT INTO look_up_case ( upper_letter, lower_letter)
   2    VALUES ('B','b');
1 row created.
SQL> INSERT INTO look_up_case ( upper_letter, lower_letter)
   2    VALUES ('C','c');
1 row created.

SQL> select upper_letter, lower_letter from look_up_case;

UPPER_LETTER LOWER_LETTER
------------ ------------
A            a
B            b
C            c
```

update with decode Statement

Now let's build an **update** statement to compare an old entry to a new entry. In this case, we are changing uppercase to lowercase. But many times, it's changing old code to new code or an old department to a new department.

```
SQL> update source_table
   2  set source_letter =
   3     decode(source_letter,
   4            'A','a',
   5            'B','b',
   6            'C','c',
   7            '*');
4 rows updated.
```

Here are the results of the update:

```
SQL>select source_letter from source_table;

SOURCE_LETTER
------------
*
a
b
c
```

update Using a Subselect

Many times people try to solve the problem of converting from old code to new code by using a subselect, rather than using the **decode** statement. They build an **update** statement that has a subselect look up the new code of each row that is being updated. Let's build a subselect to do what the **decode** program just did:

```
SQL> update source_table
  2  set source_letter =
  3    (select lower_letter
  4     from look_up_case
  5     where look_up_case.upper_letter =
  6              source_table.source_letter);
ERROR at line 1:
ORA-01407: cannot update
("TIMETRACK"."SOURCE_TABLE"."SOURCE_LETTER") to NULL
```

We are sorry to say we learned this lesson the hard way: We were writing a hospital application, in which we were updating millions of rows of data from old code to a new code. After the SQL statement ran for six hours, it bombed. The old code was missing in the lookup table. A subselect has no **if-then-else** feature. That means if the subselect can't find a match, the program halts.

Not only does the **decode** statement have an **if-then-else** clause, it is also very efficient. The **decode** statement gets loaded into memory. The **decode** version of the program ran in under two hours. It may be ugly, but it works well.

Our next chapter discusses the advanced features of PL/SQL. With the release of Oracle 9i, Oracle has integrated the SQL engine with the PL/SQL engine. This means that all the power of SQL is now available when using Oracle's PL/SQL language. Think of PL/SQL as SQL on steroids. Using the advanced features of PL/SQL, you can now create programs that are stored within the database and can be called out to handle whatever special needs you may have. If you think SQL is fast, wait until you see PL/SQL in action.

Chapter 8 Questions

Answers to questions can be found in Appendix A.

I. The dual table has how many rows?

   A. None

   B. One

   C. Two

   D. Three or more

2. The _____ is the concatenation operator.

    A. +

    B. and

    C. ||

    D. –

3. Which of the following provides the **if-then-else** capability of SQL*Plus?

    A. Subselect

    B. decode

    C. where

    D. having

4. Which of the following is not a **group by** function?

    A. max

    B. min

    C. avg

    D. sqrt

CHAPTER
9

More PL/SQL

e have come a long way so far in this book. We have looked at a number of important topics at the introductory level, but now it's time to go a bit deeper. In this chapter, we will take a more detailed look at PL/SQL. Chapter 6 discussed how to create a program using PL/SQL. We looked at its structure, the use of variables, error handling, the SQL in PL/SQL, and some basic debugging. In this chapter, we are going to turn it up a notch. We will discuss some advanced features, such as overloading and user-defined exceptions, as well as several of the built-in programs that Oracle provides with PL/SQL.

With the integration of the PL/SQL engine and the SQL engine in Oracle9i, you no longer need to worry about SQL functions not working in PL/SQL. In addition, PL/SQL runs faster due to this integration. So, now you know PL/SQL has improved over time, and it is also a product that is here to stay. Whenever we ask Oracle senior management about PL/SQL's future, they always laugh. As mentioned in Chapter 6, you can ignore the urban legend that says Oracle will be dropping support for PL/SQL in favor of some other programming language; PL/SQL is here to stay.

The following are the subjects covered in this chapter:

- Overloading and packages

- Advanced error handling

- The cursor variable

- Autonomous transactions

- Invoker rights

- Dynamic SQL

- The utl_file package and other PL/SQL improvements

Terminology

The following terminology will arm you with the technical jargon to get through this chapter.

- *Autonomous transactions* are PL/SQL programs that run independently. For example, a commit issued in a program that was called from another program does not affect the information processing in the calling program.

- *Dynamic SQL* is SQL that is written on-the-fly by the PL/SQL program.

- *Encapsulation* is a mechanism through which data and the program code that manipulates the data are held in a single object.

- *Overloading* is the ability to create multiple versions of one program that are called depending on the parameters sent to the program.

Packages and Program Overloading

The concepts of overloading and encapsulation were introduced with object-oriented programming (OOP). *OOP* allows you to think of everything associated in a program as a unit. This unit is known as an *object*, and objects include tables, programs, and methods for manipulating data. The integration of all of this allows for a modular design of your programming toolbox. A couple of examples of OOP programming languages are Java and C++.

Overloading allows you to create multiple versions of the same program, and the arguments that get passed to the program will determine the version to be run. This is done using packages, or procedures. Packages are stored programs much like stored procedures. In the case of functions, you usually have a number of procedures or functions contained in a single program. A package is made up of two distinct program units: the package and the package body. For a package to function properly, both must exist. The package program will contain all the procedure and function declarations, much like the declaration section of a PL/SQL program. The package body will contain the actual program code. Let's look at an example of how to overload a program:

```
SQL> create or replace package ian_pack1
  2  is
  3          procedure overload1(l_character_val    IN      varchar2);
  4          procedure overload1(l_numeric_val      IN      number);
  5  end;
  6  /
Package created.
SQL>
SQL> create or replace package body ian_pack1 IS
  2  --
  3          procedure overload1 (l_character_val    In      varchar2)
  4          is
  5          begin
  6              dbms_output.put_line ('Character: ' || l_character_val);
  7          end;
  8  --
  9          procedure overload1 (l_numeric_val    In number)
 10          is
 11          begin
```

```
12                        dbms_output.put_line ('Number: ' || l_numeric_val);
13        end;
14   end ian_pack1;
15   /
Package body created.
```

Here we have created a program that will output a value to the session that runs it. The catch is that we can call one program and the program will sense whether it should use the version that was created for a character value or one that is to be used with numeric values. Let's run them and see the results.

```
SQL> set serveroutput on
SQL> execute ian_pack1.overload1('My cat is named Dreidle');
Character: My cat is named Dreidle
PL/SQL procedure successfully completed.
SQL> execute ian_pack1.overload1(123456);
Number: 123456
PL/SQL procedure successfully completed.
```

Notice the way we called a procedure in a package. To call a package, you need to prefix the program with the package name and then follow it with a period (.) and the name of the procedure that you would like to run. In the previous listing, the package and procedure name are highlighted. We overloaded this procedure by calling it on two separate occasions. First, we passed a character string, and the program used the correct procedure in the package. The next time, we called the package using a numeric value of 123456, and the program returned the correct output for a numeric parameter.

> **NOTE**
> *Packages are loaded as a whole into Oracle's
> internal memory. This can provide significant
> performance improvements, especially if you
> use the programs often.*

So, you have seen the structure of packages and how to use overloading; let's move on and look at some additional error handling facilities.

Advanced Error Handling in PL/SQL

We already discussed error handling, called exception handling in PL/SQL, in Chapter 6. We discussed using the exceptions that Oracle provides and also mentioned that you can define your own exceptions. Here, we will show you how to define and use user-defined exceptions. We also introduce you to some special values available during PL/SQL program execution that are useful when you encounter errors in your program code. These special values are handy for debugging your programs, as well as providing feedback to users when something goes wrong during the running of your code.

User-Defined Exceptions

When PL/SQL programs encounter problems or undesirable conditions, an exception is raised during the processing of a program unit. You already know that Oracle9*i* provides exception handling facilities with its software. You can extend the functionality of the Oracle9*i* exception handling facility by defining your own private exceptions, known as *user-defined exceptions*.

NOTE
User-defined exceptions may be raised to handle an error or to handle a condition that may not be seen by Oracle as an error.

In order for a user-defined exception to be valid and to be used properly, you must define three components within your program code:

- Declare the exception.

- Raise the exception during program execution.

- Define the exception handle itself.

This differs from the Oracle-defined exceptions, which may be used within a program without declaring them or even raising an error condition. So, let's see how the three components come together in a program.

```
Declare
    L_counter    number := 0;
    L_name       employee.employee_name%type;
    Cursor get_employee_name is
      Select employee_name
        From employee;
    excep_old_friend          Exception;
    excep_never_met_them      Exception;
Begin
    Open    get_employee_name;
    Fetch   get_employee_name into l_name;
      If l_name = 'JACQUI DEBIQUE' then
          Raise excep_old_friend;
```

```
     Else
          Raise excep_never_met_them;
     End if;
   Close get_employee_name;
Exception
   When excep_old_friend then
          Dbms_output.put_line('I know this person');
   When excep_never_met_them then
           Dbms_output.put_line('I do not know this person');
End;
/
```

As you can see in the preceding program, the definition and use of a user-defined exception is driven by your own needs. For purposes of this example, we selected data from the EMPLOYEE table and created an exception of our own choosing.

There are three components that we need to implement in order to use this exception. First, we declare the exception, by naming it in the declaration section of the program, as we have done here.

```
excep_old_friend          Exception;
excep_never_met_them      Exception;
```

Next, we need to call, or raise, the exception within the program code when something occurs. In our case, this is when we get the name of a friend, or of a stranger. To call a user-defined exception within your program code, you simply use the **raise** command followed by the name of the exception, as in the following code snippet:

```
   Raise excep_old_friend;
```

At this point, we have told Oracle9i that we plan to use an exception (declaration section), we have told Oracle9i that we want to use it (execution section), and now we need to define what the exception is going to do. This is done in the exception section of the program. In our case, we will simply output that we know this person:

```
Exception
      When excep_old_friend then
           Dbms_output.put_line('I know this person');
```

This example has shown you how to set up user-defined exceptions and how to use them. The possibilities for implementation of these exceptions is limited only by your imagination.

Oracle-Supplied Variables for Error Handling

Along with being able to define your own exceptions within your PL/SQL program, you have access to some important variables that Oracle9i provides you for this purpose. These variables, known as pseudocolumns, are available in many different forms depending on where you are in your program. A pseudocolumn may be used in a **select** statement or during the processing of data. Some examples of pseudo-columns include

- System data (sysdate)
- Row number (rownum)
- Oracle error number (sqlcode)
- Oracle error message (sqlerrm)

We will only look at the last two because these values are often used in exception handling. They provide access to the Oracle9*i* error number and message, and therefore allow you to write programs that always end successfully, even if they encounter an error. Let's look at the same program we have been using as an example, except we will add another exception handle for any error that may occur. We do this by adding the **when others** exception.

```
Declare
    L_counter          number := 0;
    L_name employee    employee_name%type;
    Cursor get_employee_name is
        Select employee_name
          From employee;
excep_old_friend       Exception;
excep_never_met_them   Exception;
Begin
    Open  get_employee_name;
    Fetch get_employee_name into l_name;
    If l_name = 'JACQUI DEBIQUE' then
      Raise excep_old_friend;
    Else
      Raise excep_never_met_them;
    End if;
    Close get_employee_name;
Exception
  When excep_old_friend then
    Dbms_output.put_line('I know this person');
  When    excep_never_met_them then
    Dbms_output.put_line('I do not know this person');
  When others then
    Dbms_output.put_line('Houston we have a problem . . . Number: ' ||
                      sqlcode);
    Dbms_output.put_line('The message is: '|| sqlerrm);
End;
/
```

The **when others** exception can be used to handle any error that may occur for which no other exception has been defined. It must also be the last exception in your exception section, since Oracle9i stops processing when it encounters an exception that meets the criteria. Therefore, if this exception is first, Oracle will stop once it hits the **when others** condition.

In our example, we have used the pseudocolumns, **sqlcode** and **sqlerrm**. You should always use these in your program code to ensure that all your PL/SQL programs complete in a manageable way. Another technique that we use puts these values into variables that we return to the calling program.

Autonomous Transactions

When Oracle released Oracle8*i*, it provided a valuable addition—the ability to have two PL/SQL programs work together, but to commit data to the database independently. In earlier versions of the Oracle database, commits in programs called from one another were linked. This means that it did not matter which program issued a **commit** statement, since data affected in the database by either program would be committed into the database. To solve this problem, Oracle provided autonomous transactions. By using this facility, you can make your program independent, so that when you **commit** or **rollback** data in one program it will not affect any other data that may have been created outside the program.

In Oracle9*i*, you can define library additions to your programs. These libraries are called *pragmas*, which are directives to the compiler to act in a certain way. Let's look at an example of using a pragma that we will call **autonomous_transaction**. First, we will create a procedure that inserts data into the EMPLOYEE table:

```
SQL> create procedure insert_employee
  2  (in_id      in      number,
  3   in_name    in      employee.emp_name%TYPE,
  4   in_sal     in      employee.salary%TYPE,
  5   in_prov    in      employee.province%TYPE)
  6  IS
  7   PRAGMA AUTONOMOUS_TRANSACTION;
  8  BEGIN
  9   insert into employee
 10   values
 11   (in_id, in_name, in_sal, in_prov);
 12   commit;
 13  END;
 14  /
Procedure created.
```

Notice line 7. With this simple addition to the program code, we achieve PL/SQL program independence. Let's look at how this program can now be used:

```
SQL> begin
  2    insert into employee
  3    values
  4    (100, 'HARRISON ASTROFF', 10000, 'ONTARIO');
  5
  6    insert_employee
  7    (101,'JILLIAN ABRAMSON', 10000, 'CALIFORNIA');
  8    rollback;
  9  end;
 10  /
PL/SQL procedure successfully completed.
```

In this short program, we have a standard **insert** command to allow for the addition of an employee, Mr. Astroff. In the next command, we call our autonomous transaction program, **insert_employee**. Recall that this program executes a commit. Before autonomous transactions, both records would have been committed to the database. In this case, we want to roll back the first insert. Let's look at what we have in our database:

```
SQL> run
  1  select * from employee
  2* where emp_id >= 100
    EMP_ID EMP_NAME                              SALARY PROVINCE
---------- ------------------------------   ---------- ---------------
       101 JILLIAN ABRAMSON                    10000 CALIFORNIA
```

You can see that only the data that went through the autonomous transaction in our **insert_employee** stored procedure has been committed to the database; the other record has been rolled back by the program.

PL/SQL Security with Invoker Rights

When you create tables and other objects in the database, you grant users access to these objects. By granting privileges, like the ability to **insert**, **update**, or **delete** data, you control the way users access data. But you can take it one step further and use PL/SQL and invoker rights to control the privileges you grant to users. *Invoker rights* means that the user who creates the stored procedure is the only one with rights to a table affected by the procedure. For example, if you create a procedure that updates data in a table, users can run this procedure to perform the update, but they have not been granted the update privilege. The result is that the only way users will be able to update data in this table is by using this program.

With invoker rights, you can control the methods that are being used to manipulate the data in your database, without having to worry that your users will find a backdoor through which they can change data without any kind of control on your part.

Oracle-Supplied Packages

If you have not already installed Oracle9i, you will learn that it does a lot of work when it configures your database. During this configuration Oracle9i creates database files, control files, and other files that it needs in order to run properly. After the files are created and configured, Oracle will then create objects in the database that are needed to run the database. It builds the foundation of the database by creating some tables. Some of these tables are familiar, such as USER_TABLES, while others, such as X$BH, may be strange to you. Once Oracle9i has created its foundation, it then moves on and creates a number of special programs that run things behind the scenes. These are the stored procedures, packages, and functions that are used every day to perform specific tasks. For some useful information and to see what these packages look like, you can view the source code in the $ORACLE_HOME/rdbms/admin directory on UNIX.

NOTE

You should never change any of the programs that Oracle provides.

This part of the chapter introduces you to some of Oracle9i's built-in packages. Since Oracle supplies over 300 packages with Oracle9i, we will only discuss a few of our favorites that we use in conjunction with PL/SQL.

utl_file Package

When Oracle introduced PL/SQL, it provided a versatile new programming language; but what this programming language did not provide was the ability to interact with the operating system in a fruitful manner. With the introduction of the utl_file package, you can now read and write files that are held on the operating system. We use it to extract data from our database, as well as to read data into it. In Oracle9i, external tables have been added. These are basically data files that users will see as Oracle tables.

If you wish to use utl_file, you will need to do some work in your INIT.ora file. In the **utl_file_dir** parameter, you define the directories that your utl_file users will have access to. It is important that you explicitly define the directories to which users will have read and write access, since you are opening your system to users who may not have had access to the operating system before. The following is an example of the line that you may need to add to your INIT.ora file:

 `utl_file_dir = /work02/utl_file/rawdata, /work03/utl_file/errorlogs`

NOTE
You can also specify each directory in a separate
utl_file_dir *line. It's the only parameter we know of*
in the INIT.ora that will recognize multiple entries.

There are a number of different components that go along with the utl_file package. These components let you open files, read files, write files, and close files. The general process for using utl_file is as follows:

1. Declare a file handle in your declaration section.

2. Open the file in either read, write, or append mode.

3. Read or write to file.

4. Close your file.

5. Handle any errors in your exception section.

Let's look at how you perform each of these tasks.

When you first want to use utl_file, you need to declare a file handle in your declaration section. A *file handle* is a logical pointer that will hold the information about the file you are about to access, as well as the access method that you will define. The following is the line that you will add to your declaration section:

`l_file_handle UTL_FILE.FILE_TYPE; -- file handle for OS flat file`

Here we have declared a file handle as a variable name **l_file_handle** and defined it as a **utl_file.file_type**.

Next, you need to start writing the meat of your program. In the execution section, open your data file in the access mode that is appropriate to the task at hand. The modes are write (w), read (r), or append (a). The main difference between writing a file or appending to a file is that *append* will add to an existing file, whereas *write* will start a new file and erase anything that may already exist in the database.

NOTE
You may open as many as 50 files simultaneously.

To open a file, you use the **utl_file.fopen** package, for example,

```
-- Open file to write into  and get its file_handle
file_handle := UTL_FILE.FOPEN(in_dir_name, in_file_name,'R');
```

Here, we are opening a file for read. This command requires three parameters: the directory in which your file resides, the name of the data file, and the access mode. You may pass these by reference as we have done here. We prefer to do it this way because it makes our programs more flexible.

Finally, you perform your data reads. When utl_file reads from a file, it only reads one line at a time; so if you want to read more than one line in a file, you will need to work with the looping, as discussed in Chapter 6. The **loop**, together with the **utl_file.get_line** package, will loop through data in a file. The following shows how this may be performed:

```
LOOP
      utl_file.get_line (file_handle, l_text);
       l_pos           := instr(l_text,l_delimit);
       l_start_date    := substr(l_text,1,10);
       l_start_time    := substr(l_text,11,6););
       l_kb_read       := substr(l_text,17,10););
       l_web_page_name:= substr(l_text,27,1000);
                         insert into user_access_stats
                         (start_date, start_time, Kbytes_read, web_page)
                         values
                         (start_date, start_time, Kbytes_read, web_page);
END LOOP;
```

This program segment shows a simple loop that can be used to read the data from the open file. We read the individual lines with the **utl_file.get_line** into a variable named **l_text**. The arguments used here are the file handle that we received when we opened the file and the variable that holds the data to be parsed. The size of this variable should be defined as the length of the record being read, up to a size of 32,767 bytes, which is the limit set by the utl_file package. Once we have read the record, we then need to parse the text into its data components and place it into the variables that will be used to insert it into the table.

When we have read the entire data file and we are done, we will close the data file using the **utl_file.close** command. It is important to ensure that you close your files; otherwise, Oracle9*i* may continue to hold a lock on the file. So, just as a matter of practice, make sure that you close your files in your programs. To close a file, issue the following command:

```
UTL_FILE.FCLOSE(file_handle);
```

The close command, **utl_fclose**, requires only a single argument, the file handle variable. This command will then close your file in a proper manner.

Let's look at how a whole program comes together:

```
CREATE OR REPLACE PROCEDURE dw_load_incoming_stats
(in_file_name       varchar2,
 in_file_dir        varchar2,
 in_source_system varchar2)
IS
        file_handle UTL_FILE.FILE_TYPE; -- file handle of OS flat file
        l_text              varchar2(1000);
        l_start_date        varchar2(10);
        l_start_time        varchar2(6);
        l_kb_read           number;
        l_web_page_name varchar2(1000);
BEGIN
          -- Open file to write into  and get its file_handle
          file_handle := UTL_FILE.FOPEN('BCANDID',in_file_name,'R');

  BEGIN
    LOOP
          utl_file.get_line (file_handle, l_text);
          l_start_date          := substr(l_text,1,10);
          l_start_time          := substr(l_text,11,6););
          l_kb_read             := substr(l_text,17,10););
          l_web_page_name       := substr(l_text,27,1000);
                        insert into user_access_stats
                        (start_date, start_time, Kbytes_read, web_page)
                        values
                        (l_start_date, l_start_time, l_Kb_read, l_web_page_name);
                    commit;
        END LOOP;
    EXCEPTION
          WHEN NO_DATA_FOUND THEN
                null;   -- Do not worry about it, there is no more data
    END;
          UTL_FILE.FCLOSE(file_handle);   -- close the data file
        EXCEPTION
          WHEN NO_DATA_FOUND THEN
            DBMS_OUTPUT.PUT_LINE('no_data_found');
            UTL_FILE.FCLOSE(file_handle);
          WHEN UTL_FILE.INVALID_PATH THEN
```

```
            DBMS_OUTPUT.PUT_LINE('UTL_FILE.INVALID_PATH');
            UTL_FILE.FCLOSE(file_handle);
        WHEN UTL_FILE.READ_ERROR THEN
            DBMS_OUTPUT.PUT_LINE(' UTL_FILE.READ_ERROR');
            UTL_FILE.FCLOSE(file_handle);
        WHEN OTHERS THEN
            DBMS_OUTPUT.PUT_LINE('Error'||SQLERRM||'.');
            UTL_FILE.FCLOSE(file_handle);
END;
/
```

As you look closely at the listing, notice that we have added an exception section
to the program. The utl_file package has a number of special exceptions that may be
used to handle the unique problems that are associated with it. These include not being
able to open a file, having an invalid path, and others.

This should help you get started using the excellent utl_file package included with
Oracle. It is one that you should take the time to learn because it will open a whole
new world to your database—the operating system.

Dynamic SQL

You write PL/SQL programs so that they perform a certain activity on a certain table
and on a particular column, and complete a defined task. But some programs may
need to perform tasks that will only become known at the time the program is run—
at runtime. In cases like these, you need to use dynamic SQL. Oracle9i supplies two
options to achieve this goal. The first is a package called dbms_sql that allows you
to create these dynamic commands. The other is native dynamic SQL, which allows
you to achieve the same goal in a simpler format.

In programs that use dynamic SQL, these dynamic statements are stored in
character variables. These strings contain the valid SQL statements that you create
and then run. Starting with Oracle8i, native dynamic SQL became available, which
reduces some coding that you need to do. We will contrast the two methods of
performing dynamic SQL (dbms_sql versus native dynamic SQL), starting with the
dbms_sql package.

Dynamic SQL with the dbms_sql Package

The dbms_sql package is the original version of dynamic SQL that Oracle provided
when it introduced this feature into the database. It allows very tight control over
how you build, bind, and run SQL statements within PL/SQL.

We will start with a program that inserts data into the SALES_TRANSACTION table.
We create the program just like any other stored procedure. You may use these methods
in any type of PL/SQL program. We then need to cover the steps in the following
list to create a program that will dynamically create SQL, load in variables, and
run the statement.

- Define the SQL statement by placing it in a character string variable.

- Prepare memory to receive the statement by using the **open_cursor** command.

- Make sure that Oracle can run the command by parsing the statement with the **parse** command.

- If any variables need to be used in the command, bind them together with the statement using the **bind variable** command. This may not be necessary if you do not have any variables in your SQL statement.

- Run the statement using the **execute** command.

- Like the good programmers we are, tell Oracle it may free up the memory and close the statement.

As you see, the steps involved in using dynamic SQL are not trivial. You will find that although you think that your program will work, since it compiles, it may not work when you run SQL; so when you use dynamic SQL, you may have to debug your programs twice. Let's look at a sample dynamic SQL program:

```
CREATE OR REPLACE PROCEDURE insert_salestrans_dbmssql
(in_sales_date      date,
 in_store_id        number,
 in_sales_amt       number)
IS
    l_handle          INTEGER;
    l_sql_stmt        VARCHAR2(200);
    l_rows_processed BINARY_INTEGER;
BEGIN
    l_sql_stmt := 'INSERT INTO SALES_TRANSACTION VALUES
                 (:sales_date, :store_id, :sales_amt);';
    -- Open the SQL cursor handle
    l_handle := dbms_sql.open_cursor;
    -- Parse the SQL statement
    dbms_sql.parse(l_handle, l_sql_stmt, dbms_sql.native);
    -- Bind the variables with the SQL statement
    dbms_sql.bind_variable(l_handle, ':sales_date', in_sales_date);
    dbms_sql.bind_variable(l_handle, ':store_id ', in_store_id);
    dbms_sql.bind_variable(l_handle, ':sales_amt ', in_sales_amt);
     -- execute the SQL statement
     l_rows_processed := dbms_sql.execute(l_handle);
     -- close cursor (OF COURSE!)
     dbms_sql.close_cursor(l_handle);
END;
/
```

So there you have it—a program that may change each and every time you run it. That is the beauty of dynamic SQL. With it you can now have your SQL statements driven by parameters or data within your data, instead of hard coding each and every situation. Now let's move on to native dynamic SQL, Oracle8i and Oracle9i's addition to our dynamic world.

Native Dynamic SQL

The introduction of native dynamic SQL simplified the use of dynamic SQL. Using the old method, it took approximately 20 lines of program code (32 lines Canadian) to achieve our goal of inserting data into our table. We are going to perform the same task, except this time we will do it in 13 lines (the SQL portion only accounting for two of those lines). This is a significant cost savings in terms of time, typing, and complexity.

The steps that you need to follow with dynamic SQL are straightforward:

- Define the SQL statement.

- Parse, load your variables, and run the program in a single step, using the command **execute immediate**.

It almost seems too easy. Let's look at the program using dynamic SQL:

```
CREATE OR REPLACE PROCEDURE insert_salestrans_native
(in_sales_date      date,
 in_store_id        number,
 in_sales_amt       number)
IS
l_sql_stmt          VARCHAR2(200);
BEGIN
l_sql_stmt:= 'INSERT INTO sales_transactions values
            (:sales_date, :store_id, : sales_amt)';
EXECUTE IMMEDIATE l_sql_stmt
            USING in_sales_date, in_store_id, in_sales_amt;
END;
/
```

This uncomplicated method to create dynamic SQL statements within Oracle should now be part of your Oracle toolkit. You can drive SQL from within your database by creating programs that are built generically, but may then morph into something very specific.

We have come a long way in our PL/SQL journey. The subjects covered in Chapter 6 and the material covered in this chapter contain the methods and techniques that we use 95 percent of the time when we program. Take the time to play with PL/SQL. Whether you are a DBA or a developer, it is one programming language that will add value to your Oracle life. We can now move on and delve more deeply into the Oracle9*i* database from an administrative perspective. In the next chapter, we will help you qualify for your Ph.D. in Oracle database administration.

Chapter 9 Questions

Answers to questions can be found in Appendix A.

1. What is the name of Pink Floyd's first album?

  A. *The Wall*

  B. *Dark Side of the Moon*

  C. *The Piper at the Gates of Dawn*

  D. *Larry Ellison Sings the Blues*

2. What method is used to make a PL/SQL stored procedure independent?

  A. Independent transactions

  B. Autonomous blocks

  C. Integrated blocks

  D. This feature is not currently supported.

3. Name the pseudocolumn that you use to extract the Oracle error number from within a PL/SQL program.

  A. **errnum**

  B. **sqlerrm**

  C. **ohmygodsomethingiswrong**

  D. **sqlcode**

4. Packages may contain many stored procedures.

  A. True

  B. False

5. When using utl_file in Oracle9*i*, how many files may be opened simultaneously?

   A. 10

   B. 25

   C. 50

   D. 100

6. When using dynamic SQL, which command runs the program?

   A. execute immediate

   B. run

   C. execute

   D. start

CHAPTER
10

More DBA

his chapter will round out the material we covered in Chapter 7. As you dive into Oracle9i DBA land, you will encounter a very complex product, fraught with technical intricacies every which way you turn. We are going to have a look at two main items in this chapter—backup and recovery. As you hone your skills with the Oracle9i DBA tasks, these two areas will command most of your attention. This chapter, even though it covers more advanced DBA material, can be read by anyone looking for startup information on backup and recovery issues. This chapter will look at the following material:

- Backup and recovery concepts
- Export
  - The role it plays in backup
  - Important parameters
  - Modes of operation
  - Types
- Import
  - The role it plays in recovery
  - Important parameters
  - Modes of operation and types
- Media recovery features
- Writing image backups
- Recovery using image backups

Terminology

Let's get started with the technical jargon you will need to make it through this chapter.

- The assortment of database files and associated system support files that support the Oracle9i database are referred to as the *infrastructure*.
- An *extent* is a chunk of space allocated by Oracle9i when additional disk space is required for objects.
- The act of copying Oracle9i data to a secondary location is called *backup*. Although backups are classically written to tape or some other form of offline storage, they are often written to alternate locations on disk.

■ The act of copying data from a backup location and rebuilding all or portions of an Oracle9*i* database is called *recovery*.

■ The rebuilding of all or part of an Oracle9*i* information repository is sometimes referred to as *reinstantiation*.

Backup and Recovery

These two items—backup and recovery—are very close companions. It almost seems like one cannot exist without the other. This is close to the truth. In the next few sections, we are going to have a look at some issues related to backup and recovery, and touch on some Oracle9*i* specifics we cover later in the chapter. Backup is a very big topic, with complete books dedicated to the subject. Suffice it to say, the basics are all you need to leverage the backup features of Oracle9*i*.

Export

Oracle DBAs have been using export since the dawn of relational database technology. Affectionately called *exp*, the program makes a binary copy of your data, only readable by its sister program import, or *imp*. The exp program is called from the command line and passed an assortment of parameters and parameter values. These values tell export what data and data definitions you wish to extract and where you would like the export file deposited.

Export's Role in Backups

Seasoned and beginner DBAs alike incorporate export into almost all their backup routines. Leveraging the features embedded in export, its output file can be read by import to do the following:

■ Write an output file that contains all the SQL statements required to re-create the infrastructure that supports the Oracle9*i* database. A small sample of this type of SQL is shown in the next listing.

```
CREATE TABLESPACE "TOOLS" DATAFILE . . .
CREATE USER "HAROLD" IDENTIFIED BY . . .
CREATE ROLLBACK SEGMENT "RBS01" TABLESPACE . . .
```

■ Generate a series of SQL statements that can be run to create a user's tables, indexes, and constraints.

■ Make a copy of one user's data in another user's schema.

■ Move data from one server to another.

■ Populate a brand-new database after successfully running a **create database** command.

Let's get started by looking at the parameters or keywords used to influence the operation of export.

NOTE
Most of you will already be familiar with entering parameters and parameter values when invoking programs, especially if you remember the MS-DOS–based days.

Parameters Used with Export

The export task is defined by the parameters and values entered as export is invoked. Online help is available by entering the command **exp help=y**, whose output is shown next. Table 10-1 discusses the highlighted parameters.

NOTE
Export is a sophisticated and powerful backup utility; we can only scratch the surface in this brief exposé.

```
Export: Release 9.0.1.0.0 - Production on Thu Sep 13 21:55:49 2003
(c) Copyright 2001 Oracle Corporation.  All rights reserved.

You can let Export prompt you for parameters by entering the EXP
command followed by your username/password:

     Example: EXP SCOTT/TIGER

Or, you can control how Export runs by entering the EXP command followed
by various arguments. To specify parameters, you use keywords:

     Format:  EXP KEYWORD=value or KEYWORD=(value1,value2,...,valueN)
     Example: EXP SCOTT/TIGER GRANTS=Y TABLES=(EMP,DEPT,MGR)
           or TABLES=(T1:P1,T1:P2), if T1 is partitioned table

USERID must be the first parameter on the command line.

Keyword     Description (Default)      Keyword      Description (Default)
----------------------------------------------------------------------
USERID      username/password          FULL         export entire file (N)
```

BUFFER	size of data buffer	**OWNER**	list of owner usernames
FILE	output files (EXPDAT.DMP)	**TABLES**	list of table names
COMPRESS	import into one extent (Y)	RECORDLENGTH	length of IO record
GRANTS	export grants (Y)	INCTYPE	incremental export type
INDEXES	export indexes (Y)	RECORD	track incr. export (Y)
DIRECT	direct path (N)	TRIGGERS	export triggers (Y)
LOG	log file of screen output	STATISTICS	analyze objects (ESTIMATE)
ROWS	export data rows (Y)	**PARFILE**	parameter filename
CONSISTENT	cross-table consistency	CONSTRAINTS	export constraints (Y)

```
FEEDBACK              display progress every x rows (0)
FILESIZE              maximum size of each dump file
FLASHBACK_SCN         SCN used to set session snapshot back to
FLASHBACK_TIME        time used to get the SCN closest to the specified time
QUERY                 select clause used to export a subset of a table
RESUMABLE             suspend when a space related error is encountered(N)
RESUMABLE_NAME        text string used to identify resumable statement
RESUMABLE_TIMEOUT     wait time for RESUMABLE
TTS_FULL_CHECK        perform full or partial dependency check for TTS
VOLSIZE               number of bytes to write to each tape volume
TABLESPACES           list of tablespaces to export
TRANSPORT_TABLESPACE export transportable tablespace metadata (N)
TEMPLATE template name which invokes iAS mode export

Export terminated successfully without warnings.
```

Export Modes of Operation

Three modes can be used to call export:

- **Interactive mode**   After the **EXP** command, you enter a dialogue that requests session information and the details about the export method you wish to initiate.

- **Command-line mode**   You pass a number of parameters and values to **exp** as it is invoked.

- **Parameter-file mode**   You call **exp** with the **parfile=** parameter, the object of which is the name of a file that has keywords and parameter values for the session.

Let's spend a few minutes on a brief example of each mode.

Interactive Mode

The interactive mode is where you will end up "cutting your teeth" with export. The following listing shows an export session invoked in interactive mode, with discussion in Table 10-2. (The line numbers in the listing are for reference purposes only.)

Parameter	Meaning	Notes
Userid	The username and password under the auspices of which the export session will be run.	With appropriate privileges, some Oracle9*i* users can export data that they do not own.
Buffer	The chunk of memory to be allocated for the export session.	An integer value representing the buffer size is coded here—values as high as 5000000 or more are common.
File	The operating system (O/S) file that is the target of the export.	This name must conform to O/S rules.
Log	The name of the file to which a record of the export session is to be written.	
Owner	A list of one or more owners whose data is to be written to the export file.	If more than one owner is mentioned, names are separated by commas and the whole list is bounded by parentheses, as in **(allan,jean,bobday)**.
Tables	A list of tables that will be included in the export file.	If tables do not belong to the userid running the export session, the table names must be prefixed by the owner's name, as in **tables=(fred.blue,molly.yellow)**.
Parfile	The name of a parameter file that contains keywords and values as if they were passed to export on the command line.	
Filesize	The number of bytes to write to an export file when you want to create a series of export files that logically come together when read by import.	Oracle9*i* will do some rounding of the file size value entered.

TABLE 10-1.   *Common Parameters for Export*

NOTE
This listing is a sample of one export session. The response you give to each question has an effect on the nature of the export, as well as the questions that follow. For example, if we were to choose (1)E(ntire Database) rather than (2)U(sers), there would be no prompt for the user(s) to be exported.

```
 1  Export: Release 9.0.1.0.0 - Production on Sat Sep 15 13:49:35 2005
 2  (c) Copyright 2001 Oracle Corporation.  All rights reserved.
 3  Username: exporter/exporter
 4  Connected to: Oracle9i Enterprise Edition Release 9.0.1.0.0 - Production
 5  With the Partitioning option
 6  JServer Release 9.0.1.0.0 - Production
 7  Enter array fetch buffer size: 4096 > 1000000
 8  Export file: expdat.dmp > ouser
 9  (1)E(ntire database), (2)U(sers), or (3)T(ables): (2)U >
10  Export grants (yes/no): yes >
11  Export table data (yes/no): yes >
12  Compress extents (yes/no): yes >
13  Export done in US7ASCII character set and AL16UTF16 NCHAR character set
14  About to export specified users ...
15  User to be exported: (RETURN to quit) > oracle
16  User to be exported: (RETURN to quit) >
17  . exporting pre-schema procedural objects and actions
18  . exporting foreign function library names for user ORACLE
19  . exporting object type definitions for user ORACLE
20  About to export ORACLE's objects . . .
21  . exporting database links
22  . exporting sequence numbers
23  . exporting cluster definitions
24  . about to export ORACLE's tables via Conventional Path . . .
25  . . exporting table                ADDRESS
26  . . exporting partition            ADD_P01            67893 rows exported
27  . . exporting partition            ADD_P02            83938 rows exported
28  . . exporting partition            ADD_P03            48484 rows exported
29  . . exporting partition            ADD_P04            23323 rows exported
30  . . exporting partition            ADD_P05            32343 rows exported
31  . . exporting partition            ADD_P06            43443 rows exported
32  . . exporting table                EXTRA             434433 rows exported
33  . . exporting table                MAILING
34  . . exporting partition            MAILING_P02        54430 rows exported
35  . . exporting partition            MAILING_P03        90393 rows exported
36  . . exporting partition            MAILING_P04        32323 rows exported
37  . . exporting partition            MAILING_P05        36363 rows exported
38  . . exporting partition            MAILING_P06        45455 rows exported
39  . . exporting partition            MAILING_PMAX       67677 rows exported
40  . . exporting table                SALES
41  . . exporting composite partition  SALES_Q1_2001
42  . . exporting subpartition           SYS_SUBP17      543434 rows exported
```

```
43 . . exporting composite partition SALES_Q2_2001
44 . . exporting subpartition         SYS_SUBP18    454543 rows exported
45 . . exporting composite partition SALES_Q3_2001
46 . . exporting subpartition         SYS_SUBP19    334444 rows exported
47 . . exporting composite partition SALES_Q4_2001
48 . . exporting subpartition         SYS_SUBP20    333339 rows exported
49 . . exporting composite partition SALES_Q1_2002
50 . . exporting subpartition         SYS_SUBP21    545455 rows exported
51 . . exporting subpartition         SYS_SUBP22    435444 rows exported
52 . . exporting subpartition         SYS_SUBP23    234234 rows exported
53 . . exporting table                INVDET       1122112 rows exported
54 . exporting synonyms
55 . exporting views
56 . exporting stored procedures
57 . exporting operators
58 . exporting referential integrity constraints
59 . exporting triggers
60 . exporting indextypes
61 . exporting bitmap, functional and extensible indexes
62 . exporting posttables actions
63 . exporting materialized views
64 . exporting snapshot logs
65 . exporting job queues
66 . exporting refresh groups and children
67 . exporting dimensions
68 . exporting post-schema procedural objects and actions
69 . exporting statistics
70 Export terminated successfully without warnings.
```

Line(s)	Details
2	The familiar prompt for username and password. They can, as always, be entered on the same line separated by the /.
7	This buffer is an amount of memory allocated for writing information to the export file. We recommend using values in the neighborhood of at least 1000000 or more.
8	The name of the file to be created by export. It will be suffixed by the extension .dmp unless you specify something else.
9	This response defines the method—user, table, or full—to use for this export session. These three methods are discussed in an upcoming section of this chapter. We simply accepted the suggested default since we wanted to do a user-based export.

TABLE 10-2. *Details about the Export Session*

Line(s)	Details
10–12	These three lines terminate with export's suggested response (all **yes**). Any time you wish to accept the question's default answer, simply press ENTER.
12	Answering **yes** to this prompt instructs Oracle9*i* to write an SQL statement to the export file, which allows each table to be created with all its allocated space in one extent. Suppose a table has three extents allocated, sized at 32,768,000, 32,768,000, and 65,536,000 bytes, respectively. The **yes** value for this prompt will cause the initial amount of space requested for this table as its creation statement is written to the export file to be 131,072,000, or the sum of all three current extent sizes.
15–16	This is where the users to be exported are listed. We entered the username **oracle** and then, as suggested by the subsequent prompt, pressed ENTER alone to indicate that there were no more users to include.
17–69	This output describes the progress of the export session, displaying useful information such as row count, that can be used later to verify the integrity of an import run using this export file as input.
70	This trailer sums up the success or failure of the export session. Sometimes we end up looking at this line to assess the outcome of an export job using a command similar to **tail –1 ouser.log** in UNIX, looking for the text "without warnings."

TABLE 10-2.   *Details about the Export Session* (continued)

Command-Line Mode

This mode is similar to the interactive approach, but you pass parameters and parameter values to export as it is invoked. A sample of this is shown next, with (. . .) representing pieces of the listing that have been cut.

```
/d0/oraclehome/product/oracle9.0.1/dbs> exp userid=exporter/exporter \
 full=y rows=n buffer=1000000
Export: Release 9.0.1.0.0 - Production on Sat Sep 15 14:28:54 2004
(c) Copyright 2001 Oracle Corporation.  All rights reserved.
Connected to: Oracle9i Enterprise Edition Release 9.0.1.0.0 - Production
With the Partitioning option
JServer Release 9.0.1.0.0 - Production
Export done in US7ASCII character set and AL16UTF16 NCHAR character set
Note: table data (rows) will not be exported
About to export the entire database . . .
. exporting tablespace definitions
. exporting profiles
```

```
. exporting user definitions
. exporting cluster definitions
. . .
. about to export SYSTEM's tables via Conventional Path . . .
. . exporting table                  AQ$_INTERNET_AGENTS
. . .
. . exporting table             REPCAT$_PRIORITY_GROUP
. . exporting table           SQLPLUS_PRODUCT_PROFILE
. about to export ORACLE's tables via Conventional Path . . .
. . exporting table                         ADDRESS
. . .
. . exporting table                           SALES
. about to export IAN's tables via Conventional Path . . .
. . exporting table                        EMPLOYEE
. . exporting table                     FAMILY_INFO
. . exporting table           HIGH_PRICED_EMPLOYEE
. . exporting table                    RELATIONS_EXT
. . exporting table                     SUBSCRIBERS
. about to export SAMPLE's tables via Conventional Path . . .
. exporting synonyms
. exporting views
. . .
. exporting statistics
Export terminated successfully without warnings.
```

Parameter-File Mode

The secret to this mode is the single keyword parameter **parfile=**. The object of this **parfile=** is a file name that contains the parameters and values that control the export session to be invoked. The next listing shows the contents of a parameter file that could have been used to accomplish what we did in the previous section on the command-line approach.

```
/d0/oraclehome/product/oracle9.0.1/dbs> cat pfmode.parfile
userid=exporter/exporter
full=y
rows=n
buffer=1000000
/d0/oraclehome/product/oracle9.0.1/dbs>
```

Time to look at the three types of exports—full, user, and table.

Types of Exports

Not too far into Oracle9*i* land, you will find yourself using the three types of exports as part of your backup strategy. Essentially, there are similarities but also significant differences between these three types of exports. They are summarized in Table 10-3.

As you ingest this material on export, we hope it will whet your appetite and send you off to become more familiar with its power and usage. It has often been said that export and import are a DBA's best friends. Now let's move on and look at import.

Import

The import utility, called with the command **imp**, reads the files created by export and, based on the instructions you give, puts data and data definitions into the Oracle9*i* database. Attentive DBAs test the integrity of their export files using import. A successful run of an import session is the only way to check the usability of export files.

Export Type	What It Includes	Usage Notes
Full	All data, data definitions, and stored objects required to rebuild the database, except user SYS. The SYS schema is set up when the **create database** script completes, and subsequent work is done when the assortment of administration scripts are run afterward.	Code the parameter and value **full=y**.
User	Data, data definitions, and stored objects belonging to the one or more users whose names follow the **owner=** parameter.	A list of users separated by commas and bound by parentheses.
Table	Data and data definitions, but no stored objects, for user running the export or the schema whose tables are mentioned with the **tables=** parameter.	The table list is separated by commas and bound by parentheses.

TABLE 10-3. *Export Types*

Import's Role in Recovery

Import is a chameleon—it changes to suit its role in the recovery arena. Besides the jobs import can do as mentioned earlier in this chapter, import can be used to

- Restore a copy of an object as it existed at the time an export file was written. This may prove extremely helpful if a table is dropped in error, or an erroneous **update** statement changes the column values of a table by mistake.

- Assist the retrieval of some rows from a table that may have been deleted due to a programming error. When this is necessary, you import a copy of the affected table into another schema, and then get the missing rows into the real table via an **insert into . . . select * from . . .** SQL statement.

- Move data from an Oracle9i database running under one operating system to another hardware platform. It is not uncommon to move a database from Windows 2000 to Linux. Import allows this to be carried out as painlessly as possible.

Import uses mostly the same parameters as export. Let's look at the online output for import, and then discuss a few parameters specific to import.

Parameters Used with Import

The next listing shows the online help of which we speak—parameters shown in bold will be discussed in Table 10-4.

NOTE

A complete discussion of the following output would be beyond the scope of this introduction to import. We will highlight the parameters that account for the major differences between export and import.

```
Import: Release 9.0.1.0.0 - Production on Sat Sep 15 15:41:19 2006
(c) Copyright 2001 Oracle Corporation.  All rights reserved.
You can let Import prompt you for parameters by entering the IMP
command followed by your username/password:
     Example: IMP SCOTT/TIGER
Or, you can control how Import runs by entering the IMP command followed
by various arguments. To specify parameters, you use keywords:
     Format:  IMP KEYWORD=value or KEYWORD=(value1,value2,. . . .,valueN)
```

```
       Example: IMP SCOTT/TIGER IGNORE=Y TABLES=(EMP,DEPT) FULL=N
                 or TABLES=(T1:P1,T1:P2), if T1 is partitioned table
USERID must be the first parameter on the command line.
Keyword  Description (Default)          Keyword       Description (Default)
------------------------------------------------------------------------
USERID    username/password             FULL          import entire file (N)
BUFFER    size of data buffer           FROMUSER      list of owner usernames
FILE      input files (EXPDAT.DMP)      TOUSER        list of usernames
SHOW      just list file contents (N)   TABLES        list of table names
IGNORE    ignore create errors (N)      RECORDLENGTH  length of IO record
GRANTS    import grants (Y)             INCTYPE       incremental import type
INDEXES   import indexes (Y)            COMMIT        commit array insert (N)
ROWS      import data rows (Y)          PARFILE       parameter filename
LOG       log file of screen output     CONSTRAINTS   import constraints (Y)
DESTROY                     overwrite tablespace data file (N)
INDEXFILE                   write table/index info to specified file
SKIP_UNUSABLE_INDEXES       skip maintenance of unusable indexes (N)
FEEDBACK                    display progress every x rows(0)
TOID_NOVALIDATE             skip validation of specified type ids
FILESIZE                    maximum size of each dump file
STATISTICS                  import precomputed statistics (always)
RESUMABLE                   suspend when a space related error is encountered(N)
RESUMABLE_NAME              text string used to identify resumable statement
RESUMABLE_TIMEOUT           wait time for RESUMABLE
COMPILE                     compile procedures, packages, and functions (Y)
VOLSIZE                     number of bytes in file on each volume of a
                            file on tape
The following keywords only apply to transportable tablespaces
TRANSPORT_TABLESPACE import transportable tablespace metadata (N)
TABLESPACES tablespaces to be transported into database
DATAFILES datafiles to be transported into database
TTS_OWNERS users that own data in the transportable tablespace set
Import terminated successfully without warnings.
```

As you begin to work with import, you will find the nuances and ins and outs of all the parameters listed in the online help. Let's look at the modes of operation for import.

Import Modes of Operation

The meat of this section can be summed up in three words—same as export. Even though import shares some parameters with export, it can also be invoked using the interactive, the command-line, or the parameter-file method. With that said, let's look at a few examples of running import using the interactive and command-line approaches. The comments are embedded in each example. The second example, showing a command-line import, illustrates one of many things that can go wrong and the error text generated.

Parameter	Meaning	Notes
Ignore	When importing an object, if it already exists, ignore that fact and carry on with any other activities upon that object.	The default for this parameter is **n**, so be careful when bringing data into tables that already exist.
Indexfile	Names a file that will receive most of the SQL statements that can be extracted from the export file.	The output created as a result of this parameter's inclusion can be run in SQL*Plus with the removal of comment indicators and a handful of minor edits.
Resumable	Instructs import that when problems are encountered related to the text string coded with **resumable_name**, import should suspend its operation for the amount of time contained in the **resumable_timeout** parameter.	During this suspension, you can fix the problem before import resumes.
Fromuser/touser	Used in conjunction with one another to control the source and target schemas involved in an import session.	This is the best way to move data from one schema to another.

TABLE 10-4. *Import Parameter Notes*

```
# Interactive mode . . . get back a copy of ORACLE's MAIN table
# MAIN already exists (hence yes is answered to the object existence
# question); the export file is called expdat.dmp
#
/d0/app/oracle/product/9.0.1> imp
Import: Release 9.0.1.0.0 - Production on Sat Sep 15 17:44:44 2004

(c) Copyright 2001 Oracle Corporation.  All rights reserved.
Username: /
Connected to: Oracle9i Enterprise Edition Release 9.0.1.0.0 - Production
With the Partitioning option
JServer Release 9.0.1.0.0 - Production
Import file: expdat.dmp >
Enter insert buffer size (minimum is 8192) 30720> 1000000
Export file created by EXPORT:V09.00.01 via conventional path
```

```
import done in US7ASCII character set and AL16UTF16 NCHAR character set
List contents of import file only (yes/no): no >
Ignore create error due to object existence (yes/no): no > yes
Import grants (yes/no): yes >
Import table data (yes/no): yes >
Import entire export file (yes/no): no >
Username: oracle
Enter table(T) or partition(T:P) names. Null list means all tables for user
Enter table(T) or partition(T:P) name or . if done: main
Enter table(T) or partition(T:P) name or . if done: .
. importing ORACLE's objects into ORACLE
. . importing table        "MAIN"           502787 rows imported
About to enable constraints...
Import terminated successfully without warnings.
#
# Do the same import using the command-line approach.
#
/d0/app/oracle/product/oracle9.0.1/dbs> imp userid=/ tables=main
Import: Release 9.0.1.0.0 - Production on Sat Sep 15 17:49:16 2004
(c) Copyright 2001 Oracle Corporation.  All rights reserved.
Connected to: Oracle9i Enterprise Edition Release 9.0.1.0.0 - Production
With the Partitioning option
JServer Release 9.0.1.0.0 - Production
Export file created by EXPORT:V09.00.01 via conventional path
import done in US7ASCII character set and AL16UTF16 NCHAR character set
. importing ORACLE's objects into ORACLE
IMP-00015: following statement failed because the object already exists:
 "CREATE TABLE "MAIN" ("COL1" NUMBER, "COL2" DATE)  PCTFREE 10 PCTUSED 40 INI"
 "TRANS 1 MAXTRANS 255 STORAGE(INITIAL 32768 NEXT 16384 MINEXTENTS 1 MAXEXTEN"
 "TS 1017 PCTINCREASE 50 FREELISTS 1 FREELIST GROUPS 1 BUFFER_POOL DEFAULT)  "
 "             LOGGING"
Import terminated successfully with warnings.
#
# The problem was that the MAIN table already existed. To avoid the
# IMP-00015 error, you would have had to code ignore=y which is the
# same as answering yes to the "Ignore create error due to object
# existence" question asked using the interactive mode.
```

Before finishing up this section on import, let's look at import types.

Types of Imports

The export types listed in Table 10-3 are also applicable to import, with the following import-specific details:

■ With the full database import, you should ensure that the message "Import terminated successfully without warnings" appears at the bottom of the log file. This is actually the desired completion message for all imports, but especially the full import.

■ With the user import, when specifying multiple source and target users, you should include the same number of source as target, or the results can be unpredictable. Suppose three schemas are being copied from one database to two schemas in another; then the fromuser/touser portion of the import command would be as shown in the next listing.

```
fromuser=(huey,duey,luey)
touser=(foghorn,leghorn,leghorn)
```

Time to move on. We are now going to have a look at Oracle9i's media recovery features. The features are intimately tied to the redo logs and placing the database in archivelog mode. This is a very technical and complex area; the material we present is an introduction, no more.

Media Recovery Features

The act of recovering all or part of your Oracle9i database as a result of some sort of failure comes under the heading of *media recovery*. Failure usually is the result of one of the following three problems:

■ **Operator error**   Someone, for some unknown reason, does something to your data that should not have been done. A few years back, when working for a government department, a member of the financial management team did fiscal year-end processing on March 28 rather than April 1.

■ **Programming error**   Picture the following two SQL statements: the first one deletes rows from the wrong partition of a table; the latter, through the wonders of modern logic, issues the SQL statement correctly. Suppose the first one was built dynamically by an Oracle Forms application; all the user had to do was enter a fiscal year and quarter for an archival activity, and entered **1998** and **Q3**. The subsequent SQL statement wiped the wrong partition!

```
SQL> alter table client truncate partition fy98q3;
Table altered.
SQL> -- Oops!! Should have been . . .
SQL> alter table client truncate partition fy98q2;
Table altered.
```

■ **Media failure**   This is some sort of hardware issue—most commonly, the failure of a disk. When is the last time someone in the company coffee shop told you, "I lost drive D: last night—wiped—kaput—goner!" Suppose that drive was serving your corporate Oracle9i database, holding the payroll information for your few thousand colleagues.

Component	Cold Backup	Hot Backup
Control file(s)	X	
Online redo logs	X	
Data files	X	X

TABLE 10-5.   *Components of Hot and Cold Backups*

Before looking at archivelogging and the backups it allows you to write, let's spend a minute on hot and cold backups.

Hot and Cold Backups

Oracle9*i*'s media recovery features allow you to back up its files with the database open—a backup of this type is called an *online*, or *hot*, backup. Even when running in archivelog mode, you can still write backups with the database down—also called an *offline*, or *cold*, backup. Table 10-5 lists the components of the database and those that participate in both types of backups.

That's all fine and dandy, but let's look at a script that can be used to prepare a list of Oracle9*i*'s redo logs, control files, and data files.

```
SQL*Plus: Release 9.0.1.0.0 - Production on Sat Sep 45 18:09:52 2004
(c) Copyright 2001 Oracle Corporation.  All rights reserved.
SQL> connect / as sysdba
Connected.
SQL> select file_name from dba_data_files
  2  union
  3  select member from v$logfile
  4  union
  5  select name from v$controlfile;
/d1/oradata/beg9/invoice_ts1.dbf
/d1/oradata/beg9/invoice_ts2.dbf
/d1/oradata/beg9/invoice_ts3.dbf
/d1/oradata/beg9/invoice_ts4.dbf
/d1/oradata/beg9/mailing_ts1_01.dbf
/d1/oradata/beg9/mailing_ts2_01.dbf
/d1/oradata/beg9/mailing_ts3_01.dbf
/d1/oradata/beg9/mailing_ts4_01.dbf
/d1/oradata/beg9/mailing_ts5_01.dbf
/d1/oradata/beg9/mailing_ts6_01.dbf
/d1/oradata/beg9/mailing_tsmax_01.dbf
/d1/oradata/beg9/mailingx_ts1_01.dbf
/d1/oradata/beg9/mailingx_ts2_01.dbf
```

```
/d1/oradata/beg9/mailingx_ts3_01.dbf
/d1/oradata/beg9/mailingx_ts4_01.dbf
/d1/oradata/beg9/mailingx_ts5_01.dbf
/d1/oradata/beg9/mailingx_ts6_01.dbf
/d1/oradata/beg9/mailingx_tsmax_01.dbf
/d1/oradata/beg9/ora_abbey_da_xlhwczv2.dbf
/d1/oradata/beg9/ora_abbey_da_xlxrtzv7.dbf
/d1/oradata/beg9/ora_abramson_xlhwfsg2.dbf
/d1/oradata/beg9/ora_corey_xlhwfdj1.dbf
/d1/oradata/beg9/ora_rollback_xlhtdsm9.dbf
/d1/oradata/beg9/ora_system_xlhtcqp6.dbf
/d1/oradata/beg9/redo1/ora_1_xlhtbysq.log
/d1/oradata/beg9/redo1/ora_2_xlhtc9np.log
/d1/oradata/beg9/redo1/ora_xlhtbycl.ctl
/d1/oradata/beg9/redo2/ora_1_xlhtc40n.log
/d1/oradata/beg9/redo2/ora_2_xlhtcj3q.log
/d1/oradata/beg9/redo2/ora_xlhtbykt.ctl
30 rows selected.
```

Let's now look at the heart of Oracle9i's solution for these types of problems, based on the database's redo or transaction logs.

NOTE
Whole books are dedicated to backup and recovery issues like the ones discussed here. This chapter is simply an introduction to concepts and some of the procedures to use when leveraging Oracle9i features in this arena.

Running in Archivelog Mode

We have talked about redo logs in a number of places throughout this book, Chapter 2 being the first. Oracle9i writes transaction information to these redo logs as it operates. Think of redo logs as a mirror image of all the user sessions that interact with your data. In order to write consistent backups of a database, the database must first be placed in archivelog mode. The next listing compares the way redo logs are reused in archivelog mode.

```
FACT: Oracle9i uses redo logs in a circular fashion—a group fills up,
      it moves to the next group and reuses groups again when their
      turn comes up.
redo log group fills up
if database in archivelog mode then
   if cleanup has been finished on group then
      make a copy of a member of the group
```

```
            flag the group as ready to reuse
      else (cleanup not complete)
         while cleanup being performed
         loop
            wait a while
            check again
            if cleanup has been finished on group then
               make a copy of a member of the group,
               flag the group as ready to reuse
            end if
         end loop
      end if
   else (database not running in archivelog mode)
      perform cleanup
      flag redo log group as ready to reuse
   end if
```

Let's look at the steps for putting an Oracle9*i* database in archivelog mode.

Placing the Database in Archivelog Mode

Follow these steps to put the database in archivelog mode:

1. Proceed to the location of the initialization parameter file.

2. Edit that file, placing entries there for the three parameters shown in Table 10-6. Using the cell values in this table, redo log sequence 3828 will end up archived as /d0/oraarch/beg9/arch_3828.arc.

Parameter	Sample Value	Details
Log_archive_start	TRUE	Instructs Oracle9*i* to spawn a background process to automatically archive redo logs.
Log_archive_dest	/d0/oraarch/beg9/	The location where redo logs should be archived.
Log_archive_format	arch_%s.arc	The format used for naming the archived redo logs. The **%s** instructs Oracle9*i* to include a log sequence number when a member of a redo log group is archived.

TABLE 10-6. *Parameters Required for Archivelogging*

3. Enter SQL*Plus as sysdba.

4. Enter the command **shutdown immediate**.

5. Enter the command **startup mount**.

6. Enter the command **alter database archivelog;**.

7. Enter the command **alter database open;**.

The dialogue and feedback from Oracle9i is shown in the next listing.

```
oracle@mail.ntirety.com-->(beg9)
/d0/oraclehome/product/oracle9.0.1/dbs> sqlplus /nolog
SQL*Plus: Release 9.0.1.0.0 - Production on Sat Sep 45 18:09:52 2003
(c) Copyright 2001 Oracle Corporation.  All rights reserved.
SQL> connect / as sysdba
Connected.
SQL> shutdown
Database closed.
Database dismounted.
ORACLE instance shut down.
SQL> startup mount
ORACLE instance started.
Total System Global Area  109872420 bytes
Fixed Size                   279844 bytes
Variable Size              54525952 bytes
Database Buffers           54525952 bytes
Redo Buffers                 540672 bytes
Database mounted.
SQL> alter database archivelog;
Database altered.
SQL> alter database open;
Database altered.
SQL> archive log list;
Database log mode              Archive Mode
Automatic archival             Enabled
Archive destination            /d0/oraarch/beg9
Oldest online log sequence     7837
Next log sequence to archive   7842
Current log sequence           7842
```

Notice the **archive log list;** command in the listing. It tells you that archivelogging is enabled and the process that performs automatic archival is active, and it gives the destination of the archived redo logs. Now that the database is in archivelog mode, backups can be written while it is open. Before moving on to have a quick look at recovery offered when Oracle9i runs in archivelog mode, let's look at writing a hot backup.

Writing a Hot Backup

As long as the correct procedure is followed, writing a hot backup is no big deal. Before a data file is backed up, the tablespace to which it belongs must be placed in backup mode. The next commented listing shows how this is done, shelling out to the UNIX operating system to make file copies.

```
SQL*Plus: Release 9.0.1.0.0 - Production on Sat Sep 45 18:09:52 2003
(c) Copyright 2001 Oracle Corporation.  All rights reserved.
SQL> connect / as sysdba
Connected.
SQL> --
SQL> -- Place ABBEY_DATA tablespace in backup mode.
SQL> --
SQL> alter tablespace abbey_data begin backup;
Tablespace altered.
SQL> --
SQL> -- Copy all the files belonging to a tablespace while it is
SQL> -- in backup mode.
SQL> --
! cp /d1/oradata/beg9/ora_abbey_da_xlhwczv2.dbf .
! cp /d1/oradata/beg9/ora_abbey_da_xlxrtzv7.dbf .
SQL> --
SQL> -- Once the files have been copied, take the tablespace out of
SQL> -- backup mode. The secret is to have a tablespace in backup
SQL> -- mode for as short a time as possible.
SQL> --
SQL> alter tablespace abbey_data end backup;
Tablespace altered.
SQL> alter tablespace abramson_data begin backup;
Tablespace altered.
! cp /d1/oradata/beg9/ora_abramson_xlhwfsg2.dbf .
SQL> alter tablespace abramson_data end backup;
Tablespace altered.
SQL> alter tablespace corey_data begin backup;
Tablespace altered.
! cp /d1/oradata/beg9/ora_corey_xlhwfdj1.dbf .
SQL> alter tablespace corey_data end backup;
Tablespace altered.
```

Now, the icing on the cake. Having briefly looked at writing a hot backup, let's spend a few minutes on media recovery.

Media Recovery—An Example

You already know what media recovery is in a general way; specifically, it is the act of taking a copy of a database component from a past time and, using archived redo logs, rolling it forward. The *roll forward* exercise can be thought of as a phantom session that reapplies all the transaction information stored in redo logs. Picture the following scenario that lends itself very nicely to a situation in which media recovery is required. A handful of users complain that the following error is being displayed on their screens:

```
ERROR at line 1:
ORA-00376: file 3 cannot be read at this time
ORA-01110: data file 3: '/d1/oradata/beg9/ora_abbey_da_xlhwczv2.dbf'
```

It now becomes your job to investigate the reason for the problem and, if necessary, go to your most recent backup and get a copy of the offending database file. Suppose you have already looked into the issue, and need to do just that. Here's what you might do:

1. Take the offending database file offline with the following SQL statement:

   ```
   alter database datafile '/d1/oradata/beg9/ora_abbey_da_xlhwczv2.dbf'
        offline;
   ```

2. Proceed to the location of your most recent backup, and get a copy of the ora_abbey_da_xlhwczv2.dbf file, placing it in the appropriate location.

3. Attempt to bring the data file online with the **alter database datafile '/d1/ oradata/beg9/ora_abbey_da_xlhwczv2.dbf' online;** command, and receive the following feedback from Oracle9*i*.

   ```
   alter database datafile '/d1/oradata/beg9/ora_abbey_da_xlhwczv2.dbf' online;
   *
   ERROR at line 1:
   ORA-01113: file 3 needs media recovery
   ORA-01110: data file 3: '/d1/oradata/beg9/ora_abbey_da_xlhwczv2.dbf'
   ```

4. Perform media recovery by initiating a dialogue with Oracle9*i* and receiving feedback, as shown in the next listing.

   ```
   SQL> recover datafile '/d1/oradata/beg9/ora_abbey_da_xlhwczv2.dbf';
   ORA-00279: change 1676533 generated at 09/15/2003 08:13:11 needed for thread 1
   ORA-00289: suggestion : /d0/oraarch/beg9/arch_7888.arc
   ORA-00280: change 1676533 for thread 1 is in sequence #7888
   Specify log: {<RET>=suggested | filename | AUTO | CANCEL}
   {Press ENTER alone here to accept the suggested archived redo log}

   Log applied.
   ORA-00279: change 1679889 generated at 09/15/2003 10:43:32 needed for thread 1
   ORA-00289: suggestion : /d0/oraarch/beg9/arch_7889.arc
   ORA-00280: change 1679889 for thread 1 is in sequence #7889
   ```

```
Specify log: {<RET>=suggested | filename | AUTO | CANCEL}
{Press ENTER alone here to accept the suggested archived redo log}

Media recovery complete.
SQL>
```

5. Bring the offending data file back online with **alter database datafile '/d1/ oradata/beg9/ora_abbey_da_xlhwczv2.dbf' online;**, and receive feedback from Oracle9*i* as shown in the next listing.

```
Database altered.
```

6. Mission accomplished—leave SQL*Plus using the **exit** command.

This mock recovery session went well; unfortunately, this will not always be the case. Issues creep up that hinder a smooth recovery. These factors go all the way from a missing archived redo log to perhaps a corrupt data file backup. Let's close out this chapter by looking at media recovery types and a handful of unfortunate but common problems that get in the way of recovery activity.

Types of Media Recovery

Classic Oracle9*i* theory dictates two types of media recovery—complete and incomplete. Let's tackle the two types of recovery:

- Complete media recovery involves taking a copy of the entity that needs recovery (be it the whole database, a tablespace, or one or more data files) and rolling it forward to the current point in time using archived redo logs.

- Incomplete media recovery is similar, except it is done only at the database level. The database is copied back from tape and rolled forward to a point in time before the current time. Suppose it's 2:09 p.m., and for some reason you only want to roll the database forward to 11:00 a.m. This would be a candidate for incomplete media recovery. There are three types of incomplete media recovery:

  - *Cancel-based* recovery is when you start the recovery process with the statement **recover database until cancel;**. Oracle9*i* presents suggested archived redo log names and locations until you enter the word **cancel** to a request for a name. At that point, recovery stops.

  - *Time-based* recovery is started with the statement **recover database until time 'DD-MON-YYYY:HH24:MI:SS';**, where the time is something like '05-JUL-2002:14:12:00'. Oracle9*i* will roll the database forward until the most recent transaction just before 2:12 p.m. on Friday, July 5, 2002.

■ *Change-based* recovery relies on the internal system change number (commonly called *SCN*) that is incremented as changes are applied to the database and written to the online redo logs. This is the same number you may have noticed a few listings back when we were performing recovery against the datafile ora_abbey_da_xlhwczv2.dbf and Oracle9*i* displayed text similar to that shown in the next listing. The SCN is highlighted in the second line of the listing.

```
SQL> recover datafile
'/d1/oradata/beg9/ora_abbey_da_xlhwczv2.dbf';
ORA-00279: change 1676533
generated at 09/15/2003 08:13:11 needed for thread 1
```

NOTE
Incomplete media recovery is a very complex topic deliberately simplified. We wanted to mention some terminology and introduce the beginnings of this topic to familiarize you with some jargon.

More than 90 percent of the recovery exercises we have performed over the past few hundred years have involved complete media recovery. Unfortunately, sometimes that is what you start, but picture the following error message that we have seen when pressing ENTER as we did in our little recovery session a while back.

```
ORA-00279: change 1679889 generated at 09/15/2003 10:23:11 needed for thread 1
ORA-00289: suggestion : /d0/oraarch/beg9/arch_7889.arc
ORA-00280: change 1679889 for thread 1 is in sequence #7889
Specify log: {<RET>=suggested | filename | AUTO | CANCEL}
{Press ENTER alone here to accept the suggested archived redo log}

ORA-00308: cannot open archived log
'/d0/oraarch/beg9/arch_7889.arc'
ORA-27037: unable to obtain file status
SVR4 Error: 2: No such file or directory
Additional information: 3
```

For some reason, Oracle9*i* cannot open the desired archived redo log. Being the resourceful DBA that you are, you proceed to the /d0/oraarch/beg9 directory, obtaining a listing of the supposedly missing archived redo log, as shown next:

```
/d0/oracle/home> ls -l /d0/oraarch/beg9/arch_7889.arc
rw-r--r--   1 oracle   dba       209715712 Sep 15 08:42 arch_7889.arc
```

You reenter SQL*Plus and try again—same error message. Next stop? Get another copy of the archived redo log back from tape, fingers crossed, hoping that the newly restored file will be OK. Oh no! Same problem. You now have a situation in which you can only roll the database forward until the end of archived redo log arch_7888.arc, and thus are forced to perform incomplete media recovery.

Some thoughts to leave you with before closing Chapter 10 and moving on to have a look at Oracle Enterprise Manager. We have said this over and over again in this book, but it makes even more sense in the light of the major subject material of this chapter—backup and recovery. Export, import, media recovery, and the like, are huge topics. We could easily fill the one cargo hold of the *Valdez* with the amount of material that could be produced on these features alone of Oracle9*i*. We have introduced ideas, and touched on some of the backup and recovery features of this electronic offering. Allocate as much time as possible to master the techniques of which we speak in this chapter. Once you think you are on top of it, remember that you may have only scratched the surface.

Chapter 10 Questions

Answers to questions can be found in Appendix A.

1. **Filesize** is an export parameter that

    A. controls the maximum size of the export output file

    B. dictates the largest table that can be part of the export session

    C. controls the maximum size of each export output file when more than one file is created for a session

    D. determines the maximum size of the log file written

2. Media recovery involves

    A. replacing a defective disk and retrying the desired operation that failed

    B. completing transactions based on the information stored in the online redo logs

    C. archiving redo logs to more than one destination in case of media failure

    D. rolling a previous copy of a database entity forward using archived redo logs

3. Which of the following components are part of a cold, or offline, backup?

    A. Just the database data files.

    B. Only the control file(s) and the online database files.

    C. All components of the database, including data files, control files, and online redo logs.

    D. None of the above.

4. Which of the following SQL statements notifies Oracle9i that the COREY tablespace is about to be backed up?

    A. `alter database begin backup;`

    B. `alter tablespace corey start backup;`

    C. `alter database tablespace corey begin backup;`

    D. `alter tablespace corey begin backup;`

5. A database is placed in archivelog mode while it is

    A. open

    B. mounted

    C. open in restricted mode

    D. nomounted

CHAPTER
11

Oracle
Enterprise Manager

s mentioned in many places throughout this book, management and care and feeding of the Oracle9*i* database is a task that falls to many unsuspecting database administrators. In Chapters 7 and 10, we looked at database administrators' jobs and how they carry out their day-to-day activities. In this chapter, we are going to revisit some of that material through the eyes of Oracle Enterprise Manager, affectionately called *OEM* in most circles. OEM has been around since early versions of Oracle7. It is still basically the same tool as release 1.0, but the look and feel is somewhat different in this day and age. We are going to cover the following material in this chapter:

- Introduction to what can be done with OEM

- Tools in the OEM interface

- Instance startup and shutdown

- Tablespace and data file maintenance

- User maintenance

- Object maintenance

Terminology

First, here is the technical jargon you will need to make it through this chapter.

- Each Oracle9*i* database is uniquely identified on each server by an *ORACLE_SID*, which stands for Oracle system identifier. When we installed Oracle9*i* on our client, we chose the ORACLE_SID of o9ibeg.

- *Tablespaces* are made up of one or more operating system files, and are the logical containers within which Oracle9*i* data is stored.

- Oracle9*i* stores its data in chunks of database space called *data blocks*. The size of the data block can be from 2KB up to 16KB. Block sizes are typically the same as, or integer multiples of, the operating system block size, usually 512 bytes on UNIX.

- *Rollback segments* store images of data before it is changed, in case the session interacting with the data does not follow through on making its changes. You will find a more detailed discussion in the "Rollback

Segments/Undo Tablespace" section of Chapter 3, as well as other spots throughout this book.

■ *Redo logs* are the transaction logs that record the details of every interaction with the data in an Oracle9*i* database.

■ *Fault tolerance* refers to a methodology that removes a single point of failure and allows users of Oracle9*i*'s technology to have copies of their data to fall back on if and when disaster strikes.

■ A *standby database* is just that—it stands by in the background in case something goes wrong in your production environment, at which point it can be called into service.

■ Windows-based programs use a *GUI* (graphical user interface) to allow interaction with users.

■ An Oracle9*i instance* is made up of a set of Oracle processes, a portion of a computer's shared memory, and the assortment of support files that allow users to work with the data stored in an Oracle9*i* database.

NOTE
All the database objects and entities that we work with in this chapter existed on our Oracle9i database when writing these exercises. The names of these items and their locations may be drastically different when you work with OEM on your own computer. The PERSON table, for example, discussed in a number of sections throughout this chapter, will not exist unless it has been precreated by you or another DBA.

What Can Be Done with OEM: A Quick Tour

OEM offers the full range of DBA-related functionality with a familiar Windows look and feel. When we installed Oracle9*i* on our client, we chose the text **9i2k** when asked to select a nickname for the installation. In the Windows 2000 Professional Start menu, we selected Programs | Oracle – 9*i*2k | Enterprise Manager Console, as shown in Figure 11-1.

FIGURE 11-1. *OEM from the Start menu*

NOTE

You can choose any nickname you wish; even though we use this handle in this chapter, you will have to substitute your entry of choice if you do not use 9i2k.

Once OEM Console is selected, the computer will churn away for what seems to be an eternity, and then present you with a screen where you select your desired connection type. Choose the first of the following two options, and then click OK to enter the OEM interface.

- Launch Standalone hooks you up to a single Oracle9i database without the luxury of being able to manage a corporate database networked environment from one place.

- Login to the Oracle Management Server requires some setup to be done beforehand, and allows you to manage a handful of nodes and databases registered with the management server. This management server setup and node discovery is well beyond the scope of this introductory chapter.

You are then positioned at the OEM Console startup screen, as shown in Figure 11-2. Notice the Databases folder in the upper-left corner of the work area on the main console. Click the + sign to display the identifier for the default Oracle9i database; ours displays the ORACLE_SID of **O9IBEG**, whereas yours will display whatever

FIGURE 11-2.   *OEM Console startup screen*

you entered when installing your database software. Interestingly enough, you are still not logged into any database. That will come next. First, we'll discuss the assortment of management tools commonly used in OEM.

■ Instance management encompasses startup and shutdown of an Oracle9*i* database, management of Oracle's initialization parameters, and monitoring of user sessions as they interact with the database.

■ Schema management provides a point-and-click interface for working with the assortment of database objects, as defined in Chapter 4.

■ Security management includes the tasks of creating, dropping, or altering users, as well as giving out special privileges that permit specified users to interact in certain ways with the Oracle9*i* database.

■ Storage management provides an interface where you administer some of the Oracle9*i* infrastructure, such as rollback segments, tablespaces, and online redo logs.

- Workspace management allows the administrator to version-enable tables in the database, and set up a facility whereby timestamped copies of tables can be stored for comparison and life-cycle analysis purposes. Workspaces lend themselves well to what-if queries popular in many decision support systems, also called *data warehouses*.

- Data Guard management plays a significant role when implementing fault-tolerant features of the Oracle9i server such as standby databases and log management.

- Backup management tools provide access to wizards that assist backup and recovery of the Oracle9i database.

- Data management permits access to tools such as export and import, which are used to put data into an Oracle9i database or make copies of the database data in operating system files.

- SQL*Plus worksheet is a full-fledged GUI front end where you can work with SQL*Plus (the subject matter of Chapters 5 and 8), as well as PL/SQL (as discussed in Chapters 6 and 9).

OEM is a one-stop shop for management activities with the Oracle9i database. Let's look at some common activities using OEM, starting with—what a coincidence—starting up the database.

Startup

We connected to OEM console using the Launch Standalone option a few paragraphs back. To start the database, you must connect using a logical role called *sysdba*.

NOTE
Oracle user SYS automatically has this sysdba role, and for the purposes of this chapter and much of the work we highlight in OEM, we use the SYS account. The sysdba role can be granted to other users, but it's somewhat technical. Ask a more experienced DBA for assistance when you want to give out the sysdba role to others.

Let's get going. Carry out the following to start your Oracle9*i* database:

1. Right-click the database name (**o9ibeg**, in our case), and select the Connect option in the drop-down menu that appears.

2. When the dialog box appears, as shown in Figure 11-3, enter the login credentials as shown, and then click OK to continue. Notice we have selected sysdba from the Connect As pick list shown in Figure 11-3. When you successfully connect to your database, the database name will expand, indicating that you are now user **sys as SYSDBA**, and a few branches will appear underneath the database folder.

3. Right-click the database name similar to when we connected, and this time select the Startup option. When this startup window appears, more than likely the No Mount/Mount/Open radio group will have Open selected by default, both Startup Options will be deselected, and the Use Configured Parameters option will be checked. Click OK to initiate the startup.

4. When OEM begins the startup, it displays a screen similar to that shown in Figure 11-4. Click Close when the "Processing completed" message appears.

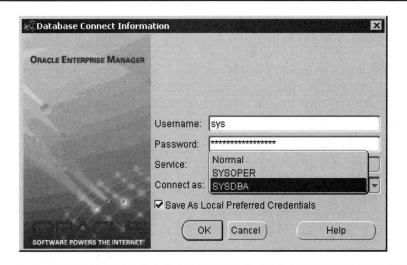

FIGURE 11-3. *Logging in with sysdba*

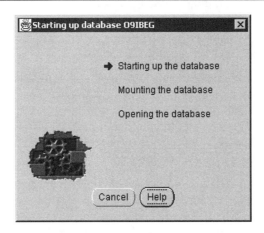

FIGURE 11-4.   *Database startup progress*

The database is now started. Before looking at shutting down the Oracle9i instance, let's stop for a minute at the Instance display underneath the database name shown in Figure 11-5.

There is a virtual cornucopia of useful information in this display, specifically the following areas:

■ **Configuration**   With the Memory tab selected, OEM displays the allocations given to key memory structures, as well as information about the maximum size of the concurrent user community (700 for our configuration).

■ **Sessions**   Lists the current connections where, in our case, sessions 1 through 6 are instance support processes, and 7 through 10 are some of your favorite Oracle Press authors, we hope (Abbey, Corey, and Abramson—fancy that!).

So, your database is started. Let's now look at shutdown.

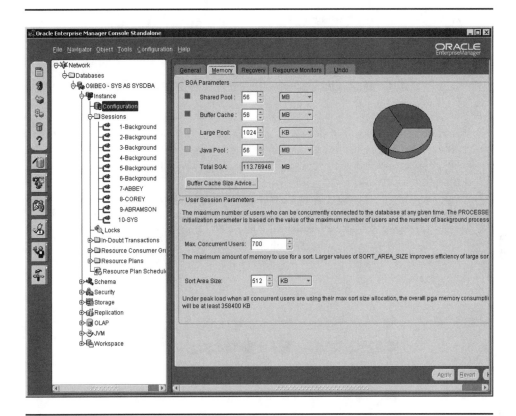

FIGURE 11-5. *Instance display*

Shutdown

While parked at a screen similar to that shown in Figure 11-5, the shutdown activity is accomplished as follows:

1. Right-click the database icon you wish to shut down, displaying a drop-down menu with options such as Connect, Disconnect, and Shutdown.

2. Click Shutdown to bring up a screen similar to that shown in Figure 11-6. Most of the time, the Immediate option is not selected; select it before moving on.

3. Click OK to commence the shutdown operation.

4. When the "Processing completed" message appears, click Close to return to OEM.

The database is now shut down, and all sessions that were connected have been gracefully closed down. Just for fun, click Sessions once to collapse the tree; then click the + sign beside Sessions—an "ORACLE not available" warning pops up. Click Cancel to dismiss the information.

Before we move on and look at some more activities and management interfaces, please restart your databases! Instead of right-clicking the database name, as indicated in the "Startup" section earlier in the chapter, try clicking Object on the menu bar at the top of the OEM console, and then click Startup. This is shown in Figure 11-7; the rest of the steps are in the "Startup" section. First, we will look at tablespace and data file maintenance. Hang on!

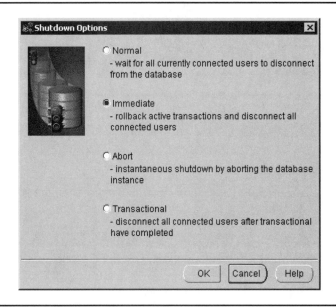

FIGURE 11-6.   *Shutdown dialog box*

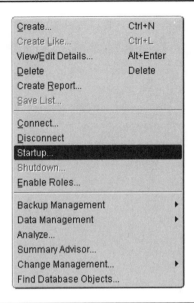

FIGURE 11-7. *Startup from the Object menu option*

Tablespace Maintenance

Work on tablespaces can also be done from the OEM main console. The first place to go is the Storage folder. Click the + beside Storage, and then expand the Tablespaces folder to bring up a screen similar to that shown in Figure 11-8.

The first task is adding a tablespace called **beginner** to our Oracle9*i* database by doing the following:

1. Highlight Tablespace in the storage tree, and then right-click to bring up a drop-down menu.

2. Click Create to bring up the Create Tablespace dialog box.

3. Fill in values for Name and Datafiles. We chose the values **beginner** and **/u01/oradata/o9ibeg**. Notice that when you fill in the tablespace name, OEM populates the File Name field with that name suffixed by .ora. If you wish to change the name and suffix as we did, click in the File Name field and override the default. You must use the mouse for this movement, not the TAB key, for some reason.

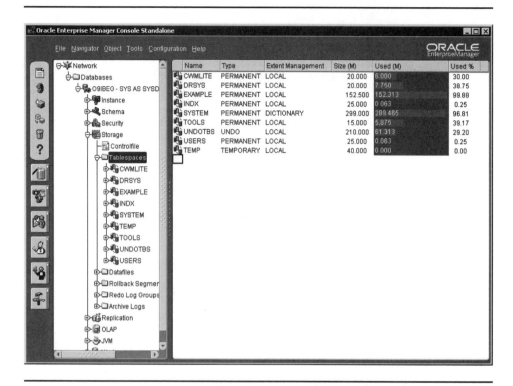

FIGURE 11-8. *Tablespaces in the Storage folder*

4. Fill in values for Size, picking MB from the pick list for unit of measurement for the file size. We chose **10**. The completed form is shown in Figure 11-9.

NOTE
We clicked the Show SQL button in the Create Tablespace dialog box to display the code in the SQL Text field at the bottom of the window.

5. We ensured that the Online and Permanent radio buttons were selected before moving on, and then clicked Create to create the Tablespace.

6. Dismiss the "tablespace created" acknowledgment box by clicking OK; when returned to the OEM display, the new tablespace will appear in its alphabetical position on the screen.

NOTE
When entering storage parameters for a new tablespace, you can specify an Oracle block size. Each database has a default block size that you can override if the appropriate parameters are set in the initialization parameter file.

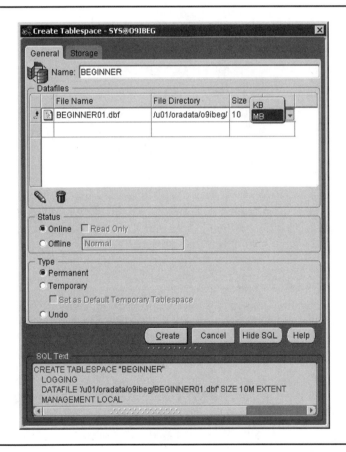

FIGURE 11-9. *Create Tablespace dialog box completed*

Suppose it's now a few weeks down the road, and the original 10MB allocated for the **beginner** tablespace turns out not to be enough. There are two ways to deal with this shortfall:

- Resize an existing file that is already part of an existing tablespace.

- Add a new file to the desired tablespace.

Let's look at both of these approaches.

NOTE
There may be some operating system limits on the maximum size of data files. One that we run across all the time is the 2GB file-size limit on many UNIX *servers.*

Resizing a Data File

The starting point for this activity is the Datafiles folder. When the list of data files is expanded, select the file to be resized, and then do the following:

1. Right-click to bring up the data file menu.

2. Select View/Edit to bring up the Edit Datafile dialog box.

3. Make the appropriate change for File Size, as shown in Figure 11-10. We chose to increase the file size from 10MB to 20MB; notice how we selected M Bytes from the File Size pick list.

Adding a Data File

Position yourself at the Tablespaces folder, and then highlight the tablespace to which you wish to add some more space.

1. Right-click the tablespace, and then select the Add Datafile option.

2. When the Create Datafile dialog box appears, type in the fully qualified name for the new data file. We entered **/u02/oradata/oibeg9/tools03.dbf** and left the M Bytes measurement with a value of **20**.

3. When ready, click Create to initiate the add activity.

4. As shown in Figure 11-11, the additional data file is now included in the readout of the tablespace file makeup. In Figure 11-8, there were 15MB allocated to the **tools** tablespace; now there are 25MB.

Before moving on to the next exercise—working with users through OEM—we want to issue a caveat about resizing data files.

Shrinking a Data File

From time to time, we allocate space to a tablespace to accommodate large amounts of data. Often, when we no longer require that extra space, we try to find the time to reclaim the unused space. We previously looked at increasing the size of a data file, but let's look at making a file smaller. Suppose we have right-clicked a data file, selected View/Edit Details, and highlighted the file to shrink. We

FIGURE 11-10. *Resizing a data file*

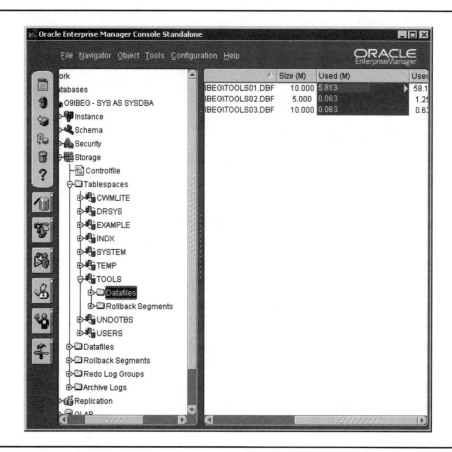

FIGURE 11-11. *List of data files with additional file*

changed the displayed value of 500MB to **10MB**, and have just clicked Apply and received a message mentioning ORA-03297 and the text "file contains used data beyond requested RESIZE value." Select a value larger than the one you entered, and try again. Remember—practice makes perfect.

User Maintenance

Users—without them a database is simply an assortment of bits and bytes; with them, a database springs to life and starts to satisfy the electronic needs of a hungry user community. Working with users in OEM starts at the Security Management main console shown in Figure 11-12. Let's start by creating a new user.

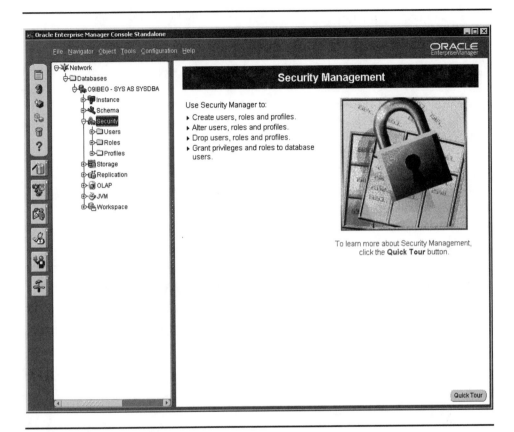

FIGURE 11-12.   *Security Management main console*

Creating a New User

Suppose we want to create a new user named ELLISON with a password of LARRY.
Here's how to do it:

1. Right-click the Users folder.

2. Select Create from the ensuing drop-down menu, bringing up the screen
   shown in Figure 11-13.

3. Enter the text **ellison** in the Name field, and **larry** in the Enter Password
   field. We clicked on Show SQL.

4. Move down to the Temporary field, and click System Assigned to bring up
   a pick list of tablespaces that can be assigned for the new user's temporary

objects. Temporary objects are built implicitly by Oracle9*i* when in need of intermediary work tables for processing SQL statements. After selecting TEMP for the temporary tablespace, the SQL code assembled in the Show SQL window is shown in the next listing.

```
create user ellison profile default
    identified by larry default tablespace users
    temporary tablespace temp
    account unlock;
grant connect to ellison;
```

5. Click Create to start the process.

6. When the user creation confirmation appears, click OK to return to the list of users, now displaying **ellison**.

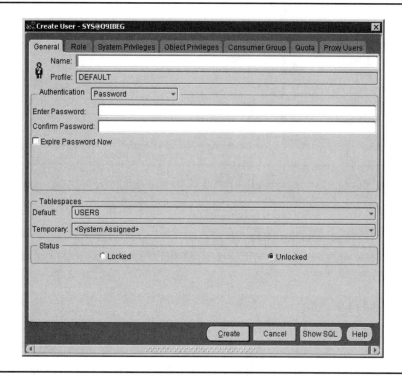

FIGURE 11-13. *Create User dialog box*

Once a user has been created, about all it can do is connect to the Oracle9*i*
database. Let's look at giving users the rights to occupy space in the database and
a few object privileges.

Rights to Occupy Space in the Database

Quotas allow users to occupy space in the database. User ELLISON that was
created in the previous section is now allowed to log in, but that's about all. Without
appropriate quotas on one or more tablespaces, users would get error messages similar
to that shown in the next listing if they were to try and create a table.

```
SQL*Plus: Release 9.0.1.0.0 - Production on Tue Aug 21 20:30:09 2003
(c) Copyright 2001 Oracle Corporation.  All rights reserved.
Connected to:
Oracle9i Enterprise Edition Release 9.0.1.0.0 - Production
With the Partitioning option
JServer Release 9.0.1.0.0 - Production
SQL> create table general (name varchar2(20),
  2   state_cd varchar2(2), area number);
create table general (name varchar2(20),
*
ERROR at line 1:

ORA-01950: no privileges on tablespace 'USERS'

SQL>
```

Let's give ELLISON some rights to occupy space.

1. Ensure that the list of users is expanded by clicking the Users folder
   beneath Security.

2. Right-click the desired user—ELLISON, in our case—and select
   View/Edit Details.

3. Select the Quota tab in the Edit User dialog box.

4. Quota allocation starts by highlighting the appropriate tablespace,
   in our case, **indx**.

5. Proceed to the None, Unlimited, Value area of the dialog box, and
   select Value. This opens a field where the quota amount can be entered
   and also enlivens the pick list beside K Bytes.

6. Enter an amount of **100** beside Value.

7. Proceed to the pick list underneath K Bytes, and select M Bytes as the session unit of measurement. The values we filled in along with the SQL that will be passed to Oracle9i are shown in Figure 11-14.

8. Click Apply, leaving you on the same quota screen, with the just-allocated amount appearing under Quota Size once the statement is processed.

The next exercise will take you to the same Edit User screens as discussed in this section.

Granting Object Privileges

There is a pretty significant catch to this section. In all the previous exercises covered in this chapter, we were logged into OEM using our preferred login credentials as the user SYS. To give out object privileges, you must first reconnect to the database as the owner of the objects.

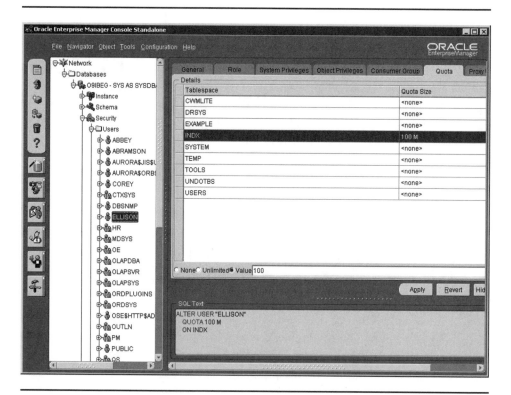

FIGURE 11-14. *Giving quota to a user*

NOTE
*Attempting to grant privileges while logged in
using an account other than the object owner will
generate error ORA-01031: insufficient privileges.
This applies to all users, even the seemingly
all-powerful SYS user.*

Let's reconnect to OEM as ELLISON by following these steps:

1. Dismiss the Edit User dialog box by clicking Cancel.

2. When returned to the OEM main console, right-click the database
   name beneath the Databases icon.

3. Click Connect from the ensuing menu.

4. Enter the username **ellison** and the password **larry**.

5. Select Normal from the Connect As pick list.

6. Click OK to log into OEM as ELLISON.

NOTE
*This login will only succeed if you have chosen
to launch OEM stand-alone; if you selected
Login to Oracle Management Server, you may
experience connection problems when trying
to connect as ELLISON.*

Now we can grant privileges on ELLISON's tables since we have reconnected.
Let's get going.

1. Expand the Security folder by clicking its + sign.

2. Expand the Users folder as well.

3. Right-click PUBLIC, and then select View/Edit Details
   from the menu that appears.

NOTE
*User PUBLIC is a logical entity to which everyone
able to access the database belongs. After you
create a new user, it automatically belongs to
this logical user.*

4. Traverse to the Object Privileges tab on the screen that appears. Note that when the Edit User dialog box appears, a long list of object privileges is already there—this is PUBLIC, and these are all the grants that are already in place.

5. Navigate to ELLISON in the list of users that appears, and then click ELLISON. You are then positioned at a screen similar to that shown in Figure 11-15. Remember, we are logged into OEM as user ELLISON, wishing to give out privileges to PUBLIC.

6. Expand the tables underneath, bringing up a list of ELLISON's tables, at this point only showing PERSON.

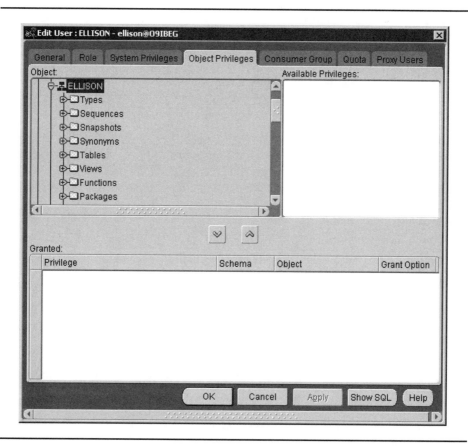

FIGURE 11-15. *Getting started with granting object privileges*

7. Click PERSON, and the object's seven privileges will appear in the right pane, starting with ALTER and ending with UPDATE.

8. Move SELECT, INSERT, UPDATE, and DELETE down to the bottom pane. The SQL that will be passed to Oracle9*i* is in the next listing.

```
grant delete on ellison.person to public;
grant insert on ellison.person to public;
grant select on ellison.person to public;
grant update on ellison.person to public;
```

9. Click Apply to begin processing. Click Cancel to return to the OEM console.

That's about it for these introductory exercises on user maintenance. We are going to touch on one last topic in this OEM chapter—object maintenance. Start your engines ladies and gentlemen.

Object Maintenance

Let's stay logged into OEM as ELLISON and make some changes to the PERSON table.

1. Expand the Schema folder and do the same with Tables.

2. Navigate to the ELLISON display, and then click to expand the list of tables.

NOTE
We are going to be making changes to ELLISON's tables, since for now those are the only tables ELLISON is allowed to modify.

3. Click PERSON to bring up the modify object worksheet, as shown in Figure 11-16.

4. Let's add a STATE_CD column with the data type **varchar2** and a maximum size of two characters, by entering these values in the Name, Datatype, and Size fields. We also ensure that we do not click in the Nulls? field, thereby making STATE_CD a mandatory column.

5. Click Apply to pass an SQL statement to Oracle9*i* that resembles the following:

```
alter table person add (state_cd varchar2(2) not null);
```

6. Let's make a few more modifications to PERSON and then get out of here. Suppose we want to expand the Name field to 50 characters and change the DOB column from optional (nulls allowed) to mandatory. Proceed to the Name field, and mouse over to the Size field, changing the 20 to **50**.

7. Navigate to the Nulls? field beside the DOB column, and click to remove the check mark. The data entry is shown in Figure 11-17.

8. Click Apply to pass the SQL to Oracle9i.

Just about anything you can do in SQL*Plus—as discussed in Chapters 5 and 8 or in the two DBA chapters, 7 and 10—can be done using OEM. Before calling this a wrap, let's look at a few more common object maintenance activities in OEM, but this time using SQL*Plus Worksheet.

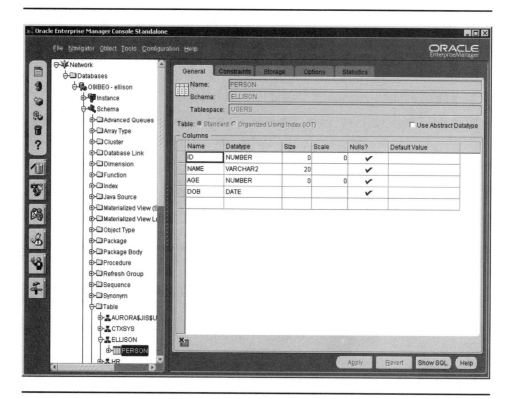

FIGURE 11-16. *Object modification worksheet*

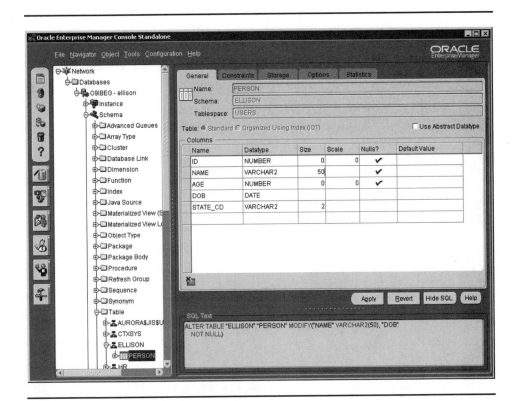

FIGURE 11-17.   *Modifying columns in the PERSON table*

Object Maintenance Using SQL*Plus Worksheet

To access the SQL*Plus Worksheet, proceed to the menu at the top of the OEM console, select Tools, and then pick Database Applications | SQL*Plus Worksheet. Once in the worksheet, we have simply entered two very simple commands to look at ELLISON's two tables—**desc state** and **desc person**. This is shown in Figure 11-18. Notice the two panes in the worksheet—the top is where commands are entered and executed, and the bottom displays output. Notice in Figure 11-18 how we executed the two commands at the same time by selecting the lightning bolt (Execute) button on the left side of the worksheet.

When working with SQL*Plus Worksheet, you might enjoy a few features that are not available via the regular SQL*Plus interface. Table 11-1 highlights these features.

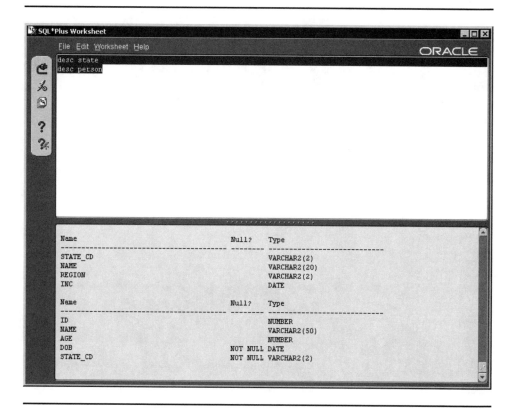

FIGURE 11-18. *SQL*Plus Worksheet dual pane display*

Keystroke	Function
F5 or CTRL-ENTER	Execute the command showing in the data entry area of the worksheet.
CTRL-H	Access the worksheet history window, where commands can be retrieved by highlighting text and pressing ENTER.
CTRL-N	Scroll forward in the command history.
CTRL-P	Scroll backward in the command history.
CTRL-O	Open the Windows Explorer dialog box to bring an SQL*Plus program into the workspace.

TABLE 11-1. *Useful SQL*Plus Worksheet Keystroke Shortcuts*

Suppose ELLISON has a table called OWNERS as described in the next listing.

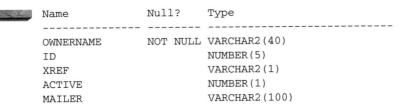

```
Name             Null?    Type
---------------  -------- ---------------------------
OWNERNAME        NOT NULL VARCHAR2(40)
ID                        NUMBER(5)
XREF                      VARCHAR2(1)
ACTIVE                    NUMBER(1)
MAILER                    VARCHAR2(100)
```

There are three things we want to do to OWNERS using SQL*Plus Worksheet:

■ Place a default constraint on ACTIVE so that when a row is created, if no value is supplied for ACTIVE, a 1 is placed there automatically.

■ Increase the size of MAILER by 20 characters.

■ Add two more columns—SELFSERVE and ADDR.

Let's get started by clearing the worksheet. Proceed to Edit on the menu at the top of the window, and select Clear All from its drop-down menu.

1. Enter the text **alter table owners modify (active default '1')**, and then press F5 to execute the command.

2. After receiving the "Table altered." feedback, enter the command **alter table owners modify (mailer varchar2(120))**, and press F5 once again, receiving acknowledgment from Oracle9*i*.

3. Finally, enter the commands as shown in Figure 11-19, which will not only complete this exercise in SQL*Plus Worksheet, but will also mark the beginning of the end of this chapter!

Hang on tight, as the OEM express comes in for a landing. OEM is a very large and powerful tool, offering a GUI interface to just about anything you may want to do with the Oracle9*i* database. We have only scratched the surface of this immense product—you should now have a flavor of the interface it provides, especially to the DBA role. The funny thing about OEM, which is true about any and all GUI tools, is that all the Oracle9*i* database engine understands is SQL statements. OEM provides a fancy, functional, and pretty point-and-click interface to formulate those commands.

Our next chapter delves briefly into the world of distributed computing. Picture a vast network of intertwined servers, working together to provide a robust solution for a multinational distributor of goods to the hungry consumer. LONS (Lots of Nice Stuff) International is one of the hundreds, if not thousands, of companies worldwide that offer this type of service, with the distributed computing capabilities of Oracle9*i* and Oracle Net as the backbone of their technology.

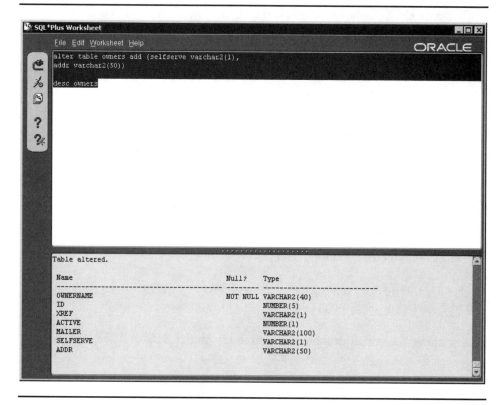

FIGURE 11-19. *Table modification command and altered table description*

Chapter 11 Questions

Answers to questions can be found in Appendix A.

1. The right to occupy space in a specific Oracle9*i* database is referred to as a

   A. resource

   B. quota

   C. table creation

   D. All of the above

2. The ORACLE_SID is an identifier used to

   A. assign names to your Oracle9*i* databases

   B. uniquely identify each database

   C. set variables when interacting with an Oracle9*i* database

   D. All of the above

3. Without any additional work being done, which user of the Oracle9*i* database automatically gets the sysdba role?

   A. ELLISON

   B. SYS

   C. OEM

   D. No user gets this role by default.

4. Which of the following shutdown options does a rollback on active transactions and disconnects all connected users?

   A. Abort

   B. Normal

   C. Sysdba

   D. Immediate

5. Suppose you own a TAILOR table. The correct syntax for giving DELETE privileges to all users of the database with one SQL statement is

   A. `Grant delete to all on tailor;`

   B. `Grant delete on tailor to all;`

   C. `Grant delete on tailor to public;`

   D. This cannot be done—you must issue a separate **delete** statement to each user of the database.

CHAPTER

12

Distributed Computing

n this Internet age, distributed computing is beginning to be taken for granted. With the almost-daily advent of new networking technology, you can achieve interconnectivity among your computers, even if they are strewn all over the office. In this chapter, we are going to look at Oracle9i's distributed features, in particular,

- Partitioning applications via distributed processing
- Oracle Net configuration files
- Database links and the role they play

Terminology

Let's get started with the technical jargon you will need to make it through this chapter.

- *CPU* stands for *central processing unit*, the heart of every computer, which works along with main memory, disk drives, and other peripherals to deliver the total computing solution.

- In a distributed computing environment, the *master site* holds data that is pushed to remote sites for the purposes of partitioned processing. The *remote site* receives information from one or more master sites and often participates in system functionality after receipt of data from the appropriate master.

- A *listener* runs on a server and detects remote requests for services. When one computer wishes to carry out work in the Oracle9i database on another machine, it's that other machine's listener that intercepts this request.

- The process of making copies of the Oracle9i data is called *backup*. The corollary is called *recovery*, which involves copying backups of your data back to their proper location after failure.

- A *port* is a logical doorway to the resources on a computer. Ports are conduits used by multiple sessions running on the same server, ensuring that when two sessions request information simultaneously, they both receive their proper responses. Ports are referred to by four-digit numbers.

A *database link* is set up on one database to allow transparent access to objects that reside in another database. Think of it as the network cable connecting two servers running Oracle9i.

- When you have a fixed amount of time to perform a task, that time period is referred to as a *window of opportunity*.

- A *protocol* defines the specific wording and control flow for communications between two or more programs, devices, or systems.

- The *interprocess communication protocol* (IPC), is sometimes used with Oracle Net when a server and a client process interact with one another on the same computer.

- An *IP address* is a four-part number used to identify computers on a network. Each part of the address commonly has from one to three digits. A couple of examples are 209.11.34.198 or 32.97.87.66. Notice how each part is separated by a dot, or period.

- A *domain name service* (DNS) is a convention used to translate cryptic IP addresses into more familiar, hierarchical names. Examples of DNS usage are **thewhitehouse.com** for 216.182.45.11, and **ioug.org** for 63.165.6.58.

Partitioning Applications via Distributed Processing

Common complaints voiced by users center on performance and availability. Instead of stacking all the cards in one place, distributed processing permits all of the following:

- CPU-intensive application functionality can be split among servers. The load on each machine ends up being lower.

- Each server can be dedicated to a specific function within an application. Suppose an online community wants a separate repository for real-time messaging (commonly called *chats*) and another for storage of email messages. The distributed solution is ideal for this requirement.

- With smaller volumes of data on each node, backup and recovery times can be reduced. The window of opportunity on each server for backup is shortened. Suppose a 43GB database is evenly split between two servers in a distributed computing environment. No matter how long it takes to back each one up, it will be 50 percent of what it would be were they together.

- When some form of failure renders an application unavailable on one node, the availability of other components may be unaffected. Often, you visit your friendly neighborhood banking machine and are told it is temporarily out of service. You then go into the branch and find the tellers working away as usual—their piece of the bank's system remains available while the ATMs are not.

Oracle Net

The precursor to Oracle Net was called SQL*Net, a name with which some readers may be more familiar. Oracle Net is the backbone of Oracle9i's distributed computing solution. It's a big topic, with many books dedicated to it alone. The heart of Oracle Net's functionality is its listener, trained to listen on a certain port. The listener passes connections through to the Oracle9i server when they contain proper authentication details. Let's spend a bit of time looking at the two major configuration files used by Oracle Net—listener.ora and tnsnames.ora. Then we'll see how they can be created with the Oracle Net Configuration Assistant.

NOTE
Looking at the outputs from the Net Configuration Assistant and then looking at the tool itself may seem backward. Most of the time, even the beginning Oracle9i administrator will simply copy the two Oracle Net configuration files rather than using this assistant, and then make modifications using a text editor.

listener.ora

The listener.ora file describes the environment within which requests for remote connections will be serviced. When the listener process is running on a machine, connection requests are intercepted on the specified ports and passed to the appropriate Oracle9i database. The next listing shows a snippet from a sample listener.ora file. The line numbers are not part of this file; they are there for the discussion in Table 12-1. Knowing your way around this file rounds out your understanding of Oracle Net.

NOTE
Most of the time, you will not have to create your own listener.ora, as it is done by the Oracle Net Configuration Assistant that is run when Oracle9i is installed.

```
1   # LISTENER.ORA Network Configuration File:
2   # Generated by Oracle configuration tools.
3   LISTENER =
4     (ADDRESS_LIST =
5       (ADDRESS= (PROTOCOL = TCP)(HOST = db.tpg.com)(PORT = 1521))
6     )
7     SID_LIST_LISTENER =
```

```
 8      (SID_LIST =
 9        (SID_DESC =
10           (ORACLE_HOME= /app/oracle/product/9.1.2)
11           (SID_NAME = o9ibeg)
12        )
13      )
14   STARTUP_WAIT_TIME_LISTENER = 0
15   CONNECT_TIMEOUT_LISTENER = 10
16   TRACE_LEVEL_LISTENER = OFF
```

So we've looked at listener.ora; now on to its close friend—tnsnames.ora—where handles are assigned that can be used to access Oracle9*i* databases using Oracle Net.

Line	Description
3	This is the name of the listener. You may use any name you want, but LISTENER is the default. From time to time, we use multiple listeners on the same server.
4	This begins the first descriptive part of this file. Notice how the file is formatted, with ADDRESS_LIST's closing parenthesis on line 6. This formatting is not mandatory, but makes the file more readable.
5	This is the heart of the address description, with the three main entries as follows: ■ **Protocol** This value is **tcp** most of the time, though not always. The most common Internet protocol is **tcp**, but you may see the value **ipc** for this parameter. ■ **Host** This is commonly the IP address for the server upon which the listener is running, though a domain name service (DNS) can appear here as well. Using DNS, the names of your servers are more readable. DNS also offers portability. For example, if a server IP changes from 196.213.21.34 to something else, the pointer of the DNS is changed and all references to the DNS transparently follow the change. This is illustrated in Figure 12-1. ■ **Port** This is a four-digit number, most commonly 1521. When an address is defined using a specific port, only connection requests on that port are intercepted by the aforementioned listener.
10	ORACLE_HOME is the location on your server where the Oracle9*i* software resides. Be it Windows 2000 or a UNIX server, this name is used to reference this directory.

TABLE 12-1.   *Discussion of listener.ora*

Line	Description
11	SID_NAME refers to the logical handle used to reference an Oracle9*i* database on a server. This system identifier is used to assist routing of connection requests to the proper database.
14-16	These entries are self-explanatory and help define the operating environment for the listener they reference. Notice how they terminate with LISTENER, the name given the listener process being defined. If your listener were called LISTENER_MEX, then the first of these three parameters would read STARTUP_WAITTIME_LISTENER_MEX instead.

TABLE 12-1. *Discussion of listener.ora* (continued)

tnsnames.ora

Many different names have been assigned to the entries in this file. When SQL*Net version 2 hit the streets around 1992, Oracle called the leading entries in this file *service descriptors*. We commonly refer to them as Net aliases. The next listing shows a sample of a tnsnames.ora file—again, the line numbers are included for the discussion in Table 12-2.

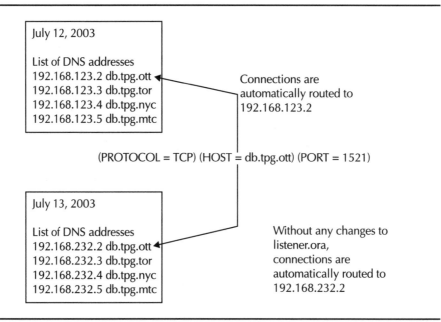

FIGURE 12-1. *Changing DNS transparently to listener.ora entries*

Line	Description
3-12	See the Note before the preceding listing.
13	This text, **o9ibeg**, is referred to as an Oracle Net alias. It can be used when connecting to the server upon which this copy of tnsnames.ora resides. Connection requests take the form *username/password@{alias}*, using, of course, **@o9ibeg** for the purposes of this discussion.
16	This is the heart of the tnsnames.ora file, where the alias's protocol, host name or IP address, and port of entry are defined. A DNS is commonly used rather than a hard-coded IP address. Note that we have entered **db.tpg.com** as used in listener.ora in the previous section.
19	This service name accompanies the entries listed in line 16 to further define the environment accessed when using specific Oracle Net aliases.

TABLE 12-2. *Discussion of tnsnames.ora*

NOTE
When the Oracle9i Network Configuration Assistant goes about its work, it sets up an alias specific to the Apache web server, as well as the IPC protocol shown in lines 4–12. We will concentrate on the more traditional TCP/IP protocol shown with the o9Ibeg alias.

```
1 # TNSNAMES.ORA Network Configuration File
2 # Generated by Oracle configuration tools.
3 EXTPROC_CONNECTION_DATA =
4   (DESCRIPTION =
5     (ADDRESS_LIST =
6       (ADDRESS = (PROTOCOL = IPC)(KEY = EXTPROC1))
7     )
8     (CONNECT_DATA =
9       (SID = PLSExtProc)
10      (PRESENTATION = RO)
11    )
12  )
13 O9IBEG =
14   (DESCRIPTION =
15     (ADDRESS_LIST =
16       (ADDRESS = (PROTOCOL = TCP)(HOST = db.tpg.com)(PORT = 1521))
17     )
18     (CONNECT_DATA =
```

```
19          (SERVICE_NAME = o9ibeg)
20      )
21  )
```

At this point, you could easily be saying to yourself, "Wait a minute, how were these files created?"

The Network Configuration Assistant

To invoke the Network Configuration Assistant, click Start I ora9i2k I Configuration and Migration Tools I Net Configuration Assistant. When the GUI interface starts, you will be presented with a screen similar to that shown in Figure 12-2.

We are only going to concern ourselves with options one and three shown in Figure 12-2. Let's get started.

1. Select Listener Configuration, and click Next.

2. You will be asked to select the activity you wish to perform—Add, Reconfigure, Delete, or Rename. Select Add, and click Next.

3. The assistant displays a suggested default listener name—LISTENER (surprise, surprise). Leave as is and again click Next.

4. You will see the protocol screen, where most of the time you will leave the selected protocol TCP/IP as is and click Next. Do that now.

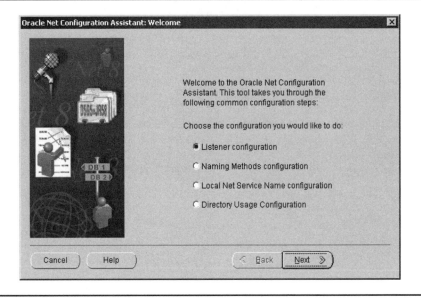

FIGURE 12-2. *Net Configuration Assistant startup*

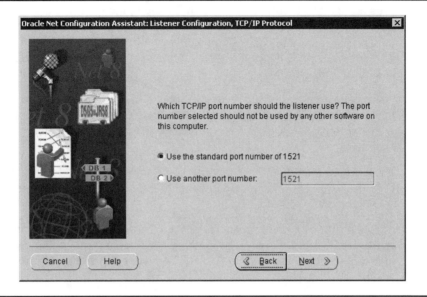

FIGURE 12-3.   *Choosing a listener port*

5. The assistant now needs to know the port. You enter it on a screen similar to that shown in Figure 12-3. Click Next to finish.

6. When asked whether you want to configure another listener, ensure that No is selected, and then click Next.

7. The assistant brings up a screen where you can start the listener you have just created. If the listener just created is displayed, click Next to continue. If necessary, pick the desired listener from a drop-down list before carrying on. A DOS window will pop up as the assistant invokes the listener startup.

8. When you are told that the configuration is complete, click Next to initiate another Net Assistant task or Cancel to leave.

That's it! You now have a properly configured and running listener. Before delving into making connections using Oracle Net aliases, let's spend a bit of time on using the Net Assistant to manufacture a tnsnames.ora file. Suppose the assistant were just invoked, as shown in Figure 12-2. This time, choose Local Net Service Name Configuration, and then click Next. Using the ensuing screens, the tnsnames.ora services file is created by following these steps.

1. You are asked what type of activity you want to pursue, except this time there is one additional choice—Test. Select Add and move to the next screen by clicking Next.

2. Even though this assistant comes with Oracle9*i*, the next screen needs to know whether the database you will be accessing is release 8*i* and later or 8.0 and earlier. There was a significant swing in the Oracle Net technology going from 8.0 to 8*i*, hence the need for this. Select Oracle8*i* or later database or service, and click Next.

3. Pick a name for the service as requested on the next screen. We chose **o9ibeg**, but you can choose whatever you want. Click Next. Again, you are presented with the protocol choice screen. Ensure that TCP/IP is highlighted, and click Next.

4. The assistant then needs to know the host name and the port to use. Enter a host (the name of the server upon which the Oracle9*i* database resides) and accept the entry 1521 for port.

5. It's D day! Time to test the connection. We advise you to test your connections as they are created. Carry on by clicking Next again. You will receive a message like the one shown in Figure 12-4 if your connection test succeeds, as ours did.

6. Click Next to bring you to the screen where you are informed of the success of the net service name configuration.

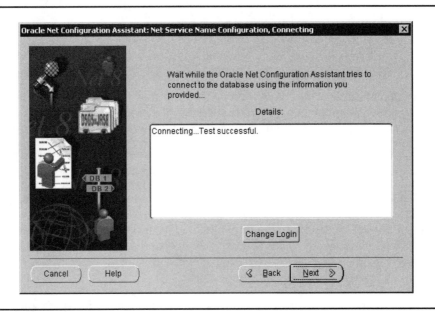

FIGURE 12-4. *A successful connection*

7. Click Next to return to the same screen shown in Figure 12-2.

8. Click Finish to exit the assistant.

Move to the front of the class—you are now an experienced Oracle Net configuration technocrat! Our next topic centers around making connections to remote databases using the connect descriptors created with the Network Configuration Assistant. But first, let's introduce the concept of database links by switching to the Oracle Enterprise Manager discussed in Chapter 11. Click Enterprise Manager Console on your Start menu; and after bringing up the console's main screen, follow these steps:

1. Expand the tree underneath your database name by clicking +.

2. Expand the Schema branch that will end up looking something like that shown in Figure 12-5.

3. Right-click the Database Link folder, and then select Create, bringing up the data entry form shown in Figure 12-6.

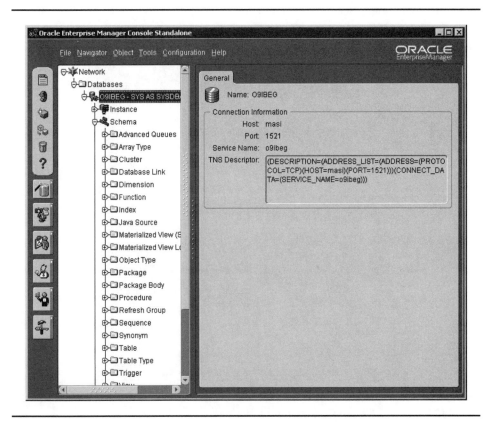

FIGURE 12-5. *Schema branch of the OIBEG9 database in OEM*

4. Select the Fixed User option to allow for username and password data entry.

5. Fill in values for Name, Username, Password, and Service Name. Our entries—**to_toronto**, **reader**, and **hrpay.to.ca**—may not be the same as those you enter. We clicked the Show SQL button to display the SQL statement that will be passed to Oracle9i to create the database link.

6. Accept your settings by clicking Create.

7. Dismiss the link-created message by clicking OK.

We have now created a database link. Let's look at a hypothetical assortment of networked Oracle9i databases and how the magic of Oracle Net can intertwine their data at the click of a mouse.

Placement of tnsnames.ora

The listener.ora configuration file resides on the server upon which the Oracle9i database runs, but the tnsnames file is a corporate entity, sitting everywhere there may be a client wanting to access a remote database. Whether you are using a two-tier or

FIGURE 12-6. *Create Database Link dialog box*

a three-tier architecture, tnsnames.ora must be accessible somehow from each client. Figure 12-7 illustrates this concept.

Let's put the icing on the cake or, in some other circles, the sesame seeds on the bagel, or the oil on the man'ousheh! All this comes together when we take a quick look at the interconnectivity provided by Oracle Net.

Establishing a Connection via Oracle Net

The distributed computing environment, being what it is, lends itself nicely to the functionality provided by Oracle Net. From day one, regardless of whether you are using Oracle9*i* on Sun Solaris, Linux Intel, Compaq TRU64, or HP, you will find that Oracle Net is your best friend. For example, the following table lists a handful of servers in a networked Oracle9*i* server environment at a large multinational

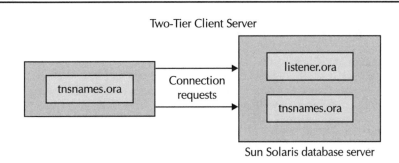

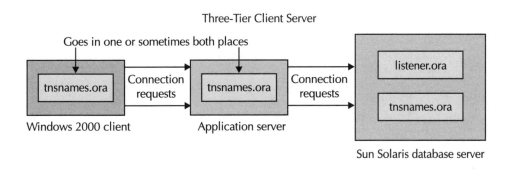

FIGURE 12-7. *Placement of listener.ora and tnsnames.ora*

manufacturer called Lons International. Using this as an example, we will have a look at the interconnection facility Oracle Net provides.

Server Location	Oracle9i Database	Connection Descriptors	Function
Toronto	Hrpay	Hrpay.tor.ca	Human resources pay
Chicago	Ap	Ap.ch.us	Accounts payable
Nice	Armtl	Armtl.nc.fr	Accounts receivable material
New Delhi	Gl	Gl.nd.in	General ledger
Buenos Aires	Mkg	Mkg.ba.ar	Marketing

The DBA has set up database links in addition to the **to_toronto** link we set up in OEM in the previous section, to resolve all the data references between the five network nodes.

```
-- Create database links between the servers . . .
--
-- This first one has been run in Chicago using OEM so just
-- run it in Nice, New Delhi, and Buenos Aires

create public database link to_toronto
        connect to reader identified by reader
        using 'hrpay.tor.ca';
-- Run this in Toronto, Nice, New Delhi, and Buenos Aires

create public database link to_chicago
        connect to reader identified by reader
        using 'ap.ch.us';
-- Run this in Toronto, Chicago, New Delhi, and Buenos Aires

create public database link to_nice
        connect to reader identified by reader
        using 'armtl.nc.fr';
-- Run this in Toronto, Chicago, Nice, and Buenos Aires
create public database link to_new_delhi
        connect to reader identified by reader
        using 'gl.nd.in';
-- Run this in Toronto, Chicago, Nice, and New Delhi
create public database link to_buenos_aires
        connect to reader identified by reader
        using 'mkg.ba.ar';
```

Melissa Cornfield, the comptroller at Lons, arrives at work most days by 9:00 a.m. local time. The traffic on the Don Valley parkway has been awful with all the construction this fall, and she is in a rush to collect some information before she heads into a senior management meeting at 11:00 a.m. Unbeknownst to her, the Oracle Discoverer interface she uses to browse her corporate data resides on servers in the five cities shown in the previous table. The location of data is transparent to Melissa and anyone else accessing the corporate infrastructure due to Oracle Net. This is because the DBAs at all the Lons servers have set up an intricate network of synonyms, three of which are shown in the following table for PERSON, JOB, and PAYROLL.

Table Name	True Location	Synonym built with
PERSON	Toronto	create public synonym person for person@hrpay.tor.ca;
JOB	Toronto	create public synonym job for job@hrpay.tor.ca;
PAYROLL	Chicago	create public synonym payroll for payroll@ap.ch.us;

This might not seem like magic at first sight, but picture the following query, issued on any of the Lons database servers. The wording of the query is exactly the same regardless of where you come from.

```
-- The tables in normal print reside in Toronto, Chicago's table is in
-- bold.
select per.full_name,per.hire_date,job.title,job.description,
       pay.starting,pay.current
from person per,job jb,payroll pay
where per.pid = pay.pid
and jb.jid = pers.jid;
```

Distributed computing with Oracle9*i* is a vast topic, and we have looked at a small part. The next chapter looks at some Internet specifics in Oracle9*i*. It seems you can't go anywhere in today's computer world without finding software prefixed or suffixed with this ninth letter of the alphabet.

Chapter 12 Questions

Answers to questions can be found in Appendix A.

1. Database links offer what major functionality to the Oracle9*i* database?

  A. The ability to link your tables with someone else's tables

  B. The ability to access someone else's data from your desktop

    C. The ability to read data directly from other vendors' databases

    D. The ability to network an assortment of databases running on different servers

2. Which file outlines the environment used by the Oracle Net process that scans the network for incoming server connection requests?

    A. tnsnames.ora

    B. INIT.ora

    C. listener.ora

    D. None of the above

3. Which file contains a list of valid Oracle Net aliases that can be used to access a database running on a specific server?

    A. tnsnames.ora

    B. INIT.ora

    C. listener.ora

    D. None of the above

4. The logical four-digit address used to access resources on a computer is called

    A. an IP address

    B. a CPU model number

    C. a port

    D. a protocol

5. ORACLE_HOME in the context of the Oracle9*i* server product is

    A. www.oracle.com/oracle9i

    B. the location of the Oracle9*i* software

    C. the location of all Oracle Net configuration files

    D. All of the above

PART IV

I Is for Internet

CHAPTER
13

The *i* in Oracle9*i*

s Oracle reminds us in their advertising, "The Internet Changes Everything." I like to watch my daughter on the Internet. Although she is only 10, she gives me tips on how to use it. When a friend wants to talk to her using an instant messenger, she calls her on the telephone and tells her to log onto the Internet. Watching this occur, I can't help but chuckle at the way my daughter's life has been simplified! Whether we use it for personal or business reasons, or both, the Internet has had a profound effect on our way of life.

The Internet has also had a profound effect on the Oracle database. It allows us to simply open a web browser like Internet Explorer or Netscape and view information no matter where we are. This is possible through the increasing portability of databases and applications, and the use of a programming language that is very generic—Java. With the adoption of Java and the Internet, we are starting to see a greater dependence on back-end servers. These servers include database servers and Internet servers. Together, they provide significant power to the types of objects that we can deploy. This chapter will discuss the Internet and its impact on the Oracle database, specifically,

- The Enterprise Java Engine (EJE)

- Java in the database

- High availability

- Internet security issues

- Real Application Clusters

- Internet File System (iFS)

Terminology

The following definitions will arm you with the technical jargon to make it through this chapter.

- The *Internet* is a global network connecting millions of computers.

- An *intranet* is an Internet-like network belonging to an organization, usually a corporation, accessible only by the organization's members, employees, or others with authorization to enter the network. An intranet's web sites look and act just like any other web sites, but the firewall, which surrounds the intranet, fends off unauthorized user access.

■ An *application server,* also called an *appserver,* is a program that handles all operations between users and the database. Application servers are typically used for complex transaction-based applications.

■ *Java* is an object-oriented programming language similar to C++ that was originally developed by Sun Microsystems. Java program files (files with a .java extension) are compiled into a format called *bytecode* (files with a .class extension), which can then be executed by a Java interpreter. Compiled Java code can run on most computers because Java interpreters and runtime environments, known as *Java Virtual Machines* (JVMs), exist for most systems.

■ *JVM* is an acronym for Java Virtual Machine. An abstract computing machine, or virtual machine, the JVM is a platform-independent programming language that converts Java into machine language and then runs it.

■ *CORBA,* which stands for Common Object Request Broker Architecture, enables pieces of programs, called objects, to communicate with one another regardless of what language they were written in or what operating system they are running on.

■ A *network protocol* is a method used to allow computers to talk to one another in a standard messaging transaction. The most common network protocol is known as TCP/IP (Transmission Control Protocol/Internet Protocol).

■ JDBC stands for Java database connectivity. If you are familiar with ODBC (database connectivity from a Windows environment), this is the Java version of that connectivity. This allows a Java program to interact with any SQL-compliant database.

■ *SQLJ* is the feature that allows Java programs to execute SQL statements and receive the results back for processing.

■ *EJB,* which stands for Enterprise Java Beans, defines an architecture in which components are deployable.

■ *J2EE* is short for Java 2 Platform Enterprise Edition. J2EE is a platform-independent Java environment from Sun for developing, building, and deploying web-based enterprise applications online.

■ *ORB,* which stands for Object Request Broker, is a component that acts as the middleware between clients and servers. The various ORBs receive the requests, forward them to the appropriate servers, and then hand the results back to the client.

- *RAC*, for Real Application Cluster, is a technology for deploying a number of servers that have independent CPUs and memory, but share the same disk drives. RAC technology allows you to scale your hardware as your needs require.

The Oracle Internet Database

The use of the Oracle database as an Internet engine began in Oracle8i. It incorporated an Internet-ready engine into the database itself, allowing you to drive applications from the database. By bringing the Internet engine into the database, Oracle has provided a scalable solution. When Oracle first introduced Java to the database (in version 8.1.5), it provided a system known as the JServer. The JServer supported Java from within the database, while leveraging the security and memory management provided by the database. Then, as Oracle tends to do with its products, when it released the next version of the database (8.1.6), the JServer was replaced with the Java Virtual Machine (JVM). With Oracle9i, the JVM has been renamed once again to the Enterprise Java Engine (EJE). The EJE has a complex architecture to allow it to support the many access methods, client types, and user access layers. Figure 13-1 illustrates the architecture of the EJE.

Figure 13-1 shows how Oracle9i deals with the Internet. As is quite obvious from the diagram, it is an alphabet soup. From EJE to IIOP to HTTP, the Internet is the world's center for TLA (three-letter acronyms).

As you can see, there are three tiers to the Internet architecture. Each tier defines a level of hardware or software. The three tiers are the clienttier, middle tier, and database tier. Each tier contains its own Java Virtual Machine. The JVM allows the software to translate code that has been written in Java and run it as appropriate to the individual program code. This is one of the major advantages of using a language like Java. Since Java provides true portability, it can be deployed on many different platforms without special programming to accommodate each special environment. Having a JVM in each tier allows each tier to translate the Java code for its own needs.

NOTE
The portability of Java requires a platform-specific Java interpreter that slows down the execution of the Java code.

Users access the system from the client tier. This may be a client-server program or a desktop computer running a web browser like Internet Explorer or Netscape. Through various network or Internet protocols, users communicate either with the

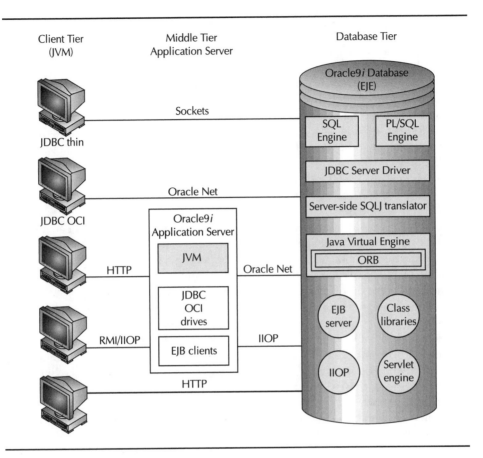

FIGURE 13-1.   *Enterprise Java Engine architecture*

database directly or through a middle-tier layer. The middle tier contains functional modules that process data. This tier usually runs on a server and is called an application server. Oracle9*i* Application Server is this middle tier of a complete Oracle solution. Oracle9*i*AS provides users with many different products that may be used to access the database, including Oracle Portal, Oracle Forms, Oracle Reports, and Oracle Discoverer, among others. The final tier, the database tier, contains the database as well as its own processes to allow for the receiving and sending of messages. The Oracle9*i* database contains an EJE so that Java can be stored in the database and then run from within the Oracle database engine. Together, these three layers form the architecture for the Oracle9*i* database.

Communicating with the Database

As you have seen in Figure 13-1, there are many methods for communicating with the database. So, whether you are communicating directly from a client workstation or via an application server, there are many different methods of access to your data and applications. Although this is not part of the Oracle9i database, it is important that you understand the different methods. A network protocol is an agreed-upon format for transmitting data between two devices. The protocol determines the type of error checking to be used; the data compression method, if any; and how the sending device will indicate that it has finished sending a message, as well as how the receiving device will indicate that it has received a message successfully. That is a lot of stuff for something to do, but that is the job of communication—making the transition from one device to another.

We are always intrigued by movies, and one movie that tries to educate us on the importance of communication is *Independence Day*, with Will Smith. In this film, Will Smith's character is responsible for putting a virus into the computer on the alien ship. This virus will, of course, destroy the alien ship and save Earth. So he loads the virus on his computer and then flies up to the mothership. He then gets his laptop computer to link to the alien computer and installs the virus. Surprisingly, earthlings and aliens use the same network protocol. As you might expect, the aliens are defeated. What we find amazing is that protocols are standard throughout the universe; how else could Will Smith have transmitted the virus, a true triumph of earthling technology? Of course, our real-life experience on Earth is quite different, and managing all these different protocols is a definite challenge to programmers and administrators.

Many different protocols are used in today's Internet world. Some depend on the access methods that you are using, while others depend on the type of programming that you are doing. Let's work our way through the protocols identified in Figure 13-1:

- Oracle Net and TCP/IP
- IIOP—presentation layer
- Sockets—transport layer
- HTTP—application layer

The standard method of passing requests to the Oracle database and getting the information uses Oracle Net and TCP/IP. Oracle Net is known as a native connection, since it is specific to the Oracle database. Using TCP/IP, it passes the request to the database and then receives it back at the client. To be able to use this method of accessing the database, you need to install Oracle Net and the required protocol (TCP/IP) on each client machine.

To understand the remaining three types of protocols, you need to understand that communication over networks occurs at many levels. Protocols have been created today with a seven-layer framework called *Open System Interconnection (OSI)*, which is a standard for worldwide communications. The seven layers are

- Application layer

- Presentation layer

- Session layer

- Transport layer

- Network layer

- Data link layer

- Physical layer

TCP/IP meshes the session, transport, and network layers a little, but essentially does what the OSI model is intended to do. When you use the Internet, you are actually interacting at the application layer through your browser, and the browser sends the information over the presentation layer with HTTP. The rest of the layers package and send the data off. Each of these layers has a purpose, and we urge you to do additional reading on the OSI seven-layer model. A complete discussion of communication protocols is beyond the scope of this book.

When you use CORBA or Enterprise Java Beans (EJBs) to deploy your applications, another protocol is used. This protocol is IIOP, or Internet Inter-ORB Protocol, the standard protocol for this type of communication. IIOP enables web browsers and application servers to exchange integers, arrays, and complex objects, unlike HTTP, which only supports transmission of textual data.

HTTP (Hypertext Transfer Protocol) is the Old Faithful of the Internet. The underlying protocol used by the today's Internet, HTTP defines how messages are formatted and transmitted, and what actions application servers and web browsers should take in response to various commands. For example, when you enter a URL like **http://www.torontodesigners.com** in your browser, this actually sends an HTTP command to the web server, directing it to fetch and transmit the requested web page.

NOTE
HTTP is called a stateless *protocol because it does not know what command was issued before it received the current one. This means that all HTTP requests are independent. Although each is independent, all HTTP requests can be associated with individual sessions.*

With HTTP, you can send requests to the database or the application server and then process data and web pages from the database.

The last type of protocol, a *socket*, is a software object that connects an application to a protocol. For example, a program can send and receive TCP/IP messages by opening a socket, and reading and writing data to and from the socket. This simplifies program development because the programmer need only worry about manipulating the socket and can rely on the operating system to actually transport messages across the network correctly. The Internet uses Secure Sockets Layer (SSL) to transport data through the wide-open environment. SSL uses encryption to protect the data as it is being transmitted. This way your information is protected from prying eyes.

So, there you have it—numerous ways that data is transported over the Web and into and out of an Oracle database. We can now move on and look at how this relates to using Java within the Oracle9*i* database.

Java in the Database

One of the valuable features of the Oracle9*i* database is the inclusion of Java within the database engine itself. The fact that Java is simple and portable means that it works well on the very diverse Internet. Oracle9*i* supports Java, in that it allows you to execute Java natively, just like PL/SQL. But the true and emerging power of Java is actually in the middle tier of a three-tier computing model with Java servlets. The Java application sends requests off to either the database or another intermediate request broker machine. These machines simply receive SQL requests, and Oracle presumably would be handling this.

The fact that Java can now handle SQL more easily means that there is less translating to do between Oracle9*i* and the overlying application. The Web has introduced a new paradigm in that it provides a nice new mini-operating system. The Web is actually pretty equal to both Windows and UNIX (and its various flavors) in that any application that can be run in a browser has little to do with the underlying operating system. The browser *is* the operating system, and that was the initial allure of Java applets. Unfortunately, their slow loading times and executions made them impractical for serious applications. But now, with server-side Java, distributed applications are all the rage, and they are perfect for Oracle, since Oracle9*i* is the foundation for serious applications that require scalability. Java can help you achieve this goal.

Java is an object-oriented programming language. In object-oriented programming, programmers define both the types of data and the types of operations that can be applied to the data structure. In this way, the data structure becomes an object that includes both data and functions, which are also known as methods. In addition, programmers can create relationships between one object and another. For example, objects can inherit characteristics from other objects. This inheritance allows an object to adopt the characteristics of the parent object. This provides for great control over the way that data is both organized and managed.

Java, like all object-oriented programming languages, supports the idea of a class. A *class* is a template for objects that share the same characteristics. Every class contains two main features: attributes and methods. *Attributes* are static or variable items that are available in inherited instances. *Methods* are the rules used against an object, such as an **insert** command that is managed by the object. So why do we want to use Java in our Oracle9*i* database? Java in the database provides us with the following advantages:

- Simplicity

- Portability

- Automatic memory management

- Security

Let's look at each of the advantages and see how Oracle9*i* provides support for Java. The first point is simplicity. Java is a simple language in the object-oriented class of programming languages, since it is consistent in its use of the object model. There are also plenty of standard Java classes that may be used and shared, providing significant time savings when programming applications. Just look up Java on the Internet, and you will see how much code already exists that you can use.

We have already talked about Java's portability. It runs on many different platforms, since you write generic code that is then translated on each machine within each JVM. Using Java within Oracle9*i* is an advantage because Oracle9*i* handles the internal allocation and deallocation of memory. However, this is not always reliable for code that is hit hard and often. This means that you do not have to worry about any type of memory management as you might have to in a language like C. Finally, when it comes to Java security, an applet is supposedly very secure. It is not supposed to allow access to the operating system file system when run. However, if the applet source is run locally, then those security constraints are lifted. The moral of the story— some things are not as secure as they may appear at first.

The JVM has mechanisms within it that verify that code has not been changed. Oracle9*i* also provides you with a security manager object that can be used to control a program.

We will discuss how to store and run Java in the database in Chapter 14. Now we will move on to see how Oracle9*i* provides high availability in the database. Although it is not directly an Internet subject, the remainder of this chapter will look at how Oracle9*i* supports the needs of the Internet database.

High Availability

The fact that the Internet is a 24-hour-a-day activity makes high availability a vital factor in the Internet database. Although your particular organization may have different requirements, we basically understand that your database needs to be available 7x24x365. Can you imagine Amazon.com not having their database up all the time?

The definition of *high availability* differs depending on the function of the information. Although Amazon.com may need to have a database up and running all the time, that may not be true for all organizations. A business that runs a data warehouse may only need it available 12 hours per day. The rest of the time may be spent loading and managing data, and if users are restricted from accessing data, it may not be a problem. You need to define what high availability means to your organization. Let's look at some of the features that Oracle9i provides to support most high-availability situations.

There are many different types of failures that can cause a system to become unavailable, including system crashes, network failures, disk failures, human errors, and planned outages. Let's look at some of the features that Oracle9i provides to help minimize these types of failures.

Protection from System Crashes

Sometimes things go wrong and a system crashes. Think of how many times you get a "blue screen" in Microsoft Windows, and you realize that computers are not stable and that failures do occur. However, getting a crash every few hours or days is not an acceptable situation in an enterprise database environment. Although Oracle9i cannot control operating system failures, it does provide significant help when things go wrong to ensure that the database recovers as quickly as possible.

To quickly recover from system crashes, Oracle9i provides you with recovery at the time of database startup. This means that any transactions that may not have been posted at the time of the crash will be posted before anyone can use the database. Also, if transactions were pending and the database was never told to make these permanent, it will remove or roll back these transactions.

Another approach that is taken to deal with system crashes is Oracle9i's standby database. A standby database provides a means to create and maintain a remote copy of a production database. When the primary database fails, Oracle will switch control to the standby database, with only a minimal interruption. As an added benefit, it is possible to access the data in the standby database and use it for read-only purposes, such as reporting. You will need to break the ties between the two databases first; afterward, you can relink the master and the standby database.

NOTE
When in standby mode, it is not possible to select from the tables. Also, the interval between archive redo log pushes may cause some data loss.

Although we all hope that our servers never stop or that operating systems are fault free, the reality is that we need to plan for these types of failures. Using Oracle9*i* features, you can minimize the impact of these sad occurrences.

Protection from Disk Failures

When disks die, where do they go? We would like to know, since it seems that disks sometimes disappear, and we don't know where they have gone. The physical disk drive still exists, but the computer can't see it anymore, or the data has gone on vacation. Disk failures are one of the most common faults that you will see when running a database. A lot of time is spent recovering disks that have failed or files that have become corrupt, so Oracle9*i* provides some features to reduce the time required to recover from these faults.

Oracle9*i* lets you multiplex files. *Multiplexing* is the ability to create multiple copies of the same file on a single machine but different disk drives. This is especially useful for files that are critical to the database's running correctly or even at all. By creating and maintaining multiple copies of the files on different areas of your disk arrays, it is possible to continue normal business operations even if one file is lost.

Another method for reducing the risks of disk failures and speeding the recovery of faults is the use of the Recovery Manager, known to its friends as RMAN. RMAN provides users with a tool for managing backups and recoveries. It contains backup strategies, and it logs all backup and recovery information.

Finally, Oracle9*i* provides the ability to repair the database. For example, it is possible that data may become corrupted. Although the disk file may still be fine, the data in the file is unreadable. The DBMS_REPAIR utility allows you to identify problems and aid in their resolution.

The most important item that you need to know here is that recovery from disk failure is only as good as your last backup; so ensure that your backups are current and that they work. You may even want to take a backup and see whether you can restore it to another machine. Backups that have never been tested are as good as no backup at all.

Protection from Human Errors

How can you avoid human errors in your database? Removing the human from the database equation may do this, but it may be difficult. You say that this is impossible; then let's look at some Oracle9i features that help save our humans when it all goes terribly wrong.

Oracle9i provides significant security features that protect the data from unauthorized access. These include Oracle9i's standard user authentication, as well as the Oracle Advanced Security. The Advanced Security protects distributed environments, providing data integrity, data privacy, authentication, and authorization. You can also use Oracle9i's profiles, privileges, and roles:

- A *profile* is a mechanism within the database that allows you to control the amount of resources for a user. For example, with a profile, you can ensure that your users change their passwords every 30 days or that they only have two sessions running at the same time.

- *Privileges,* along with roles, control user access to objects. With privileges, you can allow some users only to view data, while others may have the ability to create and update the same data.

Finally, Oracle9i allows you to create Virtual Private Databases (VPDs), which are subsets of the data in the database. You do this by defining data access rules and then assigning these to individual users. Then when users select data from the database, the database will only retrieve the data that the user has the right to see.

Security is important, but it becomes even more important when you start exposing your data to the entire world as the Internet does. Take the time to understand security and its implications before you expose your data to prying eyes.

Management of Planned Outages

Finally, on the topic of high availability, we need to look at some of the features that allow you to minimize downtime caused by planned outages. Planned outages may be needed to optimize data placement or upgrade software, among many other reasons. Oracle9i provides features that allow you to reduce your downtime by providing the ability to perform tasks while the database is still up and running, with minimal impact on users.

As you will learn later in this book, it is important to keep your data organized within the database. When data in your database gets disorganized, it is known as *fragmentation.* Database fragmentation can result in performance problems for your users. Oracle9i now allows you to reorganize data in your indexes while users are using the system. Oracle9i also lets you use data partitions. A *data partition* allows you to divide large tables into smaller, more manageable pieces. Although users do not see these pieces individually (unless they want to), it allows the administrator to manage the pieces independently. This means that if you have data that has been separated by year, you can remove data that may have been added in 1995, without affecting data in any other year or even impacting system performance.

Real Application Clusters

One of the most important scalability features introduced in Oracle9*i* is Real
Application Clusters (RACs) and Cache Fusion technology. This technology lets you
share the power of many servers in a more or less scalable manner. With clustering,
you have a group of computers that act together as a single machine. The machines
then share the disk drives and the data contained on them, but do not share CPUs or
memory. This provides great flexibility and reduces downtime. It does this by allowing
you to survive the failure of one computer, by having others that can assume the load
or by plugging in a new computer to replace it. When you have many computers
connected to one database, all of these machines act as a single machine. This also
allows you to add machines when your needs increase. Figure 13-2 illustrates how
RAC technology would look.

As you see in Figure 13-2, the database is completely shared, and the hardware is
separate. This differs from other database vendors who use a *shared nothing* approach.
In a shared nothing database, queries directed to the overall database are sent to
the individual machines, since the database is divided over many different database
servers. The workload is divided across the multiple machines. The overall results for
a query cannot be assembled until all machines in the cluster have completed their
work. This limitation means that performance gains, which would result from an even
distribution of data across the machines, are lost, and you are now dependent on the
slowest single node.

Part of the RAC technology, Cache Fusion, is Oracle9*i*'s solution for providing a
single data cache that is shared by the cluster. This technology reduces the amount
of disk access by providing the data in a memory cache. Reducing disk access increases
performance significantly, since memory access is approximately 14,000 times faster
than disk access.

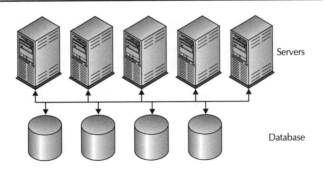

Servers

Database

FIGURE 13-2. *Real Application Cluster architecture*

This technology is particularly valuable for deploying your Internet applications. Success on the Web is measured in page hits, and when a web site becomes successful, these hits increase. The ability to add computing power in a simple manner like that of RAC technology allows you to evolve into the right size system without adding new database servers or separating your database into many pieces.

The Internet File System (*i*FS)

As the final stop on our *i* in Oracle9*i* journey, we will look at the Internet File System. The *i*FS combines the power of the Oracle database engine with the simplicity and friendliness of a traditional file system. Virtually any format of file can be put into the Oracle9*i* database and stored in its native format. Once the file is placed there, the file may be searched or queried just like any other content in the database. Even when resident in the Oracle9*i* database, *i*FS documents can be accessed as files by web browsers, as well as Windows Explorer, ftp clients, or even email programs. The end user relates to the *i*FS as just another drive on the corporate network.

The following are some of the benefits of using Oracle's *i*FS solution:

- Document storage directly in the database simplifies application developers' integration of different document types. Be it a spreadsheet, a word processing file, images, or sound files, centralized storage simplifies the integration of these different files into corporate applications.

- System administration of the *i*FS is the same as traditional network management, since *i*FS is accessed using techniques, processes, and procedures that are familiar to the database management team.

- The *i*FS may be accessed using SMB (server message block), which is a protocol for file sharing in Windows. Windows users can use drag-and-drop functionality, as well as edit documents directly on an *i*FS device. HTTP is used for browser-based access, and popular email protocols are used when *i*FS is accessed from an email program.

- Messaging hooks in *i*FS allow users to forward and reply to files as if they were email messages. Developers can use this messaging feature to trigger electronic communications between users when certain events occur. This feature can be used for auditing purposes if the organization wants to track file access.

As you might expect, *i*FS is an added value to the Oracle9*i* database and is another feature that may be part of your overall Internet implementation.

We have touched the surface of what is available in the database for use on the Internet—the Enterprise Java Engine, Java in the database, and the Internet File System. Now let's move on and look in more detail at just how we can use Oracle9*i* in our Internet world.

Chapter 13 Questions

Answers to questions can be found in Appendix A.

   1. Which of the following is not an Internet protocol?

     A. IIOP

     B. HTTP

     C. TCP/IP

     D. Internet/IP

   2. What part of the Oracle database is used to run Java?

     A. The coffee machine

     B. The Java Virtual Machine

     C. The EJB

     D. The network protocol

   3. What Oracle9*i* features may be used to minimize planned outages?

     A. Data partitioning

     B. Online index reorganizations

     C. None of the above

   4. To store a word processing file in the database, you would use what facility?

     A. A table

     B. A view

     C. *i*FS

     D. An operating system file

CHAPTER
14

All Things WWW

e have already discussed numerous subjects that circulate around the Web. In this chapter, we will look at what Oracle9i offers in the database, as well as in the middleware layer for Internet, intranet, or extranet solutions. Oracle9i now sells two products: the database and the Application Server. The two products help to form Oracle's solution for everyone who wants to store data and get data to the world. That world may be big or small, but together these products help make it smaller and more manageable.

This chapter will look at the Oracle9i solution from a few different angles. We will look at the Oracle9i Application Server—the middleware part of the solution. It listens for users to make requests to the database and then talks to the database to get the information that may be needed by the request. We will also look at Oracle Portal, which provides a simple interface to access the database, as well as another method for creating applications for users to input and retrieve data. To round it out, we will discuss using PL/SQL for the Web. Oracle9i has extended PL/SQL so that it can be used for generating web pages.

We will cover the following topics to help guide you through your Internet initiative:

- Oracle9i Application Server

- Various services provided by the Application Server

- PL/SQL for the Web

- Oracle Portal

Terminology

The following terminology will arm you with the technical jargon you need for this chapter:

- *Internet Application Server* (iAS) acts as the middle tier of a three-tier architecture. iAS acts as the go-between for the client using a web browser and the Oracle database. iAS is formerly known as Oracle Application Server (OAS) and commonly referred to as Oracle9i Application Server.

- *Oracle Portal* (formerly known as WebDB) is a GUI development tool for writing PL/SQL packages, which, in turn, generate dynamic HTML. Oracle Portal is oriented toward smaller companies that wish to get their Oracle databases onto the Internet/intranet but lack the development staff to create a complicated application.

■ The *HTTP listener* is a program that listens for web requests from a client web browser. Once a request is received, the type of request (Java, PL/SQL, HTML, etc.) is determined and forwarded to the appropriate module of the listener. For the purposes of this chapter, we'll be discussing the Apache HTTP listener, which is incorporated into *i*AS.

■ *Caching* refers to keeping frequently accessed information in a local server to permit fast retrieval. Oracle provides database caching and web caching. Database caching keeps commonly accessed data in memory such that the database doesn't have to be accessed to get the same information. Web caching keeps the contents of commonly accessed URLs on the application server rather than returning to the source web site.

■ *Three-tier architecture* is a system layout in which there is a database server tier, an application server tier, and a client tier. In this scenario, the database server is a high-end machine supporting a large database; the application server(s) is a midrange server providing communications between the database and the users; and the client tier is considered to be a thin client, where no extra software has been installed to run the application.

■ *Thin client* goes hand in hand with three-tier architecture. During the 1990s the creation of client-server applications demonstrated the degree of desktop support required for large applications. A thin client is a desktop PC requiring little or no extra software to be installed in order to run the application. Typically, a web browser like Netscape or Internet Explorer is all that is required.

■ The *thin Oracle driver* is written in Java and is downloaded at runtime. The thin driver does not require a client installation and is used with Java applets. The *thick Oracle driver* requires a dynamic link library (DLL) and Oracle Net installed on the client platform. The drivers can use the Oracle Net features and the Oracle Advanced Networking option, and can improve performance.

■ *CGI* stands for Common Gateway Interface, a specification for transferring information between an application server and a CGI program. A CGI program is any program that is designed to accept and return data that conforms to the CGI specification.

The Oracle9*i* Application Server

Application servers are programs that handle all operations between users and an organization's back-end business applications or the Oracle9*i* database itself. Application servers are typically used for complex transaction-based applications. To support high-end needs, an application server has to have built-in redundancy, high-availability, high-performance distributed application services, and support for complex database access. In the Oracle world, an evolution has occurred over the years, and it is useful to understand where this software has come from and to see where it is going.

When Oracle first launched their application server technology, it was known as the Oracle Web Server (OWS). This product was a challenge to all who used it. It was full of bugs and was a difficult product to use and administer. To help solve some of these problems and to distance Oracle from it, Oracle repackaged the product and called it Oracle Application Server (OAS). OAS was a great step forward, and it provided a stable middleware that was more reliable, yet it still had problems. Recently, Oracle once again took the rename strategy and called their new application server *i*AS, for Internet Application Server. This brand-new product that supersedes OAS provides much better stability, expandability, and features, and has succeeded where previous software versions did not.

One of the two major differences between OAS and *i*AS is the underlying web listener. A *web listener* is the software that listens for requests from users. The listener translates requests and then responds by providing the web page that may have been requested. Web listeners are critical to the Internet, and are therefore a critical piece of the application server puzzle. OAS was built upon the Spyglass HTTP listener, and it was severely lacking in stability. If you ever used OAS, you might remember all the problems you experienced. Although Spyglass was a solid product, in conjunction with OAS it did not perform as expected, and it was not an open or standard platform. Oracle understood this was not acceptable to most people and changed direction with *i*AS by making use of the world's most popular HTTP listener, Apache. Not only is Apache part of the installation of Oracle9*i*AS, but it has been bundled with all the extra modules required to get your database to communicate with the Internet.

The second major difference has to do with the performance of a web site using *i*AS. Oracle has incorporated database and middle-tier caching to permit frequently accessed URLs and information to be retrieved without requiring the site or database. Caching allows you to store data at the application server level, so that you don't have to go back to the database each time the same data is requested. This provides for some significant performance gains. As mentioned in previous discussions in the book, Oracle has always stored the most recently retrieved data from the database in memory. Caching at the application server level does the same thing for the Internet by caching data and web pages, to minimize database accesses for information that is used often.

Everything required for the middle tier is included with *i*AS. This product is oriented to act as the interface between the Internet/intranet/mobile users and the database. Figure 14-1 illustrates where *i*AS fits into the three-tier architecture—a common implementation for Internet deployment.

When we talk about three-tier architecture, as shown in Figure 14-1, we see how the Web is implemented in most organizations. The first tier is the client tier. This is your web browser. The next tier is the application server, or middleware layer. This layer handles transactions between clients and the final tier, the database. This is where the Oracle9*i* database resides in the Internet architecture.

Oracle9*i*AS is currently available in four flavors, with each containing additional software and functionality. Table 14-1 shows you the different features that you will find in each version.

We'll discuss all the features of these different versions to help you decide what is appropriate for your application and budget. Figure 14-2 shows all the components that come with the Enterprise Edition, as well as where the Wireless (Portal-to-Go) component would be situated in the architecture. Let's start by looking at the communication services.

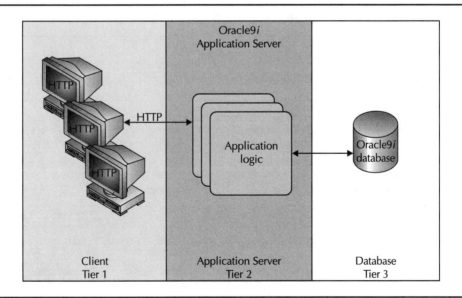

FIGURE 14-1.   *Three-tier architecture*

Version Type	Features

Minimal	Includes the HTTP listener, Oracle Portal, *i*AS wireless, and the Oracle Enterprise Manager client, specifically:
	  Communication Services
	  BC4J, JVM portions of Business Logic Services
	  Presentation Services
	  Oracle Portal

Standard Edition	Includes the options from the minimal version and adds the Java engine and Oracle Internet file system:
	  Features of minimal installation
	  Full Business Logic Services
	  Content Management Services

Enterprise Edition	Includes the options from Standard Edition, with the addition of web and database caching, Discoverer/Forms/Reports Services, and the Oracle Management server. All services are included.
Wireless Edition	Supports wireless implementations. This is the same as Enterprise Edition with the addition of Portal-to-Go.

TABLE 14-1. *Oracle9iAS Features Summary*

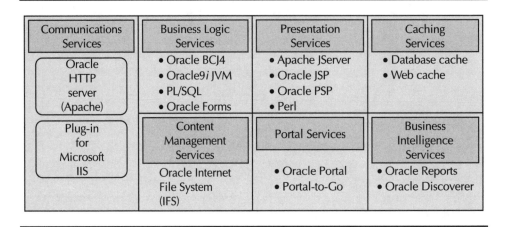

FIGURE 14-2. *Oracle9iAS architecture*

Communication Services

The communication services area is a key component to the application server solution. Imagine not being able to communicate—the thought, especially in the context of the Web, would be unimaginable. The Apache HTTP listener is the basis for all communications with Oracle9iAS. Oracle has extended the functionality of Apache by adding modules to support communications with the database. To provide this functionality, it has bundled a number of modules with the 9iAS product. The modules, mod_ssl, mod_plsql, mod_perl, mod_jserv, and mod_ose, permit you to run applications through the HTTP listener and to talk with the database. These modules allow you to communicate using any of the following options: SSL (Secure Sockets Layer), PL/SQL, Perl, Java servlets, and OSE (Oracle Servlet Engine). The fact that these modules are installed and fully configured along with Apache saves you the onerous task of installing them separately.

NOTE
Apache was developed as an open source application for UNIX systems. There is an implementation of Apache for NT, but it is not stable; this is due to the underlying architecture of Windows being completely different from UNIX. For that reason, it is recommended to run 9iAS on UNIX platforms. If you must run iAS on NT, then implement Microsoft Internet Information Server (IIS) and install iAS with the plug-in.

Let's look at each of the Oracle-specific Apache modules so you may decide how and when they should be used.

The mod_ssl Module

The mod_ssl module is provided to allow for encrypted communication. If you have ever performed banking with a web browser, you have communicated in a secure manner. Take a look the next time you transfer some money or pay a bill, and you will notice a small lock in the lower portion of your browser. This shows you that the communications that you are performing with the bank have been encrypted using SSL technology. Most sites that perform e-business functions today utilize Secure Sockets Layer (SSL); so when you order your concert tickets, you can be sure that you are using a secure form of communications. Oracle9iAS 1.0.2 uses the module open_ssl, which allows a secure HTTP connection (S-HTTP) that permits encrypted communication between the client and the database. HTTPS is used when your application sends corporate or private information over the public Internet. The encryption will help to ensure your sensitive information remains secure with minimal impact on performance.

The mod_plsql Module

The mod_plsql module is used to allow communication between the application server and stored procedures in your database. This feature allows you to leverage the power of your database along with the portability of the Internet. We use PL/SQL to minimize network and application server load. It is best to manipulate large amounts of information in the database server and then send only the results to the application server for presentation. Utilizing PL/SQL stored procedures will permit the queries to run on the database server (typically, a high-end server). For example, a PL/SQL stored procedure can be used for running "canned" reports. The result set is returned to the application server, which could then use Java servlets to display the information in a tabular format. This is an important feature, since one goal of communicating with people on the Internet is to minimize the amount of data that you transmit. By using PL/SQL and stored procedures, you will find that you can achieve this important goal.

The mod_perl Module

The mod_perl module allows you to utilize Perl (Practical Extraction and Report Language), a programming language designed for processing text. Because of its strong text-processing abilities, it has become one of the most popular languages for writing CGI scripts. Perl is an interpretive language that makes building and testing simple programs easy. This module forwards Perl requests to the HTTP server so that information requests and Perl programs may be executed within 9iAS. Perl scripts can be written to query the database and display the information. All data retrieved by a Perl script is considered to be character based, so there are no data type conversion issues, which often cause problems when programs are executed. The presentation capabilities of Perl are much better than HTML, so it should be used where the basic HTML tables for formatting are not sufficient.

The mod_jserv Module

The next module is mod_jserv, which forwards Java servlet requests to the HTTP server. A JServ engine is embedded in the HTTP server. Java servlets run on the application server and are recommended where large amounts of information are being handled. Typically, a servlet would call a PL/SQL stored procedure and display the result set in HTML format.

The mod_ose Module

Our final module is mod_ose. This module permits Apache to talk with the Oracle Servlet Engine (OSE), which runs inside the Oracle database. Typically, Java sessions are *stateless*, meaning that they do not use memory structures. The OSE provides a *stateful* environment. This improves performance, since Oracle9*i*AS is aware of previous requests that may have been made to the application server. Large Java-based applications need to keep track of past transactions, and this is normally difficult to perform in Java, since it is inherently stateless. OSE provides this "memory" to aid in the development of robust applications.

The Plug-in for Microsoft IIS

Experience has shown us that running Apache on Windows NT is not the best option for a production implementation. If you must run *i*AS on NT, then you will need to implement Microsoft IIS. This is done by using the plug-in supplied with 9*i*AS. This plug-in will provide the same functionality as the Oracle HTTP modules that we have just discussed.

You should note that each of these modules has its own configuration files that need to be coordinated with your Apache listener configuration. The configuration is all performed by editing text files, so it is best to follow the Oracle installation manuals closely and use Oracle's technet for advice. You may consult **http://technet.oracle.com** for Oracle-specific topics and the Apache web site, **http://www.apache.org**, for further assistance.

Business Logic Services

Now that you have your application server communicating with your users and the database, you will need to implement the meat of your application. To do this, you enroll the use of the Business Logic Services contained in 9*i*AS. This service will support the running of your application from the application server. The components of this area permit your applications to utilize XML, Java, or PL/SQL, or to web enable your client-server forms. Let's look at the various types of support that this service provides.

BC4J Support

Oracle Business Components for Java (BC4J) is a framework used to enforce the business rules for the application. The components are developed using JDeveloper and are compiled into Enterprise Java Bean (EJB), Session Beans, or CORBA server objects. These beans and objects are reusable to ensure the business rules are consistently applied throughout the application.

JVM Support

As discussed in the Chapter 13, the Java Virtual Machine (JVM) provides a server-side Java platform to support EJBs, CORBA, and database stored procedures. The JVM contained in 9*i*AS handles the Java services in the middle tier and the database.

PL/SQL Support

The PL/SQL component enables users to communicate with PL/SQL stored procedures that are held in the database. The PL/SQL stored procedure performs the data retrieval in the database and returns the information in HTML format. Frequently accessed data can be retrieved from the database cache rather than the database, if that feature has been configured.

Oracle Forms Support

During the 1990s, many companies invested in Oracle-based, client-server technology. Since that time, Oracle has said, essentially, client-server was a mistake, and we're sorry we sold it to you. The new vision is to reduce the amount of support required for the desktop and to have applications accessed by web browsers. If you want to get your "legacy" client-server application on the web without rewriting everything, you can use the Forms Services of 9iAS. The Forms Services consists of a listener on the application server and a Java plug-in on the client, called the JInitiator. JInitiator needs to be loaded into the client web browser to view the data forms; fortunately, it only needs to be loaded once. The only problem is that the file is 9MB, and for anyone who has tried to use Napster on a modem, this may cause a real problem. Ironically, JInitiator is not required for users of Microsoft Internet Explorer using a JVM of 5.0.0.3167 or higher; however, users of Netscape will have to use JInitiator.

So, there you have it. These are some of the options available to you to implement your business logic for deployment to the Web when using Oracle9iAS. Although these facilities are available, it is still necessary for you to write programs that make efficient use of both programming code and database access. Keep in mind, when you do start to write these applications, that you take full advantage of the environment in which you plan to implement your logic. Now we should move on to facilities that are provided to present your web pages to your end users.

Presentation Services

The next stop on our application server journey is the one that most users care about. They want to see your web pages; they want to see their data; and, most important, they want the ability to see data that is current. How many times have you gone to a web page only to discover that the information was out of date? It seems inconceivable to us in the instant information age that data could ever be old or dated.

The Apache JServ Service

Apache JServ is a pure Java servlet engine and meets all specifications established by Sun Microsystems. The Apache JServ works on any Java Virtual Machine that is compliant with Java Runtime Environment (JRE) 1.1 and will execute any Java servlet that is compliant with Java Servlet APIs 2.0. For 9iAS, JServ is configured to work with the Apache HTTP server and the embedded JVM within the application server. You can think of JServ just like a listener, as in an HTTP listener. When the HTTP listener receives a servlet request, it is routed to mod_jserv, which forwards the request to the JServ servlet engine, and the servlet engine then executes the servlet. The configuration of the Apache JServ is controlled via some special files: jserv.conf, jserv.properties, and httpd.conf. The httpd.conf file is the primary configuration file for Apache, and it needs to know the JServ component has been installed. The remaining two files are used to configure zones where the servlets are physically stored on the application server. The following is a sample of an httpd.conf file:

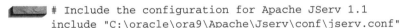

```
# Include the configuration for Apache JServ 1.1
include "C:\oracle\ora9\Apache\Jserv\conf\jserv.conf"
```

This entry in the httpd.conf file tells Apache where to find the JServ configuration file. If you do not specify this, the application server will not be able to initiate the JServ. So, if you plan to run Java servlets, you will need to investigate the JServ engine.

Using Java Server Pages

Java Server Pages (JSP) technology is based upon Java servlet technology; in fact, when the JSP scripts are compiled, Java servlets are created. Servlets are limited in their presentation capabilities, so JSP makes use of XML-like tags and scriptlets written in Java to separate the data retrieval from the presentation logic. This permits the presentation standards to be coded and stored on the application server as reusable resources (such as JavaBeans) while the content is retrieved via servlets. Developing a JSP application permits the JSP developers to concentrate on the presentation while Java developers concentrate upon the data. By using this approach, you will separate the data access and presentation, allowing each side to focus on what they do best. The configuration of the JSP is controlled via the ojsp.conf file. As with the JServ files, this file is used to inform the component of where the JSP files are located and must exist before you can use JSP functionality.

PL/SQL Server Pages

Oracle PL/SQL Server Pages (PSPs) are Oracle's version of a Java Server Page, but using PL/SQL rather than Java. The separation of presentation from data is the same in PSPs as it is in JSPs. The use of PSP or JSP depends upon the resources within your organization. Shops with Java experience will stick with JSP, while Oracle-oriented groups will stick with the PL/SQL side of things and utilize PSP.

Let's look at how you can use Oracle9*i* to create a PL/SQL web page to perform a simple display of data from the database. The code breaks down in the following manner. First, we must create a PSP file that contains the HTML that we want to display, along with the formatting and data access methods. In the following example, we will display data that is contained in a table. First, we create a PSP file, as we have done here.

```
<%@ plsql procedure="test_psp" %>
<html>
<head>
<meta http-equiv="Content-Type" content="text/html; charset=iso-8859-1">
<meta name="Author" content="Ian Abramson">
<meta name="GENERATOR" content="Mozilla/4.77 [en] (Windows NT 5.0; U) [Netscape]">
    <title>Test Page (PSP)</title>
</head>
<body>
Hello from the Oracle9i Database
<p>
  <%
  declare
  dummy boolean;
  begin
  dummy := owa_util.tableprint
      ('relations_info','border=1 cellspacing=0 cellpadding=4 width=100%');
  end;
  %>
Have a nice day!
</body>
</html>
```

The code is basically an HTML web page, with some PL/SQL commands embedded in it. The important line in our case is

```
owa_util.tableprint
    ('relations_info','border=1 cellspacing=0 cellpadding=4 width=100%');
```

This line calls a built-in Oracle9i function, asks Oracle to display the data in the RELATIONS_INFO table, and provides the guidance for formatting the table that will display the data.

We then load the PSP into the database. This becomes a stored object in the database, which could then be called from the application server or the database itself. To load the PSP into the database, you issue the following command:

```
loadpsp -replace -user ian/ian test_psp.psp
```

In its simplest form, this tells Oracle9i that you are replacing any existing program, and then tells who you are and your password. The final parameter is the name of the PSP file, which you should notice has the extension .psp. You will then be told whether your code compiles correctly. If it does, you can call it from your application server or at the SQL*Plus command line. In SQL*Plus, you would issue the command **owa_util.showpage**, which shows you the HTML code that is generated by your program. You may then cut and paste it into an HTML file to ensure the formatting is correct. If you are calling the page from 9*i*AS, you would specify the URL for this page, such as **http://ias.com:8888/pls/ian/test_psp_info**. The resulting web page then appears, as shown in Figure 14-3.

As you can see in Figure 14-3, we have retrieved some data from the database and displayed it. The process of generating these pages is relatively simple, while still providing a robust environment in which to develop your web pages.

Perl

Another method for accessing the database, as well as running SQL and presenting data to your users, is Perl. Perl is an interpretive language that is provided along with UNIX and Windows operating systems. The best part is, it is free. Oracle9*i*AS contains support for Perl in the HTTP server, which has been embedded with a Perl interpreter. The advantage to this is that rather than writing a separate process to handle the Perl scripts, you can embed them in the application server. When you

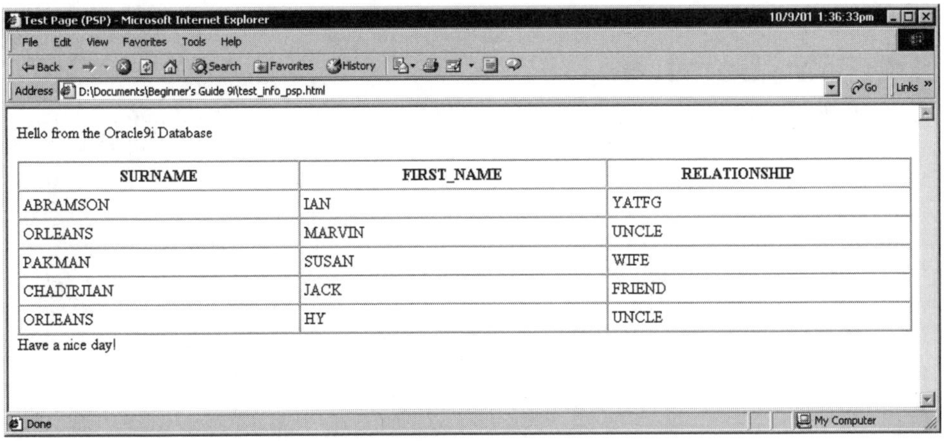

FIGURE 14-3. *PSP-generated web page*

execute a request for Perl, the request is transferred by the HTTP listener to the mod_perl module, which then moves it to the Perl interpreter for processing. The main Apache http.conf file controls the configuration of the Perl interpreter. We have included the portion of this file that handles the Perl interpreter.

```
# Extracted from http.conf
# Perl Directives
#PerlWarn On
PerlModule Apache::DBI
<Files ~ "\.pl$">
    SetHandler perl-script
    PerlHandler Apache::Registry
    Options +ExecCGI
</Files>
<Files ~ "\.cgi$">
    Options +ExecCGI
</Files>
PerlRequire /usr/src/apache_1.3.9/conf/startup.perl
```

You have many different options for displaying your information to users. You will need to choose the one that works for your individual organization and your internal skill sets. Developing applications for the Web is a challenge and, at times, a difficult process to manage; but this is the direction that applications are taking, so get on board. Let's look at some ways to improve performance by using the caching services of Oracle9iAS.

Caching Services

Caching is important because people look at the same thing many different times. It is no different in your local grocery store. Grocery stores place lots of stock on the shelves and only keep reserves in the back of the store. They do this not only so they don't need to go back to the storeroom every time a product is needed, but also to improve your shopping experience and speed you through the store. The same is true for databases and the Internet. So, whether you are retrieving data from the database or a web page from your organization's web site, you are generally doing the same thing over and over again. To improve performance, caching is available at both the database and web tiers. So when your users select data from the database, Oracle does not need to go back and read it off disk (the storeroom); it reads it out of memory (the shelves). And with memory being about 14,000 times faster than disk reads, this is a very good thing. The same can be said for the Web. By providing caching within the application server, there is no need to go back and read the HTML for a web page from disk—and on the Internet, performance is everything.

You should consider the following points to see whether caching is right for your organization:

- Are you accessing an Oracle database?

- Are your users using an Oracle database and an Oracle application server in your environment, and are they deployed on different platforms?

- Do you perform mostly read-only transactions?

- Are you willing to accept data that may be out of synch with the data in the database?

Consider the final question carefully. Since the caches hold data at the application server level, you will find that your data may become dated due to the fact that the refresh of the information on the database may differ from your refresh of the data on the application server. If the answer to most of these questions is yes, then you should consider using the caching services of Oracle9iAS.

Web caching has been offered in application servers as a performance enhancement for many years. Oracle's first venture into this arena came with Oracle8iAS when Oracle launched iCache, but web caching was only available on the NT platform. Oracle9iAS has updated the caching to work on the main application server platforms (Solaris, Linux HP-UX, and NT/2000) and has expanded it to include database caching. Oracle has labeled this version of the caching Oracle Database Cache and Oracle Web Cache, and it takes the next step in the evolution of caching.

What Is Database Caching?

Queries to the main database server can be expensive in terms of CPU cost, disk access, and network bandwidth. Frequently accessed data can be cached into a specialized database on the application server, where it can be more quickly retrieved. The database cache is specialized, in that is contains nonpersistent data (data that is dynamic and can change). You should note that you cannot perform backup/recovery on the database cache, nor should it be used as a regular transactional database. It merely exists to improve performance for data that may be retrieved through the application server.

Many companies have daily reports that query the same information. The data relating to these reports may be cached in the middle tier to permit faster access to that information. This is an important consideration in environments that have many data accesses.

Making use of the database cache requires no changes to your application or the logic of them. The functionality is controlled entirely by Oracle9iAS.

What Is Web Caching?

Web caching is a simple concept whereby frequently accessed URLs (web pages) have their contents copied and stored on the application server. Many people start their day by reading the *New York Times* or "Dilbert." By enabling web caching, you will permit the application server to hold copies of these web pages to permit faster access and reduce Internet traffic.

From a database application standpoint, web caching will permit frequently run reports to be stored in the cache without having to rerun the report. Figure 14-4 shows where the web cache server would be positioned within a standard network architecture. The server acts as a load balancer and automatically rebalances the load if one of the back-end HTTP servers were to crash. Redundancy is an important factor in ensuring that your web presence stays consistent. As you may expect with the architecture of the Internet, the requests are made from the client to the server via HTTP requests, and then these requests are forwarded to the application server. These are then processed through the application server HTTP layer and on to the database. A lost request could be that million dollar order that you had been waiting on, and sadly, it got lost.

Assuming that you have deployed your caching hardware and software as illustrated in Figure 14-4, you will find that you are well on your way to improving your web performance and allowing your organization to meet the challenges of the expanding Internet.

Content Management Services

As we discussed in the previous chapter, the Internet File System (*i*FS) stores files of any type in the database. Whether you plan to store an image, a document, or any other nondata object, *i*FS provides you with this ability. For users, the information is accessed as if the data were on a mail server, Windows file server, or web site. For this discussion, the important feature here is that *i*FS is fully supported by the application server. Let's move on and look at Oracle's Portal services, to see some other ways that you can access your database and the rest of the Internet.

Portal Services

You can use Oracle Portal services to build portal sites that integrate all of your content on a single web page. Portal sites give your users a single, centralized, personalized view of relevant applications and data. By using Oracle9*i* Application Server Portal services, you can make your portal sites accessible to both fixed and mobile clients. Oracle Portal provides portal services for users connecting from a traditional desktop. An enterprise *portal* is a Web-based application that provides a common, integrated entry point for accessing dissimilar data types on a single web page. For example, you can create portals that give users access to web applications, business documents, business intelligence reports, graphics, and URLs that reside both inside and outside your corporate intranet. If you have ever been on the Excite web site (**www.excite.com**), you have seen the portal approach to web site design. The web page in Figure 14-5,

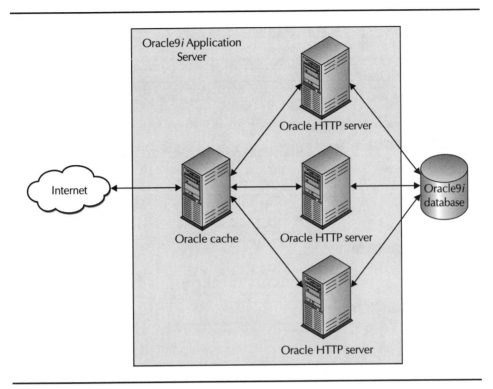

FIGURE 14-4. *Web-caching network architecture*

from the Virginia Oracle User Group (**www.voug.org**), is a wonderful example of an Oracle Portal implementation.

As you can see in Figure 14-5, they have used numerous different portlets on their web page. A *portlet* is a piece of information that can be added to a portal as an independent component. Some of these provide information, others provide access to email, while still others provide access to other areas of the VOUG web site. The web site shows you that, with some good planning, you can provide a wonderful interface and a plethora of information. Portlets are reusable interface components that provide access to web-based resources. Any web page, application, business intelligence report, syndicated content feed, or other resource can be accessed through a portlet, allowing it to be personalized and managed as a service of Oracle9*i*AS Portal. Users can select a portlet from an extensive list of portlet offerings. If users require custom solutions, authorized staff can develop their own portlets without having to code.

Another way that Oracle Portal is being implemented today is to support the mobile world. Let's take a look at Portal-to-Go.

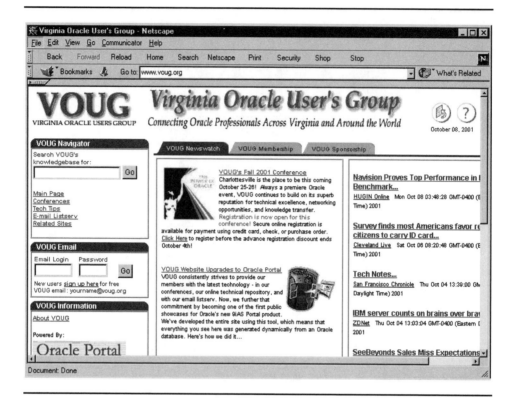

FIGURE 14-5. *Example of an Oracle Portal web page*

Portal-to-Go

Oracle Portal-to-Go is a portal service for delivering information and applications to mobile devices and wireless devices. Using Portal-to-Go, you can create custom portal sites that use different kinds of content, including web pages, custom Java applications, and XML applications. Portal sites make this diverse information accessible to mobile devices without having to rewrite the content for each target device platform. Portal-to-Go works by isolating content acquisition from content delivery. It provides an intermediary format layer, Portal-to-Go XML, between the source format and the target format. Portal-to-Go XML is a set of DTDs (Document Type Definitions), and XML document conventions used to define content and internal objects in Oracle Portal-to-Go.

Business Intelligence Services

Along with providing the services for applications that help you to run your business, Oracle9iAS provides services to help analyze the information that you have about your business. The science of business intelligence surrounds the analysis of information that is collected by your operational systems and is then formatted to provide support for decision making. Business intelligence is also known as decision support. Oracle9iAS has incorporated these business intelligence tools into the application server, whereas in the past, they were separate products. Let's look at these facilities and see what they mean to you and your organization.

Reports

With the addition of Oracle Reports Services and its Reports Servlet services to Oracle9iAS, you can now run new and existing Oracle Reports Developer reports on an internal company intranet, an external company extranet, or the Internet. Oracle Reports Services is optimized to deploy Oracle Reports Developer applications (Reports and Graphics) in a multitiered environment. It consists of the server component, runtime engines, and the servlet runner. In Oracle9i Application Server, when a client submits a request for a report, the Oracle HTTP listener routes that request to the Oracle Reports Services server component. The server routes the request to the Oracle Reports Services runtime engine, which runs the report. Then the report output is sent back to the client through the Oracle HTTP listener.

Oracle Discoverer 3i

The Oracle Discoverer 3i Viewer is an environment contained within Oracle9iAS for running and viewing Oracle Discoverer workbooks (reports) over the Web that have been created with Oracle Discoverer 3i Plus. By using Discoverer Viewer, web authors can access database information and embed it in their sites without being database experts. They can publish live reports to web sites by creating a URL that indicates to Discoverer Viewer which workbooks to open. Clicking the URL invokes the workbook query to the database and returns live results to the browser. Users interact with the query results to show more or less detailed information, to enter values into parameters, or to follow links to other applications. These tools form the strategy that Oracle has taken with their data warehouse and reporting tools. Let's take a look at one last subject—using Java in the database.

Java for the Database

Today in our ever-changing programming environment we have Java. As we have already discussed, Java is a language that is portable, due to the fact that it is run within your environment. This environment may be a web browser, a database, or an application server. In each of these environments, it is possible to run Java due to the fact that they each contain a Java Virtual Machine (JVM). The JVM reads Java requests, interprets them for their individual platform, and then executes them. JDBC is used to communicate to the database. JDBC stands for *Java Database Conectivity*; through this, Java can send requests to and receive data from the database. There are shortcomings to using Java, and these mainly surround performance, but we will leave that discussion for those with way more time on their hands. In this section, we will look at some Java code examples and see how Java can be used with a database like Oracle9i.

The most important thing application developers do is provide access to information. This access may be in the form of forms or reports, but ultimately, it is information that people will need. Here are the steps needed to execute a query using JDBC:

1. Register the driver.

2. Connect to the database.

3. Create an SQL statement.

4. Execute a query.

5. Generate a result set.

6. Process the result set one row at a time.

7. Assign results to Java variables.

8. Close resources (result set, statement, connection).

The next example shows a Java program that follows the preceding steps. You may use this to test whether your connection to the database is working.

```java
import java.io.*;
import java.sql.*;
import javax.servlet.*;
import javax.servlet.http.*;
public class thin extends HttpServlet
{
public void doGet(HttpServletRequest request,
        HttpServletResponse response)throws ServletException, IOException
{
  Connection conn = null;
  Statement stmt = null;
  ResultSet rset = null;
  response.setContentType("text/html");
  PrintWriter out = response.getWriter();
  try
  {
    Class.forName("oracle.jdbc.driver.OracleDriver");
    conn = DriverManager.getConnection
        ("jdbc:oracle:thin:@127.0.0.1:1521:orcl","system","manager");
    stmt = conn.createStatement ();
    rset = stmt.executeQuery ("SELECT sysdate FROM dual");
    out.println("<html>");
    out.println("<head><title>JDBC Servlet Thin Test</title></head>");
    out.println("<body>");
    while (rset.next())
```

```
   {
     out.println("Date: " + rset.getString(1) + "<BR>");
   }
   out.println("</body></html>");
   rset.close();
   stmt.close();
   conn.close();
 }
 catch (ClassNotFoundException e)
 {
   out.println("Can't load database driver: " + e.getMessage() + "<BR>");
 }
 catch (SQLException e)
 {
   out.println("Database Connection error: " + e.getMessage() + "<BR>");
 }
 out.close();
}
}
```

In the preceding code example, we have provided you with a sample Java program that simply connects to the database. The library function **DriverManager.get Connection** is the function that performs the connection. For more details on this and the other functions used in this example, we direct you to the documentation on the subject.

Next, you should see how Java could be used as a stored object in the database. Here, we create a stored Java object that simply prints hello to the name that we pass to the program. The Java program uses some of the Java classes that are provided with Oracle and will be familiar to you if you have programmed in Java in the past.

```
CREATE OR REPLACE JAVA SOURCE NAMED "MyHello" AS
    public class Hello {
    public static java.lang.String  printHello(java.lang.String  pvar)
{
      return "Hello " + pvar;
                 }
             }
/
```

As you may notice in the preceding code listing, we are actually creating a Java object. This is one of the objects that Oracle9*i* has added to support its Internet strategy and JVM. Next, we need to create another stored object to actually run the program. We use a stored object known as a *function* in this case. We discuss functions more fully in Chapter 9; but in this case, think of it as a wrapper for the Java program, since you cannot directly run Java code without using this type of support for it.

```
CREATE OR REPLACE FUNCTION  print_hello(pstr VARCHAR2)
      RETURN  VARCHAR2 AS
```

```
LANGUAGE    Java   NAME
    'Hello.printHello(java.lang.String)
    return   java.lang.String';
/
```

Now that we have created the Java object and wrapped it in a stored object called a function, we can run the program and verify that everything is all right. Let's see whether we can say hello to our friend George.

```
SQL> set serveroutput on
SQL> run
  1   DECLARE
  2        s varchar2(100);
  3     BEGIN
  4        s := print_hello('George');
  5        dbms_output.put_line(s);
  6*   END;
Hello George
PL/SQL procedure successfully completed.
```

Good news—we were able to get Oracle to say hello to George. (By the way, thanks to George Trujillo for helping with this example.) You should now see that using Java within the Oracle9i database is a viable option, but, compared with using PL/SQL, there are many more steps involved. However, the portability and industry standard of Java should make it an option for all organizations moving to the Web and using Oracle9i as their database.

There you have it—a journey through the Oracle9i Application Server. It is technology that continues to mature and provide you with the ability to take your operations and analysis to the Internet. It is a technology whose time has come, and it should constitute a critical part of your organization's strategy. We can now move on and look at some more advanced topics and technologies that surround the Oracle9i database and application server. We will start by looking at the tools that are available in the Oracle product line.

Questions for Chapter 14

Answers to questions can be found in Appendix A.

  1. Which of the following is *not* a service within Oracle9iAS?

   A. Presentation

   B. Business intelligence

   C. Business logic

   D. Portal

   E. None of the above

2. The configuration file for the HTTP server is called

   A. http.ini

   B. appserver.conf

   C. httpd.conf

   D. autoexec.bat

3. The program used to load a PL/SQL server page into the database is

   A. loadpage

   B. loadpsp

   C. loadplsql

   D. plsqlsploader

4. What object type is created when you write a Java program in the database?

   A. Procedure

   B. Table

   C. Java

   D. Function

5. To support access by a wireless device you would use

   A. Oracle Portal

   B. WebDB

   C. Oracle Forms

   D. Oracle Portal-to-Go

   E. a phone

PART V

Who Said You Were a Beginner?

CHAPTER
15

Forms and Reports Overview

his chapter looks at two long-term workhorses in the Oracle tools arena—Oracle Forms and Oracle Reports. We have looked at these products, Reports and Forms, in a number of previous works. Their version numbers have now climbed to 6*i*, and we expect that their next releases will bring the version numbers in line with the server—Forms and Reports 9*i*. These tools are very broad; they offer a wide range of development options, with hooks into just about every Internet feature you may want to think of and then some. We will cover the following items step by step in this chapter:

- Forms and Reports Developer environments and the choices with which you are presented

- How to build a simple form based on one table and make minor modifications

- How to build a simple report based on the same table and enhance the report by making cosmetic adjustments

Terminology

First, let's get started with the technical jargon you will need to make it through this chapter.

- *A graphical user interface,* or *GUI,* is the familiar Windows mouse-driven interface used by tools, including Forms and Reports.

- A background entity upon which user interface items are placed is called a *canvas.*

- A *trigger* is an event that fires when a certain condition has been met. In Form Builder, you can program triggers to display text as records are fetched from the Oracle9*i* database.

- The *boilerplate* text on a form or in a report is the static text that sits on the screen before any data from the Oracle9*i* database is fetched. Think of boilerplate as the series of prompts and other text on a hard copy of an application form.

Sample Data

The following listings will create and populate CITY and PROVINCE used in this chapter.

NOTE
The tables we use for the sample forms and reports do not exist in your Oracle9i database until you create them. Shortly after this book hits the shelves, we will release code that you can download from the Oracle Press web site and run against your database.

```
create table city (
  id              number(2),
  name            varchar2(40),
  last_election   date,
  mega_city       varchar2(1),
  population      number(12),
  last_census     date,
  prov_code       varchar2(2));
insert into city values (23,'Ottawa','02-AUG-00','Y',790000,
      '06-NOV-00','ON');
insert into city values (22,'Toronto','24-FEB-00','Y',25678993,
      '25-MAY-01','ON');
insert into city values (21,'Winnipeg','20-DEC-00','N',78000,
      '20-APR-00','MB');
insert into city values (20,'Regina','20-DEC-00','N',657909,
      '06-JAN-01','SK');
insert into city values (87,'Vancouver','11-MAR-99','Y',1876734,
      '13-APR-00','BC');
insert into city values (67,'Edmonton','19-NOV-99','N',898746,
      '26-SEP-99','AB');
insert into city values (17,'Montreal','11-JUL-01','N',1678424,
      '22-JUL-00','QC');
insert into city values (82,'St. John''s','29-JUN-99','N',354909,
      '22-JUL-00','NF');
insert into city values (7,'Victoria','29-MAY-01','N',79082,
      '26-OCT-97','BC');
insert into city values (8,'Calgary','10-DEC-98','N',632121,
      '03-FEB-98','AB');
insert into city values (67,'Manotick','11-APR-00','N',2990,
      '15-SEP-1997','ON');
insert into city values (94,'Quebec City','12-MAR-98','N',239676,
      '15-SEP-1996','QC');
create table province (
  prov_code    varchar2(2),
  name         varchar2(20));
insert into province values ('BC','British Columbia');
insert into province values ('AB', 'Alberta');
insert into province values ('SK','Saskatchewan');
```

```
insert into province values ('MB','Manitoba');
insert into province values ('ON','Ontario');
insert into province values ('QC','Quebec');
insert into province values ('NF','Newfoundland');
insert into province values ('NB','New Brunswick');
insert into province values ('NS','Nova Scotia');
insert into province values ('PE','Prince Edward Island');
```

Introduction to Forms and Reports

Developer 6i release 2 does not run on Windows 98—you must be using either NT 4.0 or Windows 2000 to install these two products and run through the exercises included in this chapter. The installation program will create a handful of folders for Forms and Reports, as shown in Figures 15-1 and 15-2.

Forms and Reports Components

Both Forms and Reports have three components, as described here:

- Forms and Reports Developer is where you go to make new data entry forms and reports. Using the GUI interface, after the initiation of an Oracle9i database connection, you can pick and choose the tables to include in your output and define how these tables are joined together as their data is brought into your workspace.

- Forms and Reports Runtime is used to invoke preprogrammed forms and reports and is often the only piece of the tool deployed to the users' desktop environment. A runtime module is embedded in the Developer interface as well.

- Form and Report Compiler is where you go to pass source code through a compilation exercise to produce reports and forms that can subsequently be interpreted by their respective runtime modules.

As mentioned previously, a database connection is required for running forms and reports, as well as some design activities. Let's look at initiating a database connection next.

Initiating a Database Connection

More often than not, the connections you will initiate are to remote servers using the Oracle Net transport mechanism discussed in Chapter 12.

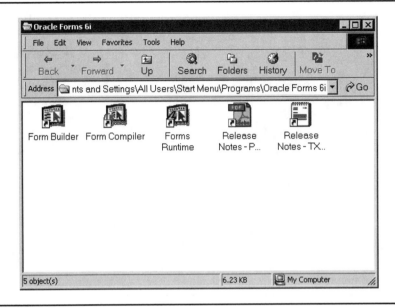

FIGURE 15-1.   *Forms Program group*

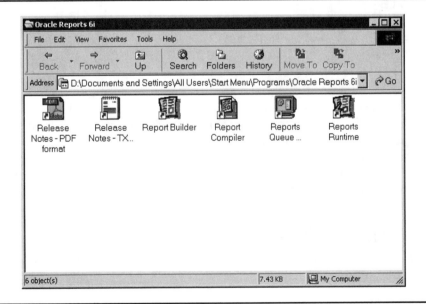

FIGURE 15-2.   *Reports Program group*

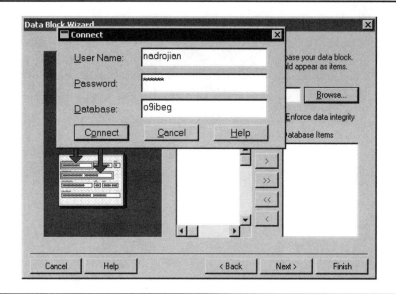

FIGURE 15-3. *Logging into an Oracle9i database*

NOTE
The account creation required to initiate a login to the Oracle9i database is the responsibility of your site's database administration. Some of this material is covered in Chapters 7 and 10.

Once you commence an activity that requires database connectivity, you will be presented with a dialog box similar to that shown in Figure 15-3. We entered **nadrojian** for User Name, **norman** for Password, and **o9ibeg** for Database; your settings may be different.

Let's get started on the meat of this chapter—building a form and then a report using Form Builder and Report Builder.

Building a Form

Start the Form Builder by clicking its icon in the Oracle Forms 6*i* folder. The screen that appears resembles that shown in Figure 15-4, where you can choose the activity to pursue.

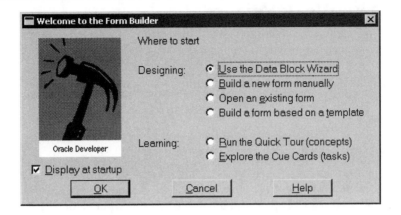

FIGURE 15-4. *Start of Form Builder*

There are four types of modules that you can create using Form Builder; together they can be combined to make a complete application:

- *Form modules* are the main component in the application build process. This is where the Developer designs, programs, and tests the way the user interacts with the Oracle9*i* objects.

- *Menu modules* are created to allow a familiar GUI method of selecting activities embedded in higher-level menus.

- *Object library modules* contain reusable objects that can be designed once and used throughout any suite of related form modules. Library modules promote consistency across forms and prevent the "reinvent the wheel" syndrome; modules that interact with the same data in roughly the same way are members of this object library.

- *PL/SQL library modules* contain code that resides on the clients and can be shared between applications as they interact with the Oracle9*i* database.

The first wizard we will visit is the Data Block Wizard. When presented with the screen shown in Figure 15-4, leave the radio button Use the Data Block Wizard selected.

The Data Block Wizard

You use the Data Block Wizard to instruct the Form Builder what table you wish to access and what columns within the table you wish to include on the ensuing form.

1. Click OK to start the first of a handful of Data Block Wizard question and answer screens.

2. Click Next.

3. Ensure Table or View is selected, and click Next.

4. The next screen is where you can log into the database to select a table. Click Browse, and enter appropriate login credentials. You will then be presented with a list of available tables, as shown in Figure 15-5. We have highlighted CITY in preparation for the next step.

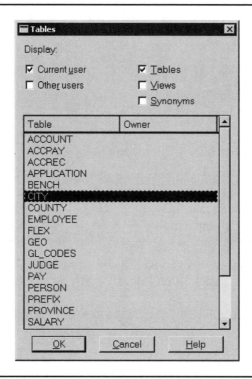

FIGURE 15-5. *List of tables for Nadrojian*

5. A list of the columns in CITY is brought back to the wizard, displaying a GUI version of a **desc city** command as if it were passed to SQL*Plus, shown next. Click NAME, and then the right arrow (→) to transfer the column name to the right pane of this page of the wizard. Do the same for PROV_CODE, POPULATION, and LAST_ELECTION.

```
SQL> desc city
 Name                Null?     Type
 ----------------    --------  -----------
 ID                            NUMBER(2)
 NAME                          VARCHAR2(40)
 LAST_ELECTION                 DATE
 MEGA_CITY                     VARCHAR2(1)
 POPULATION                    NUMBER(12)
 LAST_CENSUS                   DATE
 PROV_CODE                     VARCHAR2(2)
```

6. Click Next to see a screen similar to that shown in Figure 15-6. Leave the upper radio button selected, and click Finish.

Time for the Layout Wizard, covered in the next section.

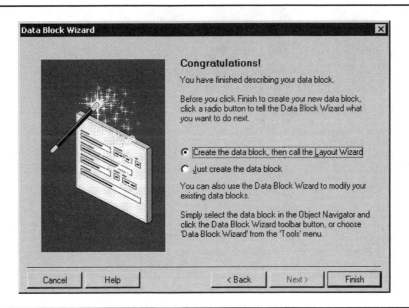

FIGURE 15-6. *Instructing Data Block Wizard of next activity*

The Layout Wizard

Almost as soon as the Layout Wizard starts, you are confronted with yet another series of questions. You need to make a selection for Canvas and the Type you wish to build. More than likely, the defaults are [New Canvas] and Content. Leave them as they are, and click Next to bring up the next page, where you can select items to be displayed from those available—remember, you picked four of CITY's fields in the Data Block Wizard. Here we go.

1. Highlight each of the columns one at a time, and click → to transfer its name from Available Items to Displayed Items. Leave the suggested Item Type of Text Item as is for all four columns.

2. Click Next to bring up the screen where you specify headings, width, and height for each column in the selected table.

3. We changed the Width and Height of these four columns as specified in Table 15-1. This screen, with the changes listed in Table 15-1, is shown in Figure 15-7.

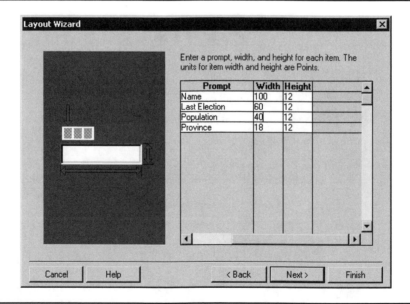

FIGURE 15-7.   *Specifying headings and other field attributes*

Field	Attribute	Old	New
Name	Width	246	100
	Height	17	12
Last Election	Width	72	60
	Height	17	12
Population	Width	84	40
	Height	17	12
Prov Code	Prompt	Prov Code	Province
	Height	17	12

TABLE 15-1.   *Changes to Column Specifications*

4. Click Next to position yourself at the screen where you select the layout style you wish to use for your form—let's choose the latter and click Next. The choices are

   ■ **Form**   One row of the CITY table's selected columns is displayed per screen, and you move up and down the list of rows with the mouse or the UP and DOWN ARROW keys.

   ■ **Tabular**   There are multiple rows displayed per screen, and you specify later how many should show at one time.

5. Hold your breath! We're just about done. The next screen that appears, as shown in Figure 15-8, is where you define the parameters that control the environment within which the rows from CITY will be displayed— Frame Title, Records Displayed, and Distance Between Records. As you can see from Figure 15-8, we entered **My First Form**, **8**, and **1**. We also checked Display Scrollbar to do just that on the form. Click Next to carry on.

6. When the next screen appears, congratulating you on the marvelous job you have done, click Next to bring up the first version of the form using all the values you have just entered in the series of dialog boxes we have filled in over the past few pages.

7. Before running the form, let's save it by clicking File at the top of the Form Builder screen, selecting Save, entering the name **city1**, and clicking Save.

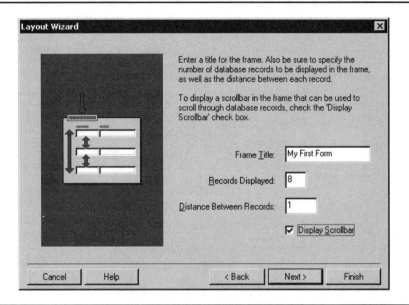

FIGURE 15-8. *Specifying additional layout properties*

8. When returned to the form, press CTRL-R to invoke Forms Runtime. As the CITY1 form appears, select Query | Execute on the menu displayed at the top of the screen to bring up a list of cities, as shown in Figure 15-9.

As you can see from Figure 15-9, the fields on the form have not been allocated enough space. In the next section of this chapter, we are going to have a look at fixing this situation. Close the CITY1 form; we will retrieve it into the Form Builder workspace at the start of the next section.

Editing an Existing Form

Invoke Form Builder 6*i* from its folder; and, if presented with the Data Block Wizard, click Cancel to dismiss it. Proceed to the File menu, and select Open. Proceed to the Files of Type, and select Forms (*.fmb) from the pick list. Double-click CITY1 to bring the file into the Form Builder. This is what we are going to do in this exercise:

■ Fix the sizes of the four fields being displayed so they are readable.

■ Right-justify the population field and put the familiar comma separators between the thousands digits.

■ Display the name of each province as it is retrieved into the workspace.

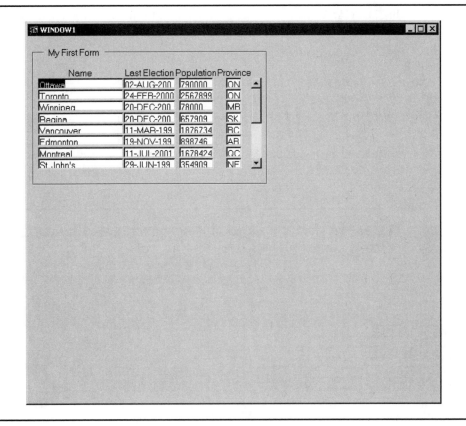

FIGURE 15-9. *Running the CITY1 form*

Fixing Field Sizes

As the CITY1 form is retrieved, if Form Builder does not expand the list of objects underneath the form name, do so by clicking the + beside its name. Proceed to the Canvases branch of the tree, and expand its list to show the single canvas name we created in the previous exercise. This is one way to go about fixing the field display sizes on CANVAS2.

NOTE
Form Builder keeps a sequential number that it uses to name canvases. The canvas we end up working on in this section is called CANVAS2; the name of yours may be different.

I. Right-click CANVAS2 and select Layout Editor from the menu that appears. You will then be positioned at a screen similar to that shown in Figure 15-10.

NOTE
We will refer to the ruler on the left side of the canvas showing numbers 0 to 384 as we massage the field display sizes in this section.

2. Click the canvas beside the words My First Form; notice how handles appear around the city window. Windows places eight small black boxes

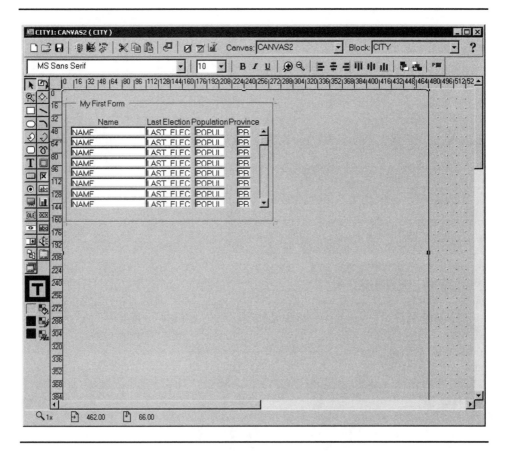

FIGURE 15-10. *CITY1 open in the Form Builder for editing*

around an object that has been selected in this fashion. These are the same handles you may be familiar with seeing in some other products, such as PowerPoint or Paint.

3. Grab the handle in the middle at the bottom, and pull it down from about 165 on the vertical ruler to roughly 288.

4. Now click inside one of the NAME fields to create a different set of handles.

5. Again, grab the middle handle at the bottom, and pull the NAME display area down to about 250 on the ruler.

6. Do the same for LAST ELECTION, POPULATION, and PROVINCE.

7. Press CTRL-R to run the form, and, if asked, enter the appropriate credentials to log into the Oracle9*i* database.

8. Select Query | Execute again from the menu.

Notice how the text in the fields is easier to read, but there is still a crowding problem. Back to the Form Builder to fix this sizing issue once and for all. Do the following once you are back in the designer:

1. Click beside My First Form, and grab the middle handle on the right side of the window; then pull the handle over to about 370 on the horizontal ruler.

2. Click in the vertical scroll bar, and move it over to about 320 on the ruler.

3. Move PROVINCE over to about 280.

4. Expand POPULATION a touch, and move it over to about 195.

5. Finally, move over LAST ELECTION and expand its width a tad as well.

6. Let's run the form again with CTRL-R; when it appears this time, press F8 instead of using the menu to retrieve the city records.

Mission accomplished. Let's look at putting some finishing touches on the POPULATION field—right justification and comma editing.

Editing and Justifying a Numeric Field

This activity is one of many you may end up going through to make the form more pleasing to the eye. Like many tasks in Form Builder, this one is quite simple. Let's get started.

1. Right-click in one of the white POPULATION fields, and select Property Palette from the menu that appears.

2. In the branch called Functional, click in the column beside Justification.

3. Bring down the pick list and choose Right.

4. Scroll down if necessary to the Data branch.

5. Click beside Format Mask, and enter **999,999,999,990**.

6. Exit the Property Palette form, and let's invoke runtime by clicking the green traffic light at the top of the layout editor window. The output after these changes is shown in Figure 15-11. Nice work!

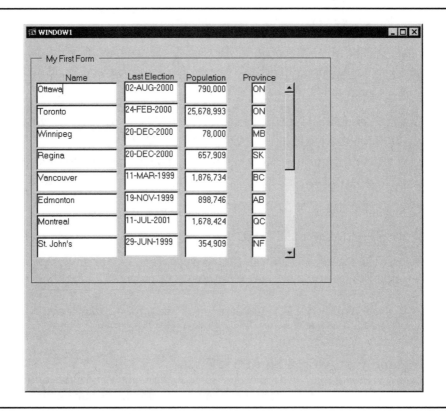

FIGURE 15-11.   *Form with formatted POPULATION field*

Displaying Additional Text

This one, if we may say so ourselves, is cute. Herein lies the heart of the magic of the relational database. This is the rule that we are going to implement electronically: each PROV_CODE value in CITY has a matching PROV_CODE value in PROVINCE. As a row is retrieved from CITY, a province name will be fetched from PROVINCE. Thus, a city in the province of ON will end up with the text "Ontario" displayed as well. Fasten your seat belts and we'll get under way.

1. First, let's grab the My First Form window and expand it to the right, out about as far as position 480.

2. Click in the vertical scroll bar, and move it over to about 450 on the ruler.

3. Next, proceed to the Text Item tool on the toolbar, the one with the lowercase letters *abc* on the white rectangle, about midway down the toolbar.

4. Click the tool, and then move the mouse over beside the PROVINCE field.

5. Create a field about the same height as PROVINCE and release the mouse. As you release, notice that Forms replicates the field just created to match the ones already on the form.

6. Resize the eight new text items displayed to match the repeating fields by selecting the item and changing the size using the handles that appear.

7. Right-click in the new field, and proceed to the Property Palette option. The changes to be made are described in Table 15-2.

Branch	Attribute	New Setting
Navigation	Keyboard Navigable	Choose No from the pick list that comes up when you enter the Yes field.
Database	Database Item	No
	Query Allowed	No
	Insert Allowed	No
	Update Allowed	No

TABLE 15-2. *Changes on Property Palette*

8. Exit the Property Palette when done.

9. Position the mouse cursor over the PROV_CODE field, right-click, and choose Smart Triggers | Other from the menu that appears.

10. When the Triggers list appears, enter the text **post-** in the Find field; and when the list automatically scrolls to POST-CHANGE, select OK to bring up the trigger text dialog box.

11. Enter text into the PL/SQL editor, as shown in the next listing.

```
select name
into :text_item7
from province
where prov_code = :prov_code;
```

NOTE
We used the "into :text_item7" syntax, as our new text item was assigned that number by Form Builder. The name it assigns for you may be different. Adjust the target field name accordingly.

12. Click Compile, and receive the feedback "Successfully Compiled" in the lower-right corner of the editor.

NOTE
If there are any compilation errors, Form Builder will display text in an error window to help you fix the problem(s).

13. Click Close.

14. Run the form with CTRL-R.

15. Press F8 when the form appears, and the results will be something like those shown in Figure 15-12.

Before moving on to Report Builder, we'll mention a few integration features that Forms brings to the application development table.

■ Forms can make extensive use of Java when deployed to the Web, thereby making it easy to plug user-developed Java objects into your applications.

■ Forms leverages true 32-bit Windows standards and protocols.

■ Since Oracle subscribes to *OTI* (Open Tool Initiative), Forms-based applications work well alongside other tools, including state-of-the-art transaction monitors.

■ Forms continues to provide open database connectivity, commonly referred to as *ODBC*, permitting seamless integration with an assortment of non-Oracle9*i* data repositories.

Suffice it to say—try it; take it for a test drive, and take advantage of its development hooks, bells, and whistles. On to Report Builder.

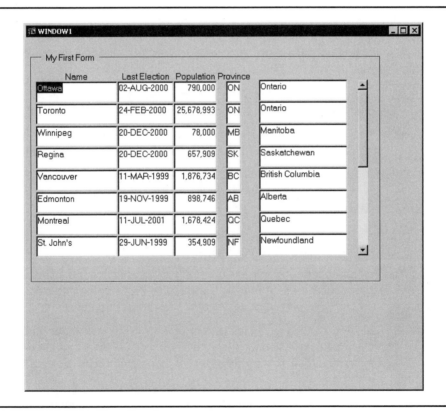

FIGURE 15-12. *CITY1 form displaying province names*

Report Builder

The nice thing about Developer 6i is that the look and feel of all its components is exactly the same. The interface with the Developer, the wizards, and the way to go about doing things is similar across the tool. Let's use our PROVINCE and CITY tables from the Form Builder and build a simple report, and then add a few bells and whistles.

The Report Wizard

Select Report Builder from the Oracle Reports6i folder to get started. As with Form Builder, you will be presented with the Welcome to Report Builder dialog box.

1. Leave Use the Report Wizard selected, and click OK to carry on.

2. When the wizard appears, click Next.

3. You are asked to specify the report style, with the following choices available:

- Tabular is the most common and simplest, where each field on a report comes from a database table.

- Form-like will remind you of some data entry screens you may have seen, with fields lined up one underneath another, each prefixed on the screen by a prompt.

- The mailing label format is just that, with data arranged in columns and rows.

- The form letter report takes fields from the database and embeds them in boilerplate text that you design in the Report Builder interface.

- The group left report takes common values from rows in a table and suppresses their repetition. It is used to restrict a column from being repeatedly displayed as values of related columns change.

- The group above report is the common master/detail layout such that the values of one data block are fetched as the values of another data block are retrieved. Reports keeps the two data blocks in synch.

- The matrix report is displayed as a grid with column values themselves becoming the row and column headers. This is a very popular report type, illustrated simply in the next listing. An interesting feature of this report type is that the number of rows and columns in the matrix is dependent on the number of distinct values in the database tables.

Had the report broken out totals for Nissan rather than lumping them in with Other, there would be five rather than four columns to report.

```
         ** Market Share for SUVs (expressed as a %) **

              Other         Ford         GM    Daml/Chry
      1998       2           39           25         33
      1999       1           44           33         22
      2000       3           41           41         15
      2001       4           38           43         15
      2002       5           40           40         15
      2003       4           42           40         14
```

■ The matrix with group report is a hybrid—a mixture of the preceding group and the matrix report, where there is a separate matrix displayed for every value in the master group.

4. On the next page, let's give our report the title **City Elections by Year**, and select the report type Matrix. Click Next.

5. When asked which query type on the next page, click SQL Statement and then Next.

6. The next screen asks whether you want to use the Query Builder or Import SQL Query—let's click the former. You are asked for login credentials to the database. We entered **nadrojian** for a username, **norman** for a password, and **o9ibeg** for the database.

NOTE
Your login information may be different, as long as it is for the user that owns the CITY table we are using in this exercise.

7. The next screen you will see is called Select Data Tables. Click CITY; Include; and, finally, Close.

8. You are then presented with the Query Builder screen, as shown in Figure 15-13. Select LAST_ELECTION and PROV_CODE, and then click OK.

9. The Report Wizard then displays your query, with its text resembling that shown in the next listing.

```
select all city.last_election, city.prov_code
from city
```

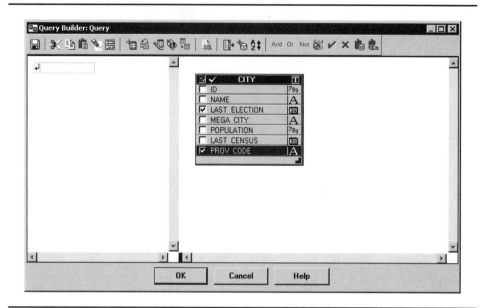

FIGURE 15-13. *Selecting columns in the Query Builder*

10. We want to add some additional SQL code to make the query suit our needs. Update the query text as shown in the next listing. This is because we want to group cities within province and display a count for each province/ election year combination.

```
select all to_char(city.last_election,'yyyy'),
       city.prov_code,count(*)
 from city
group by to_char(city.last_election,'yyyy'), city.prov_code
```

11. Now it's time to select the report fields to be displayed as row and column headers. Click Next to position yourself at the screen where you select the Matrix Row Fields. Click PROV_CODE and transfer it to the right side of the window.

12. Click Next and do the same with TO_CHAR_LAST_ELECTION on the Matrix Column Fields selection screen.

13. After clicking Next, select COUNT from the Available Fields on the Matrix Cell Fields selection screen and transfer it to the right pane by clicking Count >.

14. In the Matrix Totals screen, simply click Next.

15. When asked whether you want to make any changes to the matrix column attributes, click Next.

16. On the next screen, more than likely the Corporate 1 template will be selected as you arrive. Click Finish to produce the lovely report shown in Figure 15-14.

Nice work! Before closing this chapter, we are going to make some layout and boilerplate modifications to this report to give you an idea of how Report Builder is used to enhance its output. First, we suggest you save your report program via the

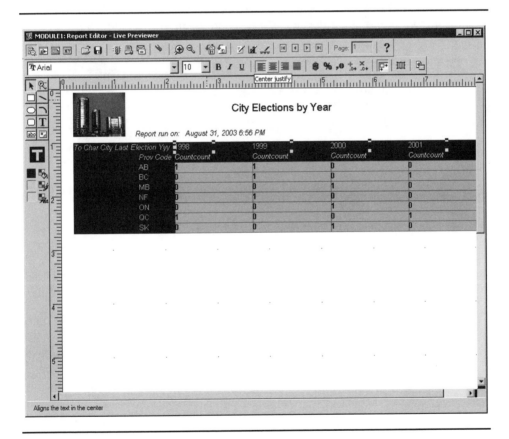

FIGURE 15-14.   *First cut at city/province matrix report*

familiar File | Save choice from the menu at the top of the window. We are going to do the following:

- Change the placement or justification of some numeric fields.

- Change a number of text fields as they appear on the screen.

- Select a different template.

Onward and upward.

Modifying the Report

The first task is so simple, we were surprised the first time we did it. We want to change the position of the four-digit year text and the number of elections that were held in each year.

1. Click the number 1999, and the handles you saw when using Form Builder will appear around the four years displayed. Click the Center Justify button, under the bubble help shown in Figure 15-14, and the years will center themselves.

2. Do the same for the count fields in the matrix. The report now looks like it did in Figure 15-14, with the minor modification we have just made.

3. Double-click the text Countcount, opening up a data entry area where the text can be changed to **# of cities**.

4. Click the Center Justify button to move these headings into the middle of their columns.

5. Using the same technique, change the text Prov Code to **Province** and To Char City Last Election Yyy to **Province \ Year**.

6. Proceed to the Tools menu option at the top of the screen, and select Report Wizard.

7. Select Template on the ensuing screen that appears, and scroll down and select NCA Yellow.

8. Click Finish, and Report Builder will rerun the report and preview the results, like those shown in Figure 15-15.

That may have been a handful, but, as is the case with all of the tools that interact with Oracle's 9i database, we could only scratch the surface of a very sophisticated offering. This chapter was supposed to tickle your fancy with what Form Builder and Report Builder can do to satisfy your data entry and reporting

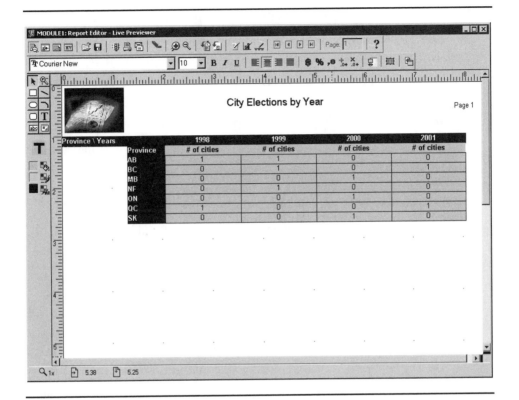

FIGURE 15-15. *The final product*

requirements. Time to move on. The next chapter looks at Oracle9*i*'s partitioning features. Partitioning is the best way to get a handle on the storage, management, and retrieval of data from very large tables—split them up into smaller physical pieces.

Chapter 15 Questions

Answers to questions can be found in Appendix A.

    1. What must you do before you are allowed to pick the tables you wish to work with when using Form and Report Builder?

        A. Connect to OEM stand-alone

        B. Connect to a local database

C. Connect to a database after providing appropriate login credentials

D. The list is always available without having to do anything once the Builder interface appears

2. The quickest way to edit numeric fields so that thousands digits commas are inserted is by

A. writing some PL/SQL code to display the field as desired

B. making these fields alphanumeric, thereby storing these commas in the database

C. specifying a format mask, defining each position with a 9, placing the commas in the appropriate position

D. giving a compiler directive to Form or Report Builder

3. When using the PL/SQL editor in Form Builder, fields on the screen are referenced in the code using what convention?

A. The name of the field is prefixed by a colon.

B. The fields are referenced by a sequential number in the code.

C. Warsaw.

D. The field name is italicized to avoid confusion at compile time.

4. When working with Developer 6i, what is the name of the programming unit that is designed to execute automatically when a specified event occurs?

A. PL/SQL editor

B. Trigger

C. Boilerplate text

D. Form or Report Compiler

5. A background entity upon which interface items are placed is called

A. boilerplate text

B. Form feature

C. Layout Wizard

D. canvas

CHAPTER
16

Partitioning Data

artitioning data—one of our favorite topics. We discussed some tools in Chapter 15 that are bundled together and called Developer9i. Regardless of what product you use to access your data, partitioning is a strong feature of Oracle9i. Oracle's partitioning directions allow DBAs to manage increasingly larger and larger tables, whose row counts can easily swell into the hundreds of millions, if not more. In this chapter, we will look at the following topics:

- Why partition your data?

- Range-based partitioning

- Indexing partitioned objects

- Overview of list and hash partitioning

NOTE
Partitioning is a very big topic. We are going to delve into some particulars of partitioning and give you a flavor of why data should be partitioned. Remember, this is designed to be a beginner's guide, not a complete primer. If it were, it could easily be a five-volume set!

Terminology

The following terminology will arm you with the technical jargon to get through this chapter.

- A *terabyte* is a trillion bytes, the equivalent of 1,099,511,627,776 bytes.

- When a query is executed against the Oracle9i database, the data that qualifies based on the criteria specified is referred to as the *result set*. Suppose we queried a rock-and-roll table and retrieved the data "Chuck Berry, Gibson, Sunburst"; those three items of information could be referred to as the result set.

- In an SQL query, the *predicate* is the portion containing the selection criteria using the SQL **where** or **and** construct. The predicate is in italics in the query **select /*+ index(idl_char$ i_idl_char1) +*/ piece#,length,piece from idl_char$ *where obj#=:1 and part=:2 and version=:3* order by piece#.**

- A *primary key* is a set of one or more columns with which each row in an Oracle9i table can be identified.

- A *partition key* is one or more columns in a table that define the range of column values placed within adjacent partitions.

- An *iterative process* is one that is repeated over and over again until done. Buying groceries and repeatedly training your lethargic teenagers to unload the car is an iterative process!

- *Range boundaries* define the upper value of a partition key column that qualifies a row for placement in a certain partition.

- *Row distribution* refers to the placement of data in a partitioned table; in an ideal world, all partitions would contain close to the same number of rows.

- A *dictionary view* is maintained by Oracle9*i* in the SYSTEM tablespace. As tables are created, information, such as their names, column names, and column data types, is tracked in the data dictionary views. The DBA does not manipulate the data dictionary manually—Oracle9*i* self-manages its own reference objects.

- *Partition elimination* involves Oracle9*i* deliberately not scanning all the partitions when assembling data that qualifies for a query. Suppose a table is partitioned by county, and a query is looking for all clients in Leviticus county with an outstanding balance; partition elimination would ensure that only the rows whose COUNTY_CODE is LV, lying in one partition, would be scanned.

- A *petabyte* is 2^{50}, or a mere 1,125,899,906,842,624 bytes. It's also sometimes referred to as a million million.

- With Oracle9*i*, a *fat table*, in our opinion, is one with more than two dozen rows. The maximum number of columns per table is still 1,000, though we have as yet to see anything anywhere close to that maximum.

Why Partition Your Data?

The answer to why you should partition your data could be a 200-page book in itself. At the dawn of our Oracle careers (it seems like light-years ago), we managed multimegabyte databases that, on odd occasions, expanded to a couple of hundred megabytes or more. The sheer volume of data in contemporary Oracle9*i* databases (often in excess of many hundreds of gigabytes) requires sophisticated storage capabilities coupled with features to ease its management. Let's look at each of these phenomena separately, and then move on to some Oracle9*i* specifics.

Volume of Data

Fact—regardless of how sophisticated database management software becomes, the data it manages resides in operating system files. Picture the files listed in the next listing; the SYSTEM, ROLLBACK, ABBEY, COREY, and ABRAMSON tablespaces reside in conventional, fairly straightforward files. This is the structure of a very simple Oracle9*i* database called beg9, which we made for this book.

```
/d0/oraclehome/product/oracle9.0.1/dbs> sqlplus /nolog

SQL*Plus: Release 9.0.1.0.0 - Production on Wed Jun 13 19:01:45 2005
(c) Copyright 2001 Oracle Corporation.  All rights reserved.
SQL> connect/ as sysdba
Connected.
SQL> select file_name,bytes from dba_data_files;
FILE_NAME                                             BYTES
--------------------------------------------------- -----------
/d1/oradata/beg9/ora_system_xlhtcqp6.dbf         104,857,600
/d1/oradata/beg9/ora_rollback_xlhtdsm9.dbf       140,509,184
/d1/oradata/beg9/ora_abbey_da_xlhwczv2.dbf       104,857,600
/d1/oradata/beg9/ora_corey_xlhwfdj1.dbf          104,857,600
/d1/oradata/beg9/ora_abramson_xlhwfsg2.dbf       104,857,600
```

NOTE

The output from this query, as is true with most we show in this book, has had some special formatting applied for readability. If you can access the tables in these listings without getting errors ORA-00942 or ORA-04043, your output may look drastically different.

Suppose this beg9 database was the foundation for a very large Oracle9*i* data warehouse that, within the first 18 months of its life, swelled to a size of 13 terabytes (14,293,651,161,088). Picture the next listing, which is a snippet of the same query from that 13-terabyte warehouse. (We inserted the numbers preceding each file name; they are not part of the query result set.)

```
SQL> select file_name,bytes from dba_data_files;
     FILE_NAME                                           BYTES
  1  --------------------------------------------------- -------------
  2  /d1/oradata/beg9/ora_system_xlhtcqp6.dbf       2,147,483,648
  3  /d2/oradata/beg9/ora_system_xlhtcqr9.dbf       2,147,483,648
  4  /d3/oradata/beg9/ora_system_xlhtcrk8.dbf       2,147,483,648
        . . .
        . . .

 19  /d3/oradata/beg9/ora_system_xlhtdyc2.dbf       2,147,483,648
 21  /d7/oradata/beg9/ora_nmart_da_ytgbx8.dbf       2,147,483,648
 22  /d9/oradata/beg9/ora_nmart_da_klkdd0.dbf       2,147,483,648
 23  /d3/oradata/beg9/ora_nmart_da_yujii9.dbf       2,147,483,648
        . . .
        . . .
```

```
378    /d3/oradata/beg9/ora_custstar_yyuio9.dbf      2,147,483,648
379    /d6/oradata/beg9/ora_custstar_iikii2.dbf      2,147,483,648
```

Ease of Management Offered by Partitioning

DBAs are continually confronted with requirements to manage larger and larger databases. The more information in a data repository, the more files form the infrastructure that supports the 9*i* instance. Management of databases with partitioned objects is easier to wrap your arms around. Let's look at four reasons why partitioned objects can lead to easier management, and then move into the meat of the partitioning discussion.

- Partitioned tables usually reside in smaller files (for example, nothing larger than 2GB). These files are more easily backed up than their bigger counterparts. Many times, we find ourselves tasked with managing Oracle9*i* databases where our predecessors have set up a network of database files sized in the 20–25GB range, and they are very difficult to back up.

- Hardware failure, though not common, will end up affecting a smaller percentage of your database if its contents are partitioned, as there are more pieces (tablespaces and stand-alone database files) that come together to form the whole information solution.

- From time to time, when working with Oracle's technical support organization (as discussed in many sections of Chapter 2, including "Oracle Support Services"), you will be asked to perform analysis on your tables. When you partition your multi-million-row tables, this analysis is faster, and the chance that you will be able to complete the exercise as requested by Oracle support is much higher.

- Portions of tables requiring maintenance can be worked with while other partitions continue to serve the user community. Suppose you archive data every six months and have a 93 million–row table partitioned into manageable buckets on CREATION_DATE. With your pre-2000 data in a few of its own partitions, it's easier to archive. Once the desired data is saved in an archive table, the desired partitions are dropped from the main table with an SQL statement similar to **alter table sale drop partition q1_1999;**. While these partitions are being dropped, the balance of the partitions in SALE are still accessible.

Performance Benefits

When large tables are split into partitions, the reduction in the amount of data assembled as systems interact with the Oracle9*i* database translates into better performance. Suppose an 84 million–row table is partitioned by **client_id**, residing in 12 partitions. The average row size per partition is just under 7 million. When running a query similar to the following, Oracle9i will scan at most a 7 million–row partition rather than an 84 million–row nonpartitioned object.

```
select client_id, sum(invoice_amt), sum(item_ct), item_no
  from order
 where client_id = 34    -- Only scans partition where client 34 resides
   and inv_date between sysdate-365 and sysdate
 group by client_id,item_no;
```

Performance gains are perhaps the biggest benefit of partitioning, regardless of the approach chosen.

Range-Based Partitioning

The simplest and earliest partitioning approach—range-based partitioning—came out circa 1997 with Oracle8.0. We have discussed the simple **create table** statement and used it in a number of places throughout this book. Partitioned tables, when created using this approach, contain extra code to set the range boundaries for each container.

Choosing a Partition Key

The first step in the partitioning process is to choose a partition key. The choices you make here will have an impact on the maintainability and row distribution down the road once the partitioned table is loaded. Before looking at specifics, we'll cover some theory on placement of rows using range-based partitioning.

There are essentially three factors that influence the choice of one or more partition key columns.

- The column must be part of SQL statement predicates as data is retrieved from partitioned tables.

- There must be enough distinct values in a column to allow for splitting of rows among the partitions.

- Once it has been determined that there are enough values, the row distribution within those values must lend itself to equal row distribution.

Let's look into each of these phenomena next.

SQL Statement Predicates

The chosen partition key column must be commonly mentioned in SQL statement predicates. Suppose we are thinking of partitioning the MESSAGE table by RECIPIENT, but find that in 132 queries we extract from our application, RECIPIENT is not used in most predicates. The SQL statement **select trunc(created),originator,count(*) from message where originator like :"SYS_B_0" group by trunc(created),originator;** is a good example of how data is retrieved, thereby making ORIGINATOR rather than RECIPIENT a partition key candidate column. Through our analysis of the MAILING table, we narrowed down the candidate columns to either ORIGINATOR or CREATED; our final decision was CREATED.

Enough Distinct Values

There must be enough column values through the table so the partitioning exercise will place roughly the same number of rows in each partition. Suppose you wanted to partition a 7 million–row table on a column that only has three distinct values in its CENTER column, which has been flagged as a candidate for the partition key. Using that as an example, Table 16-1 illustrates how a partition key could be chosen based on row counts for the three column values.

The column under consideration for the partition key clearly is not a good candidate. The **adu** partition would have almost 65 percent of the rows and the **adt** partition less than .04 percent of the rows. You then look at another candidate column, CTY, as shown in Table 16-2, which turns out to be a good candidate for the partition key.

This is an iterative process. You know your data better than anyone else, and may already have the savvy to be able to choose the partition key columns shown in Table 16-2. Equal row distribution is desirable, as discussed in the next section.

Chance for Equal Row Distribution

Table 16-3 shows a first cut at partitioning a 170 million–row table on a four-digit numeric column called ID. With range-based partitioning, you define an upper bound for each bucket. In Table 16-3, it has been determined that the partition key column candidate values run from 1455 to 9999. The Range of Values column in the table shows the begin and end column values for each partition.

CENTER	Rows with Value
adf	2,456,645
adt	2,001
adu	4,541,354

TABLE 16-1.   *Poor Distribution on CENTER Column*

CTY	Rows Within Range
Abeflantro	700,271
Boris	784,939
Cullen	848,777
Dwfwayno	804,737
Francis	823,828
Nadrojian	736,363
Norman	777,366
Traynor	730,383
Unzer	793,336

TABLE 16-2. *Good Distribution on CTY Column*

NOTE
With single-column, range-based partitioning, a key column value must be less than the upper boundary of a partition to qualify for placement therein. Looking at Table 16-3, a row whose key column value is 3211 would be placed in partition 3.

The ID column is a mediocre choice since the row distribution is not that good at the desired range boundaries. The partitions, using this set of boundaries, would contain anywhere from 11 percent to 32 percent of the 170 million rows. The next step would be to adjust the range boundaries to give a better count per partition. This is shown in Table 16-4.

Partition	Range of Values	Qualifying Rows
1	1455 to 2899	36,737,246
2	2900 to 3211	55,789,529
3	3212 to 4321	34,600,938
4	4322 to 5877	18,781,288
5	5878 to 9999	24,090,999

TABLE 16-3. *Setting Range Boundaries, Cut 1*

Partition	Range of Values	Qualifying Rows
1	1455 to 3012	32,812,798
2	3013 to 4112	35,029,339
3	4113 to 4209	33,229,299
4	4210 to 5532	36,025,681
5	5533 to 9999	32,902,883

TABLE 16-4. *Setting Range Boundaries, Cut 2*

The information shown in Table 16-4 is ideal! Not only are the rows nicely split into manageable chunks, but the row counts are within 8.9 percent of one another. Enough theory—roll up your sleeves and we will look at the SQL to define a range-based partitioned table.

Range-Based Partitioning—The SQL

The next listing presents the SQL to create the MAILING partitioned table; after the listing, we highlight the important lines using the line numbering from the listing.

NOTE
*As is the case throughout this book where we include code snippets, the SQL will not necessarily run error free if you try it out on your own Oracle9i database. We have done some preliminary setup to facilitate these code snippets—for example, the **mailing_ts1** tablespace, for one, must exist for the code to execute successfully.*

```
SQL*Plus: Release 9.0.1.0.0 - Production on Wed Jun 13 19:01:45 2005
(c) Copyright 2001 Oracle Corporation.  All rights reserved.
Connected to:
Oracle9i Enterprise Edition Release 9.0.1.0.0 - Production
With the Partitioning option
JServer Release 9.0.1.0.0 - Production
 SQL> create table mailing (
   2      originator     varchar2(40),
   3      recipient      varchar2(40),
   4      message        varchar2(4000),
   5      created        date,
   6      delivered      varchar2(1),
   7      read           varchar2(1))
```

```
 8  storage (initial 120m next 120m pctincrease 0)
 9  partition by range (created)
10  (partition mailing_p01 values less than
11              (to_date('01-JAN-2001','DD-MON-YYYY'))
12              tablespace mailing_ts1,
13    partition mailing_p02 values less than
14              (to_date('01-JUL-2001','DD-MON-YYYY'))
15              tablespace mailing_ts2,
16    partition mailing_p03 values less than
17              (to_date('01-JAN-2002','DD-MON-YYYY'))
18              tablespace mailing_ts3,
19    partition mailing_p04 values less than
20              (to_date('01-JUL-2002','DD-MON-YYYY'))
21              tablespace mailing_ts4,
22    partition mailing_p05 values less than
23              (to_date('01-JAN-2003','DD-MON-YYYY'))
24      storage (initial 300m next 100m pctincrease 0)
25              tablespace mailing_ts5,
26    partition mailing_p06 values less than
27              (to_date('01-JAN-2004','DD-MON-YYYY'))
28              tablespace mailing_ts6,
29    partition mailing_pmax values less than (maxvalue)
30              tablespace mailing_tsmax);
```

```
Table created.
```

The "Table created." message indicates that the SQL statement has been received and successfully executed by Oracle9*i*. As promised, Table 16-5 discusses the listing.

We've bitten off quite a bit so far in this chapter. Partitioning tables is one thing; let's now have a look at building partitioned indexes. The biggest bang for your partitioning dollar is having partitioned indexes underneath the tables you have so painstakingly partitioned.

Line Number	Important Points
8	This specifies the storage clause and, when coded at the table level rather than with each partition, dictates the desired space request for each partition. This is where it's easy to get yourself in trouble by wanting to allocate 3GB in total to a partitioned table and asking for that amount of space at the table level. When coded at this level, the space ends up being allocated for each partition! You can include separate storage parameters for each partition with their own **initial . . . next . . . pctincrease** entries. Look at the code for partition **mailing_p05** on line 24 to see how this is done.

TABLE 16-5. *Discussion of Range-Based Partitioning Syntax*

Line Number	Important Points
9	This is the heart of the partitioning syntax, instructing Oracle9*i* that the following code is going to outline the partition range boundaries, names, and tablespaces within which they will reside. In this case, we partitioned by range of CREATED.
10	This being the first partition description, it is prefixed with an opening parenthesis. Notice how the partition is named using meaningful text and the soon-to-be-familiar **values less than** keywords.
11	This defines the upper range boundary for the **mailing_p01** partition. In the example, we are using a DATE column so that, according to the code, rows created before January 1, 2001, will be placed in this first partition.
12	This instructs Oracle9*i* to store the **mailing_p01** partition in the **mailing_ts1** tablespace. Partitions may reside in their own tablespaces. Suppose we have 24 partitions, some containing many more rows than others. We may choose to place odd-numbered partitions in the **mailing_tsa** tablespaces and even-numbered ones in **mailing_tsb**.
13–28	The same old thing—partition range boundary definitions, partition names, and tablespace names.
29–30	Notice that the last partition in MAILING is built using the name **pmax**. You do not have to do this, but it is recommended as a reminder that this is the last partition. Notice the keyword **maxvalue**: this is a logical representation of the highest possible partition key column value and ensures that no rows can contain a column value that will not fit into any partition.

TABLE 16-5. *Discussion of Range-Based Partitioning Syntax* (Continued)

Indexing Partitioned Tables

There is quite a bit of theory and SQL syntax with which to familiarize yourself as you enter the partitioning world. The material we are going to cover in this part of the chapter is mainly applicable to range-based partitioned tables, but the theory applies to the other two types of Oracle9*i* partitioning that we will touch on briefly toward the end of the chapter—**list** and **hash**.

When indexing partitioned tables, there are two types of partitioning approaches you can use—**local** and **global**. Let's look at these first; having a basic understanding of index partitioning will allow you to hit the ground running.

Local Partitioned Indexes

Remember when we defined the MAILING table a few pages back? We specified the column names and the column data types, and then defined partition boundaries, partition names, and tablespace names. Once that table was created, a query against the owner's USER_TAB_PARTITIONS dictionary view would return the information shown next.

```
SQL*Plus: Release 9.0.1.0.0 - Production on Thu Jun 24 20:56:15 2003
(c) Copyright 2001 Oracle Corporation.  All rights reserved.
Connected to:
Oracle9i Enterprise Edition Release 9.0.1.0.0 - Production
With the Partitioning option
JServer Release 9.0.1.0.0 - Production
SQL> col table_name form a7
SQL> col partition_name form a12
SQL> col tablespace_name form a13
SQL> break on table_name
SQL> select table_name,partition_name,tablespace_name
  2    from user_tab_partitions
  3    order by 1,2,3;

TABLE_N PARTITION_NA TABLESPACE_NAME
------- ------------ -------------------------------
MAILING MAILING_P01  MAILING_TS1
        MAILING_P02  MAILING_TS2
        MAILING_P03  MAILING_TS3
        MAILING_P04  MAILING_TS4
        MAILING_P05  MAILING_TS5
        MAILING_P06  MAILING_TS6
        MAILING_PMAX MAILING_TSMAX

7 rows selected.
```

A local index, by definition, is one that is partitioned exactly like the table to which it belongs. When writing the SQL to create a local index, it closely resembles that used for the table creation, with some subtle but noticeable differences. Let's create the MAILING_N1 index on the CREATED column in MAILING, and then highlight some important pieces of the code in Table 16-6.

```
SQL*Plus: Release 9.0.1.0.0 - Production on Thu Jun 24 20:56:15 2003
(c) Copyright 2001 Oracle Corporation.  All rights reserved.
Connected to:
Oracle9i Enterprise Edition Release 9.0.1.0.0 - Production
```

```
With the Partitioning option
JServer Release 9.0.1.0.0 - Production
SQL> create index mailing_n1 on mailing (created)
  2  local
  3  (partition mailing_n1_p01 tablespace mailingx_ts1,
  4   partition mailing_n1_p02 tablespace mailingx_ts2,
  5   partition mailing_n1_p03 tablespace mailingx_ts3,
  6   partition mailing_n1_p04 tablespace mailingx_ts4,
  7   partition mailing_n1_p05 tablespace mailingx_ts5,
  8   partition mailing_n1_p06 tablespace mailingx_ts6,
  9   partition mailing_n1_pmax tablespace mailingx_tsmax);

Index created.
```

Now that this is done, we can join USER_IND_PARTITIONS with USER_PART_INDEXES, as shown in the next listing, providing us with the fruits of our labor. These two data dictionary views are where we go to find details about index partitioning operations we have successfully carried out.

Line Number	Important Points
2	The heart of local index creation—surprise surprise—the word **local**. This one word alone instructs Oracle9*i* on how to define the range boundaries for the partitioned index. They are picked up from the table partition definition in the data dictionary.
3–9	We could just as easily have left these lines out of the code, but Oracle9*i* would have used the same partition names as the MAILING table. Even worse, it would have placed each local index partition in the same tablespace as its corresponding table partition. This way, we ensure that the local index partition named **mailing_n1_p01** belongs to the **mailing_p1** table partition; even better, the **mailing_p1** table partition resides in the **mailing_ts1** tablespace, and the **mailing_n1_p01** index partition is in the **mailingx_ts1** tablespace. This is nice and clean and exactly the way smart partitioning architects go about naming partitions and tablespaces.

TABLE 16-6. *Discussion of Building a Local Index*

```
SQL*Plus: Release 9.0.1.0.0 - Production on Thu Jun 24 20:56:15 2003
(c) Copyright 2001 Oracle Corporation.  All rights reserved.
Connected to:
Oracle9i Enterprise Edition Release 9.0.1.0.0 - Production
With the Partitioning option
JServer Release 9.0.1.0.0 - Production
SQL> col table_name form a7
SQL> col index_name form a12
SQL> col tablespace_name form a16
SQL> col partition_name form a14
SQL> break on table_name on index_name
SQL>
SQL> select table_name,uip.index_name,
  2          uip.partition_name,uip.tablespace_name
  3     from user_part_indexes upi, user_ind_partitions uip
  4     where uip.index_name = upi.index_name;

TABLE_N INDEX_NAME    PARTITION_NAME    TABLESPACE_NAM
------- ------------  ----------------  --------------
MAILING MAILING_N1    MAILING_N1_P01    MAILINGX_TS1
                      MAILING_N1_P02    MAILINGX_TS2
                      MAILING_N1_P03    MAILINGX_TS3
                      MAILING_N1_P04    MAILINGX_TS4
                      MAILING_N1_P05    MAILINGX_TS5
                      MAILING_N1_P06    MAILINGX_TS6
                      MAILING_N1_PMAX   MAILINGX_TSMAX

7 rows selected.
```

To assess exactly how Oracle9i constructed the range boundaries for the local index MAILING_N1, let's query USER_IND_PARTITIONS, shown next. We also confirm what we assume by looking at USER_TAB_PARTITIONS. Notice that the HIGH_VALUE data is the same for both the index and data partitions.

```
SQL*Plus: Release 9.0.1.0.0 - Production on Thu Jun 24 20:56:15 2003
(c) Copyright 2001 Oracle Corporation.  All rights reserved.
Connected to:
Oracle9i Enterprise Edition Release 9.0.1.0.0 - Production
With the Partitioning option
JServer Release 9.0.1.0.0 - Production
SQL> col high_value form  a30 trunc
SQL> select partition_name,high_value
  2     from user_ind_partitions;
```

```
PARTITION_NAME    HIGH_VALUE
---------------   ------------------------------
MAILING_N1_P01    TO_DATE(' 2001-01-01 00:00:00'
MAILING_N1_P02    TO_DATE(' 2001-07-01 00:00:00'
MAILING_N1_P03    TO_DATE(' 2002-01-01 00:00:00'
MAILING_N1_P04    TO_DATE(' 2002-07-01 00:00:00'
MAILING_N1_P05    TO_DATE(' 2003-01-01 00:00:00'
MAILING_N1_P06    TO_DATE(' 2004-01-01 00:00:00'
MAILING_N1_PMAX   maxvalue

7 rows selected.

SQL> select partition_name,high_value
  2     from user_tab_partitions;

PARTITION_NAME   HIGH_VALUE
--------------   ------------------------------
MAILING_P01      TO_DATE(' 2001-01-01 00:00:00'
MAILING_P02      TO_DATE(' 2001-07-01 00:00:00'
MAILING_P03      TO_DATE(' 2002-01-01 00:00:00'
MAILING_P04      TO_DATE(' 2002-07-01 00:00:00'
MAILING_P05      TO_DATE(' 2003-01-01 00:00:00'
MAILING_P06      TO_DATE(' 2004-01-01 00:00:00'
MAILING_PMAX     maxvalue

7 rows selected.
```

In a nutshell, with the local partitioned index,

- There are exactly the same number of partitions in the index as in its corresponding table.

- The index creation statement makes no reference to **values less than**, as the boundary values are inherited from the table partitions.

Let's now look at the local partitioned index's cousin—the global partitioned index.

Global Partitioned Indexes

Global partitioned indexes are created with SQL code very similar to that used to create the partitioned table. Unlike local indexes, partition range boundaries are explicitly coded using the **values less than** approach. There are a handful of fundamental differences between local and global indexes, as highlighted in Table 16-7.

Characteristic	Local	Global
Same number of partitions as table to which they belong	Automatic	Manual
Same range boundaries as their table counterparts	Automatic	Manual
Must mention range boundaries when index created	Not allowed	Mandatory
Same partition key column as their table counterpart	Automatic	Optional

TABLE 16-7. *Differences Between Local and Global Partitioned Indexes*

NOTE

As per Table 16-7, it is possible to build a global index with the same number of partitions as its table counterpart and the same range boundaries. That being the case, this is something you will more than likely never do.

Enough said; let's have a look at building a global index on the MAILING table. Remember the MAILING_N1 index was built on CREATED. Suppose we wanted to build an index now on RECIPIENT. This is presented in the next listing.

```
SQL*Plus: Release 9.0.1.0.0 - Production on Thu Jun 24 20:56:15 2003
(c) Copyright 2001 Oracle Corporation.  All rights reserved.
Connected to:
Oracle9i Enterprise Edition Release 9.0.1.0.0 - Production
With the Partitioning option
JServer Release 9.0.1.0.0 - Production
SQL> create index mailing_n2 on mailing (recipient)
  2     global partition by range (recipient)
  3   (partition mailing_n2_p01
  4           values less than ('G')
  5           tablespace mailingx_ts1,
  6     partition mailing_n2_p02
  7           values less than ('P')
  8           tablespace mailingx_ts2,
  9     partition mailing_n2_p03
```

```
10                values less than ('T')
11                tablespace mailingx_ts3,
12     partition mailing_n2_pmax
13                values less than (maxvalue)
14                tablespace mailingx_tsmax);
```

Index created.

The syntactical differences between the global and local index creations are highlighted in italics in the previous listing. Table 16-8 discusses these differences.

That's all fine and dandy—but as soon as we came to grips a few hundred years ago with the theoretical and implementation differences between local and global indexes, we looked for guidance on which approach to use when. This is discussed next.

To Local or Not to Local, That Is the Question

From our partitioning experience, there are three words that sum up all index partitioning decisions wherever possible—*local is best*. Index partitioning decisions made properly today will pay off many fold down the road. Sometimes, due to the technology constraints placed on partitioned indexes, you will have no choice other than to use global indexes.

NOTE
You may sometimes find yourself forced to use global partitioned indexes when building a **unique** *partitioned index. From our experiences, index uniqueness brings some strict rules into play when trying to build local.*

In a nutshell, the reason local ends up easier (and better) wherever possible becomes apparent at partition maintenance time. Without delving very much into partition maintenance and the syntax involved, the two following activities—adding and dropping partitions—are most common with partitioned tables. Indexing (local or global) affects index maintenance operations required after partition maintenance.

Global Index Creation	Local Index Creation
Global partition by range (recipient)	Local
Values less than ('G')	{No code specified}

TABLE 16-8. *Highlight of Syntax Differences, Global vs. Local*

Adding a New Partition

The best example of adding a partition is a table that is partitioned by an ever-increasing date field. It's now approaching June 2004, and the partition that holds everything with a partition key column value greater than January 1, 2004, sits in the table's **pmax** partition. Each partition, right from the start, is designed to hold six months of data. The adding of a new partition is usually done by splitting the **pmax** partition at the desired column value. This is shown in the next listing. The heart of this discussion is the STATUS column in the second query in the listing, especially those partitions marked **unusable** after the split. Trying to access and index with status **unusable** will generate an error, and the query will abort. Index partitions marked as such after partition maintenance can entail downtime while they are rebuilt.

```
SQL*Plus: Release 9.0.1.0.0 - Production on Thu Jun 24 20:56:15 2003
(c) Copyright 2001 Oracle Corporation.  All rights reserved.
Connected to:
Oracle9i Enterprise Edition Release 9.0.1.0.0 - Production
With the Partitioning option
JServer Release 9.0.1.0.0 - Production
SQL> -- Split the pmax partition at July 1, 2004.
SQL> alter table mailing split partition
  2      mailing_pmax at (to_date('01-JUL-2004','DD-MON-YYYY'))
  3    into (partition mailing_p07,partition mailing_pmax);

Table altered.
SQL> -- Local is better than global, as you now see . . .
SQL> select uip.index_name,upi.locality,uip.status,
  2          uip.partition_name
  3    from user_ind_partitions uip,user_part_indexes upi
  4   where uip.index_name = upi.index_name
  5   order by 1,2,3,4;

INDEX_NAME LOCALI STATUS    PARTITION_NAME
---------- ------ --------  ------------------
MAILING_N1 LOCAL  UNUSABLE  MAILING_P7
                  USABLE    MAILING_N1_P01
                            MAILING_N1_P02
                            MAILING_N1_P03
                            MAILING_N1_P04
                            MAILING_N1_P05
                            MAILING_N1_P06
                            MAILING_N1_PMAX
MAILING_N2 GLOBAL UNUSABLE  MAILING_N2_P01
                            MAILING_N2_P02
```

```
MAILING_N2_P03
MAILING_N2_PMAX
```

12 rows selected.

Notice how **mailing_p7**, part of index MAILING_N1 (local), as well as all the partitions of MAILING_N2 (global) are marked as **unusable** and must be rebuilt. Only one of seven local index partitions needs rebuilding, whereas all four global index partitions need it.

Dropping a Partition

The archiving of old data is the classic example of when dropping a partition is carried out. Suppose the partition design for MAILING entails off-lining data older than four years. In the previous section, we split **pmax**, in effect adding a new partition to hold data from July 1, 2004, on. The next step would be to drop the existing **mailing_p01** partition whose data is now older than four years. Look at the following listing to see how this is done and the effect it has on the table's index partitions. The local index partitions in this case require no maintenance, and all four global partitions do.

```
SQL*Plus: Release 9.0.1.0.0 - Production on Thu Jun 24 20:56:15 2003
(c) Copyright 2001 Oracle Corporation.  All rights reserved.
Connected to:
Oracle9i Enterprise Edition Release 9.0.1.0.0 - Production
With the Partitioning option
JServer Release 9.0.1.0.0 - Production
SQL> alter table mailing drop partition mailing_p01;

Table altered.
SQL> -- Again, local is better than global . . .
SQL> select uip.index_name,upi.locality,uip.status,
  2          uip.partition_name
  3     from user_ind_partitions uip,user_part_indexes upi
  4    where uip.index_name = upi.index_name
  5    order by 1,2,3,4;

INDEX_NAME LOCALI STATUS   PARTITION_NAME
---------- ------ -------- ------------------
MAILING_N1 LOCAL  USABLE   MAILING_N1_P02
                           MAILING_N1_P03
                           MAILING_N1_P04
                           MAILING_N1_P05
```

```
                    MAILING_N1_P06
                    MAILING_N1_PMAX
MAILING_N2 GLOBAL UNUSABLE MAILING_N2_P01
                    MAILING_N2_P02
                    MAILING_N2_P03
                    MAILING_N2_PMAX

10 rows selected.
```

Well, Maggie Muggins, that was quite a day! We're just about done with this whirlwind introduction to partitioning with Oracle9i. Before leaving this section on index partitioning, we want to mention a wee bit more jargon that you may run into as soon as you test-drive some of the material we have discussed here.

Prefixed and Non-prefixed Partitioned Indexes

We discussed choosing a partition key in a previous section of this chapter, and have discussed indexing as a whole elsewhere in this book. Remember, the columns mentioned in an index creation are referred to as the index columns, and those in the partitioning section of a **create index** are called partition keys.

When an index is built on a partitioned table and the leftmost column of the index is the same as the leftmost column in the index partition key, the index is called *prefixed*. On the other hand, when this leftmost match is not implemented, the index is called *non-prefixed*. Table 16-9 looks at some examples of this phenomenon for a number of different tables, not just MAILING.

Range-based partitioning, the earliest offering in Oracle's partitioning solution, is only one of three approaches offered in Oracle9i. Let's briefly have a look at list and hash partitioning before moving on.

Partition Column(s)	Index Column(s)	Prefixed	Non-prefixed
CREATED	ORIGINATOR, CREATED		X
RECIPIENT	RECIPIENT, CREATED	X	
SDATE,OWNER	OWNER, SDATE		X
ID,CREATED	ID, LOCATION	X	
ALIAS	ALIAS	X	
ALIAS	CITY		X

TABLE 16-9.   *Examples of Prefixed and Non-prefixed Partitioned Indexes*

List Partitioning

Although we are not going to dive into list partitioning as deeply as we did range-based partitioning, let's look at some highlights. With range-based partitioning, the range boundary values coded in the **create table** statement must increase as you go further down in the defining SQL statement. For example, if the first partition holds **values less than (198)**, the subsequent boundary identifiers must be greater than 198. With list partitioning, a **create table** statement might resemble the following. The portions of the listing that differentiate list from range-based partitioning are italicized.

```
SQL*Plus: Release 9.0.1.0.0 - Production on Thu Jun 24 20:56:15 2003
(c) Copyright 2001 Oracle Corporation.  All rights reserved.
Connected to:
Oracle9i Enterprise Edition Release 9.0.1.0.0 - Production
With the Partitioning option
JServer Release 9.0.1.0.0 - Production
SQL> create table invoice (
  2     id              number(10),
  3     created         date,
  4     order_type      varchar2(1),
  5     cust_id         number,
  6     completed       varchar2(1),
  7     delivered       varchar2(1))
  8  partition by list (order_type)
  9  (partition invoice_p01 values ('A','D','T')
 10            tablespace invoice_ts1,
 11   partition invoice_p02 values ('F','P')
 12            tablespace invoice_ts2,
 13   partition invoice_p03 values ('B','J','S')
 14            tablespace invoice_ts3,
 15   partition invoice_p04 values ('X')
 16            tablespace invoice_ts4);


Table created.
```

Now that INVOICE is created, its partitioning structure, including the list of each ORDER_TYPE that is found in each bucket, can be gleaned from USER_TAB_PARTITIONS, as shown next.

```
SQL*Plus: Release 9.0.1.0.0 - Production on Thu Jun 24 20:56:15 2003
(c) Copyright 2001 Oracle Corporation.  All rights reserved.
Connected to:
Oracle9i Enterprise Edition Release 9.0.1.0.0 - Production
With the Partitioning option
JServer Release 9.0.1.0.0 - Production
```

```
SQL> col table_name form a10
SQL> col partition_name form a14
SQL> col high_value form a20
SQL> break on table_name
SQL> select table_name,partition_name,high_value
  2    from user_tab_partitions
  3   where table_name = 'INVOICE';

TABLE_NAME PARTITION_NAME HIGH_VALUE
---------- -------------- --------------------
INVOICE    INVOICE_P01    'A', 'D', 'T'
           INVOICE_P02    'F', 'P'
           INVOICE_P03    'B', 'J', 'S'
           INVOICE_P04    'X'
```

Based on the types of orders we have allowed for in INVOICE, keep in mind that the loading of the table would reject any rows whose ORDER_TYPE did not fall in one of A, D, T, F, P, B, J, S, or X, raising the following Oracle error:

```
SQL> insert into invoice (order_type) values ('C');
insert into invoice (order_type) values ('C')
                *
ERROR at line 1:
ORA-14400: inserted partition key does not map to any partition
```

Not to worry—the following set of SQL statements assess the row counts in the INVOICE partitions and, based on those findings, add the value C to the appropriate partition.

```
SQL> select count(*) from invoice partition (INVOICE_P01);
  COUNT(*)
-----------
   1245699

SQL> select count(*) from invoice partition (INVOICE_P02);
  COUNT(*)
-----------
   1440099

SQL> select count(*) from invoice partition (INVOICE_P03);
  COUNT(*)
-----------
   1839772
```

```
SQL> select count(*) from invoice partition (INVOICE_P04);
   COUNT(*)
-----------
   1029388
SQL> -- Let's add the new ORDER_TYPE to INVOICE_P04 . . .
SQL> alter table invoice modify partition
  2          invoice_p04 add values ('C');
```

Table altered.

Now for something completely different—the last of three partitioning approaches—hash partitioning.

Hash Partitioning

Using the hash partitioning approach, you specify a list of from 1 to 16 partition key columns, and Oracle9i places rows in the specified number of partitions based on the values found in those columns. Let's look at some SQL to set up an ADDRESS table using hash partitioning.

```
SQL*Plus: Release 9.0.1.0.0 - Production on Thu Jun 24 20:56:15 2003
(c) Copyright 2001 Oracle Corporation.  All rights reserved.
Connected to:
Oracle9i Enterprise Edition Release 9.0.1.0.0 - Production
With the Partitioning option
JServer Release 9.0.1.0.0 - Production
SQL> create table address (
  2      designator      varchar2(40),
  3      street          varchar2(40),
  4      municipality    varchar2(40),
  5      state           varchar2(2))
  6  storage (initial 160m next 160m pctincrease 0)
  7  partition by hash (municipality)
  8  partitions 8
  9  store in (address_ts1,address_ts2,
 10            address_ts3,address_ts4);
```

Table created.

The syntax looks much cleaner than range-based and list partitioning. Table 16-10 highlights the important parts of the listing.

Suffice to say, each partitioning approach has its advantages and its place. Before calling this chapter a wrap, let's look at that perplexing "Which approach is best for me?" question.

Line Number	Important Points
7	This instructs Oracle9*i* to perform a hash function on the one or more columns enclosed in parentheses. This function is based on some internal algorithm and is influenced by the number of partitions chosen, as well as the number of columns to be hashed.
8	This line specifies the number of partitions. This choice is influenced by the desired number of rows per partition.
9–10	These dictate the names of the tablespaces within which the hash partitions will be stored. If the number of tablespaces specified is less than the **store in** portion of the creation statement, Oracle9*i* cycles through the tablespace names provided as the rows are placed.

TABLE 16-10. *Discussion of Building a Hash Partitioned Table*

Which Approach to Use When

The bottom line of any partitioning approach is row count. Books—software documentation in particular—continually use very subjective adjectives when offering advice. This is very common: "If you have a large number of concurrent transactions, allocate a lot of rollback for your Oracle9*i* database." What does *large* and *a lot* mean? The guidelines we offer in this section are more finite. As mentioned in the "Volume of Data" section in this chapter, larger and larger data sets offer more sophisticated setup, storage, and management. Let's start by looking at the row count and access method issues, and the major advantage offered by each partitioning approach, and then briefly mention a best-of-both-worlds approach.

Row Count

Speaking of subjective—what one DBA calls a large database with very large tables, the other might call minute. Back in the mid-1980s, we managed Oracle V5 databases that checked in at 200–300MB; we were overwhelmed by tables that had more than 30,000 rows. Today, the scenario has changed, with Oracle9*i* (and its most recent predecessor 8*i*) capable of managing repositories in excess of many petabytes. When deciding the row count threshold for partitioning, there are two ways to look:

- **The row count itself**   Deciding an arbitrary but deliberate value somewhere over 2 million, and then deliberately partitioning tables whose row count is in excess of that.

- **The number of columns in a table coupled with the row count**   The fat 700,000–row table can end up occupying many more times the database space than its thinner counterparts with a mere 12 to 16 columns. The following query illustrates how to relate row counts and database space occupied by specific tables.

```
SQL*Plus: Release 9.0.1.0.0 - Production on Thu Jun 24 20:56:15 2003
(c) Copyright 2001 Oracle Corporation.  All rights reserved.
Connected to:
Oracle9i Enterprise Edition Release 9.0.1.0.0 - Production
With the Partitioning option
JServer Release 9.0.1.0.0 - Production
SQL> set numwidth 20
SQL> col sum(bytes) form 999,999,999,990
SQL> select num_rows
  2    from sys.dba_tables
  3   where table_name = 'ORDER'
  4     and owner = 'COREY';
  NUM_ROWS
-----------
 1,754,889
SQL> -- This could be deceiving, were we to take for granted that
SQL> -- ORDER is a thin table, when in fact it has over 90 columns.
SQL> select count(*)
  2    from sys.dba_tab_columns
  3   where table_name = 'ORDER'
  4     and owner = 'COREY';

  COUNT(*)
-----------
        92
SQL> select sum(bytes)
  2    from sys.dba_segments
  3   where segment_name = 'ORDER';

          SUM(BYTES)
--------------------
       3,340,032,000
```

The interesting thing here is that the less than 2 million–row ORDER table is an ideal candidate for partitioning, even though it may be on the low side of row count. It is a candidate due to its having 92 columns, which, spread over 2 million rows, translates to a data volume ideal for partitioning.

Access Method

In this context, *access method* refers to the way SQL queries against an object are worded. Suppose you are looking at partitioning a CUSTOMER table, its having been flagged due to its row count. After assessing the nature of the queries that access CUSTOMER, you figure out that the table is hit one customer at a time. Armed with this fact, you would partition the table using the range-based approach, to allow for partition elimination. The point we are trying to make here is illustrated in Figure 16-1.

Suppose a query goes out looking for customer ID 4626; only the **p003** partition will be scanned. Oracle9*i* eliminates the other partitions, knowing 4626 is not there. You could as well apply the same theory to choosing list-based partitioning. Suppose you did business in the following provinces in China: Szechwan, Hunan, Kwangsi, Ahwei, Hubei, and Fukien, and you wanted to group the two most active together and the remainder by themselves. The list portion of the partition table creation would resemble the following, allowing for partition elimination:

```
. . . partition p_minor values ('Kwangsi','Ahwei','Hubei','Fukien') . . .
. . . partition p_major values ('Szechwan','Hunan') . . .
```

If you are partitioning an object and it becomes obvious that range-based or list partitioning would not allow for partition elimination, the hash partitioning approach is the way to go. Suppose you had a table keyed on CUST_ID and you were looking at which partitioning to use. The lowest value in the column is 9000 and the highest is 77899. Most queries on the table are by a wide range of customer IDs; and if the table were partitioned by range, these queries would more than likely hit a lot of partitions. With this understanding, partition elimination would not come into play, and thus the hash partitioning approach seems ideal. Simply put, Table 16-11 illustrates the fundamental benefits that can be gained by the three partitioning approaches.

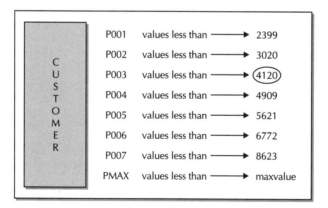

FIGURE 16-1. *Partitioned CUSTOMER table*

Desired Outcome	Range	List	Hash
Partition elimination	X	X	
Equal row count per partition			X

TABLE 16-11.   *Gains from Different Partitioning Approaches*

Composite Partitioning—A Hybrid

Often in data warehousing applications, you can take advantage of the benefits of range or list partitioning and hash partitioning at the same time. The syntax requirements for implementing composite partitioning are more cryptic when you first get started. The secret here is to hash partition within higher-level range or list partitions. This is illustrated in the next and final listing in this chapter.

```
SQL*Plus: Release 9.0.1.0.0 - Production on Thu Jun 24 20:56:15 2003
(c) Copyright 2001 Oracle Corporation.  All rights reserved.
Connected to:
Oracle9i Enterprise Edition Release 9.0.1.0.0 - Production
With the Partitioning option
JServer Release 9.0.1.0.0 - Production
SQL> create table sales
  2  ( prod            number(6),
  3    cusnum          number,
  4    sold            date,
  5    channel         varchar2(1),
  6    volume          number(3),
  7    amount          number(10,2))
  8  partition by range (sold)
  9  subpartition by hash (channel) subpartitions 8
 10   (partition sales_q1_2001 values less than
 11          (to_date('01-APR-2001','DD-MON-YYYY')),
 12    partition sales_q2_2001 values less than
 13          (to_date('01-JUL-2001','DD-MON-YYYY')),
 14    partition sales_q3_2001 values less than
 15          (to_date('01-OCT-2001','DD-MON-YYYY')),
 16    partition sales_q4_2001 values less than
 17          (to_date('01-JAN-2002','DD-MON-YYYY')),
 18    partition sales_q1_2002 values less than
```

```
19                   (to_date('01-APR-2002','DD-MON-YYYY'))
20              subpartitions 4,
21    partition sales_q2_2002 values less than
22                   (to_date('01-OCT-2002','DD-MON-YYYY'))
23      (subpartition sq2_2002_sp1,subpartition sq2_2002_sp2,
24       subpartition sq2_2002_sp3,subpartition sq2_2002_sp4,
25       subpartition sq2_2002_sp5,subpartition sq2_2002_sp6));
```

```
Table created.
```

Table 16-12 discusses important sections of the previous listing. We deliberately skimmed the surface on this partitioning approach; we simply wanted to show that it existed, and, due to some of its complexities, it could consume a few chapters on its own.

Time to move on. Once you get the cobwebs out of your head formed by the volume of technical material presented in this chapter, you will possess enough knowledge to take a seat on the partitioning wagon. Be it day one or year 22 working with the Oracle technology, partitioning is a dream come true. We hope that this chapter has helped turn what seems to be a partitioning nightmare into a dream right from the start.

Line Number	Important Points
9	This is the heart of the composite partitioning approach—the subpartition column is defined, as well as the number of buckets for the subpartitioning exercise. The hash key of the partition can be more than one column.
10–17	This is standard code like you would see in range-based partitioning. Each partition would be split into eight subpartitions based on the code in line 9.
18–20	With this partition, it is split into four rather than eight subpartitions since **subpartitions 4** is mentioned at the partition level. When not mentioned at this level, a partition assumes the table-level subpartition default. This is one way of overriding table defaults; the other way is discussed in lines 23–25 next.
23–25	This partition is split into six subpartitions, each assuming an **sq2_2002_sp**n subpartition name.

TABLE 16-12. *Discussion of Building a Composite Partitioned Table*

Chapter 16 Questions

Answers to questions can be found in Appendix A.

I. Range-based or list partitioning is the best approach to use if you are looking for

   A. the easiest partitioning approach

   B. an almost guaranteed equal row distribution in each partition

   C. partition elimination as queries are processed

   D. local rather than global indexes

2. While hash partitioning a table into 16 partitions (**p01** through **p16**), and mentioning a list of eight tablespaces (**ts01** through **ts08**) in the **store in** portion of the code, which partitions would share tablespace **ts08**?

   A. **p08** through **p16**, since the tablespace list is 8, whereas there are 16 partitions

   B. An Oracle error will be raised, as there must be the same number of tablespaces as partitions.

   C. **p08** and **p16**

   D. **p08**

3. An index is partitioned on ID, with an ITEM_1 partitioned index on ID and SYNCH_DATE. The ITEM_1 index is called

   A. non-prefixed

   B. prefixed

   C. This is impossible.

   D. function based

4. Partition elimination means

   A. deciding not to partition a table

   B. eliminating the hash partition approach

   C. Oracle9*i* does not scan partitions whose partition key column values cannot possibly be part of a query result set.

   D. not using the Oracle9*i* Partitioning option

5. When selecting rows from a specific partition, the syntactically correct way to mention the table and appropriate partition name is

   A. table name followed by the partition name

   B. table name followed by a colon followed by the partition name

   C. table name followed by the partition name enclosed in parentheses

   D. table name followed by the keyword **partition**, followed by the partition name enclosed in parentheses

CHAPTER
17

Data Warehousing
and Summarization

I f you use databases, you can be pretty well assured that you are collecting data. You may be collecting data that is about the business that you run. The data may be about books that you have sold, airline reservations you have taken, people who have subscribed to your service, or even marks attained by students in your school. There is no limit to the amount of data that can be collected today. Of course, when you build these systems, you build reports. The reports tell you how your business is doing at a point in time, but they don't usually help you understand how well your business is doing or the types of customers that you have. A *data warehouse* is built primarily to help you understand the business you are running. It helps you see how your business is doing over time, it helps you understand your customers, and it can even help you evaluate the quality of the work you are performing.

To put it simply, a data warehouse helps turn data into information. You systematically collect information from one or more data sources and collect the information into a central data repository. You then provide the information in a simple integrated structure, which allows an organization, or an individual, to make decisions based on better information. You have to remember that even though you may build a data warehouse, you can still make bad decisions with good data. This chapter will not provide you with decision-making skills; just buying this book proves you can make good decisions. A data warehouse will improve your entire organization's decisions.

Critical to the success of any project is assembling the right team. Just like the teams that win the Super Bowl, the World Series, and the Stanley Cup, the data warehouse team is composed of many different skill sets that work toward a common goal of building the right data warehouse for your organization. You should always consider having an individual who specializes in data warehouses as part of your team. Building a data warehouse is not the same as any other system you may have built in the past, so ensure that you have someone who can help guide you through the process. Data warehouses cannot be prebuilt; they must be built to your own (or your organization's) needs and requirements. This is one type of system that should not be created based on technology but should be driven by the business.

Oracle9i is a product that is built for data warehouses. We have seen and used many different databases, and we keep coming back to Oracle when we create data warehouses. Whether your data warehouse is going to contain 100MB of data or multiple terabytes, Oracle9i provides facilities that will help you organize and optimize its performance.

This chapter will cover the following topics:

- What a data warehouse is
- Data warehouse design

- Data warehouse storage considerations

- Data warehouse backups

- Loading the data warehouse

- Materialized views

- Oracle functions and features for summarization

Terminology

The following terminology will arm you with the technical jargon you need for this chapter:

- A *data warehouse* is an integrated view of a majority of the data for an organization.

- A *data mart* is a set of tables that focus on a single task. This may be for a department, such as sales, or a single task, such as handling customer products.

- An *operational system* is a computer system that is used to help operate a business, for example, a reservation system in a travel agency.

- A *federated data warehouse* is a data warehouse that is developed in pieces and then integrated together.

- *Normal form* is a method for designing a database. Normal form adheres to a set of rules that define the most efficient way to store data in a relational database.

- *Denormalization* is a method of database design in which tables may not adhere to the rules of normal form, so that storage space is sacrificed for speed.

- *Star schema* is a special type of organization of data tuned for quick access. It is by nature simple to understand and navigate.

- A *fact table* is the central table of a star, or snowflake, schema. Usually, the fact table is the collection of the key values from the dimension tables and the base facts of the table's subject.

- A *dimension table* holds the attributes about a specific characteristic of the data. For example, dimension tables may be tables about customers, stores, products, and so on.

- *OLAP* is the acronym for Online Analytical Processing. This is the area of data warehousing that provides users with the ability to analyze their information.

- *Data mining* is the area of data warehousing that uses advanced mathematical techniques to discover previously undiscovered trends.

What Is a Data Warehouse?

Knowing what a data warehouse is, is basic to understanding how to design and construct one. How you create a data warehouse that will help your organization improve its performance is critical. A data warehouse is not an operational system; it is quite different. It is created for what may seem like some simple purposes, including reporting and analysis, but you should not minimize the importance of these tasks in today's competitive environment. A data warehouse has four distinct characteristics that make it different from your operational system:

- **Subject oriented**   The warehouse is organized around a specific business process or knowledge area such as sales, logistics, or customer profiles.

- **Integrated**   The warehouse is integrated so that you can relate one business area to another within your organization. For instance, you may want to compare sales versus inventory. The warehouse should become the one place in your organization where people come to perform all analysis; so integration is critical.

- **Nonvolatile**   The warehouse is static; it does not change like an operational system. You load data into the warehouse on a regular basis; but once the data is loaded, you do not change it in the warehouse. If data changes, you use mechanisms in the warehouse to store how the data has changed. If you create a report today and want to run the same one in 2005, the results should be the same. Data in the warehouse is loaded once and read many times.

- **Time based**   The basic power of the warehouse is that the information contained in it is based on specific point-in-time loads. The date component may be based on the date of a sale, the daily rollup of sales, the weekly sales, the monthly sales, or annual sales. The warehouse provides users with the ability to perform analysis over time, which is the basis for truly understanding how an organization is performing.

Each of the preceding points defines the nature of the data in the warehouse. The warehouse becomes the place in your business that people have all the information needed to support strategic and tactical decisions that may need to be made.

In addition to building the right data stores, you will need to present this information to your users. To do this, you use a technology known as *Business Intelligence* (BI), a collection of facilities that allow you to deliver information in a productive manner to the user community. BI comes in many forms, including Online Analytical Processing (OLAP) and many derivatives that provide information access to your warehouse via easy-to-use interfaces delivered to the desktop. Oracle Discover and Business Objects are examples of this technology. For a more complete discussion of BI technology, we refer you to *Oracle8i Data Warehousing*, by Abbey, Abramson, Corey, and Taub (Osborne/McGraw-Hill, 2000). Here, we will discuss design and then features. Once you have decided that a data warehouse is right for your organization, you should definitely look at how Oracle9*i* can help you in achieving your warehousing goals.

Designing the Data Warehouse

When you embark on your data warehouse construction plan, you first need to design the best possible solution. The design of a warehouse is critical to its overall success. If you consider the construction of a building like the Empire State Building, it was built with a solid plan. If not, it may have fallen down when King Kong climbed to the top. The same can be said for a data warehouse—designing a solid plan and then building a solid data foundation will provide your warehouse with the greatest opportunity for success.

Designing the warehouse is not a job for the novice. It should be undertaken, or at least verified, by someone with experience. You would not attempt to climb to the top of Mount Everest without a Sherpa guide; don't try to design a warehouse without guidance. Ask for help and build upon experience. Before we start designing the warehouse, let's take a look at the architecture to get an idea of the whole solution and then focus on design. Figure 17-1 illustrates how data flows through the warehouse and the overall data warehouse architecture.

As you can see in Figure 17-1, a warehouse is more than a simple database. It is part of a process. The data warehouse always starts with source data. Your data sources are operational data systems, as well as external data like census information. You must understand these systems completely, or your data warehouse will not achieve your information goals. Once you have identified your source systems, you will need to extract data from these systems. You will need to design extracts from these systems so that the information you want is prepared for movement into the warehouse.

Now you will need to populate the warehouse with data. The process of populating a warehouse is usually known as extraction, transformation, and loading, or ETL to its friends. There are many methods that you can use to take data from the source

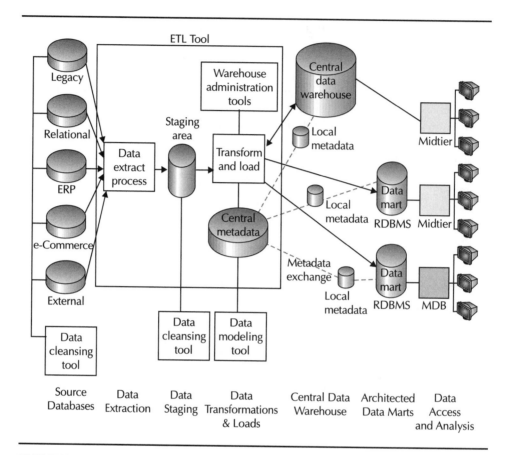

FIGURE 17-1. *Data warehouse architecture*

to the data warehouse target. Among the choices are PL/SQL or SQL alone, or products like Oracle Warehouse Builder, Informatica, or some other ETL tool. We recommend that you always consider an ETL tool for this part of your warehouse architecture, since it will simplify the long-term maintenance of your warehouse loading routines.

Next, the figure shows the two main data structures of your data warehouse. The first is the warehouse itself. It is here that you provide a complete enterprise view of your business. The central data warehouse will contain all the information from within and outside your organization in an integrated manner. The other structure is the data mart. A *data mart* is a data store that is focused on a business process or a department within your organization, such as sales. Finally, there are the methods used to deliver the information to your end users. By delivering this information in a simple and useful way, you will find that users will be more ready to accept the warehouse.

Let's look at how to design the structures used to store the information within the warehouse.

Dimensional Database Design

The current favorite design methodology is known as *dimensional data warehousing*. A dimensional data warehouse is based upon two basic pieces known as facts and dimensions. *Fact tables* contain the information that you wish to measure. They are based upon the tasks that you want to support. For example, you may have a fact table that contains the daily sales by store, or the number of goals scored by position. *Dimension tables* are the windows into the information that you want to measure. The dimensions provide the information to be used in your **where** clauses. Dimension tables will include tables about customers, stores, geographical information, or salespeople. Together, facts and dimensions form a structure called a *star schema*. A schema is simply a data structure that contains a number of tables. These tables are usually organized using the normalized method of design. Normalized databases are tuned to store data very efficiently. Figure 17-2 illustrates what a star schema looks like.

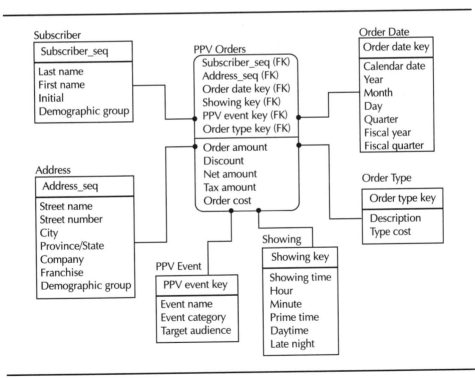

FIGURE 17-2. *Data warehouse star schema*

The fact table is the table PPV ORDERS, and the dimension tables include the SUBSCRIBER, ADDRESS, ORDER DATE, ORDER TYPE, SHOWING, and PPV EVENT. This type of structure is very simple for end users to understand and navigate. The structure and relationships are obvious and allow for powerful analysis. Now that you have a better idea of how to design a warehouse, let's move on and look at some the features that directly influence the performance of a data warehouse that uses Oracle9i. We will start by looking at some storage considerations for the warehouse.

Data Warehouse Partitioning

In the previous chapter, we provided you with a detailed view of how to use and implement partitions in an Oracle9i database. The next piece you need to understand is why you need them. When we teach courses about building data warehouses using Oracle9i, we discuss partitioning. We feel that when you implement a data warehouse, one feature that you are sure to use with Oracle9i is the partitioning option.

Data in a warehouse is very well suited to being partitioned. There are two main reasons for partitioning data. First, it allows physical separation of data, which helps to optimize queries and storage. The other reason is for the rotation of data. When you perform analysis on data in a data warehouse, this analysis is usually time based. This means, for example, that you may want to know what your sales have been for the last 12 months. Data that is older than 12 months may not be important anymore, and, therefore, it may then be archived. Partitioning makes it easy to roll data off that is no longer needed. Let's look at how we would implement partitioning in a data warehousing environment.

We have decided that we need to store a large amount of data that will need to be analyzed based on monthly comparisons. In the days before partitioning we had a limited number of options—none of them very good. We could create one big table, or we could create a number of tables and join them in a view. With one large table, it is possible that Oracle would have to search through the entire table, even when we may have wanted to look at data from only a small portion of the table, so this is not a good thing. Combining tables into one view, known as a *partition view*, is no longer recommended either because, as you know, accessing views tends to be slower than direct access to tables. Since Oracle first added the partition functionality to the product in Oracle8, it should be considered mandatory in all data warehouses. Figure 17-3 illustrates how partitioning compares to single table accesses.

As depicted in Figure 17-3, when users access a table, some users will be selecting data, while others will be loading data, and still others will require data for secondary purposes like a remote data mart. When many users access the data simultaneously,

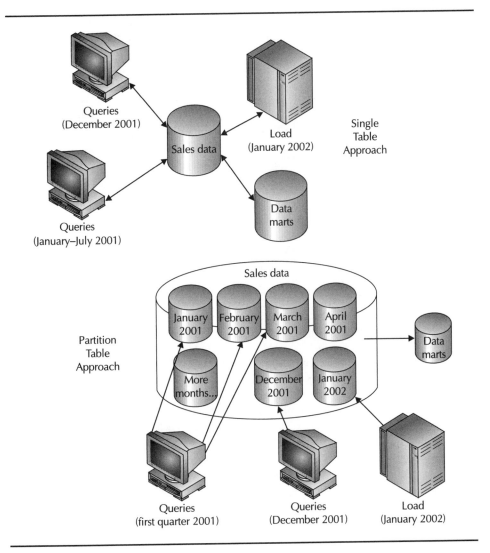

FIGURE 17-3. *Partition table vs. nonpartitioned data access*

something needs to give. By using partitioning, as shown in Figure 17-3, each user can access data in the areas they care about. For example, if all you want to see is data in the first three or six months of the year, there should be no need to look at data in the last six months; or when you are loading data into the database, you shouldn't have to contend with resources that may be used for a query for historical data. This provides users a cleaner path with less contention to the area of the table that concerns them.

In Chapter 16, we discussed how to implement partitioning. We will not go into as much detail on the creation of partitions, but more on the use and maintenance of them in a warehouse. Normally, when partitions are created in a warehouse, these partitions are created based on time. Since most analysis is performed at the day, week, or month level, these are commonly used as partition keys. The following example shows the syntax for creating a month-level range partition table:

```
create table sales_transactions
(sales_date   date,
 store_id     number(10),
 sales_amt    number)
 partition by range (sales_date)
(partition sales_dec_2000 values less than
        (to_date('01-JAN-2001','DD-MON-YYYY')),
 partition sales_jan_2001 values less than
        (to_date('01-FEB-2001','DD-MON-YYYY')),
 partition sales_feb_2001 values less than
        (to_date('01-MAR-2001','DD-MON-YYYY')),
 partition sales_other_2001 values less than   (MAXVALUE));
```

We have created a table that will be partitioned by month, and to do this we use the technique known as *range partitioning*. We have divided data into month partitions starting with January 2001. The other months follow right after this. So here we have a table that will be partitioned by month, the most common of partition methods. After creating tables using this strategy, a whole world of possibilities opens up for you in the areas of loading and backup. We will look at these later in this chapter.

Before we move on, let's look at the newest form of partitioning. Oracle9i provides the ability to create partitions based on a list of values; this is known as *list partitioning*. The syntax for this technique is as follows:

```
CREATE TABLE SUBSCRIBERS
(AREA_CODE   NUMBER,
 LAST_NAME   VARCHAR2(30),
 FIRST_NAME varchar2(30),
 PHONE_NUM   varchar2(10),
 NO_MARKETING varchar2(1))
 PARTITION BY LIST (AREA_CODE)
```

```
(PARTITION SUB_416 VALUES (416)
        tablespace ABRAMSON_416,
 PARTITION SUB_514 VALUES (514)
        tablespace ABRAMSON_514,
 PARTITION SUB_705 VALUES (705)
        tablespace ABRAMSON_705,
 PARTITION SUB_TOLLFREE VALUES (800,888)
        tablespace ABRAMSON_TOLLFREE,
 PARTITION SUB_OTHERS VALUES (212,604,613,819));
```

In this code, we have created a table that will separate the data based on area codes.

There are many areas where this knowledge of partitioning will come in handy, but it is especially useful when you are backing up your data warehouse or any database that has a large amount of data to be backed up.

Backing Up the Warehouse

We have already discussed how to back up a database in Chapter 10. Data warehouse backups may be problematic due to the large size of the database. It is very common for warehouses to have sizes that exceed 1TB (terabyte), and based on current technology, backing up this much data can take an extensive amount of time. One installation that we work with has a data warehouse that currently contains 1.3TB of data. It takes ten hours to back up this database, but we need to get it done in two hours. We could move to archivelog mode and perform hot backups; but since the daily loads exceed 3GB of data, there is a concern that the load processes will slow down due to the archiving. Therefore, we need to improve the backup times of the data warehouse.

Think about data in a data warehouse—you can assume that a mature data warehouse will contain dynamic data that constitutes only a small portion of your total database. A majority of data in a data warehouse does not change over time. The old adage of Load Once and Read Many (LORM) or Write Once and Read Many (WORM) is definitely an important part of data warehousing. The question becomes, Why do I need to back up the same unchanging data time after time? The answer is you don't, if you use read-only tablespaces. *Read-only tablespaces* are tablespaces that have been told that no writing is to occur in them. The benefit of this is that you only need to back up a read-only tablespace once. You may do this immediately after you have put the table into read-only mode, and you never have to back it up again unless you put the tablespace back into read-write mode. To set a tablespace to read-only mode, issue the following command:

```
SQL> alter tablespace abramson read only;
Tablespace altered.
```

It's as simple as that. Now if you want to use the tablespace after you have set it to read-only, you will receive an error. In the next code example, we try to create a table in the read-only tablespace ABRAMSON. Let's see what happens.

```
SQL> create table test
  2  (col1 number)
  3  tablespace abramson;
create table test
*
ERROR at line 1:
ORA-01647: tablespace 'ABRAMSON' is read only, cannot allocate space in it
```

You can see that this would not be possible once a tablespace is set to read-only. However, if you can imagine that you may one day need to use this tablespace again, you can reset the tablespace back to read-write mode by issuing the following command:

```
SQL> alter tablespace abramson read write;
Tablespace altered.
```

Based on this new information, let's see how our 1.3TB data warehouse does if we put all of our static data that was older than one month into read-only mode. Luckily, we partitioned our data into month-based partitions, so doing this is relatively simple. The following table shows how our data is organized and where we use read-only tablespaces:

Data Type	Partition Method	Tablespace Mode	Data Volume
Current data	Monthly	Read-write	400GB
Historical Data	Monthly	Read-only	850GB
Dimension Data	None	Read-write	100GB

As a result of this approach, our full backup still occupies ten hours; but now when we back up the active portion of the data warehouse, the time is reduced to two hours. Our backup schedule becomes one full backup per month and two weekly incremental backups of active data and other necessary Oracle files. Previously, an average of eight full backups were performed in a month. This new approached saves a total 54 hours during each month. This time is now available for loading or using the warehouse. Now that we have all this extra time, let's move on and look at loading data into the warehouse.

Loading Your Data Warehouse

One of the most critical functions you will perform in a data warehouse is loading the data into it. A data warehouse without data is just a warehouse with empty shelves. The biggest problem administrators have when managing a data warehouse is that the time needed to load a warehouse is always longer than the available time. You will usually need to start loading at 12:00 p.m. and finish by 6:00 a.m. The problem occurs when it really takes nine hours to load the 30GB of daily data, so it is imperative that you select methods that can take advantage of any way to minimize the amount of time needed to load your data. There are many methods you may use to improve performance, including

- Import
- SQL*Loader
- Array loads with SQL processing
- PL/SQL

Some of these methods have already been discussed. You are already aware that you can use Import to load data from another Oracle database. Since export files that are used by the Import utility are created using the Export utility, you are limited on your options here. This restriction of loading data only from an Oracle database limits the flexibility of using Import, since a data warehouse usually collects data from multiple data sources, including non-Oracle sources. In addition, you cannot perform any type of validation using this option. So using Import may provide you with fast loading, but it will form only a portion of your warehouse loading solution.

Along with Import, you can use SQL*Loader. With SQL*Loader, you have the option of loading data that is in a fixed format. A *fixed format* file is one that has a defined layout—if the Name field is in position 10 to 40, you will always find that data there. The other type of file that can be read is a *delimited file*, which has a separator, such as a comma or tab, between data fields. This is normally done to minimize the amount of space used by the file. We will look at SQL*Loader in a little more detail in the next section.

The next two options both revolve around SQL and PL/SQL. Using SQL or PL/SQL allows you to load data using the power of the Oracle internal languages. Oracle9*i* now allows you to use external tables. These tables are held in files in the operating system. Let's look closer at some of these options. They will all load the same files into the database. The file that we will be using will be the same one in each method. The following is the file that we need to load:

```
IAN|ABRAMSON|FATHER
SUSAN|ABRAMSON|MOTHER
BAILA|ABRAMSON|DAUGHTER
JILLIAN|ABRAMSON|DAUGHTER
DREIDLE|ABRAMSON|CAT
KOOGLE|ABRAMSON|HAMSTER
```

As you can see, this is a simple delimited file. We have delimited the values using the | character. You can use any character to delimit data, but be aware that if you use the character in your data, this will confuse the loading program.

The table that we will be using is defined as follows:

```
SQL> create table family_info
  2  (first_name        varchar2(30),
  3   surname           varchar2(30),
  4   relation          varchar2(30));
```

Now let's see a few ways that we can get external data into our database.

Using SQL*Loader to Load the Warehouse

SQL*Loader is a utility that allows you to load data into the database from an operating system file. These files need to be standard format (as in ASCII standard format) so that the database utility may read the file. So if you have an ASCII file and want it in the database, you need to create a special file that is used by SQL*Loader as a guide to loading the data. This file is known as a *control file*. Every control file contains information on the following items:

■ The name of the table into which data is to be inserted

■ How to load the data

■ Delimiters, if any are used

■ The columns into which you want to put data and their data types

■ The position of the fields in the case of a fixed format file

As you can see, there are many things that you need to include in a control file. The following is an example of the control file needed to load our data into the table we created.

```
LOAD DATA
INFILE test.txt
INTO TABLE family_info
REPLACE
FIELDS TERMINATED BY '|'
( first_name     char,
  surname        CHAR,
  relation       char
)
```

NOTE
*You must create a control file
for each and every data load.*

Now we have the control file we need. Next, we need to run the command to
let Oracle know we want to load data into the database. When we run the SQL*Loader
utility we issue the command **sqlldr**. This command may differ on your particular
platform, but generally it is **sqlldr**. For full details on the command on your particular
platform, we suggest that you check the documentation or look in your $ORACLE_
HOME/bin directory and see whether you find an executable program with a name
similar to sqlldr. Like many utilities that Oracle provides, you can specify a number
of different parameters. To see all the parameters supported by SQL*Loader, issue the
command **sqlldr help=y**. The following listing shows you the simplest issuance
of the SQL*Loader command. We provide our username and password and tell
SQL*Loader the name of the control file that we created. The command runs,
and we see that it loads six rows.

```
oracle@mail.ntirety.com-->(beg9)
/d0/oraclehome/ian> sqlldr ian/ian control=test
SQL*Loader: Release 9.0.1.0.0 - Production on Mon Sep 3 16:38:00 2001
(c) Copyright 2001 Oracle Corporation.  All rights reserved.
Commit point reached - logical record count 6
```

When Oracle loads data using SQL*Loader, many files may be created during
a loading session, the most important of which is the SQL*Loader log file. The following
is the log file that was generated by our load example:

```
/d0/oraclehome/ian> vi test.log
"test.log" 49 lines, 1542 characters
SQL*Loader: Release 9.0.1.0.0 - Production on Wed Sep 5 19:16:03 2001
(c) Copyright 2001 Oracle Corporation.  All rights reserved.
Control File:   test.ctl
```

```
Data File:        test.txt
  Bad File:       test.bad
  Discard File:   none specified
  (Allow all discards)
Number to load: ALL
Number to skip: 0
Errors allowed: 50
Bind array:       64 rows, maximum of 256000 bytes
Continuation:     none specified
Path used:        Conventional
Table FAMILY_INFO, loaded from every logical record.
Insert option in effect for this table: REPLACE
    Column Name                      Position   Len  Term Encl Datatype
------------------------------- ---------- ----- ---- ---- -----------
FIRST_NAME                           FIRST     *    |        CHARACTER
SURNAME                              NEXT      *    |        CHARACTER
RELATION                             NEXT      *    |        CHARACTER
Table FAMILY_INFO:
  6 Rows successfully loaded.
  0 Rows not loaded due to data errors.
  0 Rows not loaded because all WHEN clauses were failed.
  0 Rows not loaded because all fields were null.
Space allocated for bind array:                    49536 bytes(64 rows)
Read   buffer bytes: 1048576
Total logical records skipped:         0
Total logical records read:            6
Total logical records rejected:        0
Total logical records discarded:       0
Run began on Wed Sep 05 19:16:03 2001
Run ended on Wed Sep 05 19:16:03 2001
Elapsed time was:     00:00:00.24
CPU time was:         00:00:00.06
```

This log file tells us about the fields that we are loading. It shows you the files that are being used by the program and then the details of the load. This file also shows you that it took less than one second to load the table. The most important detail that this file tells us is that we have successfully loaded six rows with no failures. In a case in which rows do get rejected, you will see a log of the problems that were found. You then can either change your data or change the control file to handle the issues. The handling of these types of errors is beyond the scope of this discussion, but it will be critical when you want to use SQL*Loader. SQL*Loader is a great way to load your database, but it's limited in terms of handling problems. So we need to find some more sophisticated methods that will allow us to validate data as we are loading it. External tables are our next step in our data loading adventure, so let's move on.

Using External Tables to Load the Warehouse

If you are building a data warehouse, external tables are a great asset. You should understand by now that getting data into the warehouse is one of the most important functions that you will need to perform. External tables allow you to define a table that is actually not a table at all in the traditional sense of the word. With an external table, the data is held in an operating system file. This allows you to define a file as a table and select data from a file just as you would from a table. You can use **where** clauses or parallelize the command to improve performance. Before you create an external table, you need to create an object known as a directory in the database. A *directory* assigns a logical name to a physical directory in the operating system and must be defined in advance of creating your external table. The following is the syntax for creating an external table:

```
SQL> CREATE or REPLACE directory admin as '/d0/oraclehome/ian';
Directory created.
```

We have named our directory admin, but the choice is yours. It should have a meaningful name just as any other object name has in your database. Now we are ready to define our external table by issuing the following command:

```
SQL> CREATE TABLE relations_ext
  2  (
  3   first_name      varchar2(20),
  4   surname         varchar2(20),
  5   relationship    varchar2(20)
  6  )
  7   ORGANIZATION EXTERNAL
  8   (TYPE oracle_loader
  9    DEFAULT DIRECTORY admin
 10    ACCESS PARAMETERS
 11    (
 12    RECORDS DELIMITED BY newline
 13    BADFILE 'test2.bad'
 14    DISCARDFILE 'test2.dis'
 15    LOGFILE 'test2.log'
 16    FIELDS TERMINATED BY "|"
 17    (
 18    first_name      CHAR,
 19    surname         CHAR,
 20    relationship    CHAR
 21    )
 22    )
 23    LOCATION ('test.txt')
 24    )
```

```
25*  REJECT LIMIT UNLIMITED

Table created.
```

We have successfully created our external table. Table 17-1 explains the important lines in this code example.

You may notice that the creation of an external table is very much like using SQL*Loader; but since we can use the power of SQL in combination with the speed of SQL*Loader, it should be considered as an alternative when loading data into the warehouse.

To prove that this works, let's select data from our new table.

```
SQL> select * from relations_ext;
FIRST_NAME            SURNAME               RELATIONSHIP
--------------------  --------------------  --------------------
IAN                   ABRAMSON              FATHER
SUSAN                 ABRAMSON              MOTHER
BAILA                 ABRAMSON              DAUGHTER
JILLIAN               ABRAMSON              DAUGHTER
DREIDLE               ABRAMSON              CAT
KOOGLE                ABRAMSON              HAMSTER
6 rows selected.
Elapsed: 00:00:00.09
```

External tables open a new path for accessing data, which allows you to leverage SQL when loading your data. Let's move on and see how we can use PL/SQL to load data into the warehouse.

Line #	Description
1–6	Define the columns of the table. These should match your data in the file that you want to load.
7	Define the table as an external table.
10–16	Tell Oracle how to load the file, along with the files that will be used for logging the load and any problem records.
18–20	Define the file layout for the file being loaded. If this was a fixed format file, then it would include the position of the fields, just as you would do in a SQL*Loader control file.
23	Specify the name of the file that will be loaded.

TABLE 17-1. *Discussion of External Table Definition*

Using PL/SQL to Load the Warehouse

PL/SQL has been the only integrated solution for loading the warehouse before the release of Oracle9*i*. In Chapter 9, we introduced you to the package utl_file. This package is important for loading data, since it allows you to read data files, parse the data, and then load it into the database. This section will not delve into the utl_file package, but instead will show you how it may be used to load our famous file into the database.

NOTE
The utl_file package has been available since Oracle7; so if you are not currently running Oracle9i, you should consider this approach an alternative to using external tables.

Let's look at a PL/SQL program that we can use to read the file, parse the data, and then insert it into our table. The program is a complex one. We use the built-in function utl_file. The loading in this case is more complex due to the fact that the file is delimited. To read this data, we need to move through the data, and we do this by knowing the character being used to delimit each field. Let's look at the code that we use to make this all happen:

```
SQL> get utl1
  1  CREATE OR REPLACE PROCEDURE load_family_info
  2  (in_file_name                   varchar2,
  3   in_dir_name                    varchar2,
  4   out_rows_processed      OUT    number,
  5   out_return_code   OUT    number)
  6  IS
  7   file_handle        UTL_FILE.FILE_TYPE;-- file handle of OS flat file
  8   retrieved_buffer  VARCHAR2(100);      -- Line retrieved from flat file
  9   l_text                       varchar2(1000);
 10   l_new_text                   varchar2(1000);
 11   l_stripped_text              varchar2(1000);
 12   l_delimit                    varchar2(1)    :='|'; --The field delimiter
 13   l_counter                    number         := 0;
 14   l_pos                        number         := 1;
 15   l_new_pos                    number         := 0;
 16   l_end                        number         := 1000;
 17   l_new_end                    number         := 0;
 18   l_readpos                    number         := 0;
 19   l_family_tab                 family_info%ROWTYPE;
 20  BEGIN
 21  dbms_output.put_line('Start');
```

```
22   -- Open file to write into and get its file_handle
23   dbms_output.put_line('Open File');
24   file_handle := UTL_FILE.FOPEN(in_dir_name,in_file_name,'R');
25   dbms_output.put_line('File OpenedDone');
26   BEGIN
27      LOOP
28            -- Read each row of the file
29            utl_file.get_line (file_handle, l_text);
30            l_readpos := l_readpos + 1;
31            -- First Name field
32            l_pos      := instr(l_text,l_delimit);
33            l_new_text := substr(l_text,l_pos+1);
34            l_new_pos  := instr(l_new_text,l_delimit);
35            l_family_tab.first_name := substr(l_text,1,l_pos-1);
36            l_text     := l_new_text;
37            -- Surname
38            l_pos      := instr(l_text,l_delimit);
39            l_new_text := substr(l_text,l_pos+1);
40            l_new_pos  := instr(l_new_text,l_delimit);
41            l_family_tab.surname := substr(l_text,1,l_pos-1);
42            l_text     := l_new_text;
43            -- Relationship
44            l_pos      := length(l_text)+1;
45            l_family_tab.relation := substr(l_text,1,l_pos-1);
46            insert into FAMILY_INFO
47            (first_name,
48             surname,
49             relation
50            )
51            values
52            (l_family_tab.first_name,
53             l_family_tab.surname,
54             l_family_tab.relation);
55            l_counter := l_counter + 1;
56      END LOOP;
57            out_rows_processed := l_counter;
58            commit;
59            out_return_code    := 0;
60      EXCEPTION
61            WHEN NO_DATA_FOUND THEN
62                    null;
63      END;
64      -- Close the file that was opened
65   UTL_FILE.FCLOSE(file_handle);
66    EXCEPTION
67      --Handle utl_file errors.
68      WHEN NO_DATA_FOUND THEN
69        DBMS_OUTPUT.PUT_LINE('no_data_found');
```

```
70            UTL_FILE.FCLOSE(file_handle);
71      out_return_code      := SQLCODE;
72       WHEN UTL_FILE.INVALID_PATH THEN
73         DBMS_OUTPUT.PUT_LINE('UTL_FILE.INVALID_PATH');
74         UTL_FILE.FCLOSE(file_handle);
75         out_return_code      := SQLCODE;
76       WHEN UTL_FILE.READ_ERROR THEN
77         DBMS_OUTPUT.PUT_LINE(' UTL_FILE.READ_ERROR');
78         UTL_FILE.FCLOSE(file_handle);
79         out_return_code      := SQLCODE;
80       WHEN UTL_FILE.WRITE_ERROR THEN
81         DBMS_OUTPUT.PUT_LINE('UTL_FILE.WRITE_ERROR');
82         UTL_FILE.FCLOSE(file_handle);
83         out_return_code      := SQLCODE;
84       WHEN OTHERS THEN
85         DBMS_OUTPUT.PUT_LINE('Error:'||SQLERRM||'.');
86         UTL_FILE.FCLOSE(file_handle);
87         out_return_code      := SQLCODE;
88  END;
89  /
```

Now that we have successfully created our load procedure, let's run it. As a habit, we like to describe the procedure before we run it to make sure that we get our parameters right. Also, in this case, we need to define some variables that will be used to return some values back to us. So let's see how this all works.

```
SQL> describe load_family_info
PROCEDURE load_family_info
 Argument Name                   Type                      In/Out Default?
 ------------------------------  ------------------------  ------ --------
 IN_FILE_NAME                    VARCHAR2                  IN
 IN_DIR_NAME                     VARCHAR2                  IN
 OUT_ROWS_PROCESSED              NUMBER                    OUT
 OUT_RETURN_CODE                 NUMBER                    OUT
SQL> -- Now let's set up the parameters.
SQL> var rows number
SQL> var ret_cd number
SQL> set serveroutput on
SQL> -- Let us now get on with running our program.
SQL> execute load_family_info('test.dat','/d0/orahome/ian',:rows,:ret_cd);
Start
Open File
File OpenedDone
PL/SQL procedure successfully completed.
```

We have successfully loaded the data into our table. You have seen many ways to load data using Oracle9i. There are tools out there that have been designed to do the same task; they are outside the scope of this book. We do encourage you to look at these before you embark on a data warehouse project. They will help you develop loading routines for your warehouse. Now we should move on and see some of the data warehouse functions that Oracle9*i* provides for us.

Oracle9*i* Data Warehousing Functions

Oracle9*i* provides a number of facilities that can be used to analyze data. These functions are not limited to use in a data warehouse, but they do tend to be used more often in these types of systems. Summarization is the friend of the data warehouse designer. It allows you to improve the performance of most data warehouses because you can work with smaller data sets. Whenever we have the chance to summarize data in the warehouse, we take it. Oracle9*i* could be called the *summary engine*; its arsenal of views, snapshots (or materialized views) lets you create logical and physical data summarizations. But this isn't all. Oracle9*i* has many additional analysis features that let you create a wide range of data analysis reports.

You don't have to settle for being able to sum, count, or average your data; now you can rank data, create moving aggregates, or perform some really significant data analysis. Oracle9*i* has provided all of these capabilities and more. Summary is good, mathematics is good, so let's unleash these powers and move on to a discussion of data summarization features in Oracle9*i*.

Materialized Views

Views provide a way to present a different look at the data that resides within the base tables; they allow you to tailor the presentation of data to different types of users. Views are often used to provide an additional level of table security by restricting access to a predetermined set of rows and/or columns of a table. As you know, views are local views of the data, and as such they are not stored in the physical database. They are created on-the-fly, so they are usually slow and result in performance problems.

To directly address the performance issue, Oracle created snapshots and materialized views, which are summarized data objects stored in the database. This allows for the data warehouse to support new features like query rewrite. *Query rewrite* allows Oracle to look at your database and decide whether it should access the data in the tables or look at a precomputed summary instead. This feature works behind the scenes and is invisible to end users. As you might expect, any feature that helps to improve performance in the data warehouse is a welcome addition; so let's move on and look at materialized views, and start to tap the potential of the Oracle9*i* data warehouse.

Materialized views are schema objects that can be used to summarize, precompute, replicate, and distribute data. They are suitable in various computing environments, including data warehousing, decision support, and distributed or mobile computing. Within the realm of data warehousing, a materialized view is commonly used to store summary and precomputed results. Materialized views provide significantly faster data warehouse query processing. The time necessary to calculate these summarizations is performed in advance of the data request. Prior to Oracle8, materialized views were called *snapshots.* Frankly, we still don't know why the name changed. Is bigger better? You decide. We'll be using both terms.

NOTE
For the purposes of this chapter, we'll keep our coverage of materialized views simple and just look at the basic concepts and the syntax behind them. When you get started with these views in your own warehouse, this chapter will have given you a framework to build upon.

Given that materialized views are such a big item in the warehouse, we're going to have a brief look at them from the ground up. We'll look at some master and remote site setups, and then look at materialized view maintenance. Figure 17-4, in a nutshell, shows the high-level architecture of implementing snapshots.

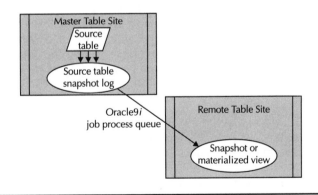

FIGURE 17-4.   *Materialized views architecture*

There are five pieces to the diagram shown in Figure 17-4.

- **Master site**   One or more tables whose data feeds the snapshot reside here.

- **Source table**   The data being made into a snapshot is held in this table.

- **Source table snapshot log**   Transactions that interact with the source tables can be stored locally in that table's snapshot log.

- **Oracle9i job process queue**   These processes propagate the contents of the snapshot log to the remote site.

- **Remote site**   Transactions are processed as they arrive—updating, deleting, or inserting new rows into the snapshot.

Sound like magic? In a way it is; in a way it isn't. Let's look a little deeper into the technology.

NOTE
We've just started this section of the chapter, and already we are stumbling over the use of the term materialized views. *Even though it's supposedly passé, we're going to use the name* snapshot *from now on. Either works in SQL*Plus with Oracle9i, though this may not be the case much longer.*

Before you run off and try to implement these views in your warehouse, the schemas within which they will be built must first be prepared. The owner of the one or more tables that feed data into the snapshot needs a special system privilege to get started. This is given out using a command similar to the following:

```
SQL> grant create materialized view to dw_owner;
Grant succeeded.
```

NOTE
The appropriate objects and system privileges were in place on our database instance when we ran the code shown in this chapter. If these pieces are not in place on your warehouse, you will not be able to build the appropriate schema.

Once the appropriate system privilege has been given out, the user is ready to start. In the next section, we'll look at the setup on the master site for the two kinds of snapshots—simple and complex.

Setup on the Master Site

The setup on the master site is dictated by the type of snapshot you intend to create on the remote site—simple or complex. Oracle9*i* determines whether a snapshot is complex or simple based on the following two criteria; if you can answer yes to both of the following, your target snapshot is deemed simple and can be fast refreshed.

■ There is only one source table involved in the query.

■ There are no summary (aggregation) or **group by** operations being performed on the source table's columns, as defined here:

■ **Aggregation** This is a fancy word for some form of summarization. Often this is the summing of a numeric column from the snapshot's base table(s).

■ **group by** This command instructs Oracle to lump values together in like columns.

The following code demonstrates how you could create a snapshot that sums all the sales for a given set of counties, by county:

```
create materialized view county_summ as
. . .
. . .
select county, sum(days30), sum(days60) . . .
  from county, accrec
. . .
. . .
 group by county;
```

Simple Snapshots The system privilege **create materialized view** allows the snapshot log to be created on the master site and allows the **create materialized view** command to succeed on the snapshot site.

The following code illustrates the makeup of a table whose contents will feed a simple snapshot:

```
create table clients (
    client_id        number,
    company_name     varchar2(100),
    contact_name     varchar2(100),
    contact_phone    varchar2(20),
    contact_fax      varchar2(20),
    comments         varchar2(4000),
    client_address   varchar2(4000),
    dba_id           varchar2(50),
    email            varchar2(300),
    monthly          number(10,2),
```

```
        short_name           varchar2(10),
        notify_list          varchar2(4000),
        active               varchar2(1),
        team                 number);
alter table clients add constraint clients_pk primary key
        (client_id);
```

Assuming that user dw_owner has the right system privileges, the code shown in the following listing will set up the snapshot log on the fictitious CLIENTS table.

```
SQL> create snapshot log on clients;
Materialized view log created.
```

That's where the heart of the difference between simple and complex snapshots lies—the former can use a snapshot log, the latter cannot.

Complex Snapshots   The next listing shows the code that created the DAILY_SALES table referred to in this section, as well as its primary key definition.

```
create table daily_sales (
        transaction_date date,
        company_num      number,
        gross_sales      number(12,2),
        discount_amt     number(12,2),
        tax_amount       number(12,2));
alter table daily_sales add constraint daily_sales_pk
        primary key (transaction_date,company_num);
```

Setup Common to Simple and Complex Snapshots   This is where the differences end; the balance of the master site setup is independent of the snapshot type. Notice how Oracle9i snapshots require a primary key on the base table—evidenced by our setting up the clients_pk and daily_sales_pk primary key constraints on CLIENTS and DAILY_SALES. Oracle9i returns the following error if you try to build a snapshot log to support a simple snapshot on a table without a primary key.

```
ERROR at line 1:
ORA-12014: table 'DAILY_SALES' does not contain a primary key
             constraint
```

The other piece in the setup equation takes place in the initialization parameter file for the master site's database. The following parameter must be set:

- **Job_queue_processes**   Defines the number of J000-type processes that will be spawned as the database is started. These J000 processes ensure that the transactions against the master table are propagated to the remote site. To enable snapshot refreshes, this parameter must be set to an integer value; the most common entries are 2, 8, and 16.

NOTE
*In previous versions of the Oracle database there was an INIT.ora parameter called **job_queue_ interval**. This parameter was required in order to let Oracle know how often it should check to see whether snapshots needed updating. This parameter is no longer valid in Oracle9i.*

Believe it or not, that's about it for the master site. The remote site is next.

Setup on the Remote Site

The owner of the snapshot on the remote site needs the same **create materialized view** system privilege as was used on the master site. The snapshot owner also needs to set up a database link that can be used to refer to the table on the master site. Let's inspect some code that sets up this database link, dissecting the lines as they appear in the listing.

```
SQL> create database link to_prod
  2  connect to Dryden identified by thegoalie
  3  using 'prod.tpg.world';
Database link created.
```

Using the line numbers from the listing, these are the important points:

- **Line 1** Select a database link name, maximum 30 characters, governed by the naming conventions dictated by Oracle9i. We recommend something intuitive so that the database link meaning can be deduced from its name.

- **Line 2** Provide login credentials to the master site in the form of a username and password.

NOTE
Avoid embedding a password in a database link name. If the user's password is ever changed, the database link will be rendered useless until it's re-created with the changed login credentials.

■ **Line 3** Reference a valid Oracle Net alias that has been set up in Oracle9i's network configuration file called tnsnames.ora. If you are not familiar with the contents of or the role played by this file, check with a colleague who is.

Voilà! We're now ready to define the snapshot.

Creating the Snapshot

The result of the defined query then forms the information contained in the snapshot. Once you've created your snapshot, you must define how and when you plan to build and update the view. A snapshot must be refreshed, based on the rule that you define when it's created. So let's look at an example of the script needed to create one simple and one complex snapshot, and then pick apart each statement's components.

Setting Up a Simple Snapshot The following listing shows how CLIENTS can be captured into a snapshot on a remote site. After connecting to that site and setting up the required database link, the following code sets up the snapshot:

```
SQL> create materialized view clients
  2      storage (initial 4m next 4m pctincrease 0)
  3      refresh fast
  4      start with sysdate next sysdate+1 as
  5      select * from clients@to_prod;
Materialized view created.
```

Of note in the previous listing are three lines:

■ **Line 3** The refresh method is defined and—this being a simple snapshot— is set to **fast**. This means that transactions against the snapshot's base table (CLIENTS on the master site) will be stored in CLIENTS' snapshot log and forwarded to the remote site in a repetitive timeframe as outlined in Line 4.

■ **Line 4** This instructs Oracle9i to build the snapshot at once and to refresh it every day.

■ **Line 5** All the columns from CLIENTS will end up in the snapshot on the remote site.

That's about it—pretty simple you say? Why do you think they are called simple snapshots? Let's look at the more complex companion next.

Setting Up a Complex Snapshot   Although most of the code for complex snapshots is the same as that used for the simple variety, there are a few differences, as highlighted after the next listing.

```
SQL> create materialized view daily_sales_summ
  2   storage (initial 100m next 100m pctincrease 0)
  3        tablespace daily_mat_views
  4   refresh force
  5   start with sysdate next sysdate+10/1440 as
  6      select trunc(transaction_date) as transaction_date,
  7              company_num,
  8              sum(gross_sales)        as daily_gross_sales,
  9              sum(discount_amt)       as daily_store_discount_amt,
 10              sum(tax_amount)         as daily_store_tax_amt,
 11              sum(gross_sales-discount_amt-tax_amount)
 12                                      as daily_net_sales
 13        from daily_sales@to_prod
 14      group by trunc(transaction_date), company_num;
Materialized view created.
```

Using the line numbers from the listing, let's look at the important syntax and concepts.

- **Lines 2 and 3**   As with the table definitions you're used to running, the snapshot is placed in a specified tablespace with its own storage parameters.

- **Line 4**   This is the heart of the snapshot technology—periodic refreshes.

  - **force**   Oracle first tries to perform a fast refresh. If a fast refresh isn't possible, then it performs a complete refresh.

  - **fast**   This term first identifies the changes that occurred in the master file since the most recent refresh of the snapshot, and then applies them to the snapshot.

  - **complete**   This term reruns the query to replace the existing snapshot data.

In our DAILY_SALES_SUMM snapshot, we must use **force** or **complete**; the query used to build the snapshot is deemed by Oracle9i to be complex. **force** means that Oracle will try a fast refresh, even though the data may be defined as stale within Oracle.

- **Line 5** This is where the initial and subsequent refreshes of the snapshot are defined. In this example, the first refresh will occur at once, and subsequent refreshes will be carried out every 10/1440 of a day—do the math: there are 1,440 minutes in a day and this interval is ten of those minutes.

- **Lines 6–14** These lines define the query that is used to assemble data in the snapshot. Note how the database link **to_prod** is mentioned with the DAILY_SALES table name. This causes the snapshot to read data from the specified master site using the logon we mentioned when creating the database link.

Why We Use Snapshots

Prior to our becoming familiar with and using snapshot technology, we used to create summary tables. We often wrote special programs to perform the updates and then needed to support this functionality through scheduled updates. Snapshots provide the following benefits, especially crucial in the data warehouse world.

Oracle9i techies—ourselves included—would rather use tables to access data in the warehouse than use the more traditional view mechanisms.

There can be a vast network of calls to the Oracle9i database engine for each query that accesses the view. Suppose there happened to be a dozen queries running simultaneously; there would be so many assembling processes (the solid lines to the traditional view) that there wouldn't be much white space left. Oracle9i commonly spawns many more processes to access information in its data dictionary when it queries traditional views rather than their underlying tables. Because a snapshot is its own table, the likelihood of these processes' chewing up valuable CPU cycles and I/O resources is drastically diminished.

Now let's have a look at the impact of the snapshot just created on the warehouse instance.

Impact on the Data Dictionary

The data warehouse administrator will end up going continually to the master and remote sites' data dictionaries during snapshot management. The impact on and use of dictionary information is higher on the remote site, but some snapshot-specific material is held on the master site as well.

The Master Site The data dictionary view USER_SNAPSHOT_LOGS is shown next. This is followed by a discussion of the impact that view has on the creation of the snapshot log on CLIENTS.

NOTE
There would be no entries in USER_SNAPSHOT_ LOGS for the snapshot on DAILY_SALES, as it is a complex snapshot.

```
Name               Null?     Type
------------------ --------  -----------
LOG_OWNER          NOT NULL  VARCHAR2(30)
MASTER             NOT NULL  VARCHAR2(30)
LOG_TABLE          NOT NULL  VARCHAR2(30)
LOG_TRIGGER                  VARCHAR2(30)
ROWIDS                       VARCHAR2
PRIMARY_KEY                  VARCHAR2
OBJECT_ID                              VARCHAR2(3)
FILTER_COLUMNS               VARCHAR2
SEQUENCE                               VARCHAR2(3)
INCLUDE_NEW_VALUES                     VARCHAR2(3)
CURRENT_SNAPSHOTS            DATE
SNAPSHOT_ID                  NUMBER(38)
```

The information in the snapshot log is shown in Table 17-2.

Column	Value	Description
LOG_OWNER	MV_CREATOR1	
MASTER	CLIENTS	The table upon which the snapshot is based.
LOG_TABLE	MLOG$_CLIENTS	Nobody should perform any operations on this underlying log table. It is there for Oracle9*i*'s snapshot technology and nothing else!
LOG_TRIGGER	NULL	
ROWIDS	NO	An Oracle9*i* snapshot built on a primary key, not ROWID.
PRIMARY_KEY	YES	
FILTER_COLUMNS	NULL	
CURRENT_SNAPSHOTS	16-OCT-04	The time and date of the last time the snapshot was refreshed.
SNAPSHOT_ID	224	The ID of any snapshots based on the snapshot log on the CLIENTS table. It is not populated until a snapshot is built on a remote site.

TABLE 17-2.   *Contents of USER_SNAPSHOT_LOGS*

NOTE
There are often multiple rows returned for each snapshot log because it is possible to have data pushed to multiple snapshots from the same table.

Now let's look at the remote site setup for our CLIENTS and DAILY_SALES_SUMM snapshots.

The Remote Site   On the remote site, we're going to look at the impact on the data dictionary from the creation of the DAILY_SALES_SUMM snapshot, and its impact on USER_SNAPSHOTS and USER_JOBS. The former registers the existence of the snapshot and tracks characteristics such as the master table and where the data is being pulled from. The latter keeps information about the job that is responsible for performing snapshot refreshes.

NOTE
There is quite a bit more information stored in the data dictionary on the snapshot site. For the purposes of this discussion, we will only look at relevant columns in USER_SNAPSHOTS—one of the two views we will cover.

The fields in italics in the following listing will be discussed in more detail in Table 17-3.

```
Name                 Null?     Type
-----------------    --------  --------------
OWNER                NOT NULL  VARCHAR2(30)
NAME                 NOT NULL  VARCHAR2(30)
TABLE_NAME           NOT NULL  VARCHAR2(30)
MASTER_VIEW                    VARCHAR2(30)
MASTER_OWNER                   VARCHAR2(30)
MASTER                         VARCHAR2(30)
MASTER_LINK                    VARCHAR2(128)
CAN_USE_LOG                    VARCHAR2
UPDATABLE                      VARCHAR2
REFRESH_METHOD                 VARCHAR2(11)
LAST_REFRESH                   DATE
ERROR                          NUMBER
FR_OPERATIONS                  VARCHAR2(10)
```

```
CR_OPERATIONS              VARCHAR2(10)
TYPE                       VARCHAR2(8)
NEXT                       VARCHAR2(200)
START_WITH                 DATE
REFRESH_GROUP              NUMBER
UPDATE_TRIG                VARCHAR2(30)
UPDATE_LOG                 VARCHAR2(30)
QUERY                      LONG
MASTER_ROLLBACK_SEG        VARCHAR2(30)
STATUS                     VARCHAR2(7)
REFRESH_MODE               VARCHAR2(8)
PREBUILT                   VARCHAR2
```

Let's move on to USER_JOBS, the data dictionary location of information pertaining to the snapshot just created and any other repetitive tasks that may have been submitted for execution by Oracle9*i*'s job scheduler. In the "Setup on the Master Site" section a little earlier in this chapter, we mentioned the **job_queue_processes** parameter that must be set in the warehouse's initialization parameter file to propagate changes to remote snapshots. The USER_JOBS view is listed next; Table 17-4 looks at those fields italicized in the listing.

Column	Value	Description
MASTER	DAILY_SALES	The same as the like-named column in USER_SNAPSHOT_LOGS on the master site.
MASTER_LINK	@TO_PROD	The Net8 alias we used when the snapshot was created.
TYPE	FAST	The refresh type (usually **fast**, but sometimes **complete** or **force**).
NEXT	16-OCT-04	Always shows the next time the snapshot will be refreshed.
START_WITH	16-OCT-04	Same as NEXT.
REFRESH_MODE	PERIODIC	Indicates how and when the snapshot will be refreshed.

TABLE 17-3. *Contents of USER_SNAPSHOTS*

```
Name                Null?        Type
---------------     --------     --------------
JOB                 NOT NULL     NUMBER
LOG_USER            NOT NULL     VARCHAR2(30)
PRIV_USER           NOT NULL     VARCHAR2(30)
SCHEMA_USER         NOT NULL     VARCHAR2(30)
LAST_DATE                        DATE
LAST_SEC                         VARCHAR2(8)
THIS_DATE                        DATE
THIS_SEC                         VARCHAR2(8)
NEXT_DATE           NOT NULL     DATE
NEXT_SEC                         VARCHAR2(8)
TOTAL_TIME                       NUMBER
BROKEN                           VARCHAR2
INTERVAL            NOT NULL     VARCHAR2(200)
FAILURES                         NUMBER
WHAT                             VARCHAR2(4000)
NLS_ENV                          VARCHAR2(4000)
MISC_ENV                         RAW(32)
INSTANCE                         NUMBER
```

Column	Value	Description
JOB	47	A unique identifier assigned by Oracle9i to the job created as the snapshot is defined. It assigned 47 in our warehouse; yours will more than likely be different.
LAST_DATE	16-OCT-04	The last calendar date the job ran to refresh the snapshot.
LAST_SEC	18:09:12	The hours, seconds, and minutes of the last refresh (that is, the exact time the job last ran).
NEXT_DATE	16-OCT	The calendar date of the next refresh of the snapshot.
NEXT_SEC	18:19:12	The exact time of the next refresh.
BROKEN	N	A flag that indicates whether the job that performs the refresh is working (BROKEN=N) or not working (BROKEN=Y). When it is set to Y, the job will not execute.
INTERVAL	10/1440	The interval between successive refreshes.

TABLE 17-4. *A Look at USER_JOBS*

Now that was a mouthful. Let's move on and have a look at managing these snapshots, give you a heads-up on what may go wrong, and point you to some code that you may find helpful when you manage the network of materialized views that feeds your warehouse.

Snapshot Management

All too many administrators spend inordinate amounts of time managing snapshots and their associated refresh jobs. There's some homework that must be done before you can implement the smooth operation of an environment that uses this technology. We keep running across time-consuming management issues and believe that you would be wise to read on and become more aware of key areas that will occupy your time in a snapshot-intensive data warehouse environment. We are by no means touching all bases—just hitting the ones that creep up most often.

NOTE

It's best to come up to speed now on how to fix a warehouse plagued with inoperable (but fixable) snapshots, rather than to try to do so at 3:00 a.m. with a key senior management meeting early the next morning! Agree?

Changing Columns in One or More Base Tables

As we all know, data and data structures in the warehouse can be very dynamic. Altering the structure of a table that feeds a snapshot requires snapshot maintenance on the other end. When we speak of *base tables*, we refer to the tables whose data is summarized in a snapshot. Picture the following scenario:

- The DAILY_SALES table has changed, and now the tax amount is broken up into tax_amounts and tax_amountf for state and federal tax amounts.

- As shown previously, this table feeds data that is summarized into the DAILY_SALES_SUMM snapshot.

- We want to turn on the data warehouse users to the information contained in these two new columns.

To accomplish this task, given that DAILY_SALES has been altered to include these two new columns, proceed according to the following steps:

1. Inform the appropriate personnel that the DAILY_SALES_SUMM snapshot will be temporarily unavailable.

2. Proceed to the remote site and issue the command **drop snapshot daily_sales_summ;**.

3. Issue the following SQL statement to re-create the snapshot (with the inclusion of the new columns italicized):

```
SQL> create materialized view daily_sales_summ
  2  storage (initial 100m next 100m pctincrease 0)
  3      tablespace daily_mat_views
  4  refresh force
  5  start with sysdate next sysdate+10/1440 as
  6     select trunc(transaction_date) as transaction_date,
  7            company_num,
  8            sum(gross_sales)  as daily_gross_sales,
  9            sum(discount_amt) as daily_store_discount_amt,
 10            sum(tax_amountf) as daily_fed_tax_amt,
 11            sum(tax_amounts) as daily_state_tax_amt,
 12            sum(gross_sales-discount_amt-
 13                            tax_amountf-tax_amounts)
 14               as daily_net_sales
 15       from daily_sales@to_prod
 16     group by trunc(transaction_date), company_num;
Materialized view created.
```

Before completing this discussion and introduction to snapshots, let's look a bit at manually refreshing your snapshots. This is a common—but not necessarily frequent—exercise once snapshots have been defined.

Manually Refreshing a Snapshot

Inherent in the snapshot technology is the word *automatic*. A corollary of Murphy's Law states that all things that are automatic aren't. Periodically, you may have to refresh a snapshot manually. Remember, there are three main methods to refresh—**fast**, **complete**, and **force**. Suppose it's 3:00 a.m., and due to the luck of the draw, you're paged by your snapshot site with the following series of error messages from the CLIENTS snapshot routines:

```
Errors in file /oracle/admin/ntirety/bdump/tpg_snp0_12408.trc:
ORA-12012: error on auto execute of job 44
ORA-12034: snapshot log on "DW_OWNER"."CLIENTS"
           younger than last refresh
ORA-06512: at "SYS.DBMS_SNAPSHOT", line 604
ORA-06512: at "SYS.DBMS_SNAPSHOT", line 661
ORA-06512: at "SYS.DBMS_IREFRESH", line 577
ORA-06512: at "SYS.DBMS_REFRESH", line 211
```

Without delving into the reasons for this set of error conditions (which are beyond the scope of this introductory chapter), the following listing shows how to manually refresh our CLIENTS snapshot. The refresh is a two-stage process: the first statement performs a complete refresh; the second runs job 44 to perform the next fast refresh.

```
SQL> -- Perform a complete refresh by issuing a call to a SYS
SQL> -- packaged
SQL> exec dbms_snapshot.refresh ('CLIENTS','C');
PL/SQL procedure successfully completed.
SQL> -- Run job 44 to do fast refresh.
SQL> exec dbms_job.run (44);
PL/SQL procedure successfully completed.
```

NOTE
*There are some setup steps that have to be done before these procedures are available for use in the warehouse—mainly **catsnap.sql**, **dbmssnap.sql**, and **prvtsnap.plb**.*

Even though the bulk of the work we've done in warehouses involves complex snapshots, CLIENTS is a good example of a simple snapshot and how foreign key references from other tables can affect the way it's refreshed.

We've barely skimmed the surface in this discussion of snapshots; it was intended to be an introduction with some preliminary specifics—nothing more, nothing less. Let's move on and look at how we can use Oracle9*i* to help summarize data in the warehouse.

Extended Aggregate Operations

The power and ease of maintenance that Oracle9*i* provides comes in many forms. The data warehouse is obviously a focus for the Oracle engine; to that end, Oracle9*i* has provided us with many powerful features. We've already discussed materialized views. Oracle9*i* has some additional SQL extensions that are new to the product and that are a great help in the data warehouse world.

In the past, we had to have help when we needed to present data to users. SQL*Plus was pretty cool, but was limited. The end users who could write SQL have been known to create reports to do some pretty cool data analysis, but it was a hit-or-miss proposal sometimes. They needed more; they needed to truly understand their data. To get the results they needed, they turned to third-party products like

Oracle Discoverer or Cognos Impromptu. These products have great capabilities, including complex data grouping and dynamic summarization features. Oracle8—and to an even greater degree, Oracle9i—have provided some excellent and productive functions to allow complex analysis without the need for an extra-cost product. This stuff all resides in the database and, believe it or not, is part of the standard Oracle9i product: you spend your money on a great database, and all these SQL extensions come for free!

Oracle9i now has extensions that allow users to develop SQL queries that perform functions similar to the **group by** clause of a **select** statement. However, these extensions—**rollup** and **cube**—are **group by** on steroids. **rollup** creates subtotals at any level of aggregation needed, from the most detailed up to a grand total. **cube** is similar to **rollup**, enabling a single statement to calculate all possible combinations of subtotals. These summaries are widely performed on data warehouses every day and provide for timely analysis information.

Get out your thinking caps for a pop quiz: what is the critical dimension in a data warehouse? . . . Time. No, not time for your answer, but time itself. Oracle9i has also provided SQL extensions that allow you to window your data, enabling you to take better advantage of your data by doing time-slice analysis.

To summarize, Oracle9i now allows you to perform data analysis using functions in the areas of

- Cross-tabular analysis
- Ranking functions
- Windowing function
- Lag and lead functions
- Additional statistics functionality

One of the most important concepts in data warehousing is the idea of multidimensional analysis. Dimensions in this context are categories, such as time, product, store, sales rep, and so on. By combining dimensions during analysis, you can investigate different perspectives and discover some interesting relationships.

There are a few important concepts that you need to understand before we move on to the technical portion of this section of the chapter. We'll use some or all of these concepts when we're performing the analysis:

- Processing order
- Result set partitioning
- Windowing

Let's look at each of these concepts and how they relate to Oracle9*i* summarization features. First is the processing order. A query that uses analytic functions requires three steps, or stages. The first stage completes all the joins and includes the **where**, **group by**, and **having** clauses. This provides the data set that will be used by the function. During the second stage, all calculations are computed. Finally, Oracle9*i* performs the **order by** clause, and the data is then displayed to the user.

We also need to discuss result set partitions. Analytic functions allow you to separate your data into groups called *partitions*. Don't get this term confused with table partitions. In table partitioning, you're physically partitioning the data into separate disk locations. In data partitioning, you can think of separating your data into smaller partitions for analysis. The **group by** function is a powerful SQL tool; Oracle's analytic functions now provide additional power to the **group by**. Partitions can be based on any column or expression. You can perform analysis on one large partition or many smaller ones. The important thing to remember about partitioning is that the size of a partition will depend on a number of factors, including data set size and the granularity of the analysis being performed.

The final concept we need to talk about is windowing. *Windowing* allows you to define the range of rows within a partition on which the analysis will be performed. The window can be defined as a physical number of rows or an interval, such as time. The window can also be a moving window, and the movement can happen at the starting or terminating size of window. As you can see, this is not your usual old SQL; you now have a few more things to think about when you write your Oracle9*i* SQL.

But Oracle provides even more functionality. Its cross-tabular capabilities, for example, allow you to create reports that slice your information across aggregation points and dimensions. The ranking functions allow you to rank your data and perform operations like percentiles. The windowing functions allow you to perform cumulative and moving averages. Now you can look at your data changes over time to view trends. You can also perform functions like sums, variance, and standard deviation, among many others. The lag and lead functions allow you to compare values in different time periods. Finally, Oracle has added some new statistics functions, just to give us an olive for our warehouse martini. Let's now move on and look at some of these features in more detail and see how they can help you get more out of your data warehouse.

The rollup Function

The **rollup** and **cube** functions are simple extensions to the **select** statement's **group by** clause. **rollup** creates subtotals at any level of aggregation needed, from the most detailed up to a grand total. **cube** is an extension similar to **rollup**, which enables you to use a single statement to calculate all possible combinations of subtotals. **cube** can generate the information needed in cross-tab reports with a single query.

rollup's action is straightforward: it creates subtotals that "roll up" from the most detailed level to a grand total, following a grouping list specified in the **rollup** clause. **rollup** takes as its argument an ordered list of grouping columns. First, it calculates the standard aggregate values specified in the **group by** clause. Then, it creates progressively higher-level subtotals, moving from right to left through the list of grouping columns. Finally, it creates a grand total.

rollup will create subtotals at $n+1$ levels, where n is the number of grouping columns. For instance, if a query specifies **rollup** on grouping columns of YEAR, MONTH_NAME, and COMPANY ($n=3$), the result set will include rows at four aggregation levels.

```
select d.year, d.month_name month, s.company_num,
sum(s.gross_sales) as tot_sales,
sum(s.discount_amt) as tot_discount,
sum(s.tax_amount) as tot_tax,
sum(s.gross_sales-s.discount_amt-s.tax_amount) as tot_net_sales
from  daily_sales s, report_date d
where s.transaction_date = d.calendar_date
group by ROLLUP(d.year, d.month_name, s.company_num);
```

The results of this query show you how these values roll up under the date dimension that we created earlier in this chapter:

```
YEAR  MONTH  COMPANY_NUM TOT_SALES TOT_DISCOUNT   TOT_TAX TOT_NET_SALES
----- ------ ----------- --------- ------------ --------- -------------
1999 APRIL         100   1250.38      131.29    206.99        912.1
1999 APRIL         200   2877.5       265.5     372.49       2239.51
1999 APRIL                4127.88     396.79    579.48       3151.61
1999                      4127.88     396.79    579.48       3151.61
                          4127.88     396.79    579.48       3151.61

7 rows selected.
```

As you can see, the values have been summarized at the year, month, and company levels, and the levels of aggregation. The year, month, and a grand total for the sample data set have all been calculated for us. Let's move on and see the **cube** function.

The cube Function

The easiest way in Oracle9i to generate the full set of subtotals needed for cross-tabular analysis is to use the **cube** function. **cube** allows a **select** statement to calculate subtotals for all the combinations of a group of dimensions. It also calculates a grand total. This is the set of information typically needed for all cross-tabular reports, so **cube** can calculate a cross-tabular report with a single **select** statement. Like **rollup**, **cube** is a simple extension to the **group by** clause.

cube takes a specified set of grouping columns and creates subtotals for all possible combinations of them. In terms of multidimensional analysis, **cube** generates all the subtotals that could be calculated for a data cube with the specified dimensions.

If you have specified **cube** (time, region, department), the result set will include all the values that would be included in an equivalent **rollup** statement, plus additional combinations. If there are n columns specified for a **cube**, there will be $2n$ combinations of subtotals returned. (If you remember your Statistics 101 class, you already knew this answer.) Let's look at how you initiate a **cube** query.

```
select d.year, d.month_name month, s.company_num,
sum(s.gross_sales) as tot_sales,
sum(s.discount_amt) as tot_discount,
sum(s.tax_amount) as tot_tax,
sum(s.gross_sales-s.discount_amt-s.tax_amount) as tot_net_sales
from  daily_sales s, report_date d
where s.transaction_date = d.calendar_date
group by CUBE(d.year, d.month_name, s.company_num);
```

The results of this query show you how these values cube under the date dimension that we created earlier in the chapter. Notice that this data is the same data set that we used during the **rollup** example, yet the resulting combinations are much more complete. These data combinations allow for many ways to look at your data, which forms the basis for data analysis. We call this "slice and dice" analysis, because you can slice and dice the data in so many different ways.

YEAR	MONTH	COMPANY_NUM	TOT_SALES	TOT_DISCOUNT	TOT_TAX	TOT_NET_SALES
1999	APRIL	100	1250.38	131.29	206.99	912.1
1999	APRIL	100	1250.38	131.29	206.99	912.1
1999	APRIL	200	2877.5	265.5	372.49	2239.51
1999	APRIL	200	2877.5	265.5	372.49	2239.51
1999	APRIL		2877.5	265.5	372.49	2239.51
1999	APRIL		1250.38	131.29	206.99	912.1
1999	APRIL		4127.88	396.79	579.48	3151.61
1999		100	1250.38	131.29	206.99	912.1
1999		100	1250.38	131.29	206.99	912.1
1999		200	2877.5	265.5	372.49	2239.51
1999		200	2877.5	265.5	372.49	2239.51
1999			2877.5	265.5	372.49	2239.51

1999			1250.38	131.29	206.99	912.1
1999			4127.88	396.79	579.48	3151.61
	APRIL	100	1250.38	131.29	206.99	912.1
	APRIL	100	1250.38	131.29	206.99	912.1
	APRIL	200	2877.5	265.5	372.49	2239.51
	APRIL	200	2877.5	265.5	372.49	2239.51
	APRIL		2877.5	265.5	372.49	2239.51
	APRIL		1250.38	131.29	206.99	912.1
	APRIL		4127.88	396.79	579.48	3151.61
		100	1250.38	131.29	206.99	912.1
		100	1250.38	131.29	206.99	912.1
		200	2877.5	265.5	372.49	2239.51
		200	2877.5	265.5	372.49	2239.51
			2877.5	265.5	372.49	2239.51
			1250.38	131.29	206.99	912.1
			4127.88	396.79	579.48	3151.61

```
28 rows selected.
```

These results show you all the various data combinations that would be seen in a cross-product table. The data provides details as well as aggregates at the various levels as defined in the date dimension. Let's now look at how we would rank data using Oracle9i.

Ranking Functions

How many times have you asked yourself, "Who are the top hockey players in the Ice Gardens Hockey League (especially the top goalies)?" "Who are the ten best salespeople in your organization?" or "What are the top ten ways Canadians are different from Americans?" All right, maybe not all of these can be answered from data in our database. The ranking query provides the ability to easily determine rankings that would have been difficult to make using Oracle before Oracle9i.

Ranking functions allow you to compute the rank of a record with respect to the other records in your data set. There are four types of ranking functions:

- **rank** and **dense_rank**
- **cume_dist** and **percent_rank**
- **ntile**
- **row_number**

The **rank** and **dense_rank** functions provide you with simple ranking facilities. The **cume_dist** and **percent_rank** provide you with rankings based on distribution and percentiles. **ntile** provides you with the facility to create tertiles, quartiles, deciles, and other statistical summaries. The **row_number** functions allow you to assign a row number to each row within the partition. Let's look at these ranking functions and see some of the power that they provide.

rank and dense_rank

The **rank** and the **dense_rank** functions differ only slightly; they both rank your data into groups, but **dense_rank** does not leave any ranking gaps. Table 17-5 shows the scores from a golf tournament; look closely to see how the ranking functions differ.

As Table 17-5 illustrates, when the row values are the same, the ranking in the **rank** column is relative to the row position. So if, like David Duvall and Sergio Garcia, you finished in a tie for second place, your rank would be two, but the person who finished after you—Nick Faldo—would be in the fourth row and would be in fourth place. However, in the **dense_rank** ordering, Nick would finish in third place. Although he still collects a great paycheck, I think his ego would prefer to finish with the **dense_rank** of third instead of the **rank** of fourth.

Player Name	Score	rank	dense_rank
Tiger Woods	67	1	1
David Duvall	68	2	2
Sergio Garcia	68	2	2
Nick Faldo	69	4	3
Mike Weir	70	5	4
John Daly	70	5	4
Davis Love III	71	7	5

TABLE 17-5. *rank vs. dense_rank*

Let's look at some real-life examples of these ranking functions:

```
1  select company_id, sum(post_requests),
2  RANK () OVER
3  (ORDER by sum(post_requests) desc) as ranking,
4  DENSE_RANK() OVER
5  (ORDER by sum(post_requests) desc) as dense_ranking
6  from READER_STATISTICS_DETAILS
7  where company_id < 100
8* group by company_id

SQL> /
```

COMPANY_ID	SUM(POST_REQUESTS)	RANKING	DENSE_RANKING
48	1282	1	1
98	238	2	2
24	208	3	3
67	93	4	4
40	68	5	5
65	63	6	6
37	59	7	7
13	52	8	8
21	44	9	9
56	40	10	10
4	22	11	11
42	21	12	12
55	19	13	13
78	17	14	14
19	14	15	15
73	14	15	15
59	13	17	16
26	12	18	17
69	11	19	18
1	10	20	19
33	10	20	19
81	9	22	20

As you can see, the companies that are in the 20th and 22nd places with the **rank** function are ranked in the 19th and 20th places with the **dense_rank** function.

This is the simplest form of ranking in Oracle9*i*; however, the database also provides you with the capabilities to do multiple rankings. This allows you to use multiple criteria for ranking data. When you are setting up your **order by** criteria, the ranking will process the data from the far right expression back toward the center.

cume_dist and percent_rank

The functions **cume_dist** and **percent_rank** allow you to investigate percentile computations. **cume_dist** is defined as the inverse of percentile; it computes the position of specified values relative to the data set. The calculation for the **percent_rank** function is slightly different and is based on row counts. The formulas used by these functions are illustrated in Table 17-6.

As Table 17-6 illustrates, the formulas are quite similar and come down to differences in the way the data sets calculate their result set. Let's look at the results that each function provides on the same data set. First, we will examine the **cume_dist** function:

```
SQL> run
  1  select company_id, sum(post_requests),
  2  CUME_DIST () OVER
  3  (ORDER by sum(post_requests) asc) as
  4  from READER_STATISTICS_DETAILS
  5  where company_id < 50
  6  group by company_id
  7* order by sum(post_requests) desc;
COMPANY_ID SUM(POST_REQUESTS) CUME_DIST
---------- ------------------ ---------
        48               1282         1
        24                208 .95833333
        40                 68 .91666667
        37                 59      .875
        13                 52 .83333333
        21                 44 .79166667
         4                 22       .75
        42                 21 .70833333
        19                 14 .66666667
        26                 12      .625
         1                 10 .58333333
        33                 10 .58333333
        17                  8        .5
        34                  8        .5
        36                  7 .41666667
        11                  6      .375
        28                  6      .375
         2                  3 .29166667
         6                  2       .25
        25                  1 .20833333
        27                  1 .20833333
        14                  0      .125
        15                  0      .125
        45                  0      .125

24 rows selected.
```

The data provides us with the highest ranked value falling into the highest rank of 1 going all the way down to lowest rank of .125. The **percent_rank** function

Function	Formula
cume_dist	$\dfrac{number\ of\ values\ in\ set\ coming\ before\ the\ value}{set\ size}$
percent_rank	$\dfrac{rank\ of\ row\ within\ the\ partition - 1}{number\ of\ rows\ in\ the\ partition - 1}$

TABLE 17-6. *Mathematical Formulas for **cume_dist** and **percent_rank** Functions*

provides us with different results due to the manner in which it uses the row counts in its numerator:

```
SQL> run
  1  select company_id, sum(post_requests),
  2  PERCENT_RANK () OVER
  3  (ORDER by sum(post_requests) asc) as CUME_DIST
  4  from READER_STATISTICS_DETAILS
  5  where company_id < 50
  6  group by company_id
  7* order by sum(post_requests) desc

COMPANY_ID SUM(POST_REQUESTS) CUME_DIST
---------- ------------------ ---------
        48               1282         1
        24                208 .95652174
        40                 68 .91304348
        37                 59 .86956522
        13                 52 .82608696
        21                 44  .7826087
         4                 22 .73913043
        42                 21 .69565217
        19                 14 .65217391
        26                 12 .60869565
         1                 10 .52173913
        33                 10 .52173913
        17                  8 .43478261
        34                  8 .43478261
        36                  7 .39130435
        11                  6 .30434783
        28                  6 .30434783
         2                  3 .26086957
         6                  2  .2173913
        25                  1 .13043478
```

```
      27                    1 .13043478
      14                    0          0
      15                    0          0
      45                    0          0
```

24 rows selected.

As you can already see, Oracle9*i* provides some highly capable functionality to do complex data analysis. This is the tip of the proverbial iceberg, and you might need a degree in statistics to see how these can be utilized by your users; but it's imperative that you work with your end users to teach them about the functions that exist within the Oracle9*i* kernel.

Windowing Functions

The windowing of information is a requirement for data analysis in the warehouse. Time is the friend of the warehouse. We always want to see how we are doing over time. The windowing functions now allow you to do such time analysis as averages and totals over time. These functions must be used in the **select** and **order by** clauses in your query. Let's look at an example and see what comes out the other side.

This example calculates the average bytes over time. We can see how the average changes based on the cumulative averages over time.

```
SQL> run
1  select      company_id, start_time, round(KB_PER_SECOND,2) KB_PER_SECOND,
2      round(avg(KB_PER_SECOND)  OVER
3              (PARTITION by COMPANY_ID ORDER BY start_time
4               ROWS UNBOUNDED PRECEDING),2) as AVG_KB_PER_SEC
5  from READER_STATISTICS_DETAILS
6  where company_id <= 10
7  and    post_requests != 0
8* order by company_id, start_time
COMPANY_ID START_TIME KB_PER_SECOND AVG_KB_PER_SEC
---------- ---------- ------------- --------------
         1 0145                 .15            .15
         1 0350                 .16            .16
         1 0815                 .08            .13
         1 1916                3.54            .98
         1 1944                   0            .79
         1 2219                 .16            .68
         1 2222                 .08             .6
         1 2223                 .32            .56
         1 2224                 .33            .54
         1 2301                 .89            .57
         2 0035                 .06            .06
```

```
2 0333                 .02              .04
2 1933                   0              .03
4 0431                 .02              .02
4 0458                 .09              .05
4 0527                 .02              .04
4 0548                 .12              .06
4 1306                 .27               .1
4 1328                 .11              .11
4 2356                 .01              .09
6 1729                1.18             1.18
6 2103                 .05              .62
22 rows selected.
```

As this example illustrates, the values are averaged over the entire sample. This is done by using the clause **rows unbounded preceding**. The example doesn't place any restrictions on the window, so we see that the averages are based on the entire sample. The sample in this case is based on the COMPANY_ID field.

NOTE
The windowing function calculates the values for all rows in the resulting data set, so watch out that you can utilize the result in a meaningful manner.

In addition to performing bounded analysis by defining the bounds of the window, the window bounds define a logical offset. The next example illustrates range windowing. The **range** keyword is used to tell SQL that we are doing a bounded range.

```
SQL> run
  1   select      company_id, start_time, round(KB_PER_SECOND,2) KB_PER_SECOND,
  2   round(avg(KB_PER_SECOND)  OVER
  3     (PARTITION by COMPANY_ID ORDER BY to_number(start_time)
  4            RANGE 100 PRECEDING),2) as AVG_KB_PER_SEC
  5   from READER_STATISTICS_DETAILS
  6   where company_id <= 10
  7   and    post_requests != 0
  8*  order by company_id, start_time

COMPANY_ID START_TIME KB_PER_SECOND AVG_KB_PER_SEC
---------- ---------- ------------- --------------
         1 0145                 .15            .15
         1 0350                 .16            .16
         1 0815                 .08            .08
         1 1916                3.54           3.54
```

1 1944	0	1.77
1 2219	.16	.16
1 2222	.08	.12
1 2223	.32	.19
1 2224	.33	.22
1 2301	.89	.36
2 0035	.06	.06
2 0333	.02	.02
2 1933	0	0
4 0431	.02	.02
4 0458	.09	.05
4 0527	.02	.04
4 0548	.12	.08
4 1306	.27	.27
4 1328	.11	.19
4 2356	.01	.01
6 1729	1.18	1.18
6 2103	.05	.05

```
22 rows selected.
```

In this example, we defined the range as being 100; so if you look at COMPANY_ID = 4, you will see how the values are summarized between 1306 and 1328. However, you can see that by 2356, the previous values are not used in the average value computation.

When defining your bounds, you must be very aware of data types. In our example, the column of START_TIME was used to define the data set partition; but because we stored it as a varchar2 in the table, we needed to do a number conversion. This may or may not cause your results to be inaccurate, so care must be taken because your range data type must match the column. You can also partition by days, months, or years when you're doing date analysis.

Windowing is great; now you can use the database to perform functions that previously needed a third-party product or a really sharp pencil to calculate. Oracle9i has put this into their database for the low cost of $0.00. For that price, we'll also throw in some very useful statistical functions.

Statistical Functions

Oracle9i's statistical analysis support allows for calculations like variance, standard deviation, and others. We aren't going to discuss each of theses function types here. If you do need them, we suggest that you get your degree in statistical analysis and *then* start using them. Our discussion in this forum is limited to an overview of how to use these functions.

Just like any function in Oracle9i, these statistical functions are used in SQL statements. You may use them just as you do the **sum**, **avg**, and **count** functions.

They may be used in the select portion of a **select** statement or in the **where, order by**, or **group by** statements. They may also be utilized in a function-based index. These are the deepest and most powerful functions in your Oracle9*i* database, so know where you tread. Let's now take a quick look at how one of these functions, the **var_samp** (variance by sample), is used in a **select** statement and the result that it provides.

```
SQL> run
  1  select company_id, var_samp(kb_per_second)
  2  from   reader_statistics_details
  3  where company_id <= 25
  4* group by company_id
COMPANY_ID VAR_SAMP(KB_PER_SECOND)
---------- -----------------------
         1               6.0694495
         2               7.1148554
         4                18.85182
         6               2.2121609
        11               3.9701146
        13               14.048105
        14               5.3138384
        17               1.1947914
        19               1.5446113
        21               1.9679998
        24               1.8215652
        25               .51178571
13 rows selected.
```

Now you've seen how Oracle9*i*'s powerful summarization functionality can provide you with another useful tool in your data warehouse toolkit. So get out your hammer and start building your data analysis library! From materialized views to SQL aggregate operations, Oracle9*i* provides the data warehouse with some significant features that allow it and the data analyst to support many diverse summarization activities. Although the Oracle database does provide these features, it can be used with a variety of end-user tools that can present the data in a nicely formatted report.

We have looked at so much of Oracle that is used for data warehousing. If you don't have a data warehouse, you may find that these features will help you in your applications.

Chapter 17 Questions

1. What type of database design is normally used in today's data warehouses?

    A. Data warehouse normalized design level 7

    B. Star schema

    C. Normal database

    D. The scheming design

2. To reduce the amount of data that you back up on a regular basis, you should use

    A. smaller tablespaces

    B. smaller extents

    C. write-only tablespaces

    D. read-only tablespaces

3. What type of view helps in creating summary tables?

    A. Data views

    B. Snap views

    C. Materialized views

    D. A room with a view

4. Which of the following are Oracle9*i* summary functions?

    A. cube

    B. square

    C. rollup

    D. variance

APPENDIX A

Answers to End-of-Chapter Questions

Chapter 1: Oracle: The Company and the Software

1. Larry Ellison, Bob Miner, and _____ founded Oracle.

   D. Ed Oates

2. Oracle shipped the first commercial release of a relational database in what year?

   A. 1979

3. Oracle competes with

   E. All of the above

4. Oracle's database was the first to introduce the _____ consistency model.

   A. read

5. Oracle's first international office was located in what country?

   D. Denmark

Chapter 2: Road Map to Services

1. The TAR, or technical assistance request, is the vehicle used to access the following organization at Oracle:

   C. Tech Support

2. If you use command-line ftp to transfer files to support services when logging TARs, what username or login account would you use to access Oracle's servers?

   C. anonymous

3. When logging an iTAR, what is the single most helpful thing you can do to speed up the process?

   B. Assemble relevant trace and log files and upload them somehow to Oracle Support Services.

4. Oracle's one-stop shop for software downloads and technical information on their products is

   B. Technet

5. The best corporate site to go for E-Business and Oracle Applications information is

D. AppsNet

Chapter 3: The Oracle Server

1. Which background process is responsible for cleanup of aborted user sessions?

D. pmon

2. The online redo logs contain

D. a record of all transactions whether committed or rolled back

3. Which of the following INIT.ora parameters is the primary determining entry that controls what features are enabled when the Oracle9*i* instance starts?

B. compatible

4. Ready-to-execute SQL statements are placed where in the SGA?

B. Library cache

5. As Oracle9*i* runs, what portion of the instance is protected by latches?

D. Memory structures in the SGA

Chapter 4: Database Objects

1. A _____ is a database object that contains your data.

D. table

2. Until it is executed, a _____ contains no data, just a stored SQL statement.

A. view

3. A _____ must always return a value.

C. function

4. A _____ allows a user to work with data in a remote database.

B. database link

5. A _____ is an easy way to manage groups of privileges.

A. role

Chapter 5: SQL*Plus 101

1. The proper way to terminate a SQL*Plus session is to issue the _____ command.

   D. exit

2. The _____ command displays all the columns and attributes of the named table.

   B. describe

3. Which of the following is an example of DML?

   A. select

4. DDL stands for

   D. data definition language

Chapter 6: PL/SQL 101

1. Which of the following sections are included in a PL/SQL program?

   A. Execution

   C. Declaration

   D. Exception

2. Which one of the following may not be included in the declare section of a PL/SQL program?

   C. Loops

3. Which of the following is a valid looping structure?

   C. do while l_test is TRUE loop ... (program)... ; end loop;

4. All SQL that may be run in SQL is supported in PL/SQL for Oracle9i.

   A. True

5. What built-in Oracle function do you use to get output to your SQL*Plus session?

   B. dbms_output

Chapter 7: DBA 101

1. The system global area (SGA) is an area of memory that is

  A. shared by all users

2. To start and stop the database, you must first connect to the database using

  D. connect/as sysdba

3. These are all valid shutdown commands except

  B. shutdown now

4. A segment in the database that stores a before image or "undo" copy of a data block, before it was modified, is called a

  B. rollback segment

Chapter 8: More SQL*Plus

1. The dual table has how many rows?

  B. One

2. The _____ is the concatenation operator.

  C. ||

3. Which of the following provides the **if-then-else** capability of SQL*Plus?

  B. decode

4. Which of the following is not a **group by** function?

  D. sqrt

Chapter 9: More PL/SQL

1. What is the name of Pink Floyd's first album?

  C. *The Piper at the Gates of Dawn*

2. What method is used to make a PL/SQL stored procedure independent?

  B. autonomous blocks

3. Name the pseudocolumn that you use to extract the Oracle error number from within a PL/SQL program.

   D. sqlcode

4. Packages may contain many stored procedures.

   A. True

5. When using utl_file in Oracle9i, how many files may be opened simultaneously?

   D. 100

6. When using dynamic SQL, which command runs the program?

   A. execute immediate

Chapter 10: More DBA

1. **Filesize** is an export parameter that

   C. controls the maximum size of each export output file when more than one file is created for a session

2. Media recovery involves

   D. rolling a previous copy of a database entity forward using archived redo logs

3. Which of the following components are part of a cold, or offline, backup?

   C. All components of the database, including data files, control files, and online redo logs

4. Which of the following SQL statements notifies Oracle9i that the COREY tablespace is about to be backed up?

   D. `alter tablespace corey begin backup;`

5. A database is placed in archivelog mode while it is

   B. mounted

Chapter 11: Oracle Enterprise Manager

1. The right to occupy space in a specific Oracle9i database is referred to as a

   B. quota

2. The ORACLE_SID is an identifier used to

    B. uniquely identify each database

3. Without any additional work being done, which user of the Oracle9*i* database automatically gets the sysdba role?

    B. SYS

4. Which of the following shutdown options does a rollback on active transactions and disconnects all connected users?

    D. Immediate

5. Suppose you own a TAILOR table. The correct syntax for giving DELETE privileges to all users of the database with one SQL statement is

    C. `Grant delete on tailor to public;`

Chapter 12: Distributed Computing

1. Database links offer what major functionality to the Oracle9*i* database?

    D. The ability to network an assortment of databases running on different servers

2. Which file outlines the environment used by the Oracle Net process that scans the network for incoming server connection requests?

    C. listener.ora

3. Which file contains a list of valid Oracle Net aliases that can be used to access a database running on a specific server?

    A. tnsnames.ora

4. The logical four-digit address used to access resources on a computer is called

    C. a port

5. ORACLE_HOME in the context of the Oracle9*i* server product is

    B. the location of the Oracle9*i* software

Chapter 13: The *i* in Oracle9*i*

1. Which of the following is not an Internet protocol?

    D. Internet/IP

2. What part of the Oracle database is used to run Java?

    B. The Java Virtual Machine

3. What Oracle9*i* features may be used to minimize planned outages?

    A. Data partitioning

    B. Online index reorganizations

4. To store a word processing file in the database, you would use what facility?

    C. *i*FS

Chapter 14: All Things WWW

1. Which of the following is *not* a service within Oracle9*i*AS?

    E. None of the above

2. The configuration file for the HTTP server is called

    C. httpd.conf

3. The function used to load a PL/SQL Server Page into the database is

    B. loadpsp

4. What object type is created when you write a Java program in the database?

    D. Function

5. To support access by a wireless device you would use

    C. Oracle Forms

Chapter 15: Forms and Reports Overview

1. What must you do before you are allowed to pick the tables you wish to work with when using Form and Report Builder?

    C. Connect to a database after providing appropriate login credentials

2. The quickest way to edit numeric fields so that thousands digits commas are inserted is by

    C. specifying a format mask, defining each position with a 9, placing the commas in the appropriate position

3. When using the PL/SQL editor in Form Builder, fields on the screen are referenced in the code using what convention?

   A. The name of the field is prefixed by a colon.

4. When working with Developer 6*i*, what is the name of the programming unit that is designed to execute automatically when a specified event occurs?

   B. Trigger

5. A background entity upon which interface items are placed is called

   D. canvas

Chapter 16: Partitioning Data

1. Range-based or list partitioning is the best approach to use if you are looking for

   C. partition elimination as queries are processed

2. While hash partitioning a table into 16 partitions (**p01** through **p16**), and mentioning a list of eight tablespaces (**ts01** through **ts08**) in the **store in** portion of the code, which partitions would share tablespace **ts08**?

   A. **p08** through **p16**, since the tablespace list is 8, whereas there are 16 partitions

3. An index is partitioned on ID, with an ITEM_1 partitioned index on ID and SYNCH_DATE. The ITEM_1 index is called

   B. prefixed

4. Partition elimination means

   C. Oracle9*i* does not scan partitions whose partition key column values cannot possibly be part of a query result set

5. When selecting rows from a specific partition, the syntactically correct way to mention the table and appropriate partition name is

   D. table name followed by the keyword **partition**, followed by the partition name enclosed in parentheses

Chapter 17: Data Warehousing and Summarization

1. What type of database design is normally used in today's data warehouses?

   B. Star schema

2. To reduce the amount of data that you back up on a regular basis, you should use

   D. read-only tablespaces

3. What type of view helps in creating summary tables?

   C. Materialized view

4. Which of the following are Oracle9i summary functions?

   A. cube

   C. rollup

Index

Symbols

* (asterisk), 122, 123–124, 212
/**/ command, 215–216
|| (concatenation) operator, 216
/ (forward slash), 124
* operator, 214
+ operator, 214
/ operator, 214
– operator, 214
" (quotation marks), 233
; (semicolon), 124, 150, 155
@ sign, 207, 208
' (single quotes), 232–233
/ (slash), 212
1_counter variable, 159

A

abs function, 215
Adams, Steve, 54
add_months function, 220
administration. *See* database
    administrators

aggregate operations, 467–480
aggregation, 455
aliases, 108, 320, 321
alphanumeric items, 17
alter procedure command, 117
alter rollback segment command, 192
alter table add constraint command, 117
alter table command, 117
alter tablespace command, 188–189
alter tablespace offline command, 189
analyze command, 117
Apache HTTP listener, 351, 355
Apache JServ presentation services,
    358–359
Apache server, 357
application servers (appservers), 61,
    335, 337, 352–367
applications. *See also* software;
    specific applications
    availability of, 317
    browser-based, 11, 12
    described, 37, 143
    failures, 317
    Oracle Applications, 7–8, 10

overloading, 243–244
partitioning, 317
permissions for, 103–104
appservers (application servers), 61,
  335, 337, 352–367
AppsNet, 37–40
arc0 (archiver) process, 67
archive log list command, 278
archivelog mode, 275, 276–278
archiver (arc0) process, 67
arithmetic operations. *See*
  mathematical operations
arithmetic operators, 147
arithmetic values, 152
ASCII files, 444
asterisk (*), 122, 123–124, 212
attributes, 341
audit trails, 99–101
autoextend feature, 189
autonomous transactions, 242, 248–249
autonomous_transaction pragma, 248
avg function, 226

B

background processes, 181–182
backups
  cold, 275–276
  data warehouses, 441–442
  described, 260, 316
  distributed processing and, 317
  export utility role in, 261–262
  full, 269
  hot, 275–276, 279
  management tools for, 290
  table, 269
  user, 269
  vs. recovery, 261
BC4J (Business Components for
  Java), 357
BEGIN keyword, 148, 149
Benioff, Marc, 12

BI (Business Intelligence) services,
  366–367, 435
bitmap indexes, 98
BLOB data types, 119
blocks. *See* data blocks; Oracle blocks
blocksize keyword, 77
boilerplate text, 376
Boolean data type, 152
bounded ranges, 478–479
break command, 135–139
break logic, 135
break on clause, 135–139
break on report, 138–139
break points, 138–139
browsers. *See* web browsers
btitle command, 131–133
buffers
  database, 180
  described, 61
  dirty, 66
  export file, 266
  redo logs, 67, 180–181
  SQL buffer, 212
bugs. *See* errors
Business Components for Java
  (BC4J), 357
Business Intelligence (BI) services,
  366–367, 435
bytecode format, 335

C

cache. *See also* memory
  application servers and, 352
  data cache, 80–81
  database caching, 351, 363
  described, 62, 351
  *i*Cache, 363
  library cache, 81–82
  shared program cache, 181
  transaction cache, 180–181
  web caching, 351, 362–365

Cache Fusion technology, 345
caching services, 362–364
canvas, 376
case expressions, 156–157
ceil function, 215
central processing unit (CPU), 61, 316
CGI (Common Gateway Interface), 351
CGI programs, 351
CHAR data types, 119
character data, 216
character sets, 146–147
checkpoint activities, 61
checkpoint (ckpt) process, 67, 182
.class extension, 335
classes, 341
client-server technology, 61, 358
clusters, 110–111, 345
Codd, Dr. E. F., 5
code
    bytecode format, 335
    comments, 148, 215–216
cold backups, 275–276
column statement, 124–125
columns
    base table, 465–466
    break points, 137–138
    comparing contents, 236–237
    computing values, 137–138
    date column, 220
    described, 92
    grouping, 226, 227–228
    including on forms, 382
    indexes, 420
    naming, 92
    number of, 424–425
    order by clause, 127–128
    partition key, 423–424
    primary key, 120
comma-delimited files, 232–233
command files, 205
command-line editor, 212–213
comments, 148, 215–216

commit statement, 248
commit transactions, 62, 78, 82
Common Gateway Interface, 351
Common Object Request Broker
    Architecture. *See* CORBA
communication services, 355–357
compute sum command, 137–138
concatenation operator (||), 216
conditions, 154
configuration files, 318–322
connect / as sysdba command, 183
connections, database, 288, 292,
    324–326, 378–380
constraints, 91, 92, 98
content management services, 364
contention, 62
control files
    creating, 196–197
    creating list of, 275–276
    data warehouses, 444–445
    described, 73–74, 196
CORBA (Common Object Request
    Broker Architecture), 335
cos function, 215
count function, 226
CPU (central processing unit), 61, 316
crashes, 342–343
create cluster command, 110–111
create database statement, 183
create directory command, 108
create function command, 104–105
create index command, 117
create library command, 108
create operator object, 107
create package command, 106
create procedure command, 105–106,
    167, 168
create rollback segment command,
    190–191
create statement, 90, 117–118
create table command, 92–94, 117
create table statement, 421

create tablespace command, 77,
   186–188
create undo tablespace command, 188
create user command, 197
create view command, 94–95
CSI (customer support identifier), 20
.ctl extension, 63
cube function, 468–472
cume_dist function, 473, 474–477
cursor for loop, 163–165
cursors, 161–165
customer support identifier (CSI), 20

D

Dahlinger, Michael, 50
data
   character data, 216
   corruption, 343
   in data warehouses. *See* data
      warehouses
   deleting, 109, 120, 229–231
   duplicate, 228–231
   finding, 228–229
   grouping, 226–231
   loading into database, 120–122,
      443–452
   materialized views, 95–96,
      452–467
   multidimensional analysis,
      468–469
   partitioning. *See* partitioning
   windowing functions, 469,
      477–479
Data Block Wizard, 382–383
data blocks. *See also* Oracle blocks
   described, 179, 286
   size of, 297
   specifying, 297
data cache, 80–81
Data Definition Language. *See* DDL

data dictionary, 90, 92, 178, 460–465
data files
   adding to tablespaces, 188–189,
      298–299
   creating list of, 275–276
   described, 77–78
   maximum size of, 298
   reducing size of, 299–300
   resizing, 298, 299
   shutting off autoextend feature
      for, 189
   SQL creating, 232–233
Data Guard management, 290
Data Manipulation Language. *See* DML
data marts, 433, 436
data mining, 434
data normalization, 179
data partitions, 344
data reads, 252
data sets, 209
data types. *See also specific data types*
   bounded ranges and, 479
   dates and, 219–220
   DDL and, 118
   described, 118, 143
   PL/SQL, 149
data warehouses, 431–481
   aggregate operations, 467–480
   analyzing data, 452–467
   architecture of, 435, 436
   backing up, 441–442
   changing base table columns,
      465–466
   creation of, 432
   data in, 435, 441
   described, 432, 433
   designing, 435–438
   external tables, 443, 447–448
   federated, 433
   loading data into, 443–452
   materialized views, 95–96,
      452–467

need for, 10
overview, 434–435
partitioning, 438–441
PL/SQL, 443, 449–452
populating, 435–436
purpose of, 432
snapshots. *See* snapshots
sources of data, 435
SQL, 443
SQL*Loader, 443, 444–446
terminology, 433–434
workspaces, 290
data warehousing, 431–481
dimensional, 435–438
multidimensional, 468–469
Oracle9*i* functions for, 452–467
processing order, 469
result set partitioning, 469
windowing, 469, 477–479
database administrators (DBAs)
advanced operations, 259–284
basic operations, 177–199
control files, 196–197
creating user accounts, 197–198,
301–303
database backups. *See* backups
database exports. *See* exports
database overview, 179
database recovery. *See* recovery
instances. *See* instances
operator error, 274
redo log files, 193–195
rollback segments, 190–193
shutting down database. *See*
database shutdown
SQL*Plus and, 114–115
starting up database. *See*
database startup
tablespaces. *See* tablespaces
terminology, 178–179, 260–261
user privileges, 197–198
database caching, 351, 363

database files, 63, 64, 280, 281
database links
creating, 108–110
deleting data, 109
described, 108, 316
distributed computing and,
325–326, 328
inserting data, 109
linking to other databases,
109–110
passwords and, 457
retrieving data, 109
snapshots and, 457, 458
updating data, 109
database management, 405
database management system
(DBMS), 4, 8
database objects. *See* objects
database shutdown
described, 60
with OEM, 293–295
with shutdown command,
184–185
database startup
described, 60
with OEM, 287–295
with startup open command,
182–183
database writer (dbwr), 66, 67, 182
databases. *See also* Oracle9*i* database
buffers, 180
connections, 288, 292, 324–326,
378–380
denormalization, 433
exports. *See* exports
fragmentation, 344
initiating connection, 378–380
Internet database, 333–347
Java for, 367–370
loading data into, 120–122,
443–452
logging into, 291, 380

managing, 4, 8, 405
normal form, 433
overview, 179
placing in archivelog mode,
    277–278
primary, 342
production, 205–209, 342
quotas, 303–304
relational vs. nonrelational,
    179, 209
shared, 345
shared nothing, 345
shutting down. *See* database
    shutdown
standby, 287, 290, 342–343
starting up. *See* database startup
timeline, 4–12
versions, 4–12
Databases folder, 288–289
date arithmetic, 225
date column, 220
date data type, 151, 219–220
DATE data types, 119
date format masks, 223–225
date functions, 220–225
date values, 151
date variable, 151–152
dates
    comparing, 220
    data types for, 219–220
    display of, 223–225
DBA_ROLLBACK_SEGS view,
    191–192
DBAs. *See* database administrators
DBA_USERS view, 198
db_cache_size parameter, 80
.dbf extension, 63
DBMS (database management system),
    4, 8
dbms_output.put_line function, 174
DBMS_REPAIR utility, 343
dbms_sql package, 254–256

dbwr (database writer), 66, 182
DDL clauses, 117
DDL (Data Definition Language), 90,
    116–120
DDL locks, 83
debugging PL/SQL, 173–174, 245
decision support, 367
decision support systems, 290
declare section, 143
decode statement, 236–238
delete statement, 120, 230–231
deleting data, 109, 120, 229–231
delimited files, 443, 444
denormalization, 433
dense_rank function, 473–474
describe command, 118–120
Developer 6i, 378–399
dictionary, data, 90, 92, 178, 460–465
dictionary view, 71, 75, 403
Digital Equipment Corporation
    (DEC), 5, 6
dimension tables, 433, 437
dimensional data warehousing,
    435–437
directories
    aliases for, 108
    creating, 108
    external tables, 447
    home directory, 84, 319
dirty reads, 7
disks, 343, 345
distinct option, 226, 227
distributed computing systems,
    315–330
Distributed Lock Manager, 9
distributed networks, 61
distributed processing, 317
DML (Data Manipulation Language),
    91, 120–128
DML locks, 83
.dmp extension, 266
DNS (domain name service), 317, 319

documentation
    online, 37–38, 48–50
    resources, 37–38, 48–50
    TARs, 21–23
    technical bulletins, 33, 34
    technical libraries, 24–28
domain name service (DNS), 317, 319
drivers, 351
drop rollback segment command, 193
drop statement, 117–118
drop table command, 117
drop tablespace command, 189–190
dropping items
    redo log files, 194–195
    tables, 231–232
    tablespaces, 189–190
dual table, 213
dup_val_on_index exception, 166
dynamic SQL, 242, 254–257

E

E-Business Suite, 38, 39
edit command, 213
editors, defining, 213
EJB (Enterprise JavaBeans), 335
EJE (Enterprise Java Engine), 336, 337
Ellison, Larry, 4–6, 8–12
else action, 236
else statement, 155
elseif conditions, 156
emacs editor, 213
email
    caveats, 47–48
    etiquette, 47
    list servers, 41, 44–45, 47
    protocols, 346
encapsulation, 243
encryption, 355
END keyword, 148, 149
Enterprise Java Engine (EJE), 336, 337

Enterprise JavaBeans (EJB), 335
enterprise portals, 364
error messages, 33, 50, 69, 150
error numbers, 28–29, 50, 150, 165
error stacks, 17
errors. *See also* troubleshooting
    described, 20
    Form Builder, 392
    human, 343–344
    media recovery and, 280–281
    ORA-01031, 305
    Oracle, 20
    PL/SQL, 165–169, 244–248
    programming errors, 274
    variables and, 246–248
    when other exceptions and, 247–248
ETL (extraction, transformation, and loading), 435–436
ETL tools, 436
exception handling, 165–167
exceptions
    common, 165, 166
    described, 143
    Oracle-defined, 245
    PL/SQL, 165–167
    user-defined, 245–246
    utl_file package, 254
exclusive mode, 82
executable section, 143
executables, 60
execute command, 169, 171
exit statement, 158
explicit cursors, 161–162
export (exp) utility, 261–269
    command-line mode, 263, 267–268
    example listings, 263–268
    interactive mode, 263–267
    modes of operation, 263–268
    parameter-file mode, 263, 268
    parameters, 262–263

exports
    export utility for, 261–269
    management tools for, 290
    types of, 269
extent management dictionary,
    186–187
extent management local allocate
    clause, 187–188
extents, 178, 186–187, 260
extraction, transformation, and loading
    (ETL), 435–436
extranets, 367

F

fact tables, 433, 437
failures
    application failures, 317
    causes of, 274
    disk failures, 343
    hardware failures, 274
false value, 152
Fast Form, 7
fat tables, 403
fault tolerance, 9, 287
federated data warehouse, 433
fields, form, 387–391
file handles, 251, 252
file transfer protocol (ftp), 17
files
    appending to, 251
    ASCII files, 444
    closing, 252–253
    comma-delimited files, 232–233
    command files, 205
    control files, 444–445
    converting tables to, 232–233
    database files, 63, 64, 280, 281
    delimited files, 443, 444
    fixed format files, 443
    flat files, 205, 232–233
    iFS documents, 346

include files, 204, 206–209
multiplexing, 343
opening, 251–252
saving reports to, 129, 132
trace files, 23
writing to, 251
finding items, 228–229
fixed format files, 443
flat files, 205, 232–233
floor function, 215
.fmb extension, 386
footers, report, 131–132
for loop, 159–160, 163–165
foreign keys, 133–135
Form and Report Compiler, 378
Form Builder
    building forms, 380–381
    editing forms, 386–393
form letter reports, 394
Form modules, 381
format command, 125–127
format masks, 125–127
form-like reports, 394
forms
    building, 380–393
    columns in, 382
    components, 378
    Data Block Wizard, 382–383
    displaying additional text in,
        391–393
    editing, 386–393
    field attributes, 384–385
    field sizes in, 387–389
    headings, 384–385
    introduction, 378–380
    Layout Wizard, 384–386
    numeric fields, 389–391
    sample data, 376–378
    terminology, 376
Forms and Reports Developer, 378
Forms and Reports Runtime, 378
Forms Program group, 379

forums
discussion, 38–39
MetaLink, 28–30
fragmentation, 344
Free Agent, 41–42
ftp (file transfer protocol), 17
ftp servers, 21–23
full backups, 269
full imports, 269, 273
functions
database objects, 104–105
described, 167, 171, 243
group by functions, 226–231, 469
included with database, 214–233
Java and, 369–370
math, 214–216
PL/SQL, 167, 171–172
ranking functions, 469, 472–477
statistical functions, 469,
479–480
string functions, 216–219
windowing functions, 469,
477–479

G

Google search engine, 51–53
grant command, 117
grant connect, resource statement,
197–198
grants, 91, 104, 178
graphical user interface (GUI), 17, 61,
287, 376
group above reports, 394
group by command, 226–231, 455
group by functions, 226–231, 469
group left reports, 394
grouping data, 226–231
GUI (graphical user interface), 17, 61,
287, 376

H

hardware failure, 274
hash partitioning, 423–424, 426–427
having clause, 228–229
headers, report, 131–132
Henley, Jeff, 9
high-availability systems, 342–344
home directory, 84
Honeywell Systems, 7
hot backups, 275–276, 279
HTTP (Hypertext Transfer Protocol),
339–340, 346
HTTP listener, 351, 352, 355, 359
HTTP requests, 364
HTTP server, 356, 364
http.conf file, 359
Hypertext Transfer Protocol. *See* HTTP

I

*i*AS. *See* Oracle9*i* application server
IBM, 5, 6
*i*Cache, 363
if logic structures, 154–156
*i*FS (Internet File System), 346–347, 364
if-then construct, 154–155
if-then-else construct, 155, 236–238
if-then-elseif construct, 156
IIOP (Internet Inter-ORB protocol), 339
IIS (Internet Information Server),
355, 357
implicit cursors, 161–162
import (imp) utility, 269–274
data warehouses and, 443
modes of operation, 271–273
online help, 270–271
parameters, 270–271, 272
uses for, 270
imports
full, 269, 273
management tools for, 290

types of, 269, 273–274
user, 269, 274
Incident Support, 18–19
include files, 204, 206–209
indexes, 96–98
    80/20 rule, 98
    bitmap, 98
    columns, 420
    described, 91, 96
    global, 415–420
    local, 412–420
    non-unique, 97–98
    order of, 97
    partitioned, 410, 411–420
    problems with, 98
    unique, 97–98, 417
    uses for, 96–97
Informatica ETL tool, 436
infrastructure, 260
inheritance, 341
initcap function, 214, 218
initialization parameter file. *See*
    INIT.ora file
INIT.ora file, 68–73, 183
insert statement, 120, 121–122
instance alert log, 23
Instance display, 292
instances
    background processes, 65–67,
        181–182
    DBA tasks for, 180–186
    described, 60, 180, 287
    displaying information about, 292
    managing with OEM, 289
    multiple, 60
    SGA and, 180–181
instr function, 218
integrity constraints, 91, 92
Internet, 364, 367. *See also* web sites;
    World Wide Web
Internet Application Server (*i*AS). *See*
    Oracle9*i* application server

Internet architecture, 333–347
    described, 334
    high-availability systems, 342–344
    search engines, 51–54
    terminology, 334–336
    three tiers of, 336–337
Internet database, 333–347
Internet engine, 336–340
Internet Explorer, 358
Internet File System (*i*FS), 346–347, 364
Internet Information Server (IIS),
    355, 357
Internet Inter-ORB protocol (IIOP), 339
interprocess communication protocol
    (IPC), 317
intersect operator, 211
intranets, 334, 367
invoker rights, 249–250
IP addresses, 317
IPC (interprocess communication
    protocol), 317
IRI Software, 11
*i*TARs, 30–34
iterative process, 403
Ixora web site, 54, 56

J

J2EE (Java 2 Platform Enterprise
    Edition), 335
Java
    in database, 340–341, 367–370
    described, 4, 335
    security and, 341
Java 2 Platform Enterprise Edition
    (J2EE), 335
Java applets, 340
Java Database Connectivity (JDBC),
    335, 367–368
.java extension, 335
Java interpreters, 335, 336
Java objects, 369

Java program files, 335, 368–369
Java Runtime Environment (JRE), 358
Java Server Pages (JSP), 358–359
Java servlets, 356, 359–360
Java Virtual Machine. *See* JVM
JDBC (Java Database Connectivity), 335, 367–368
JInitiator plug-in, 358
job process queue, 454
job_queue_interval parameter, 457
JRE (Java Runtime Environment), 358
JServ presentation services, 358–359
JServ servlet engine, 356
JServer, 336
JSP (Java Server Pages), 358–359
JVM (Java Virtual Machine)
    business logic services, 357
    described, 335, 336
    environment, 367, 369
    JVM support, 357
    PL/SQL and, 144
    security features, 341

K

keyboard shortcuts, SQL*Plus Worksheet, 310
keys, 133–134

L

Lane, Ray, 9–10
last_day function, 214, 221
latches, 62, 82, 83–84
Laursen, Andy, 9
Layout Wizard, 384–386
LazyDBA list server, 44–48
least recently used (LRU) algorithm, 81
length function, 217
lgwr (log writer), 67, 182

libraries
    runtime, 64
    shared, 108
    technical, 24–28
library cache, 81–82
library modules, 381
links. *See* database links
Linux systems, 11–12
list command, 212
list partitioning, 421–423, 440–441
list servers, 40–41, 43–48
listener process, 318–320
listener.ora file, 318–320, 327
listeners
    Apache listener, 351, 355
    choosing port for, 322–323
    described, 316
    HTTP listener, 351, 352, 355, 359
    Spyglass listener, 352
    web listener, 352
literal strings, 233
Load Once and Read Many (LORM), 441
loading data
    into data warehouses, 443–452
    into databases, 120–122, 443–452
LOB data types, 119
locks, 62, 82–83
.log extension, 63
log files
    management, 290
    redo logs. *See* redo log files
    snapshot logs, 454, 460–462
    SQL*Loader, 445–446
log writer (lgwr), 67, 182
LONG data types, 119
loops
    for loop, 159–160, 163–165
    PL/SQL, 158–160, 163–165
    through file data, 252
    variables in, 160
    while loop, 158–159

LORM (Load Once and Read Many), 441
lower function, 217
lpad function, 217
LRU (least recently used) algorithm, 81
ltrim function, 217

M

mailing label format reports, 394
mainframes, 5, 6
Martin, Scott, 9
massively parallel system (MPS), 9
master sites
    data dictionary, 460–462
    described, 316
    distributed computing and, 316
    snapshots, 454, 455–457
materialized views, 95–96, 452–467.
  See also snapshots
mathematical formulas, 475, 476
mathematical functions, 214–216
mathematical operations, 144, 147, 152
mathematical operators, 214–216
matrix reports, 394–395
matrix with group reports, 395
max function, 226
maxvalue keyword, 411
media recovery, 274–283. *See also*
 recovery
    archivelog mode, 276–278
    cancel-based, 281
    cold backups, 275–276
    complete, 281, 282
    errors, 280–281
    example, 279–283
    hot backups, 275–276, 279
    incomplete, 281, 282
    time-based, 281
    types of, 281–283
memory. *See also* cache
    allocations, 292
    buffers, 61

cursors and, 162
Oracle Server, 80–82
shared, 63, 76
shared access and, 345
system global area, 179
memory allocations, 70
Menu modules, 381
messaging feature, 346
MetaLink, 23–30
methods, 340, 341
Microsoft Corporation, 8, 11
min function, 226
Miner, Bob, 4, 6, 10
minicomputers, 5, 6
minus operator, 211
mobile devices, 366
mod function, 215
mod_jserv module, 356
mod_ose module, 356–357
mod_perl module, 356, 362
mod_plsql module, 356
mod_ssl module, 355–356
months_between function, 221
most recently used (MRU)
 algorithm, 180
MPS (massively parallel system), 9
MRU (most recently used)
 algorithm, 180
multidimensional analysis, 468–469
multiplexing, 193–194, 343

N

native dynamic SQL, 256–257
Net Configuration Assistant, 318,
 322–326
Net8 protocol, 318, 338
Netscape Communicator, 358
network access, 64
Network Configuration Assistant, 321,
 322–326
network PC, 10
network protocols, 335, 338

newsgroups, 40, 41–43
newsletters, 38
new_time function, 221
next_day function, 222
nicknames
    objects, 101–102
    Oracle9*i* database, 287, 288
    SQL*Plus, 134–135
no_data_found exception, 166
normal form, 433
not null attribute, 92
not null clause, 120
null attribute, 92
null values, 120
NUMBER data types, 119
number sequences, 102–103
number variable, 151

O

OAS (Oracle Application Server),
    350, 352. *See also* Oracle9*i*
    application server
Oates, Ed, 4, 5, 6
OAUG (Oracle Applications User
    Group), 38
Object library modules, 381
Object Request Broker (ORB), 335
object-level grants, 91, 104
object-oriented programming (OOP),
    243, 340
objects, 89–112
    clusters, 110–111
    creating, 190
    database links, 108–110
    described, 243
    directory object, 108
    functions, 104–105
    indexes, 96–98
    inheritance, 341
    Java and, 340–341
    Java objects, 369–370

library object, 108
maintenance, 307–312
managing with OEM, 289
materialized views, 95–96
nicknames, 101–102
operator object, 107
packages, 106
privileges, 304–307
procedures, 105–106
roles, 103–104
sequences, 102–103
synonyms, 101–102
tables, 91–96
tablespaces and, 189, 190
terminology, 90–91
triggers, 99–101
OEM (Oracle Enterprise Manager), 61
oerr command, 50
offline backups. *See* cold backups
ojsp.conf file, 359
OLAP (Online Analytical Processing),
    434, 435
Online Analytical Processing (OLAP),
    434, 435
online backups. *See* hot backups
online documentation, 48–50
OOP (object-oriented programming),
    243, 340
open command, 163
Open System Interconnection (OSI), 339
operating systems, 20, 28, 61
operational system, 433
operator error, 274
operators
    creating, 107
    described, 204
    mathematical operators, 214–216
    set operators, 204, 209–212
    SQL*Plus, 209–212, 214, 216
    table comparisons, 209–212
ORA-01031 error code, 305
ORA-02429 error code, 98

Oracle9i application server
(Oracle9iAS), 350, 352–367
Oracle9i database. *See also* databases
    communicating with, 338–340
    connections, 288, 292, 324–326,
      378–380
    functions included with, 214–233
    as Internet engine, 336–340
    Java in, 340–341
    loading data into, 120, 121–122
    nicknames, 287, 288
    online documentation, 48–50
    retrieving information from,
      122–128
    setup overview, 84–85
    shutdown. *See* database shutdown
    startup. *See* database startup
Oracle Advanced Security, 344
Oracle Application Server (OAS),
    350, 352. *See also* Oracle9i
    application server
Oracle Applications, 7–8, 10
Oracle Applications User Group
    (OAUG), 38
Oracle AppsNet, 37–40
Oracle blocks, 186. *See also* data blocks
Oracle Business Components for Java
    (BC4J), 357
Oracle CASE, 8
Oracle Corporation, 4–13
Oracle Database Lite, 19
Oracle Database Personal Edition, 19
Oracle Database Standard Edition, 18
Oracle databases, 4–12. *See also*
    databases; Oracle9i database
Oracle Discoverer, 367, 468
Oracle Discoverer workbooks, 367
Oracle drivers, 351
Oracle Enterprise Manager (OEM),
    285–313
    connecting to, 305
    database startup, 287–295

    described, 61, 286
    object maintenance, 307–312
    overview, 287–290
    shutting down, 293–295
    starting up, 288–289
    tablespace maintenance, 295–300
    terminology, 286–287
    user maintenance, 300–307
Oracle Financials, 8
Oracle Forms, 357
Oracle9iAS. *See* Oracle9i
    application server
Oracle instances. *See* instances
Oracle Magazine, 54
Oracle Management Server, 288
Oracle Net Configuration Assistant,
    322–326
Oracle Net product, 318–329
Oracle Portal services, 364–366
Oracle Portal-to-Go service, 366
Oracle processes, 179
Oracle Product Support, 18
Oracle products, 4–13
Oracle Reports Developer, 367
Oracle Reports Services, 367
Oracle Server, 59–86
    architecture, 63–65
    background processes, 65–67
    control file, 73–74
    data files, 77–78
    INIT.ora file, 68–73
    latches, 82, 83–84
    locks, 82–83
    memory structures, 80–82
    redo logs, 74–77
    rollback segments, 78
    terminology, 60–62
    undo tablespace, 78–79
Oracle Servlet Engine (OSE), 356–357
Oracle Support Services (OSS), 16–23
Oracle system identifier
    (ORACLE_SID), 84, 286

Oracle Technology Network (OTN), 35–37
Oracle Updates Subscription Services, 18
Oracle User Forum and Fan Club, 54, 55
Oracle Warehouse Builder, 436
Oracle Web Server (OWS), 352
Oracle-defined exceptions, 245
ORACLE_HOME directory, 84, 319
ORACLE_SID (Oracle system identifier), 84, 286
ORB (Object Request Broker), 335
order by clause, 127–128
O/S. *See* operating systems
OSE (Oracle Servlet Engine), 356–357
OSI (Open System Interconnection), 339
OSS (Oracle Support Services), 16–23
others exception, 166
OTN (Oracle Technology Network), 35–37
outages, 344
overloading, 243–244
OWS (Oracle Web Server), 352

P

packages
    creating, 106
    dbms_sql package, 254–256
    described, 243
    Oracle-supplied, 250–257
    overloading, 243–244
    PL/SQL, 106, 243–244, 250–257, 350
    utl_file package, 250–254, 449
parameters
    archivelog mode, 277
    export utility, 262–263
    import utility, 270–271, 272
partition elimination, 403

partition keys, 403, 406–409, 420, 423–424
partition view, 438
partitioned indexes, 410
partitioning, 401–430
    access method, 425–427
    advantages, 403–406
    applications, 317
    composite, 427–428
    data vs. table, 469
    data warehouses, 438–441
    database management, 405
    distinct values, 407
    distributed processing, 317
    equal row distribution, 407–409
    hash, 423–424, 426–427
    indexing partitioned tables, 411–420
    list, 421–423, 427
    list partitioning, 440–441
    performance and, 405–406
    range-based, 406–411, 421, 427, 428
    result set partitioning, 469
    row count, 424–425
    table vs. data, 469
    terminology, 402–403
partitions, 344, 469
passwords
    database links and, 457
    SQL*Plus, 115
    user accounts, 198
percent_rank function, 473, 474–477
performance
    Internet, 364
    partitioning and, 405–406
    resources for, 26, 27
    scripts for, 26, 27
    shared access and, 345
Perl interpreter, 361–362
Perl language, 356, 361–362

permissions
   applications, 103–104
   users, 103–104, 197–198
petabytes, 403, 424
platform information, 26
PL/SQL, 141–176, 241–258
   advanced features, 241–258
   anonymous, 167
   architecture, 144
   arithmetic operators, 147
   autonomous transactions, 242,
      248–249
   business logic services, 357
   case expressions, 156–157
   character set, 146–147
   control structures, 152–160
   cursors, 161–165
   data types, 149
   data warehouses, 443, 449–452
   debugging, 173–174, 245
   described, 142
   errors, 165–169, 244–248
   exception handling, 165–167
   functions, 104–105, 167, 171–172
   if logic structures, 154–156
   invoker rights, 249–250
   library modules, 381
   loops, 158–160
   Oracle products and, 145–146
   overview, 144–146
   packages, 106, 243–244,
      250–257, 350
   procedures, 105–106
   program overloading, 243–244
   relational operators, 147–148
   security, 249–250
   SQL in, 160–166
   stored procedures, 167–171,
      356, 358
   structure, 147–152
   terminology, 142–143, 242–243
   variables, 148, 149–152

PL/SQL blocks, 143
PL/SQL engine, 144
PL/SQL Server Pages (PSPs), 359–361
plug-ins, 357, 358
pmon (process monitor), 66, 182
portals
   enterprise portals, 364
   Oracle Portal services, 364–366
   web sites, 364–366
Portal-to-Go service, 366
Porter, Mark, 9
portlets, 365
ports, 316, 322–323
power function, 215
precedence, 147
predicates, SQL, 402, 406–407
presentation services, 358–362
presentations, 38
primary database, 342
primary key columns, 120
primary key constraints, 92, 98
primary keys, 133–135, 402
privileges
   described, 344
   invoker rights, 249–250
   managing, 103–104
   object, 304–307, 344
   roles, 103–104
problems. See troubleshooting
Procedural Language Structured Query
   Language. See PL/SQL
procedures, 105–106
process monitor (pmon), 66, 182
processes
   background, 181–182
   Oracle, 179
   support, 63, 65–67, 76
   user, 179
product version, 29
production databases, 205–209, 342
profiles, 344
program control, 153

programming errors, 274
programs. *See* applications
Property Palette option, 391
protocols
    described, 317
    email, 346
    Net8, 318, 338
    network, 335, 338
    stateless, 339
    TCP/IP, 338
ps–ef command, 181
pseudocolumns, 247
.psp extension, 361
PSPs (PL/SQL Server Pages), 359–361
PUBLIC user, 305

Q

queries
    access method, 425–427
    executing with JDBC, 368
    main database server, 363
    rewriting, 96
    SQL*Plus, 233–235
query rewrite feature, 96, 452
quotas, 303–304
quotation marks ("), 233

R

RACs (Real Application Clusters),
    336, 345–346
raise_application_error function, 165
RAM, 61
range boundaries, 403, 408–416, 421
range-based partitioning, 406–411,
    421, 427, 428
rank function, 473–474
ranking functions, 469, 472–477
RAW data types, 119
RDBMS (relational database
    management system), 4, 6

read consistent model, 6–7, 78, 79
ReadMe files, 26
read-only tablespaces, 441–442
Real Application Clusters (RACs),
    336, 345–346
reco (recoverer) process, 67
recover database command, 281
recoverer (reco) process, 67
recovery
    described, 61, 316
    disk failure, 343
    distributed processing and, 317
    import utility role in, 270
    management tools for, 290
    media. *See* media recovery
    resources for, 26
    system crashes, 342
    vs. backups, 261
Recovery Manager (RMAN), 343
redo log files
    adding, 195
    archivelog mode and, 276–278
    archiver process, 67
    archiving, 277
    buffers, 67, 180–181
    creating, 194
    creating list of, 275–276
    DBA tasks for, 193–195
    described, 180, 193, 276, 287
    dropping, 194–195
    location of, 277
    multiplexing, 193–194
    naming, 277
    overview, 74–77
    switching, 194–195
    unable to open, 282–283
    vs. redo log groups, 74
redo log groups, 74. *See also* redo
    log files
relational database management
    system (RDBMS), 4, 6
relational databases, 179, 209
relational operators, 147–148

Relational Software Inc. (RSI), 5–6
release notes, 26
rem command, 215–216
remote sites
    data dictionary, 462–465
    described, 316
    distributed computing and, 316
    snapshots, 454, 457–458
replace function, 219
replace procedure command, 168
Report Builder, 394–399
    creating reports, 394–398
    modifying reports, 398–399
Report Wizard, 394–398
reports
    break on report, 138–139
    components, 378
    cross-tabular, 469
    footers, 131–132
    headers, 131–132
    include files and, 206–209
    introduction, 378–380
    line size, 128, 132
    modifying, 398–399
    Oracle Discoverer workbooks, 367
    Oracle Reports Developer, 367
    Oracle Reports Services, 367
    page size, 128, 132
    Report Builder, 394–399
    Report Wizard, 394–398
    Reports Servlet services, 367
    sample data, 376–378
    saving to files, 129, 132
    signifying end of, 138–139
    styles of, 394–395
    terminology, 376
    web caching and, 364
Reports Program group, 379
Reports Services, 367
Reports Servlet services, 367
resource limiters, 70
reverse clause, 159–160

revoke command, 117
RMAN (Recovery Manager), 343
roles, 91, 103–104
roll forward mechanism, 280–283
rollback segments, 190–193
    creating, 190–192
    decreasing size of, 192–193
    described, 190, 286–287
    location of, 190
    placing online, 192
    taking offline, 192
    undo information and, 62, 78, 188
rollback transactions, 78, 82
rollup function, 468, 469–470
round function, 215, 222
row distribution, 403
row_number functions, 473
rows
    exceptions, 166
    grouping, 226–227
    returning, 210–211
    specifying search conditions,
        228–229
rpad function, 217
RSI (Relational Software Inc.), 5–6
rtrim function, 218
runtime libraries, 64

S

Salesforce.com, 12
schemas, 289, 433, 437
SCN (system change number), 282
Scott, Bruce, 4
scripts
    creating control file list, 275–276
    creating data file list, 275–276
    creating redo log list, 275–276
    performance scripts, 26, 27
SDL (Software Development
    Laboratories), 4
search conditions, 228–229

search engines, 51–54
searching for items, 228–229
secure HTTP (S-HTTP), 355
Secure Sockets Layer (SSL), 340, 355
security
    invoker rights, 249–250
    Java and, 341
    managing with OEM, 289, 301
    Oracle Advanced Security, 344
    PL/SQL, 249–250
select cursor, 163–164
select statement, 120, 122–128, 161,
    163, 172
semicolon (;), 124, 150, 155
sequences, 102–103
server message block (SMB), 346
servers
    Apache server, 357
    application servers, 61, 335,
      337, 352–367
    Cash Fusion technology, 345
    ftp servers, 21–23
    HTTP server, 356, 364
    Internet Information Server,
      355, 357
    JServer, 336
    Oracle9i application server,
      350, 352–367
    Oracle Management Server, 288
    Oracle Server. See Oracle Server
    Oracle Web Server, 352
    Real Application Clusters (RACs),
      336, 345
service descriptors, 320
session identifier (SID), 78
set feedback off command, 232–233
set heading off command, 232–233
set linesize command, 128, 132
set operators, 204, 209–212
set pagesize command, 128, 132,
    232–233
set serveroutput on command, 174

set termout on/off command, 129
set trimspool off command, 232–233
severity levels, 16–17
SGA (system global area), 179, 180–181
share mode, 82, 83
shared items
    databases, 345
    disk access, 345
    libraries, 108
    memory, 63, 76
    program cache, 181
shared nothing database, 345
shared pool, 181
shared_pool_size parameter, 81
show all command, 130–131
show sga command, 180
S-HTTP (secure HTTP), 355
shutdown abort command, 185
shutdown command, 184–185
shutdown immediate command, 185
shutdown normal command, 184
shutting down database. See database
    shutdown
SID (session identifier), 78
SID (system identifier), 84
SID_NAME, 320
Siebel, Tom, 12
sign function, 215
single quotes ('), 232–233
skip option, 136–137
slash (/), 212
SMB (server message block), 346
smon (system monitor), 66, 182
snapshot logs, 454, 460–462
snapshots. See also materialized views
    complex, 456–457, 459–460
    creating, 458–460
    managing, 465
    manually refreshing, 466–467
    master sites, 455–457
    purpose of, 460
    simple, 455–457, 458

snowflake schema, 433
sockets, 340
software. *See also* applications
    downloads, 36
    version of, 20
Software Development Laboratories
    (SDL), 4
soundex function, 219
source tables, 454
spool command, 129, 232–233
Spyglass HTTP listener, 352
SQL buffer, 212
SQL statements, 406–407
SQL (Structured Query Language).
    See also PL/SQL
        creating data files, 232–233
        creating SQL programs, 231–233
        data warehouses, 443
        described, 17, 62
        dynamic SQL, 242, 254–257
        queries. *See* queries
SQLJ feature, 335
sqlldr command, 445
SQL*Loader, 443, 444–446
SQL*Net. *See* Oracle Net
SQL*Plus
        accessing, 114–115
        advanced features, 203–239
        alternate names, 134–135
        basic features, 113–140
        break on clause, 135–139
        command line, 115–116
        command-line editing, 212–213
        customizing environment,
            128–133
        Data Definition Language,
            116–120
        Data Manipulation Language,
            120–128
        date functions, 220–225
        deploying in production,
            205–209

dual table, 213
ending session, 116
environment settings,
    130–131, 132
Get Started Checklist, 115
icons, 116
if-then-else logic, 236–238
include files, 206–209
joining tables, 133–135
object maintenance, 309–312
operators, 209–212, 214, 216
Oracle functions, 214–233
passwords, 115
queries, 233–235
shutting off session display, 129
terminology, 204–205
SQL*Plus Worksheet, 290, 309–312
SQL*Star, 8
sqrt function, 214, 215
SSL (Secure Sockets Layer), 340, 355
stacks, 17
standby databases, 287, 290, 342–343
star schema, 433, 437
startup nomount command, 183–184
startup open command, 182–183
stateless protocol, 339
statistical functions, 469, 479–480
stddev function, 226
storage management, 289
stored procedures, 167–171, 356, 358
string functions, 216–219
strings, literal, 233
Structured Query Language. *See* SQL
subqueries, 233–235
subselects, 233–235
substr function, 219
sum function, 227
summarization, 452
summary engine, 452
support levels, 18–19
support processes, 63, 65–67, 76
synonyms, 91, 101–102

SYS account, 290
sysdba role, 290
system change number (SCN), 282
system crashes, 342–343
system global area (SGA), 179, 180–181
system identifier (SID), 84
system monitor (smon), 66, 182
system tablespace, 186
system-level grants, 91

T

table imports, 269
tables
    accessing, 382
    backing up data, 269
    base tables, 465–466
    based on existing tables, 93–94
    changing contents of, 120
    comparing, 209–212
    converting to files, 232–233
    creating, 92–94, 117, 118, 209
    described, 91
    dimension tables, 433, 437
    dropping, 231–232
    dual tables, 213
    examining, 118–120
    external, 443, 447–448
    fact tables, 433, 437–438
    fat tables, 403, 424–425
    hash-partitioned, 423–424
    indexing partitioned tables,
        411–420
    joining, 94–95, 133–135, 210
    loading data warehouses,
        447–448
    modifying, 307–309, 312
    overview, 91–94
    partitioned. *See* partitioning
    removing, 117, 118
    removing contents of, 120
    returning rows in, 210–211

size of, 424–425
source tables, 454
structure of, 179
timestamped, 290
viewing contents, 210
tablespaces
    adding data files to, 188–189,
        298–299
    blocksize keyword and, 77
    creating, 77, 295–297
    data files and, 77–78
    DBA tasks for, 186–190
    decreasing space in, 299–300
    described, 186, 286
    dropping, 189–190
    extent management, 187–188
    increasing space in, 298–299
    maintenance of, 295–300
    objects associated with, 189, 190
    OEM and, 295–300
    quotas, 303–304
    read-only, 441–442
    rollback segments and, 190
    system tablespace, 186
    taking offline, 189
    undo tablespace, 78–79, 85, 188
tabular reports, 394
TARs (technical assistance requests)
    creation process, 31–34
    described, 32–34, 61
    *i*TARs, 30–34
    logging with OSS, 20–23
    opening by phone, 20–23
    overview, 18–19
    reference number for, 21
    support levels, 18–19
    supporting documentation, 21–23
    tombstone information, 31, 32
TCP/IP protocol, 338
technical assistance requests. *See* TARs
technical bulletins, 33, 34
technical libraries, 24–28

technology tracks, 37
terabytes, 402
terminology
    data warehousing, 433–434
    database administrators,
        178–179, 260–261
    database objects, 90–91
    distributed computing systems,
        316–317
    forms, 376
    Internet, 334–336
    Oracle Enterprise Manager,
        286–287
    Oracle Server, 60–62
    Oracle services, 16–17
    partitioning, 402–403
    PL/SQL, 142–143, 242–243
    reports, 376
    SQL*Plus, 204–205
    World Wide Web, 350–351
thick Oracle driver, 351
thin client, 351
thin Oracle driver, 351
threads, 28
three-tier architecture, 351, 353
time values, 151
time zones, 221, 223
tnsnames.ora file, 320–323, 326–327
to_char function, 222
to_date function, 151–152, 222
tombstone information, 17, 29, 31
too_many_rows exception, 166
trace files, 23, 64, 69
transaction cache, 180–181
transactions
    autonomous, 242, 248–249
    commit, 62, 78, 82
    failed, 67
    rollback, 78, 82
triggers
    for audit trails, 99–101
    creating, 99–101
    described, 91, 99

Form Builder, 376, 392
    uses for, 99–101
troubleshooting. *See also* errors
    application failures, 317
    corrupted data, 343
    crashes, 342–343
    disk failures, 343
    hardware failures, 274
    human errors, 343–344
    index problems, 98
    media failures, 274
    operator errors, 274
    outages, 344
    PL/SQL, 173–174, 245
    programming errors, 274
    system crashes, 342–343
    unable to open redo log, 282–283
true value, 152
trunc function, 216, 223
ttitle command, 131–133

U

UFI (user friendly interface), 6
undo information, 62, 78, 188
undo tablespace, 78–79, 85, 188
Uniform Resource Locators (URLs),
    17, 364. *See also* web sites
union all operator, 210–211
union operator, 210
UNIX systems, 10, 181, 355
update statement, 120, 238
upper function, 217
URLs (Uniform Resource Locators),
    17, 364. *See also* web sites
user friendly interface (UFI), 6
user imports, 269, 274
user processes, 179
user-defined exceptions, 245–246
users
    backing up data, 269
    creating, 197–198, 301–303

maintenance of, 300–307
passwords, 198
permissions, 103–104, 197–198
size of community, 292
utl_file package, 250–254, 449

V

validation, 443
value_error exception, 166
VARCHAR data types, 119
varchar2 variable, 150–151
variables. *See also specific variables*
    assigning values to, 149–152
    described, 143
    for error handling, 246–248
    in loops, 160
    PL/SQL, 148, 149–152
    pseudocolumns, 247
    viewing contents of, 171
variance function, 227
var_samp function, 480
v$control data dictionary view, 73
vi editor, 213
views
    described, 91, 94
    dictionary view, 71, 75, 403
    issuing selects against, 94–95
    materialized views, 95–96,
        452–467
    partition view, 438
    uses for, 94
Virtual Private Databases (VPDs), 344
v$logfile data dictionary view, 75
v$parameter data dictionary view, 71
VPDs (Virtual Private Databases), 344

W

Walker, Jeff, 7, 9, 10
warehouses. *See* data warehouses

web browsers
    browser-based applications, 11, 12
    *i*FS documents, 346
    Internet Explorer, 358
    Java and, 340
    Netscape Communicator, 358
    search engines, 51
    three-tier architecture and, 353
web caching, 351, 362–365
web listener, 352
web pages, 362–363, 364
web sites. *See also* Internet
    favorites, 54–56
    *i*AS and, 352
    Oracle Support Services (OSS),
        18, 19
    portals, 364–366
    resources, 51–56
when others exception, 247–248
where clause, 133–134, 172
while loop, 158–159, 159, 160
white papers, 26, 38
window of opportunity, 316, 317
windowing functions, 469, 477–479
Windows 98 systems, 378
Windows 2000 systems, 378
Windows NT systems, 355, 357, 378
wireless devices, 366
wizards
    Data Block Wizard, 382–383
    Layout Wizard, 384–386
    Report Wizard, 394–398
Wohl, Ron, 10
workarounds, 17
workspace management, 290
World Wide Web (WWW), 349–371.
    See also Internet
WORM (Write Once and Read
    Many), 441
Write Once and Read Many
    (WORM), 441

INTERNATIONAL CONTACT INFORMATION

AUSTRALIA
McGraw-Hill Book Company Australia Pty. Ltd.
TEL +61-2-9417-9899
FAX +61-2-9417-5687
http://www.mcgraw-hill.com.au
books-it_sydney@mcgraw-hill.com

CANADA
McGraw-Hill Ryerson Ltd.
TEL +905-430-5000
FAX +905-430-5020
http://www.mcgrawhill.ca

**GREECE, MIDDLE EAST,
NORTHERN AFRICA**
McGraw-Hill Hellas
TEL +30-1-656-0990-3-4
FAX +30-1-654-5525

MEXICO (Also serving Latin America)
McGraw-Hill Interamericana Editores S.A. de C.V.
TEL +525-117-1583
FAX +525-117-1589
http://www.mcgraw-hill.com.mx
fernando_castellanos@mcgraw-hill.com

SINGAPORE (Serving Asia)
McGraw-Hill Book Company
TEL +65-863-1580
FAX +65-862-3354
http://www.mcgraw-hill.com.sg
mghasia@mcgraw-hill.com

SOUTH AFRICA
McGraw-Hill South Africa
TEL +27-11-622-7512
FAX +27-11-622-9045
robyn_swanepoel@mcgraw-hill.com

**UNITED KINGDOM & EUROPE
(Excluding Southern Europe)**
McGraw-Hill Education Europe
TEL +44-1-628-502500
FAX +44-1-628-770224
http://www.mcgraw-hill.co.uk
computing_neurope@mcgraw-hill.com

ALL OTHER INQUIRIES Contact:
Osborne/McGraw-Hill
TEL +1-510-549-6600
FAX +1-510-883-7600
http://www.osborne.com
omg_international@mcgraw-hill.com

Knowledge is power. To which we say,

crank up the power.

Are you ready for a power surge?

Accelerate your career—become an **Oracle Certified Professional (OCP)**. With Oracle's cutting-edge *Instructor-Led Training*, *Technology-Based Training*, and this *guide*, you can prepare for certification faster than ever. Set your own trajectory by logging your personal training plan with us. Go to **http://education.oracle.com/tpb**, where we'll help you pick a training path, select your courses, and track your progress. We'll even send you an email when your courses are offered in your area. If you don't have access to the Web, call us at 1-800-441-3541 (Outside the U.S. call +1-310-335-2403).

Power learning has never been easier.

University

Get Your FREE Subscription to *Oracle Magazine*

Oracle Magazine is essential gear for today's information technology professionals. Stay informed and increase your productivity with every issue of *Oracle Magazine*. Inside each **FREE,** bimonthly issue you'll get:

- Up-to-date information on Oracle Database Server, Oracle Applications, Internet Computing, and tools
- Third-party news and announcements
- Technical articles on Oracle products and operating environments
- Development and administration tips
- Real-world customer stories

Three easy ways to subscribe:

1. Web Visit our Web site at www.oracle.com/oramag/. You'll find a subscription form there, plus much more!

2. Fax Complete the questionnaire on the back of this card and fax the questionnaire side only to **+1.847.647.9735.**

3. Mail Complete the questionnaire on the back of this card and mail it to P.O. Box 1263, Skokie, IL 60076-8263.

If there are other Oracle users at your location who would like to receive their own subscription to *Oracle Magazine*, please photocopy this form and pass it along.

☐ YES! Please send me a FREE subscription to *Oracle Magazine*.   ☐ NO

To receive a free bimonthly subscription to *Oracle Magazine*, you must fill out the entire card, sign it, and date it (incomplete cards cannot be processed or acknowledged). You can also fax your application to **+1.847.647.9735**. Or subscribe at our Web site at www.oracle.com/oramag/

SIGNATURE (REQUIRED)	X	DATE	

NAME	TITLE
COMPANY	TELEPHONE
ADDRESS	FAX NUMBER
CITY	STATE · POSTAL CODE/ZIP CODE
COUNTRY	E-MAIL ADDRESS

☐ From time to time, Oracle Publishing allows our partners exclusive access to our e-mail addresses for special promotions and announcements. To be included in this program, please check this box.

You must answer all eight questions below.

1 What is the primary business activity of your firm at this location? *(check only one)*
- ☐ 03 Communications
- ☐ 04 Consulting, Training
- ☐ 06 Data Processing
- ☐ 07 Education
- ☐ 08 Engineering
- ☐ 09 Financial Services
- ☐ 10 Government—Federal, Local, State, Other
- ☐ 11 Government—Military
- ☐ 12 Health Care
- ☐ 13 Manufacturing—Aerospace, Defense
- ☐ 14 Manufacturing—Computer Hardware
- ☐ 15 Manufacturing—Noncomputer Products
- ☐ 17 Research & Development
- ☐ 19 Retailing, Wholesaling, Distribution
- ☐ 20 Software Development
- ☐ 21 Systems Integration, VAR, VAD, OEM
- ☐ 22 Transportation
- ☐ 23 Utilities (Electric, Gas, Sanitation)
- ☐ 98 Other Business and Services
- _____

2 Which of the following best describes your job function? *(check only one)*

CORPORATE MANAGEMENT/STAFF
- ☐ 01 Executive Management (President, Chair, CEO, CFO, Owner, Partner, Principal)
- ☐ 02 Finance/Administrative Management (VP/Director/ Manager/Controller, Purchasing, Administration)
- ☐ 03 Sales/Marketing Management (VP/Director/Manager)
- ☐ 04 Computer Systems/Operations Management (CIO/VP/Director/ Manager MIS, Operations)

IS/IT STAFF
- ☐ 07 Systems Development/ Programming Management
- ☐ 08 Systems Development/ Programming Staff
- ☐ 09 Consulting
- ☐ 10 DBA/Systems Administrator
- ☐ 11 Education/Training
- ☐ 14 Technical Support Director/ Manager
- ☐ 16 Other Technical Management/Staff
- ☐ 98 Other _____

3 What is your current primary operating platform? *(check all that apply)*
- ☐ 01 DEC UNIX
- ☐ 02 DEC VAX VMS
- ☐ 03 Java
- ☐ 04 HP UNIX
- ☐ 05 IBM AIX
- ☐ 06 IBM UNIX
- ☐ 07 Macintosh
- ☐ 09 MS-DOS
- ☐ 10 MVS
- ☐ 11 NetWare
- ☐ 12 Network Computing
- ☐ 13 OpenVMS
- ☐ 14 SCO UNIX
- ☐ 24 Sequent DYNIX/ptx
- ☐ 15 Sun Solaris/SunOS
- ☐ 16 SVR4
- ☐ 18 UnixWare
- ☐ 20 Windows
- ☐ 21 Windows NT
- ☐ 23 Other UNIX _____
- ☐ 98 Other _____
- 99 ☐ **None of the above**

4 Do you evaluate, specify, recommend, or authorize the purchase of any of the following? *(check all that apply)*
- ☐ 01 Hardware
- ☐ 02 Software
- ☐ 03 Application Development Tools
- ☐ 04 Database Products
- ☐ 05 Internet or Intranet Products
- 99 ☐ **None of the above**

5 In your job, do you use or plan to purchase any of the following products or services? *(check all that apply)*

SOFTWARE
- ☐ 01 Business Graphics
- ☐ 02 CAD/CAE/CAM
- ☐ 03 CASE
- ☐ 05 Communications
- ☐ 06 Database Management
- ☐ 07 File Management
- ☐ 08 Finance
- ☐ 09 Java
- ☐ 10 Materials Resource Planning
- ☐ 11 Multimedia Authoring
- ☐ 12 Networking
- ☐ 13 Office Automation
- ☐ 14 Order Entry/Inventory Control
- ☐ 15 Programming
- ☐ 16 Project Management

- ☐ 17 Scientific and Engineering
- ☐ 18 Spreadsheets
- ☐ 19 Systems Management
- ☐ 20 Workflow

HARDWARE
- ☐ 21 Macintosh
- ☐ 22 Mainframe
- ☐ 23 Massively Parallel Processing
- ☐ 24 Minicomputer
- ☐ 25 PC
- ☐ 26 Network Computer
- ☐ 28 Symmetric Multiprocessing
- ☐ 29 Workstation

PERIPHERALS
- ☐ 30 Bridges/Routers/Hubs/Gateways
- ☐ 31 CD-ROM Drives
- ☐ 32 Disk Drives/Subsystems
- ☐ 33 Modems
- ☐ 34 Tape Drives/Subsystems
- ☐ 35 Video Boards/Multimedia

SERVICES
- ☐ 37 Consulting
- ☐ 38 Education/Training
- ☐ 39 Maintenance
- ☐ 40 Online Database Services
- ☐ 41 Support
- ☐ 36 Technology-Based Training
- ☐ 98 Other _____
- 99 ☐ **None of the above**

6 What Oracle products are in use at your site? *(check all that apply)*

SERVER/SOFTWARE
- ☐ 01 Oracle8
- ☐ 30 Oracle8*i*
- ☐ 31 Oracle8*i* Lite
- ☐ 02 Oracle7
- ☐ 03 Oracle Application Server
- ☐ 04 Oracle Data Mart Suites
- ☐ 05 Oracle Internet Commerce Server
- ☐ 32 Oracle *inter*Media
- ☐ 33 Oracle JServer
- ☐ 07 Oracle Lite
- ☐ 08 Oracle Payment Server
- ☐ 11 Oracle Video Server

TOOLS
- ☐ 13 Oracle Designer
- ☐ 14 Oracle Developer
- ☐ 54 Oracle Discoverer
- ☐ 53 Oracle Express
- ☐ 51 Oracle JDeveloper
- ☐ 52 Oracle Reports
- ☐ 50 Oracle WebDB
- ☐ 55 Oracle Workflow

ORACLE APPLICATIONS
- ☐ 17 Oracle Automotive

- ☐ 35 Oracle Business Intelligence System
- ☐ 19 Oracle Consumer Packaged Goods
- ☐ 39 Oracle E-Commerce
- ☐ 18 Oracle Energy
- ☐ 20 Oracle Financials
- ☐ 28 Oracle Front Office
- ☐ 21 Oracle Human Resources
- ☐ 37 Oracle Internet Procurement
- ☐ 22 Oracle Manufacturing
- ☐ 40 Oracle Process Manufacturing
- ☐ 23 Oracle Projects
- ☐ 34 Oracle Retail
- ☐ 29 Oracle Self-Service Web Applications
- ☐ 38 Oracle Strategic Enterprise Management
- ☐ 25 Oracle Supply Chain Management
- ☐ 36 Oracle Tutor
- ☐ 41 Oracle Travel Management

ORACLE SERVICES
- ☐ 61 Oracle Consulting
- ☐ 62 Oracle Education
- ☐ 60 Oracle Support
- ☐ 98 Other _____
- 99 ☐ **None of the above**

7 What other database products are in use at your site? *(check all that apply)*
- ☐ 01 Access
- ☐ 02 Baan
- ☐ 03 dbase
- ☐ 04 Gupta
- ☐ 05 IBM DB2
- ☐ 06 Informix
- ☐ 07 Ingres
- ☐ 08 Microsoft Access
- ☐ 09 Microsoft SQL Server
- ☐ 10 PeopleSoft
- ☐ 11 Progress
- ☐ 12 SAP
- ☐ 13 Sybase
- ☐ 14 VSAM
- ☐ 98 Other _____
- 99 ☐ **None of the above**

8 During the next 12 months, how much do you anticipate your organization will spend on computer hardware, software, peripherals, and services for your location? *(check only one)*
- ☐ 01 Less than $10,000
- ☐ 02 $10,000 to $49,999
- ☐ 03 $50,000 to $99,999
- ☐ 04 $100,000 to $499,999
- ☐ 05 $500,000 to $999,999
- ☐ 06 $1,000,000 and over

If there are other Oracle users at your location who would like to receive a free subscription to *Oracle Magazine*, please photocopy this form and pass it along, or contact Customer Service at +1.847.647.9630

Form 5   OPRESS